Royal Romances

"Leslie Carroll is well on her way to officially becoming *the* 'notorious royal' historian when it comes to nonfiction on royal couples of past and present. . . . For anyone who wants the facts delivered in all of their original spice—*Royal Romances* (and I can vouch the same for the other *Royal* books of this series) will have you hooked from the first page . . . and you won't put it down until the last. Honestly, writing history as entertaining and engaging as this is truly an art. You need to add this one to your history book collection—it's a must. Excellent."
—HF Book Muse

Royal Pains

"For those who enjoy reading about the scandals of the noble class and want to learn more about the darker side of various royal families, this is a thoroughly enjoyable, quick read."
—*Booklist*

"If you love history and you love scandal, give *Royal Pains* a go. Between shaking your head at some of the antics and feeling glad Ivan the Terrible never picked you to be his Czarina of the Week, you'll learn the odd bit of history. Or you could watch the non–Moogles and Googles shows on the History Channel, but those are few and far between. Stick with Leslie Carroll; her bank account and history majors everywhere will thank you."
—Book Slut Gwen

"This installment in Leslie Carroll's *Royal* series is as thought provoking as the first two."
—Historical-Fiction.com

Notorious Royal Marriages

"For those who tackled Hilary Mantel's *Wolf Hall*, and can't get enough of the scandal surrounding Henry VIII's wives, [*Notorious Royal Marriages* is] the perfect companion book."
—*The New Yorker*

continued . . .

ALSO BY LESLIE CARROLL

Royal Romances

Royal Pains

Notorious Royal Marriages

Royal Affairs

INGLORIOUS *Royal* MARRIAGES

A DEMI-MILLENNIUM OF UNHOLY MISMATRIMONY

LESLIE CARROLL

NEW AMERICAN LIBRARY

New American Library
Published by the Penguin Group
Penguin Group (USA) LLC, 375 Hudson Street,
New York, New York 10014

USA I Canada I UK I Ireland I Australia I New Zealand I India I South Africa I China
penguin.com
A Penguin Random House Company

First published by New American Library,
a division of Penguin Group (USA) LLC

First Printing, September 2014

 REGISTERED TRADEMARK—MARCA REGISTRADA

LIBRARY OF CONGRESS CATALOGING-IN-PUBLICATION DATA:

Carroll, Leslie, 1959–
    Inglorious royal marriages: a demi-millennium of unholy mismatrimony / Leslie
Carroll.
    v. cm
    ISBN 978-0-451-41676-6
    1. Marriages of royalty and nobility—Europe—History.   2. Kings and rulers—
Sexual behavior—History.   3. Queens—Sexual behavior—History   4. Europe—
Politics and government.   I. Title.
    D107.C288 2014
    940.09'9—dc23   2014001661

Printed in the United States of America
10 9 8 7 6 5 4 3 2 1

Set in Sabon
Designed by Spring Hoteling

For anyone who has ever been—in the words of the immortal Shakespeare—"madly mated." You know who you are.

Contents

"Marriages are like death. The time and
season are marked, you can't escape."

—Liselotte, duchesse d'Orléans,
second wife to Philippe d'Orléans, the brother of Louis XIV

INGLORIOUS
Royal
MARRIAGES

Foreword

"*And* love is a thing that can never go wrong; / And I am Marie of Roumania," the American humorist Dorothy Parker satirically quipped in the Roaring Twenties, when the glamorous sovereign, one of Queen Victoria's multitudinous grandchildren, was the most famous royal on the planet. The instant recognition of Marie's name, and her reputation as the victim of an unhappy arranged marriage, have become lost to subsequent generations, but her rocky nuptial road mirrors that of countless royal spouses.

Naturally, their ancient and venerated families expected these unions to be glorious—conferring additional distinction or fame upon their respective dynasties—not to mention "glorious" as in "magnificent" and "grand." But all too often, the opposite occurred, and the royal marriages that began with such high hopes for the couple and the kingdom became *in*glorious—bringing shame and dishonor to one or both partners. Their marriages, and by extension their families, were instead disgraced by scandal and reduced to ignominy. Some of the unions profiled in this book were viewed at the time as inglorious because traditional gender roles were reversed, with wives assuming the reins of power. Or because they failed to fulfill their primary contractual duty by remaining childless for years. Or both.

Because these royal unions were intended to be political and dynastic strategic alliances, nearly all of them were arranged, even through the Victorian era and beyond. No one expected the spouses to be *in* love, or even to love each other, and yet their families and friends would always act surprised when the man and wife barely got along and the marriage failed. A much-anticipated "glorious" life of glamour, wealth, and power was doomed or destroyed, not only by such connubial disasters as adultery or infertility, but by the banalities of real life and the natural emotional reactions to marital neglect. The only reason so many of these unions lasted was because divorce was invariably unthinkable or legally unattainable. The rare royal divorces brought scandal and disgrace on the entire dynasty. As Czar Nicholas II opined—at the end of the nineteenth century—when two of his first cousins horrified the family by calling it a day, the death of a dear loved one would have been preferable to a divorce. One wonders whether Nicholas might have felt differently had *he* been trapped in a miserable union instead of having the good fortune of wedding his one true love.

Every royal marriage in this volume makes the hit parade of history's myriad mismatches. And as much as it's true that some marriages were more terrible than others, it's hardly surprising that there were so many bad ones; several of the girls were only in their mid-teens when their parents sacrificed them on the altar of matrimony to grooms who were total strangers, barely older than their brides. For centuries, this practice was not considered unusual. Even nowadays, some couples do wed in their late teens. But they usually know each other before they get hitched; and, being commoners, their responsibilities scarcely compare to those of young royals of centuries past.

The idea that these mere adolescents were routinely expected to make the weighty decisions required of governing a kingdom, to lead armies, set policy, and be the arbiters of the nation in fashion and culture is mind-boggling today. Their brains had not yet fully matured; how could they have the requisite judgment to wisely rule? By the time these children—and that's what they were—had wed at the age of fifteen or sixteen, they had reached their legal, if not emotional, adulthood, and no longer had a regent to do the heavy lifting. Yes, they had ministers, and in some situations there was a parliament, but the monarch had a tremendous amount of authority and, in many cases, the last word.

When you add to the burden of king- or queenship that of parenthood at such a tender age, as well as the fact that there was usually no rapport between the spouses, it's no wonder so many of these marriages were miserable. But what if there were no children—a different problem altogether? Royal wives had one major duty, even if they were the rulers: to bear an heir for the kingdom. When trouble in the bedroom, for any number of reasons, resulted in childlessness for an extended number of years, or even for the duration of the marriage, it was the wife who was blamed. She could be sent back to her native land in humiliated disgrace or shoved into a convent and forced to become an abbess—the inglorious marriage annulled so that her husband could try again with a more potentially fertile womb. The world would know that she had failed her spouse, her family, and her country.

More often, however, the couples remained together, although some wives might have found one of the prior alternatives preferable to the daily torment they endured within their marriage. Royal women were expected to accept their husband's behavior, no matter what he did. If he strayed, whether from frustration, disinterest in her, or a hyperactive libido, not only did propriety demand that she remain faithful to him nonetheless, but she was to turn a blind eye to his infidelities. Some wives even had to tolerate the presence of their husband's paramours at court, or worse, within their households, feigning cordiality in public while dwelling in a private hell they could never reveal. It often mortified them to be gracious to their husband's mistresses, and sapped their dignity day by day. Imagine the emotional and psychological cost. But part and parcel of the woman's role was to put up, shut up, and bear an heir—to be the well-dressed womb with no point of view.

And when she crossed the invisible boundaries prescribed for her sex by evincing an interest in affairs of state or any area perceived to be a man's sphere, including having the temerity to question her husband's extramarital infidelities, she was cast as hysterical, a harridan, or an unnatural woman. Society was rarely kind to females, but in many ways, royal women enjoyed an even narrower world with fewer choices than commoners. They could not seek employment or professionally practice a craft. They might become patrons of artists, industries, or charities, but could never be entrepreneurs. It was imperative for a royal wife to be charming and gracious, but if she was outspoken or had strong opinions, she was viewed as a meddler. She was supposed to be elegant, but if she was too glamorous or flamboyant, she was derided for behaving like a royal mistress.

Yet many of the queens and other first ladies of their respective realms managed to overcome their marital disappointments in a variety of ways, from taking the reins of power to indulging in adulterous affairs. The aforementioned Marie of Roumania, who was compelled by her mother to wed her jug-eared, shy, unassertive, and boring cousin Ferdinand, became the "face" of her little-known country during the First World War, regaining massive swaths of land during the peace talks at Versailles through her personal charm and what I have dubbed "couture diplomacy"—simply knowing the right thing to wear!

Others became warrior queens like Margaret of Anjou; yoked to the childlike Henry VI of England, whose sudden paralytic illness rendered him incapable of ruling his realm, she raised an army during the Wars of the Roses, hell-bent on saving her husband's throne.

Some royals were united with men who batted for the other team: For Marie of Roumania's younger sister Victoria Melita, known as "Ducky," things didn't go so swimmingly in the marriage bed. Her first husband, also a first cousin, the Grand Duke of Hesse, preferred footmen and stable boys—which was less of a scandal than Ducky's subsequent divorce and elopement with another first cousin, a Russian grand duke! The hypocrisy is astounding. Until very recently, divorced persons were personae non grata at the English court and were not even permitted into the Royal Box at Ascot, although for centuries, known adulterers swanned about with impunity within the royal inner circle.

During the seventeenth century, Charles II's beautiful, high-spirited sister "Minette" wed the younger brother of Louis XIV, her French cousin Philippe d'Orléans, a man who wore more makeup and perfume than she did. Although the duc d'Orléans was able to fulfill his marital duty with Minette, when she died young he didn't find it as easy to propagate with his second wife, a butch-looking, zaftig German princess. One night, she caught him hanging holy medals about his genitalia, insisting that the hardware enabled him to rise to the necessary level of performance. Philippe's father, Anne of Austria's husband, Louis XIII of France, wasn't particularly interested in women either. It took nearly a quarter century before Anne bore an heir. Although there were a number of miscarriages, absent a live birth *she* was blamed for the problems in the boudoir, and stigmatized for her barrenness.

In some marriages, the love was hopelessly one-sided. Both England's Mary I (Henry VIII's older daughter, known as "Bloody Mary") and the diminutive Portuguese-born princess Catherine of Braganza were tragically in love with their husbands. But their respective spouses, Philip II of Spain and Charles II, never returned their affection. Nicknamed the "Merry Monarch" for the jubilant and libidinous era inaugurated by his Restoration of the monarchy, Charles went so far as to flaunt his numerous mistresses in front of his love-struck wife for the duration of their twenty-three-year marriage! And Henry VIII's elder sister Margaret Tudor was the dupe of not one but *three* husbands who were incapable of fidelity.

At least these women survived to complain about their mistreatment—unlike Lady Jane Grey, wed against her will, and a victim of her parents' and in-laws' ambition. Ditto the two gorgeous Medici princesses Isabella Romola de Medici and Eleonora di Garzia di Toledo, who learned the hard way that in Renaissance Italy powerful husbands could behave with impunity—their wives . . . not so much.

Italian men created their own rules, as Marie Antoinette's elder sister Maria Carolina learned when she wed Ferdinand IV, king of Naples. She had no choice but to feign amusement when he dumped hot pasta on their subjects' heads at the opera house; and she could only rail at him or wring her hands when he made passes at every *signorina* in sight. Married to a buffoon, Maria Carolina became the decision maker at a crucial point in Neapolitan history, with Napoleon encroaching from all sides.

An overarching behavioral pattern emerges in many of the unions profiled here. Perhaps it was the fact that these royal couples couldn't easily extricate themselves from a bad marriage. Consequently, a parabola of matrimonial misery can be drawn, beginning with mutual indifference on the part of the spouses, who in most cases scarcely knew each other, but certainly hadn't viewed their mates with anything approaching passionate attachment. As the marriage progressed, familiarity did indeed breed contempt, if not utter loathing—often fertile ground for adultery. However, by the end of some of the lengthier marriages, the sparring spouses had become as comfortable together as a pair of bedroom slippers, settling into a benign state of tolerance and acceptance, occasionally sharing a platonic friendship that was solidified by their mutual devotion to their children. By the time death took one of them from the other, the survivor was often surprised by the intensity of his or her grief: It was a poignant realization, but a little too late to do anything about it.

The remarkable real-life stories in *Inglorious Royal Marriages* are interconnected; among the heroes and heroines of these connubial catastrophes are some of Europe's most famous monarchs, as well as others whose lives may be less familiar to readers. Providing context and key events of their reigns, including Readeption, Reformation, restorations, and revolutions, this compendium of royal love gone wrong proves that once again, real life is often stranger—and juicier—than fiction!

HENRY VI

AND

MARGARET OF ANJOU

MARRIED: 1445–1471

*I*t is said that history is written by the winners. Given the manner in which both sides of a conflict are often portrayed, this contention is unsurprising. For example, two of the fifteenth century's biggest losers were England's unpopular King Henry VI and his French-born wife, Margaret of Anjou. They were on the wrong side of fortune in what was then called the Cousins' War—a bloody, decades-long dispute that would eventually be known as the Wars of the Roses, after the red and white floral badges adopted by the feuding royal houses of Lancaster and York.

History has not been kind to either spouse. Even Henry's contemporary chroniclers drew biased portraits, based upon their own partisanship, fear of reprisals, or propaganda generated by years of civil war and multiple shifts in the political landscape, including regime changes.

Henry VI, who ascended the throne at the age of nine months, was the youngest English monarch to wear the crown, and the only one ever to be rightfully acknowledged and crowned as the king of *France* as well. Nonetheless, he is still perceived as one of the worst, and certainly among the weakest, sovereigns in English history. His reign was thirty-nine long years, and from the time he was a teen, he proved himself to be overly prudish and pious, credulous and malleable. He's remembered as a failure, the only English king to lose his crown twice, his sovereignty ending in civil war.

Yet where has posterity largely placed the blame for Henry's catalog of misjudgment and poor governance? On his *wife*, Margaret of Anjou, "she-wolf of France."

This slur on Margaret's character has endured for more than four centuries, and it came from the quill of a dramatist. William Shakespeare's indelible portrayals of the key figures in the Wars of the Roses have forever shaped the way we view them, and although Shakespeare relied upon contemporary chronicles as a springboard for his history plays, scholars ever since have continued to promulgate his theatrical portrayal of Margaret as fact.

In *Henry VI, Part 3*, Act I, scene iv, line 110, Shakespeare places the words "She-wolf of France, but worse than wolves of France . . ." into the mouth of Margaret's greatest enemy, Richard, Duke of York—the father of the man who will one day depose her husband and seize his throne. The "she-wolf" insult, which is utterly in character for the duke, comes at the top of a lengthy diatribe jam-packed with insults against Margaret, blaming her for the death of his teenage son, the Earl of Rutland. Very dramatic in the play, but the real Margaret wasn't even present when Rutland was slain.

In Act V at line 80 in scene iv, York's insult will be paralleled when *Margaret* calls his son, Edward IV, usurper of her husband's crown, a "wolf." I've yet to come across another analysis of Margaret of Anjou that refers to the *other* bookend of this lupine metaphor. Instead of recognizing a literary device lifted from a drama, generations of scholars have swallowed the misogynistic invectives spewed in York's forty-two-line monologue, taking his words at face value. They have reconstructed Margaret's historical persona based upon an insult uttered by a playwright's *fictional* depiction of another historical figure, portrayed in the text as her mortal enemy.

Consequently, based largely on propaganda and dramatizations, we are left with this portrait of Margaret and Henry as a mismatched royal couple: a termagant madly mated to a monk. There are elements of truth to this simplistic synopsis. But the whole story, as one might expect, is much more intriguing and nuanced.

The marriage of Henry VI and Margaret of Anjou is inextricably entwined with the events of the Cousins' War, the seeds of which were sown before Henry ascended the throne in 1422. While the scope of this chapter is not intended to provide a literal blow-by-

blow account of this lengthy conflict, some background information might be helpful.

Flash back in time to the reign of Edward III, which lasted from
1327 to 1377. Edward had thirteen children, five of whom were
sons. By making his sons the first English dukes, Edward created a
social stratum of royal magnates who wielded significant power and
expressed their sibling rivalry in land grabs. Eventually, their fraternal tension would be reduced to two factions: the cousins of the
Lancastrian line versus those of the York line, a veritable battle
royal for which side of the family had the greater claim to the crown.

The Lancastrians descended from Edward's third surviving son,
John of Gaunt, 1st Duke of Lancaster, who had inherited that title
from his father-in-law. The York branch of the family descended
from Edward's fourth son, Edmund of Langley, Duke of York.

By 1399, Richard II, who was Edward III's grandson and the son
of his eldest boy, Edward, "the Black Prince," had been on the
throne for nearly twenty-two years and had no heir to show for it.
That year also marked the death of the powerful John of Gaunt.
Gaunt's son, Henry of Bolingbroke, became the new Duke of Lancaster, and usurped the crown from his cousin Richard, declaring
himself King Henry IV.

Henry IV's grandson was Henry VI, Margaret of Anjou's husband.

Additionally, because his grandfather had deposed Richard II,
many still believed that the Lancastrian Henry VI had no right to
wear the crown at all, and they continued to view his whole line as
usurpers.

There was a popular saying at the time: "Woe to thee, O land,
when thy king is a child." It was never truer than in the case of tiny
Henry VI, whose parents were the English warrior king Henry V
and Catherine of Valois, a daughter of the mentally unsound French
King Charles VI. In 1420, five years after Henry V vanquished the
French in the Battle of Agincourt, the Treaty of Troyes was signed,
proclaiming Henry's offspring the heirs to the French throne, and
overlooking Charles's own son. Charles died on October 11, 1422,
less than two months after the infant Henry VI ascended the English throne. Henry VI was then proclaimed king of France as well.

During Henry's minority, while his uncle Humphrey, Duke of Gloucester, acted as his regent and protector of England, France was governed by another regent, his uncle John of Lancaster, the Duke of Bedford. On November 5, 1429, seven-year-old Henry was crowned king of England at Westminster Abbey. On December 16, 1431, he was crowned king of France at Notre Dame—but Bedford had badly miscalculated the mood of the French. Many refused to recognize Henry as their sovereign, and didn't like being ruled from afar by a little English boy's regent. They wanted a French grown-up on their own throne, preferring to recognize the dauphin, the son of Charles VI, as King Charles VII of France, despite the fact that the Treaty of Troyes had overlooked him.

In 1435, during renegotiations of the treaty, France completely rejected the pact, Bedford died in the middle of the discussions, and a new concord, the Treaty of Arras, was concluded between former French foes Charles VII and Philip of Burgundy, cutting the Lancastrians out of the picture entirely.

Two years later, sixteen-year-old Henry VI declared himself of age and repurposed his regency council. He also fired his tutor, the Earl of Warwick, from whom he had learned all the arts of chivalry and military strategy. When the time came to utilize these lessons, Henry would evince little interest in employing them.

Unfortunately, Henry lacked the experience and skill to manage England's nobles, so he tried to buy their support with money and lavish land grants, which his treasury could ill afford. His council cautioned him about such profligacy and urged him to conserve his funds. But Henry was not a strong leader and had tremendous difficulty asserting his authority with the same men who had run things for years during his minority.

Henry inherited a nearly bankrupt treasury, a council split into factions, an increasingly powerful aristocracy, and a corrupt legal system. He also inherited an unwinnable conflict—the so-called Hundred Years' War, begun by Edward III in 1337 for control of the French throne—that continued to drain England's resources. Most devastating of all, Henry was essentially powerless to curb any of these problems.

Although he had been a natty dresser as a boy, favoring colorful garments in the latest fashions, around the time he turned sixteen he went through a monkish phase, deciding that his former sartorial indulgences had been a display of worldly vanity. He started wearing long tunics and gowns with round hoods. His entire wardrobe was dark gray. Henry's courtiers were dismayed by the image he projected, complaining that he dressed "like a townsman."

Even after his marriage, the king continued to show so little regard for finery that in 1459 he gave his best gown to the prior of St. Albans, but then discovered he had nothing else to wear on state occasions and couldn't afford to buy a new ensemble! Much to Henry's annoyance, his treasurer bought back his garment from the prior for fifty marks.

The king's ascetic wardrobe may have gone hand in glove with his religious outlook as well. By this time, Henry was renowned for his piety. Not only did he view himself as the guardian of public morals, but he practiced what he preached. Henry never swore, nor would he tolerate it from others. Spending the lion's share of his leisure hours reading religious books and moral tracts, he believed that if his subjects did so, too, their character would be improved by it. And he was, at least compared to other men, extremely prudish. He warned the boys at Eton College, Windsor (which he founded), to stay away from the castle, where they might be corrupted by the courtiers' debauchery. Nudity offended him, and he vented his displeasure at a lord who produced a Christmas pageant featuring topless dancing girls. The king stormed out of the performance, averting his eyes as he cried, "Fie, fie, for shame!"

He "avoided the company of women," wrote John Blacman, whose memoir chronicled Henry's reign, adding that the king was "a pupil of chastity—chaste and pure from the beginning of his days and eschewed all licentiousness in word or deed while he was young." Even four years after his marriage, when he journeyed to Bath in 1449, Henry was horrified to see men and women bathing naked together in the famous spa waters.

A medieval monarch had to be a brave leader in the field, but Henry VI had no wish to fight against his fellow Christians. He was the first English king since the Norman Conquest never to have led an army against a foreign enemy. Although he desired France as much as his predecessors had, he harbored a distaste for the destruction of war and the devastating loss of life.

Couldn't France be gained through peaceful means instead?

By 1441, Henry VI had developed, in the words of a contemporary chronicler, "an earnest desire to live under the holy sacrament of marriage." He doubtless knew his duty to sire an heir, and by this point in time he wasn't *so* disinterested in women that looks were unimportant in choosing a bride. He demanded portraits of all prospects.

In order to solidify the peace between their realms after 104 years (and counting) of conflict, Henry recognized that his best alliance, regardless of physical appearance, would be with the French. He viewed the field of France as a vast chessboard. So his first choice was the daughter of the comte d'Armagnac, in order to checkmate Armagnac's rival, the Duke of Burgundy.

Henry's chief adviser, his cousin Cardinal Beaufort, proposed another girl instead: the niece of King Charles VII by marriage—Margaret of Anjou. However, Henry still wanted to see the goods before he agreed to the purchase. But how to get a portrait of Margaret?

The following anecdote may have been written much later on, and it probably contains a bit of fictional embellishment, but some historians present it as fact, and it's a marvelous adventure story, right out of a medieval *romaunt*.

Living on parole in London was a French chevalier from Argon named Champchevrier. This knight had given his word of honor (his "parole") to remain in London to Sir John Fastolf, the English knight who had taken him prisoner.

Never mind Champchevrier's promise to Fastolf (a name, albeit spelled a bit differently, that will be familiar to Shakespeare aficionados): King Henry himself needed a Frenchman! He dispatched Champchevrier on a secret diplomatic mission to Anjou to secure a portrait of his potential bride. The chevalier did so, but the irate Fastolf—who had not been told why his prisoner had "escaped" to France—demanded to know why he'd broken his parole. Sir John then insisted, by the laws of chivalry, that his prisoner be returned to him!

What happened next was a veritable comedy of errors.

Believed to have violated his parole to Sir John Fastolf, Champchevrier was arrested in France—with Margaret of Anjou's portrait on him. This was highly irregular. After the French authorities were willing to grant his desperate request to see the king of France, the chevalier told Charles VII that he was not an escaped parolee, but was on a secret diplomatic mission from Henry VI. He produced the portrait of Charles's niece and stated the reason for his flight from England. Happy to consider a marriage between Margaret and Henry, Charles released Champchevrier and sent the knight on his merrie way back to olde England.

Receiving the portrait in October 1443, Henry VI apparently became uncharacteristically smitten with the image of "the excellent, magnificent, and very bright Margaret," who was all of thirteen years old at the time. He contacted the Earl of Suffolk to go ahead and broker his marital alliance.

Unfortunately, the princess, who still bore her childhood nickname, *la petite créature*, wasn't that much of a catch. Although her uncle the king was the man who by popular acclaim and diplomatic treaty had nudged Henry off the French throne, her father, the nearly impoverished René, duc d'Anjou, was only the *titular* king of Naples and Sicily, Jerusalem and Hungary. He didn't actually wear the crowns of *any* of those realms, and in the case of Naples he'd been compelled to cede the title to Alfonso of Aragon. Even René's duchy of Anjou had been occupied by the English when he inherited it in 1434.

Margaret's mother, Isabelle, was the daughter of the duc de Lorraine, Charles the Bold. The women in her family were not only sophisticated and well educated, but they were accustomed to taking the reins of power and assuming authority when necessity demanded it. Her own mother had been such an object lesson; Isabelle had continued to claim her husband's rights and wage his battles for him while René was a prisoner of war awaiting ransom. Margaret's paternal grandmother, Yolande of Aragon, whom she lived with for eight years during her childhood, had ruled as regent for her oldest son, resisting the English at her peril by supporting the disinherited dauphin Charles, even marrying him to her daughter

Marie. Yolande's gamble had paid off. The dauphin came out on top; he was now Charles VII of France and Marie was his queen.

Although Henry VI had chosen a bride who would turn out to be an utter mismatch for him in so many respects, in a way he had inadvertently lucked out, because in the long run he could not have made a better selection. Henry was someone who became literally helpless in a crisis, whereas Margaret had not only the temperament but came from a family of women who knew how to meet a challenge head-on.

The betrothal with Margaret was part and parcel of negotiations for a lasting peace treaty between England and France. By January 1444, a cessation of hostilities seemed to be on the horizon, with a summit organized between both sides at which the peace and the king's marriage plans would be discussed.

Negotiating on England's behalf, the Earl of Suffolk discovered that René of Anjou lacked the funds to adequately dower his daughter. René also had the chutzpah to demand the counties of Maine and Anjou in exchange for his blessing. But the blood of countless fathers, husbands, and sons had been shed to conquer these territories for England. René's terms, *plus* an impoverished Margaret, would make Henry's countrymen livid.

But peace at any price was Henry's goal. So he and his council kept the terms of his marriage negotiations a secret from his subjects. At least England got to retain Normandy in the north and Aquitaine in the south. Henry also agreed to waive his right to Margaret's dowry and promised to pay for their wedding out of his privy purse.

Only a temporary truce was concluded through these negotiations, but the union of Henry and Margaret was viewed as a first step down the path to peace. The terms of the royal marriage were cemented by the Treaty of Tours, signed on May 22, 1422.

In order to save his future son-in-law some face (and money), at the eleventh hour the father of the bride appealed to the clergy of Anjou to kick in a few sous toward his daughter's nuptials. They spent 10.5 percent of their revenues to purchase a trousseau for Margaret and to pay for her betrothal celebration on French soil. Two days after the treaty was signed, Margaret and Henry were formally betrothed in Tours, amid tremendous pomp and ceremony, with Suffolk representing Henry.

Margaret's proxy wedding to Henry didn't take place until March 1445, when the French court, itinerant as most medieval courts were, had moved to Nancy. Once again, the Earl of Suffolk stood in for Henry at the altar. Margaret was gowned in white satin embroidered with gold and silver marguerites (the French word for daisies), her personal emblem. Marguerites were also embroidered on banners and hangings and on the bride's other garments.

An opulent banquet followed the ceremony, inaugurating a week of celebratory feasting and tournaments—presided over not by Margaret's aunt, queen Marie, but by Charles VII's glamorous blond mistress, Agnès Sorel. (Charles's love affair with Agnès is profiled in another volume in this series, *Royal Romances*.)

Although Henry's treasury was threadbare, he never stinted on gifts for his wife, even before their wedding. One was a hackney, "splendidly equipped, with an empty saddle," which he had sent to Rouen, where Margaret was enjoying some of the proxy wedding festivities prior to her departure for England.

On March 15, 1445, Margaret entered Paris. On Henry's behalf, she was welcomed by the thirty-three-year-old Richard, Duke of York, and a parade of six hundred archers. York presented Margaret with another one of Henry's wedding gifts: a palfrey handsomely caparisoned in crimson and gold velvet embellished with golden roses.

As the church bells pealed, Margaret's entourage promenaded through the streets of the capital. From there, her party continued to make its way toward the coast. She was York's guest at Pontoise, where he hosted two state dinners in her honor. At the time, their relationship was perfectly civil—although some two decades later, the pair would become mortal enemies.

England's Parliament had voted Henry VI more than £5,129 to bring his bride across the Channel, but expenses had skyrocketed, with delays due to weather, and the cost of transporting an entourage of hundreds of noblemen and women in fifty-six ships.

The Earl of Suffolk coached Margaret on her new role as queen of England prior to her departure from France. Although she spoke no English, she would turn out to be a quick student of her new tongue. Aware of the young queen's impoverished state—not merely her lack of a dowry, but her unglamorous attire—the earl was concerned that despite the contribution from her local clergy, fifteen-year-old Margaret was being sent abroad looking more like a pauper than a princess. The trousseau was paltry, although a merchant of Angers had contributed eleven ells of violet and crimson cloth of gold at thirty crowns per ell, plus a thousand small pieces of fur, and another furrier had furnished 120 pelts of white fur edging to embellish her robes.

Her arrival came on the heels of an embarrassing scandal. Margaret was so poor that she had to pawn some of her silver plate to pay her sailors' wages, and was compelled to purchase secondhand plate to replace it when she arrived at Rouen. Already there was grumbling in England that René of Anjou had "too short a purse to send his daughter honourably to the King, her spouse." An early foe of the royal marriage was Henry's uncle and former regent, Humphrey, Duke of Gloucester, who complained that Parliament had "bought a queen not worth ten marks."

Despite the massive cost overruns in bringing his bride to England, Henry wanted to see her well bestowed, authorizing the treasurer of his exchequer to deliver a number of jewelry items, including "Rubees, Perles," diamonds, and "greet Saphurs" (great sapphires) to "oure right entierly Welbeloved Wyf the Queene."

Meanwhile, Margaret's bridegroom so anxiously awaited her arrival that he disguised himself as a squire so that he could deliver a letter to her. As she perused it, he observed her. According to the Milanese ambassador, Henry was convinced that "a woman may be seen over well when she reads a letter."

Some scholars claim that Margaret became so absorbed in the correspondence that she scarcely noticed the messenger; nor did she appreciate Henry's trick. The Milanese ambassador reported that "the Queen was vexed at not having known it, because she had kept him on his knees." However, "Afterwards the King wrote to her, and they made great triumphs."

This messenger-with-a-letter charade was straight out of the playbook of courtly love. Margaret's father was France's most renowned poet and troubadour, and she was raised in sophisticated courts. It's more likely that she knew the game and was playing her part—the innocent damsel caught unawares who is "shocked" when the messenger reveals himself to be her swain.

So, now that the twenty-three-year-old Henry, long in the tooth for a royal bridegroom of his era, finally had the chance to see his queen in person, what *did* Margaret really look like?

She was only fifteen, which was not unusual for royal brides of the Middle Ages. Beyond that, it is difficult to separate her actual physical characteristics from the usual hyperbolic descriptions of medieval queens and the generic depictions in the fine art of the era. The nineteenth-century historian Georges Chastellain described her as "all that is majestic" in woman, believing her to be one of the most beautiful in the world. "She was indeed a very fair lady, altogether well worth the looking at, and of high bearing withal." Chastellain's portrayal of Margaret as "fair" corresponds to the depictions of her as honey haired, because queens of her day were portrayed as earthly representations of the Virgin and generally idealized as blondes, the era's *belle idéale*. And most artists who made portraits of Margaret likely never saw her. But it contradicts the Milanese ambassador's description to his boss's wife, Bianca Maria Sforza, that the queen of England was "a most handsome woman, though somewhat dark and not so beautiful as your serenity." So perhaps Margaret had a sallow, if not dusky complexion, and she may have been a brunette.

A contemporary French chronicler, Thomas Basin, described Margaret as "a good-looking and well-developed girl, who was then mature and ripe for marriage." From this description, which nonetheless remains in the eye of the beholder, one might conjecture that by the age of fifteen, Margaret had the body of a nubile young lady, rather than that of a coltish girl. But we still lack verifiable details on her hair and eye color, or her height and weight. Her personality and temperament, however, were described by Charles, duc d'Orléans, who observed that "this woman excelled all others, as well in beauty as in wit, and was of stomach and courage more like to a man than a woman."

Margaret would prove to be mercurial, too, known to change her mind "like a weathercock"—a complaint voiced by her male contemporaries. And she could be terribly vindictive to those who crossed her. But she was also fiercely loyal, and chiefly so to her husband, even when his ineffectiveness as a ruler and military leader exasperated her.

Margaret of Anjou had likely been told little about her husband before they met. So what did she see when she first laid eyes on the king of England after her arrival at Southampton on April 9, 1445?

Remarkably, no contemporary physical description of Henry VI survives, other than the observation that he had a childlike face. In 1910, after his skeleton was exhumed, it revealed that he had been well built and about five foot ten, which was considered quite tall for the day, with a fairly small head covered with brown hair. With respect to his personality, fifteenth-century chronicler Philippe de Commynes, who wasn't born until two years after Henry's marriage, ungenerously described the king as "a very ignorant and almost simple man," the word "simple" meaning "gullible" or "guileless" at the time.

Officiated by the king's confessor, Master William Ayscough, Bishop of Salisbury, the royal wedding took place on April 22, at Titchfield Abbey. Unlike the proxy wedding on French soil, the English ceremony was a quiet affair. Henry had pawned the crown jewels to pay for the event, only to realize that he needed them for the ceremony! So he redeemed the glittering treasures, placing some of his personal jewelry and plate into hock instead. Handsomely reset for her, Margaret's wedding band was a "ryng of gold, garnished with a fayr rubie" that Henry's cousin, Cardinal Beaufort, had given to *him* at his coronation. Clearly clueless regarding the etiquette about bringing wedding gifts to the church, an anonymous admirer gave Margaret a unique present—a pet lion—that was actually brought to the abbey. The king of the beasts was promptly sent to the royal menagerie, located at the Tower of London.

Because the treasury was so low on funds, Margaret would not receive the customary dower for fifteenth-century English queens until eleven months after her wedding. Her dower (the portion of her husband's property allotted for her use and enjoyment during her widowhood) amounted to ten thousand marks per annum, estates in the midlands worth two thousand pounds per annum, and additional lands in other parts of the kingdom.

On May 28, 1445, Margaret made her state entrance by barge into London, where for the next three days she was feted with numerous pageants and allegorical tableaux emphasizing her role as the bringer of peace and plenty. Lyrical poetry compared her to the Virgin Mary.

The streets of London were abundantly decorated with marguerites, both actual and figurative. But her parade met with a mixed reception. While some cheered her and sported marguerites in their caps, others scowled and grumbled, still smarting over the lack of a dowry from her father.

Nevertheless, Margaret looked positively bridal in a white damask gown, her golden coronet studded with precious gems. A pair of white palfreys whose caparisons matched her ensemble drew her carriage along the route to Westminster Abbey, where she was crowned on May 30, 1445. Three more days of celebration followed.

The royal honeymoon had begun at Titchfield Abbey, but according to one report that has been handed down through history, the newlyweds may not have had much fun, because the bishop had cautioned the groom against self-indulgence. When it came to having his "sport" with his new bride, Ayscough had put the fear of damnation into his protégé, warning Henry not to "come nigh her" any more often than absolutely required for procreative purposes. This admonition makes little sense, however. The bishop understood the importance of siring an heir for the health, security, and stability of the realm. It would, however, take Margaret eight years to conceive, so Henry might not have tried very often after all.

At least he was faithful to her, unlike many a royal husband. Henry also treated Margaret generously and kindly, and according to John Blacman's memoir, the king "kept his marriage vow wholly and sincerely, even in the absences of the lady," which "were sometimes very long." Nor "when they lived together did he use his wife unseemly, but with all honesty and gravity."

Yet the pair were hardly well mated, despite their mutual respect. Temperamentally, Margaret and Henry were polar opposites, with divergent interests in their leisure activities. Henry preferred to pore over scripture and other pious tracts, while Margaret liked the light and lascivious writings of Boccaccio.

At the outset, these differences didn't seem to cause much of a problem. During their first several years of marriage, Henry and Margaret spent considerable time together, evidently enjoying each other's company. At that time, she was no more than a traditional consort, acting as an intercessor and mediator for subjects and servants who sought the king's ear or his aid. She made philanthropic gifts, distributed patronage, and devoted her energies to the welfare of husband and household. And Margaret performed all her duties well. The one thing that was atypical of her was her failure to provide an heir.

Yet even though she was careful to tread softly, the English resented Margaret from the get-go. She was poor, she was French, and, where one issue was concerned, she was politically active. When it became known that the price of peace between England and France was the forfeiture of the hard-won territories of Maine and Anjou, Margaret was viewed as a meddler, sticking her female nose into the masculine sphere of government when she should have been making babies instead.

In December 1445, when the queen was still a newlywed, she wrote to Charles VII of France, agreeing to do her best to advance the peace process by delivering Maine. Clearly this topic had been a frequent source of discussion between husband and wife. Henry alluded to as much in his subsequent letter to Charles, written on December 22, in which he agreed to surrender Maine to him by April 30, 1446, not only because he desired peace, but "favouring also our most dear and well-beloved companion the queen, who has requested us to do this many times. . . ."

Contrary to the contention put forth by Margaret's enemies— that the teenage queen nagged her much older husband into such a major foreign policy decision—Henry had already promised the forfeiture of Anjou and Maine as the price of a lasting peace. The correspondence at the end of 1445 was just another step toward transforming words into deeds. And although Margaret was a good daughter and a loyal niece, after she married Henry—and particularly in later years, after the birth of their only son—her primary allegiance was to her husband, and her unceasing aim was to keep the English throne secure for their heir. In acting to return the two provinces to France, she was being less pro-French than pro-Henry. Margaret's biographer Helen Maurer suggests that she might have been well versed in Christine de Pisan's *Treasure of the City of Ladies*, a popular handbook and survival guide for medieval noblewomen that stressed, among other necessary skills and virtues, those of the mediator, playing the yin to her husband's yang.

Etiquette at the English court was rigid, and Margaret expected to be treated with the same respect and obeisance from her inferiors that they accorded to her husband. Her fans might view this behavior as fair enough, but her enemies saw it as arrogance. The mayor of Coventry was particularly chagrined when Margaret demanded that he carry his mace of office when he was escorting her from his city, even in the king's absence, and every supplicant seeking aid or redress from her—from the lowliest tradesman to a duchess or prince of the blood—was expected to approach her throne on their knees.

Having grown up poor, for a princess, Margaret soon learned to turn her power and authority as queen into personal financial advantage. Soon after her marriage, she obtained a license to export wool and tin, enabling her to evade customs duties and pocket the profits.

Margaret also introduced France's art of silk weaving to England, becoming patroness of a guild comprised solely of women, the Sisterhood of Silk Women, located in Spitalfields in the East End of London. Spitalfields silk remained internationally renowned through the nineteenth century. In the furtherance of England's interests in the textile market, Margaret also paid for the outfitting of merchant ships bound for Mediterranean ports.

Her own wardrobe was fairly modest for a queen. She did wear Venetian silk and cloth of gold, as well as jewelry, but her purchases were not unduly extravagant. However, during the first year of their marriage, Henry ordered extensive, and expensive, renovations to her rooms at Eltham Palace, which boasted their own kitchen and scullery as well as halls for entertaining—and Margaret did love to throw parties. It was common knowledge that her satellite court was *much* livelier than her husband's. Henry's focus was on religion and education instead, founding Eton College and King's College, Cambridge, although shortly after Henry's 1448 foundation of the latter institution, Margaret was inspired to found Queens' College, Cambridge. Henry, however, was actively involved in his educational projects, whereas Margaret does not appear to have taken any further personal interest in her own foundation.

By July 27, 1447, the terms were concluded for Henry to quit delaying and turn over Maine by November 1. On the following day, he nominated commissioners to transfer both Maine and Anjou to Charles VII. The English blamed Margaret for this surrender.

By this time, two of Henry's most powerful mentors—the Duke of Gloucester and Cardinal Beaufort—had died, and Margaret's influence on her husband increased. Every time Henry wrote a letter to someone, his queen followed up with a similar missive, demanding that she, too, be kept apprised of events and political matters, particularly if negotiations with France were involved. She also insisted on being kept in the loop with regard to financial and military affairs. All official papers were to be submitted to her for inspection, and even the highest-ranking government officials, including Suffolk, lacked the authority to act without her approval. At the time, she was only eighteen years old!

By the end of 1447, the court party, headed by Margaret and the earls of Suffolk and Somerset, controlled the king and government. However, the queen's insistence on micromanaging may not have been an effort to meddle or usurp Henry's authority at all. If the situation were viewed without the lens of a misogynist Francophobic medieval chronicler, it could be argued that Margaret knew her husband and his weaknesses better than anyone, and may have been acting in his best interests by keeping tabs on everything that was going on, making sure that no one else had a chance to control him or try to take over the government and possibly usurp the throne.

The Duke of York, who viewed Somerset as his greatest rival at court, then took it upon himself to campaign for government reform. York saw himself as a loyalist to Henry for wanting to rid the court of corruption. But the opposition, comprised of anyone excluded from the court party, looked to York to lead their faction. That led to Henry removing him from the center of power by appointing him Lord Lieutenant of Ireland for ten years.

By February 1448, when Henry had *still* not handed over Anjou and Maine, Charles VII took matters into his own hands and besieged the city of Le Mans in Maine. The English forces were unable to hold the city, and on March 16, Henry agreed to formally surrender, but only if the truce between France and England would extend until April 1450.

Predictably, the surrender went over poorly in England. In an effort to smooth things over, Margaret urged Henry to promise compensation to the English landowners who had been dispossessed in Maine and were now returning, landless, to England. Henry pledged, but never paid up, engendering further ill will against the crown.

In the spring of 1448, to reward the leaders of the court party for their service, Henry elevated Somerset from earl to duke. William de la Pole, the Earl of Suffolk, was also made a duke—the first time ducal rank was conferred on anyone other than a member of the royal family. Somerset and Suffolk now shared the same rank as York, who began using the surname Plantagenet, a resounding slap in the face to Henry VI, whose grandfather had snuffed out the last of that line, Richard II, and usurped Richard's throne.

York saw Somerset's elevation to a dukedom as a deliberate attempt by the king to block his own dynastic and political ambitions, as well as a prelude to naming Somerset as his heir in the continued absence of offspring. After three years of marriage, the combination of the royal couple's still-childless state, widespread dislike of Margaret, and Henry's ineffectiveness as a ruler made fertile ground for the seedlings of civil war. The enmity between York and Somerset now hardened into a deadly rivalry with clear factions. By March 1449, pressures to do something about the situation across the Channel were such that the peace-loving Henry broke the truce with France, authorizing his troops in Breton to attack Fougères. In June, he launched a full-scale attack on Normandy. Charles VII retaliated by formally declaring war against England.

The English scapegoated their sovereigns for these catastrophes. Rumors were spread that Margaret was illegitimate, and therefore unfit to be queen. Parliament called for a Resumption Act, whereby the crown would reclaim the lands Henry had given away to his cronies, but, predictably, the magnates who had received such largesse balked, preventing the act from becoming law. Henry's response was to dissolve Parliament.

According to a contemporary chronicler, by the 1450s "the realm of England was out of all good governance, for the King was simple [naive] and led by covetous counsel, and owed more than he was worth. His debts increased daily, but payment there was none. Such impositions [taxes] as were put to the people were spended in vain, for he kept no household nor maintained no wars."

In May 1450, the gentry of Kent rose up in revolt, led by Jack Cade, a prosperous gentleman who had penned a manifesto of grievances against the government. Cade's objections to its corruption were shared by Parliament, as well as several members of the nobility. Running with an age-old lie that the lately murdered Duke of Suffolk had been Margaret's lover, Cade frightened the citizens of Kent into believing that the queen intended to obtain vengeance by invading the county and burning their homes to the ground.

Although Cade's Rebellion began in the southeast of England, it swiftly gained momentum and was not restricted to the underclasses. Protestors included sheriffs, local officials, and two members of Parliament. Their concerns were universal. The violence soon spread to London. The king led his troops through the streets of the capital, but then bungled the city's defense by splitting his army in two; the result was a bloodbath, with the rebels getting the better of the royalist troops. Henry's soldiers mutinied. The madness continued into the summer. On June 29, the Bishop of Salisbury, who had officiated at Henry and Margaret's wedding, and who some believe had cautioned the king to abstain from recreational sex with his wife, was torn to pieces by a frenzied mob, killed, in the opinion of Judge Gascoigne, "because he was the confessor of Henry VI and did not remedy the defects around the King nor depart from the King because these were not remedied."

On July 2, Cade led his followers across London Bridge and was presented with the keys to the city. But rioting and looting subsequently erupted throughout London. When Cade himself participated in the pillaging, his supporters accused him of hypocrisy and the tide began to turn for the royal army.

At the height of the rebellion, the royal spouses parted ways. Resisting pleas from London's Lord Mayor to remain in the city, Henry fled the capital instead, first to Greenwich, then west to the castle of Berkhamsted in Hertfordshire, and then to Kenilworth Castle in the Midlands. Margaret stayed behind at Greenwich throughout the rioting. It was she who was instrumental in putting an end to the mayhem by lending her name as guarantor of a general pardon to the rebels, although Cade was ultimately captured and stabbed in a standoff.

Cade's Rebellion was unsuccessful in that neither his manifesto nor the violence changed the way Henry ruled. But it did prove how easy it was to foment civil war, and was only a taste of the strife that Margaret and Henry would face for the next eleven years. Additionally, it exposed Henry's weakness and Margaret's strength: He had panicked in a crisis, returning to London only after his *council* had restored law and order, while Margaret stayed put. In her consort's role as mediator, acting not on her own behalf, but always in her husband's interests, *she* saw the calamity through to a resolution that would mitigate the damage.

Meanwhile in France, Somerset surrendered Caen to the French. By the end of August 1450, England's only remaining possessions in France were Aquitaine and the tiny strip of land surrounding Calais. The reputations of Henry and Margaret were permanently tarnished by the humiliating defeats their armies had suffered across the Channel.

Somerset's ignominious losses on behalf of the crown so infuriated York that he returned from Ireland without Henry's permission, determined to lead an opposition party that demanded good governance and the sacking of Henry's advisers.

On November 6, 1450, when Henry opened Parliament at Westminster, some of the most powerful magnates arrived with armed forces behind them. Every day, a skirmish between the troops of Lancaster and York was expected; the antagonistic relationship between the dukes of York and Somerset was a powder keg waiting for a match. Riots *did* break out in the streets during this period, the first recorded occasion of "a great division between York and Lancaster," according to a chronicle of the times.

In May 1451, the subject of the royal couple's childless state after six years of wedlock reared its head again when Thomas Young, an MP for Bristol and a York supporter, was thrown into the Tower of London for daring to suggest that "because the king had no offspring, it would be for the security of the kingdom that it should be openly known who should be heir apparent and named the Duke of York."

On August 23, English forces surrendered Aquitaine to King Charles VII. By the autumn of 1451, it was clear that despite the rising tensions between the Lancastrian party and the Yorkists, the king had no intention of instituting any governmental reforms, although *nothing* Henry had done was a success. He had lost France. His kingdom was controlled by the fifteenth-century equivalent of special interest groups. His treasury was deeply mired in debt. And he had no heir.

Margaret's own spies informed her that York was mustering an army, and she urged her husband to do the same. Henry balked. Margaret then appealed to his chivalry and affection for her. If Henry should be killed by York's men, what would happen to her? Finally, but with great reluctance, the king agreed to take the necessary steps to raise an army.

York issued a manifesto that openly blamed Somerset for ruining the country and giving the king advice that was disastrous to the realm. By February 16, 1452, civil war was imminent. Margaret and Henry, at the head of his army, marched toward Coventry, hoping to head York off as he moved toward the capital. By many accounts, the opposing armies were almost evenly matched in terms of numbers: twenty-four thousand troops under the king and twenty thousand under York.

The forces met up in Kent, but it was Margaret, not her husband, who formed part of the party that was dispatched to negotiate a peaceful denouement; at that point, neither side was keen on actually coming to blows. However, York would return his allegiance to Henry only if the king punished the Duke of Somerset.

Henry ordered Somerset's arrest, on the proviso that York disbanded his troops—but no one was permitted to tell Margaret about it! Yet when the queen saw Somerset being force-marched out of his tent the following day, the sovereigns had a royal blowup. York arrived midargument to offer his obeisance to Henry, then realized he had walked in on a furious marital row. York also wondered why Somerset and the queen were present, because his deal with the king had been negotiated in secret. Then all four of them began to quarrel. Margaret shouted for *York's* arrest, but her husband refused to comply. However, perhaps to appease her, Henry rescinded his order for Somerset's arrest.

In a calculated move to ensure more adherents at a time of impending crisis, in 1452, Henry elevated to the peerage his half brothers Edmund and Jasper. They were his mother's sons from her second marriage to the Welshman Owen ap Maredudd ap Tewdwr; the Anglicized spelling, "Tudor," was not adopted until 1459. Edmund was made Earl of Richmond, and Jasper, Earl of Pembroke. Henry was extremely generous to his half brothers, with gifts of land, material goods, and opportunities for political influence. In return the Tudors would always remain loyal to the Lancastrian cause.

At long last, after nearly eight years of marriage, in April 1453, Margaret realized she was pregnant, and visited the shrine of Our Lady of Walsingham—where women often made pilgrimages in the hope of conceiving. There, she left an offering of pax, or thanks, for the long-awaited baby she was carrying. Yet rather than rush off to Henry with the terrific news that an heir was finally on the way, the queen confided her condition obliquely, through his chamberlain, Richard Tunstall, to tell, as Henry later wrote, "the first comfortable relation and notice that our most dearly beloved wife the Queen was *enceinte*, to our most singular consolation and to all true liege people's great joy and comfort."

Regardless of the roundabout manner in which he learned of his wife's pregnancy, Henry was so thrilled that he granted Tunstall an annuity of forty marks. Then he spent a whopping two hundred pounds on a commission with the royal jeweler, John Wynne of London, to create a "demi-cent" and to deliver it "unto our most dear and most entirely beloved wife, the Queen."

Meanwhile, in France, Charles VII triumphantly took Bordeaux on October 19, 1453. Three hundred years of British rule in Aquitaine had come to an end. Calais was now all that remained of the once-sizable English possessions on the Continent. In the eyes of his subjects, Henry VI was a disgrace to the memory of his father. York was perhaps the most livid of all, having personally spent years of his life and huge, unreimbursed sums from his own purse to maintain Henry V's conquests in France.

The king was now suffering from more than humiliation. During the first few days of August he was clearly ailing, showing signs of stress from the past several months of civil tension. On August 15, Henry was having dinner at Clarendon, his hunting lodge near Salisbury, when he complained of feeling inordinately sleepy. The next morning he had symptoms one might associate with a stroke: His head was lolling, he was paralytic, and he had lost the power of speech.

According to the Paston Letters—a collection of fifteenth-century correspondence between members of the Paston family, as well as letters written to others—Henry had sustained a "sudden and thoughtless fright."

No one knows what precipitated the event. His army's defeat in Bordeaux had shocked him, but did it send him *into* shock? Various medical speculations on the nature of Henry's illness have been made, from depressive stupor to catatonic schizophrenia. But whatever caused his state is less important than its impact on history.

When Henry showed no signs of improvement after several days, concern turned to panic. The queen conveyed her husband back to Westminster, continuing to conceal his condition from the public—something that could never happen today, with social media and a twenty-four-hour news cycle. Margaret most feared the Duke of York's discovering the situation, as he might take the opportunity to stage a coup. But when it proved too difficult to keep Henry's secret at Westminster, the queen removed him from the hub of government and brought him to Windsor.

Seven months pregnant, Margaret of Anjou became the de facto ruler of England.

Henry had suffered a complete breakdown of some kind, the manifestations of which were beyond mental or emotional incapacity. John Whethamstead in his *Registrum*, which chronicled the era, describes the episode as "a disease and disorder of such a sort . . . that he lost his wits and memory for a time, and nearly all his body was so unco-ordinated and out of control that he could neither walk nor hold his head up, nor easily move from where he sat," adding that the king had become "as mute as a calf." Henry was monitored around the clock by several pages and grooms, fed by these attendants, and supported by two of them whenever he was required to move from room to room.

Describing his condition as *non compos mentis*, a term that doctors applied at the time to madmen whose mental illness revealed itself later in life, the king's physicians tried all manner of cordials, ointments, laxatives, suppositories, and baths. They continued to assure Margaret that her husband would eventually recover, even though they had no firm diagnosis to give her. Perhaps, they theorized, he was possessed by devils. Henry's council authorized the physicians to bleed him as often as possible in order to purge him of the evil humors that were undoubtedly responsible for his loss of faculties.

With Henry utterly incapacitated and his unpopular wife, who displayed a tin ear for English politics, running the show, there was now no hope for unifying the court's squabbling factions.

At ten a.m. on October 13, 1453, Margaret gave birth to a son. Finally, after eight long years, the House of Lancaster had its heir. The queen named the boy after his father's favorite saint, Edward the Confessor, whose feast day was also being celebrated on the date of the prince's birth. But back at Windsor, Henry remained oblivious to the blessed event.

The infant's birth meant that York and Somerset could no longer squabble over the right to be named Henry's heir, but it created a new set of problems: While Henry remained incapacitated, who would govern the realm during his heir's minority? And if the king should die while his son was a baby, England would be in for a lengthy regency, just as it had been when *he* was an infant.

Later that month, swaddled in an embroidered chrisom-cloth and russet-colored cloth of gold, Edward was baptized in an opulent ceremony at Westminster. Neither of his parents attended the christening—the king's illness precluded his presence, and the queen could not appear in public until she had been churched, the ritual conducted forty days after childbirth to once again welcome a mother into the bosom of the Church.

It was necessary for Edward to be formally acknowledged by a council of magnates as heir to England's throne. And when York's name was deliberately omitted from the list, the duke took revenge through a convenient loophole: He reminded the other nobles that in accordance with established protocol, until the prince was presented to the king himself and acknowledged by him as his son, the succession could not be established. And, of course, Henry remained "uncurious and unconscious," in the words of a contemporary chronicler, despite several efforts to rouse him and make him bless the infant.

Because the public was unaware of their sovereign's condition, all they learned, as word began to spread, was that he had failed to acknowledge Margaret's son—only a partial truth—so rumors circulated, particularly during the winter of 1453 to 1454, that Edward was Somerset's bastard, or that the child was a changeling smuggled into Margaret's bed after she had given birth to a stillborn. This propaganda was all too credible, given Henry's well-known prudish views on sex, his pious habits, and the fact that the royal couple had never before conceived during their first seven years of marriage.

Meanwhile, York accumulated allies, including Henry's childhood tutor, one of England's wealthiest landowners, the Earl of Warwick, Richard Neville. Warwick had been a supporter of the Lancastrians until Henry confiscated one of his vast Welsh estates and gave it to Somerset. Charismatic and a smooth operator, the earl went about publicly proclaiming that Edward was not Henry's son, and therefore the king would *never* acknowledge the child. York cagily kept his mouth shut, but by his not defending Margaret's honor, his silence spoke volumes.

Margaret never allowed these rumors of her adultery to crush her pride. On November 18, 1453, she was churched, quite grandly, at Westminster. Her robe was trimmed with 540 sable pelts. In her train were seven baronesses, eight countesses, and a half dozen duchesses, including the wives of both Somerset and York. The prince's birth consolidated Margaret's power rather than weakened it. From that moment on, the queen intended to dominate the political stage. Her aim was to protect Edward's inheritance—the throne of England—at all costs, and her chief ambition was to crush the Duke of York. Because the king remained incoherent, Margaret of Anjou became the duke's greatest adversary and the primary obstacle between him and the crown.

As York gained support, Margaret, too, continued to further her aim. In January 1454, after another, last-ditch attempt was made to get Henry to recognize his son, according to the Paston Letters, the queen, "being a manly woman, using [being used to] rule and not being ruled," and unaware of when, or if, the king might ever awaken from his stupor, made a pitch to become Edward's regent. But because she was hampered by her gender as well as her French origins, her efforts didn't go over too well. However, Margaret's biographer Helen Maurer points out that Margaret could not have become regent anyway, because in the Middle Ages a wife was legally her husband's property, viewed by the law as an extension of himself. She could act as her husband's representative and agent, provided her actions expressed his will and had his authority, but on a legal technicality the king could not grant away any aspect of his decision-making capacity to Margaret as an independent person. Henry would only have been deeding such authority right back to himself, because a man and wife were viewed by the law as one and the same being. Additionally, during this era a regent was expected to lead the army and be the first man in the king's council, which was a boys-only clubhouse.

Finally, when Parliament convened on February 14, the Lords confirmed Edward's title as heir apparent, and York was compelled to assent to their decision. On March 15, the boy was made Prince of Wales, Earl of Chester, and a Knight of the Garter. Twelve days later, it was York whom the Lords named as Regent, awarding him the title Protector of the Realm.

On April 3, York commanded that Margaret and the prince be removed from Westminster to Windsor, ostensibly to be with the king, but it was a clear message that he wanted the queen far from the seat of government. A consort's place was in the home. But there was something sinister at work. Margaret was essentially under house arrest! When she found out that she was not permitted to quit Windsor, she became more convinced than ever that the nobles intended to make York the king of England.

And then suddenly, after sixteen and a half months of catatonia . . . there was a Christmas miracle!

On December 25, 1454, "by the grace of God the King recovered his health," described by one observer, "as a man who wakes after a long dream." He had absolutely no memory of anything that had transpired during the entire period of his illness. As soon as his powers of speech were restored, Henry ordered a Mass of thanksgiving, sending emissaries with offerings to Canterbury, as well as to the shrine of Edward the Confessor in Westminster Abbey.

On December 28, according to the Paston Letters, "the Queen came to him and brought my lord Prince with her. And then he asked what the Prince's name was, and the Queen told him Edward, and then he held up his hands and thanked God therefor. And he asked who were the godfathers, and the Queen told him, and he was well pleased."

On January 9, 1455, Edmund Clere, an esquire of the king's household, wrote to John Paston of the king's remarkable recovery. Henry had spoken to two clerics on January 7 ". . . as well as he ever did, and when they came out, they wept for joy."

Henry's recovery did not, however, mean that his throne was secure. By the spring of 1455, Somerset was still spreading rumors that York intended to depose the king. Margaret and Somerset had convinced Henry of York's plans as well.

Although Henry had declared that anyone who raised an army against him was a traitor, the respective royal houses finally came to blows on May 22, 1455, at St. Albans. The king nominally led his own army into battle, as the Duke of Buckingham was the actual commander of his forces. Henry sat astride his warhorse while arrows rained down around him. By the end of the day, Somerset was dead, Buckingham taken prisoner, and Henry had been pierced in the neck by an arrow. Inexplicably, he granted forgiveness to the Duke of York and his adherents.

The duke took possession of Henry's wounded body, and although the king still wore his crown, it had become clear that thenceforth the Yorkists would control the government. By the autumn of 1455, York was king in all but name. It is possible that the king suffered another neurological episode around this time, because Margaret's request to care for him was granted and York sent Henry to Margaret at Greenwich. The queen's intention was to get her husband into her protection so that she could influence him as well as look after his welfare. The Paston Letters report on October 28, 1455, that "summe men ar a-aferd that he is seek ageyn."

Nevertheless, Henry rallied enough to appear in Parliament and reassert his authority, revoking York's appointment in February 1456. However, by this time, Londoners in particular were fed up with Lancastrian mismanagement. Yet rather than blame the misrule on the king, his wife became the target of their ire.

But if Londoners didn't like the queen, the feeling was mutual. Margaret quit the capital and began to drum up support for her husband from the safety of Kenilworth. Unfortunately, this separation from the king meant that Henry was left under York's influence back in London.

To alleviate the threat, that summer Margaret convinced Henry to remove his court to the Lancastrian bastion of Coventry in the Midlands. Henry gave her chancellor, Laurence Booth, the privy seal, and with that imprimatur in her possession she had total power over the administrative nuts and bolts of her husband's government.

The queen then embarked on an effort of good public relations, appearing in public with her son, promoting English trade and industry, founding schools and hospitals, and shoring up the people's goodwill. Yet while Margaret focused on consolidating her power, there were riots in London. The queen began to stockpile arms as she continued to endure the rampant gossip that would plague her for the next several years: that the Prince of Wales was a love child. More than one court favorite was cited as the boy's father.

In December 1457, taking a more active role than her husband in their efforts to secure his throne, Margaret introduced military conscription to ensure that the Lancastrians would have enough soldiers to defend the crown. Although conscription had been used in France, the English had never before availed themselves of the system, and the queen's new measures were extremely unpopular. As Margaret drummed up support in the event of another inevitable skirmish with the Yorkists, Henry, ever determined to broker peace, was quoting biblical passages, citing Saint Matthew: "Every kingdom divided against itself is brought to desolation."

While Yorkist propaganda successfully claimed that the king had been led astray by evil counselors, including his wife, that he had placed himself above the law, and banished "all righteousness and justice" from the kingdom, Margaret harbored the overwhelming fear that the Prince of Wales would never succeed her husband. In one of the Paston Letters dated February 9, 1456, John Bocking wrote to John Fastolf, "The Quene is a grete and strong labourid woman, for she spareth noo peyne to sue hire thinges to an intent and conclusion to hir power." In other words, by the early part of 1459, Margaret had become commander in chief of the royal forces.

Unfortunately for her, the Yorkists achieved another resounding victory in July 1460 at the Battle of Northampton. Henry was captured by a Yorkist archer who brought the king to his tent, where the Earl of Warwick and York's son the Earl of March (the future Edward IV) swore fealty to Henry, but refused to free him.

Margaret, who had been at Eccleshall Castle during the battle, was devastated by the news of her husband's capture. She took flight with their son, heading through Cheshire toward Wales, but was robbed of her jewels and the other luxury goods she carried by one of her own servants, John Cleger. Cleger even threatened to kill the queen and her son—at which point, rather than defend their mistress, several of Margaret's entourage deserted her. Margaret and Edward managed to escape while the covetous Cleger rifled through her baggage.

Temporarily frightened, but ultimately undeterred, the queen then made a clever political feint, spreading the word that she'd gone to France to enlist troops there. In fact, she traveled in the other direction, going only as far as Denbigh, a market town in Wales. She began what would be a quest for any and every kind of aid (troops, money, alliances) that would take her from England to Scotland to France, while Henry remained under York's watchful eye.

On October 7, 1460, Henry attended the opening day of Parliament, but after that, he stayed in the queen's apartments in Westminster Palace. York entered London with great pageantry and arrogantly asserted his claim to the throne, expecting a warm reception. Instead, he was greeted with an embarrassed silence from the Lords. Weak though he was, and despite his rampant misgovernment, Henry had been king for thirty-eight years, and the Lords saw no reason for him to be deposed.

After considerable negotiation between Henry and York, an Act of Accord was announced on October 31. The decision made by Parliament formalized the new order of succession. Henry VI would remain on the throne for the duration of his lifetime, but Edward of Lancaster, Prince of Wales, was effectively disinherited in favor of the Duke of York, who was now proclaimed Henry's heir apparent.

Henry dispatched a messenger to Margaret, asking her to bring their son to London. If she failed to do so, she would be declared a rebel.

From this point on, the power struggle between the houses of Lancaster and York was no longer about governmental reform. It was for the crown itself. And, as demonstrated by the outcomes of the various Wars of the Roses, might would make right.

With York proclaimed heir to the throne and Protector of England for the second time, he now ruled the realm in Henry's name. Margaret was at Hull when she learned of their son's dispossession. Naturally she became even more determined to recruit men who would stand up for the Lancastrian cause, mustering twenty thousand by the time she reached the city of York. She made a formal public protest against the Act of Accord and announced her intention to lead her forces into London and free her husband from his enemies.

Before she could do so, on December 30, York was killed at the Battle of Wakefield—a skirmish between his troops and Margaret's forces. The duke's corpse was beheaded, and further humiliated when a paper crown was placed upon his decapitated head. York's seventeen-year-old son, the Earl of Rutland, was killed and beheaded as well.

After Wakefield the fight for the English throne became even more violent. The most popular Yorkist talking point was that the Lancastrians were usurpers, their dynasty founded upon a regicide—the murder of Richard II. The Lancastrians contended that *they* had held the throne for the past three generations, and with even more right to it.

Following many months of separation, the royal family was tearfully reunited after the second battle of St. Albans in February 1461. But Margaret's hesitation to march her troops into London (where carts of victuals intended for her soldiers had been intercepted by pro-York citizens) was a fatal mistake for the Lancastrians. On February 27, the eighteen-year-old Earl of March, Edward of York, eldest son of the decapitated duke, rode into the capital with twenty thousand knights and thirty thousand foot soldiers behind him, taking possession of the city. As Londoners cried, "Avenge us on King Henry and his wife!" the earl was proclaimed King Edward IV. He vowed not to be crowned until Henry and Margaret had been executed or exiled, declaring that Henry had forfeited his right to the throne by violating the Act of Accord and permitting his wife to take up arms against the crown's rightful heirs.

For the next several years, Margaret and Henry were more or less in self-imposed exile as they eluded capture by Edward's forces. Henry first sought sanctuary in the Convent of Greyfriars at Kirkcudbright, while the queen and Prince of Wales traveled to the Scottish court. They were still in Scotland when, with great fanfare, Edward IV was crowned king of England in Westminster Abbey on June 28, 1461.

On November 4, acts of attainder were passed in Parliament dispossessing 150 loyal Lancastrians of their estates, including Henry VI. *He*, and not Edward IV, was referred to as "the usurper," Margaret was "late called Queen of England," and Edward of Lancaster was described as Margaret's son, but not Henry's. Edward IV even had the duchy of Lancaster declared forfeit to the crown, and henceforth, all English subjects were forbidden, upon pain of death, to communicate with Henry and Margaret.

After her fund-raising sojourn in Scotland, Margaret went to France with the Prince of Wales, seeking an alliance with their king. Her uncle Charles VII had died and his son was on the throne as Louis XI. On June 28, 1462, Margaret signed a hundred-year truce with France on Henry's behalf. It stated that all English subjects were prohibited from setting foot on French soil unless they were loyal to her husband; nor were they to enter into any compacts with Henry's known enemies or any other of his rebellious subjects (in other words, Edward IV).

The price of this treaty: Calais.

Margaret possessed nearly superhuman indomitability and courage, and she never lost her resolve to recapture Henry's throne. She reconnoitered with her husband at Berwick, just south of England's border with Scotland, and, leaving their son there, the deposed sovereigns sallied forth to invade England. With only eight hundred men in addition to their respective entourages, they were woefully outnumbered by Edward IV's army. Then a storm and a disastrous shipwreck destroyed their plans.

Margaret's travails continued into 1463. Alternately on the offense and on the defense, she was robbed of her jewelry, nearly murdered, and she and the Prince of Wales were kidnapped. The queen managed to break free and get to Edinburgh, but was so impoverished that she had to borrow a groat from an archer to make an offering on Saint Margaret's feast day. That summer, leaving Henry behind at Bamburgh Castle in Northumbria, Margaret resumed her Continental peregrinations in search of alliances and funds, but she was not met with open arms.

After the Lancastrians suffered another humiliating military defeat at the Battle of Hexham on May 15, 1464, Henry remained a fugitive for more than a year, transferring from one safe house to another. But in July of 1465, his luck ran out when he was recognized at Waddington Hall by a Yorkist sympathizer. A skirmish broke out and Henry fled into nearby Clitherow Forest, where he was taken captive.

Henry was transported south to London in the most ignominious conditions—bound to a small horse without spurs, his legs tied to the stirrups with leather thongs. A rope tethered him to the saddle, and the straw hat of a penitent had been placed upon his head. Paraded through the streets of London, he was pelted with rocks and refuse. Insults rained down on him as well, some of them deriding his wife. One heckler even accused the former queen of being "shameless with her body."

Henry was then incarcerated in the Tower of London. Accounts diverge regarding the welcome he received there, some averring that he was respectfully treated, others that he was left in poor hygienic conditions. "Anybody was allowed to come and speak to him," insisted John Warkworth, a chronicler of the reign of Edward IV, and one visitor managed to attack the deposed king with a dagger, wounding him in the neck. Henry forgave his assailant, chastising him for doing "foully to smite a king anointed so." Margaret was devastated by the news of Henry's capture. She would have liked nothing better than to raise an army and rescue him, but he was being held alive in exchange for her good behavior.

Meanwhile, Edward of Lancaster was maturing quickly and would soon be able to avenge his father's deposition. The ambassador from Milan observed that Margaret and Henry's son, "though only thirteen years of age, talks of nothing else but cutting off heads or making war, as if he had everything in his hands or was the god of battle."

Henry remained in the Tower for the next five years. In the interim, disaffected with Edward IV, Warwick the "kingmaker" turned his coat. At the urging of the French sovereign, the earl brokered an unholy alliance with Margaret to help Henry regain his crown. Warwick's price was the marriage of his younger daughter, Anne Neville, to Margaret and Henry's son, with the promise that the earl would be named Regent and Governor of England if

Henry became king again, but died before Edward of Lancaster attained his majority.

The fifteenth-century chronicler Philippe de Commynes registered his shock at this new alliance. Margaret had repeatedly condemned Warwick, and with good reason! In the past he had slandered her character and consistently worked not only to dethrone, but to imprison Henry. Now she was prepared to wed their only son to "the daughter of him that did it!"

On July 25, 1470, Edward of Lancaster was betrothed to Anne Neville in Angers Cathedral. Politics make strange bedfellows, but this union was not a recipe for success. Sixteen-year-old Edward had a penchant for violence, bearing a perpetual grudge against the world and a thirst for revenge. Each teen had been raised to despise the other's parents, and Margaret had agreed to the match only as a means of restoring her husband to the throne. A papal dispensation was required before the kids could wed, because they were related— cousins in the fourth degree, both being great-grandchildren of John of Gaunt.

On September 13, 1470, Warwick and his supporters arrived on English soil and proclaimed Henry VI "the very true and undoubted King of England," calling upon the people to take up arms against the usurper Edward IV. The earl issued a proclamation stating that his invasion had been authorized "by the assent of the most noble princess, Margaret, Queen of England, and the right high and mighty Prince Edward."

With popular opinion—and an army—against him, Edward IV fled for the Continent and Henry VI was released from the Tower of London, emerging from his long incarceration, according to the chronicler John Warkworth, "as a man amazed, utterly dulled with troubles and adversities." Nor was he ". . . worshipfully arrayed as a prince, and not so cleanly kept as should seem such a prince."

Enthroned for a second time on October 3, 1470, Henry had been propped up on the throne by Warwick, who set the crown upon his head and made a great show of reverence before him, but the sovereign seemed more confused than pleased about it. No wonder, when his nemesis bowed before him! Observers noted that Henry sat on the throne as limp as a sack of vegetables. The *Great*

Chronicle of London stated, "He was a mere shadow and pretence." The real ruler of England was Warwick, functioning as Henry's lieutenant. The restored king's mind had been unstable before his imprisonment, but incarceration had surely dulled it further. However, despite the medieval chroniclers' assertion that "what was done in his name was done without his will and knowledge," most modern historians believe that Henry was not deranged, and fully lucid.

In the royal records this period was referred to as "the 49th year of the reign of Henry VI and the first of his readeption to royal power," otherwise known as the Readeption. The math ignored the fact that for the previous decade, Edward IV had been on the throne.

The Readeption Parliament confirmed Edward of Lancaster's right to be king, reinstating Henry's son in the line of succession. But he wed Anne Neville without the necessary papal dispensation, because it took too long to arrive. Permission was procured instead from another authority, the Eastern Orthodox Patriarch of Jerusalem, and the teens were married on December 13, 1470, in a lavish ceremony officiated by the Grand Vicar of Bayeux. Yet Margaret forbade her son to consummate his nuptials. Should Warwick's star plummet (and no one but the members of the Commons liked him), his daughter would hardly be an appropriate match for the Prince of Wales.

Shortly after the wedding, Henry VI authorized a two-thousand-pound expenditure from his exchequer for Warwick to collect Margaret and the newlyweds in France and escort them back to England, reuniting them with the king. But Warwick spent the money elsewhere and went only as far as Dover to await the queen's arrival. Unfortunately, no one told Margaret about the change in plans, and when Warwick never arrived in Rouen, she had to rethink her strategy to reach England. Three times she endeavored to embark from Normandy, but met with punishing storms.

Edward IV was also on the Continent, in self-imposed exile since Henry VI's readeption. By now he had raised enough support to plan an invasion and retake the throne. The fate of England rested on who landed first: Margaret of Anjou or Edward IV.

Margaret delayed her departure after learning of Edward IV's possible invasion; she feared that her ships would be caught in the cross fire. Finally, on March 24, 1471, with great trepidation she sailed from Harfleur with the Prince and Princess of Wales, a handful of trusted advisers, and three thousand French chevaliers and squires. Many of the Lancastrian lords had left London in order to greet Margaret upon her arrival in the West Country—so they were not in the capital to prevent Edward IV and his forces from marching right through the city gates.

On April 9, the Tower was taken for Edward, giving him clear access to the capital. Two days later, he entered London in triumph, welcomed by the citizens with open arms. He went to St. Paul's Cathedral, where the Archbishop of Canterbury gave thanks for his restoration to the throne, declaring Henry VI deposed.

At the bishop's palace, the forty-nine-year-old Henry embraced Edward, humbly declaring, "My cousin of York, you are very welcome. I know that in your hands my life will not be in danger." After ordering Henry transferred to the Tower, later that day in Westminster Abbey, Edward IV was recrowned king of England. There was no more hope for the Lancastrians. Warwick was killed at the Battle of Barnet on April 13, cementing the victory for Edward IV and the Yorkists. By that evening, Henry VI was once more considered a prisoner of the state.

Although Margaret reportedly fainted at the news of Warwick's death, she swiftly rallied her strength and her forces, never losing sight of her purpose. It was imperative to save the kingdom for her son! Margaret and Edward of Lancaster sent out summonses to their supporters, rallying them, in the chronicler Hall's words, "to the banner of the red rose."

By the end of April, the stage was set for a genuine battle royal between the forces of Margaret of Anjou and those of Edward IV. But on May 4, Edward of Lancaster was felled in his first taste of warfare at the Battle of Tewkesbury. Historians' accounts differ, depending on the chroniclers' allegiances. The *Croyland Chronicle* of 1486, written when the first Tudor, Henry VI's half brother's son, Henry VII, was on the throne, stated that Edward of Lancaster died "either on the field or after the battle, by the avenging hands of certain persons."

Sixteenth-century Tudor historians Vergil and Edward Hall

claim that the prince was taken alive during the battle, and that after the fighting was over he was hauled before Edward IV, who received him graciously and asked why the youth had taken up arms against him. The prince hotly replied, "I came to recover my father's heritage. My father has been miserably oppressed and the crown usurped." While the story may be apocryphal, the angry quote wouldn't be out of character for the younger Edward.

As the story continues, Edward IV became irate at such disrespect and slapped Edward of Lancaster across the mouth with his gauntlet. The king's two brothers, the dukes of Clarence and Gloucester, along with their pal Sir William Hastings, then turned the prince into a human pincushion with their swords.

However he died, Edward of Lancaster's corpse was interred in the church of the monastery of the black monks at Tewkesbury. The epitaph for the only child of Henry VI and Margaret of Anjou, dead at the age of seventeen, read:

Here lies Edward, Prince of Wales,
Cruelly slain while a youth.
Anno Domini 1471.
Alas, the savagery of men,
Thou art the sole light of thy mother,
the last hope of thy race.

During the battle, Margaret had gone into hiding with Anne Neville, but the pair were discovered at Little Malvern Priory in Worcestershire and taken into custody on May 7, 1471, by Sir William Stanley, who informed the deposed queen of her son's death. Hysterical, Margaret had to be dragged from the abbey. She and Anne were brought before Edward IV on May 11. Margaret hurled so many invectives at the usurping king that he considered executing her. But the code of chivalry did not permit knights to abuse damsels in such legitimate distress. After Edward assured her that he would deal leniently with her and treat her with respect, Margaret politely replied that she would place herself "at his commandment."

On May 14, Edward IV departed for London with Margaret of

Anjou in his entourage. He entered the city a week later at the head of a triumphant procession. Like a conquering Caesar he paraded his spoils of war: his vanquished. Ahead of the king, perched atop a litter, rode Margaret of Anjou. She was taunted and pelted with refuse by the jeering crowd.

Henry VI remained imprisoned in the Tower. And perhaps he might have languished there, but a Lancastrian uprising fomented by the Earl of Warwick's cousin, Thomas, Bastard of Fauconberg, sealed Henry's death warrant. As long as Henry lived, someone somewhere would be tempted to incite rebellion in his name and attempt to resuscitate the House of Lancaster's claim to the throne. Civil war would rage indefinitely. The crown would perpetually have to raise revenues to muster troops and defend itself.

The *Warkworth Chronicle*, a late medieval account of events, stated, "And in the same night that King Edward came to London, King Henry, being in ward in prison in the Tower of London, was put to death, between eleven and twelve of the clock, being then at the Tower the Duke of Gloucester." These accounts were written some years later, during the reign of Henry VII. In 1485 at Bosworth Field, the last major battle of the Cousins' War, Henry, then Earl of Richmond, slew Richard III (the former Duke of Gloucester), who in 1483 had usurped the throne he was supposed to be keeping warm for Edward's young son.

Naturally, it was in the interests of Tudor chroniclers to further blacken the name of the man whose crown Henry VII placed upon his own head, declaring himself the new king of England. Nevertheless, it was *also* entirely in character for Richard to play the consigliere for Edward IV and to do his older brother's violent bidding, even though no one has, beyond a shadow of a doubt, placed Gloucester's hands on the weapon(s) that eliminated Henry VI.

Tradition has it that Henry was praying in a niche within his chamber in the Wakefield Tower when he was murdered on the night of May 21, 1471. But the court's official story was that Henry had died of grief upon hearing of his son's death and the capture of his wife. However, no one believed it. The Milanese ambassador thought that the king was directly involved, remarking that Edward IV "caused King Henry to be secretly assassinated in the

Tower. He has, in short, chosen to crush the seed." Philippe de Commynes was convinced that the Duke of Gloucester (who'd also probably stabbed Edward of Lancaster) "killed poor Henry with his own hand, or else caused him to be killed in his presence."

And Vergil, a Tudor chronicler, averred that it was generally believed that "Gloucester killed him with a sword."

A sword thrust from Richard, Duke of Gloucester, or from anyone else, may have been harder to prove, but poor Henry VI did not go gently into the good night. When his bones were exhumed in 1910, his skull was found to be "much broken," the result of a severe blow, if not many, to the head.

Shortly after the king's demise, Henry's corpse was carried through the streets of London to St. Paul's, where it lay in state overnight, "opyn vysagid, that he mygth be knowyn," according to the *Great Chronicle of London*. The contemporary accounts report, as Shakespeare would later dramatize, that the dead king's body bled afresh onto the pavement, to the shock of onlookers. According to the *Great Chronicle* it was proof positive of Gloucester's guilt in Henry's judicial murder.

Margaret of Anjou's whereabouts on the night her husband was brutally killed are unknown, and her reaction to the news of his death is unrecorded, although it's a safe bet that she was both hysterical and vitriolic. Her requests to gain custody of his corpse were denied.

Henry VI's funeral was held at the monastery of the Black Friars. His body was then taken by barge up the Thames to Chertsey Abbey, where it was modestly interred in the Lady Chapel. Although Henry had been a weak ruler, he was renowned as a pious man, and this reputation was magnified to the nth degree after his death. Lancastrian propaganda all but canonized him as soon as he died (the corpse's bleeding-afresh phenomenon surely contributed to the myth), and word quickly spread that Henry had died a martyr. Soon people were making pilgrimages to Chertsey, where it was claimed 155 miracles took place at the late king's tomb. His former subjects venerated him as a saint—his incompetent administration of the realm all but forgotten.

In 1484, Richard III ordered Henry's body to be reinterred at

St. George's Chapel, Windsor. It was discovered that the corpse appeared uncorrupted and smelled just as sweet after thirteen years. To true believers, it was further proof of divine intervention. Richard even ordered Henry's royal effects to be displayed near the tomb as relics.

The room within the Tower where Henry was murdered was turned into a shrine as his cult spread, although it was dismantled in the 1530s by Henry VIII's commissioners. Nevertheless, every year on the night of May 21, the governors of Eton College, which Henry founded, place a bouquet of lilies (for France, perhaps) and red roses (for Lancaster) at the spot where Henry was supposedly felled.

Soon after her husband's death, Edward IV ordered Margaret of Anjou to be transferred from the Tower to Windsor Castle, where she remained under house arrest until July 8, 1471. After that, she was moved to Wallingford Castle, near the home of her good friend Alice Chaucer, dowager Duchess of Suffolk. Edward IV appointed Alice to be Margaret's guardian—considered a kindness on his part, as things could have gone much worse for the former queen and she could have met with a violent end.

After Alice died in 1475, Margaret was ransomed by the king of France, Louis XI, and returned to her homeland. On January 29, 1476, she was compelled to sign a formal renunciation, releasing all rights that her marriage in England had given her. Margaret's father supported her until his death in 1480. After the demise of René of Anjou, Margaret subsisted on a meager royal pension in exchange for relinquishing to the crown all claims to her Angevin territorial inheritances *and* her mother's properties in Lorraine. It was more than adequate compensation, Louis XI insisted, for the substantial expenses he had incurred on Margaret's behalf since 1462.

On August 25, 1482, at the age of fifty-two, Margaret of Anjou died in tremendous poverty after suffering from a short, unspecified illness, and was entombed beside her parents at Angers Cathedral. Her remains were desecrated—removed and scattered—when the cathedral was ransacked during the French Revolution.

It is spectacularly ironic that Margaret of Anjou bears such a ghastly reputation for acting in what was deemed an "unwomanly" manner when everything she did would, by the same lights, be considered the most natural behavior for any woman: Even at her own peril, she always wanted what was best for her husband and their only son. Her union with Henry, though a mismatch of temperaments, was in many ways doomed to failure because medieval England was prejudiced against a French-born queen, especially a dowerless one whose marriage terms included the return of two provinces the English had shed much blood to conquer. As a couple, Henry and Margaret endured perpetual ignominy: eight years of a childless marriage, his recurring bouts of "madness," and the countless rumors questioning the paternity of their only child, which, by default, falsely tarred Margaret as an adulteress. Their subjects certainly saw the marriage as an inglorious one: In their opinion England's malleable sovereign, a pious pacifist, had wed a pushy foreign wife who tried to control the government in his stead.

And yet, what their critics fail to recognize is that Henry VI and Margaret of Anjou were devoted spouses during an immensely tumultuous age. Throughout their thirty-six-year marriage, no one was a fiercer advocate for Henry than his wife. For decades, their traditional roles were reversed: Henry was the damsel in distress, while Margaret acted as his knight in shining armor, more actual than metaphorical.

Henry was a weak king who twice lost his crown and died ingloriously—but not without his "right entierly Welbeloved Wyf" putting up the fight of her life to prevent his downfall.

MARGARET TUDOR

AND

JAMES IV OF SCOTLAND

MARRIED: 1503–1513

AND

ARCHIBALD DOUGLAS, 6TH EARL OF ANGUS

MARRIED: 1514–1527

AND

HENRY STEWART, 1ST LORD METHVEN

MARRIED: 1528–1541

*S*candal seemed to follow Henry VIII's elder sister wherever she went. While her first marriage was a glorious union on paper, in practice it was tarnished by her husband's flagrant infidelity. Margaret subsequently married beneath her—twice. But wedding for love was considered inglorious for a queen, who was supposed to make grand international alliances that would further her kingdom's interests. Margaret's choices instead angered her subjects, not to mention her brother.

Named for her paternal grandmother, Margaret Beaufort, Margaret Tudor was the second child of Henry VII, the first Tudor king. Henry, Earl of Richmond, had gained the throne by defeating

Richard III at the Battle of Bosworth in 1485. Legend has it that the murdered king's crown was plucked from the branches of a thornbush and placed on the earl's victorious head. From that moment on, Henry Tudor, who traced his lineage to the Lancastrian line of kings, would need to hold on to this crown, obtained so tenuously, by any means necessary. That meant securing as many allies as possible. The best way to cement such alliances was through marriage.

He began with his own—to the niece of Richard III, the beautiful blond Elizabeth of York, eldest daughter of Richard's predecessor, Edward IV. Their wedding united the long-feuding houses of York and Lancaster—those cousins who scrabbled for decades in what we now call the Wars of the Roses.

The eldest daughter of Henry and Elizabeth, Margaret Tudor was raised as a proper Renaissance princess, learning to dance, speak Latin, play the lute and clavichord, and prove her mettle at the archery butts. Negotiations for her own royal marriage began in 1496, when she was only six years old. The designated groom was her father's closest neighbor and ofttimes enemy, King James IV of Scotland. But negotiations were forestalled by the threat of Perkin Warbeck, a pretender to the English throne who claimed to be the nephew of Richard III. Warbeck was backed by the Scots, who believed his contention.

In any event, Margaret's proposed match with James was not met with full approval in England. Some of Henry's council objected to it on the grounds that Scotland was not only a poor and, in their view, backward country, but that a union between their king and Henry's daughter would place the Stewarts, James's family line, in direct succession for the English throne. The far-thinking Henry VII cannily countered, "Supposing, which God forbid, that all my male progeny should become extinct and the kingdom devolve by law to Margaret's heirs, will England be damaged thereby, or rather benefited? For since the less becomes subservient to the greater, the accession will be that of Scotland to England, not of England to Scotland."

Additionally, a papal dispensation was necessary for Margaret to wed James, because they stood within the prohibited degree of kinship. They both descended from a common ancestor, their great-great-grandfather John Beaufort—the oldest son of John of Gaunt and his third wife, Katherine Swynford.

James IV had been crowned king of Scotland on June 24, 1488, just two weeks after the death of his father, following the Battle of Sauchieburn, near Stirling. During the fighting, a skirmish between King James III's adherents and a group of rebels that included his own son James and the 5th Earl of Angus, the king was thrown from his horse and dragged, bruised and bleeding, into the mill of Bannockburn by the miller and his wife. The injured king demanded to see a priest, whereupon the miller's wife ran into the street and called for a cleric to attend the king. A passerby responded, but turned out to be no man of the cloth. When the wounded James III asked this "priest" to shrive him, and to give him the sacrament, the stranger hastily agreed to oblige—which he did by drawing a sword and driving it through the king's body several times.

Upon learning that he might have played a role in his father's demise, young James took to wearing a heavy iron chain about his waist in an act of perpetual penance.

In theory, James IV looked like a perfect match for Margaret Tudor, even though he was several years older: He was an accomplished musician, interested in the sciences, a patron of the arts, a sportsman who was fond of hunting and hawking, a nimble dancer, and was fluent in ten languages—the last of the Scots monarchs to speak the Scots Gaelic dialect. He even enjoyed embroidery! However, he was also quite the womanizer, juggling a series of mistresses, often simultaneously.

While the negotiations for his marriage to Margaret Tudor continued, James continued to sport with his inamoratas, Janet Kennedy and Margaret Drummond, although he had fewer playmates by the time he got married. Mistress Drummond died of food poisoning a few months after James's marriage negotiations were concluded in January 1502. According to the terms of the contract, Henry VII promised his daughter a dowry of ten thousand pounds; James pledged an additional thousand pounds Scots annually, plus estates yielding a further income of six thousand pounds.

However, the proxy wedding ceremony in England wasn't conducted for another year. In the interim, Margaret's older brother, Arthur, Prince of Wales, had died. On January 15, 1503, the Earl of Bothwell represented the thirty-year-old Scots king at the altar, followed by the tolling of church bells, the illumination of bonfires, and much feasting, jousting, and dancing. Margaret, a pretty girl with a cherubic face and the characteristic Tudor red-gold hair, was only thirteen years old, about the average age for a royal bride of the era.

Elizabeth of York died just a month later, nine days after giving birth to a daughter on February 2. Margaret was left to prepare for the marriage in Scotland without her mother's wisdom and guidance, mourning also her infant sister, who did not live much longer. She finally set off on the thirty-three-day journey north to her new homeland on July 8, arriving in Edinburgh in early August.

Bride and bridegroom saw each other for the first time during a courtly charade on August 3. The custom of the times demanded that James appear to be on a hunting expedition, and, hearing that his bride was near at hand, canter over to pay her a surprise visit. Dressed to impress, the king was attired in crimson and cloth of gold, his long, flowing hair and the length of his beard a thing to behold. Instead of his crossbow, in the manner of lovers, he wore a lyre across his back. James bowed low and kissed Margaret's hand and she curtsied deeply. After he kissed the hands of each of her attendants, James led Margaret a few steps away for their first private conversation.

A few more days of celebration followed, featuring allegorical pageants and a musical flirtation between the pair as they displayed their respective talents. Finally the Scots king and the English princess were wed at Holyroodhouse on August 8, 1503. As Ishbel C. M. Barnes relates in her biography *Janet Kennedy, Royal Mistress: Marriage and Divorce at the Courts of James IV and V*, John Young, Somerset Herald, a member of Margaret's retinue, left a detailed account of her first wedding.

> Between eight and nine o'clock everyone was ready, nobly clothed: and the ladies came richly dressed, some in gowns of cloth of gold, others in crimson velvet and black, others

in satin or damask with hoods, chains and collars on their necks and accompanied by their gentlewomen, to hold company with the queen. The queen was brought from her chamber to the church crowned with a very rich crown of gold [it was studded with pearls and precious gemstones], led on the right hand by the Archbishop of York and on the left hand by the earl of Surrey, her train was carried by the countess of Surrey. . . .

Thus the queen was . . . placed near to the font . . . and all her noble company being in order on the left side of the church. Then entered the Archbishop of Glasgow and the other clergy. He was followed by the king, accompanied by his household, his nobles, lords, knights, squires and gentlemen who all stood in order on the right side of the church.

Then the king came near the queen and made reverence and she to him, very humbly. The king was in a gown of white damask, figured with gold and lined with sarsenet. He had on a jacket with sleeves of crimson satin and black velvet, under that a doublet of cloth of gold and a pair of scarlet hose, his shirt was embroidered with gold thread, his bonnet was black and he wore his sword. The queen was dressed in a rich robe like the king, with a rich collar of gold and pearls on her neck and the crown upon her head.

The Archbishop of Glasgow then performed the marriage and the Archbishop of York read the papal bulls consenting to the marriage. . . . The mass followed and later a vast dinner was served [the guests dining off golden plates, partaking of a gilded boar's head, an enormous ham, and a dozen more dishes], the lords and ladies eating in separate halls. Then followed dancing, the king went alone without the queen to evensong and supper followed. After the supper night approached and everyone withdrew to his lodging to rest "and the Kinge had the Qwene aparte, and they went togeder." The feasting, jousting and dancing continued until Sunday the thirteenth of August. "And that doon, every Man went his Way."

Throughout the various celebrations James had been quite solicitous of his young bride's welfare. For most of the wedding ceremony, his arm was protectively encircled about her waist. A short coronation ceremony for Margaret followed the wedding. James himself placed the scepter in her hand.

Scotland's great contemporary poet William Dunbar soon dubbed the royal couple "the Thistle and the Rose." Dunbar's poem of the same title eerily prophesied the union of Scotland and England one hundred years hence, an event that would indeed come to fruition in 1603, when Margaret Tudor's great-grandson would become James I of England upon the death of Elizabeth I.

Sixteen years her senior, James treated his pretty, redheaded child bride generously, giving her gowns and jewels and spending money as she desired. But the largesse never quite made up for the initial shock that met her at Stirling Castle, one of her dower properties, when she saw that it had been turned into a nursery for his numerous illegitimate children. As it was a badge of honor in Scotland, instead of a blight on one's character, to beget a bastard with the king, James couldn't understand Margaret's distaste for the semiroyal bairns, whom she ordered banished from her new property with all due haste.

Nor did James's generosity, which included naming a ship in his wife's honor and presenting her with a jeweled "serpent's tongue" one New Year's as a safeguard against poisoning, compensate for the fact that he continued to pay regular visits to Janet Kennedy, his mistress since 1498. For some reason, James couldn't understand why his young wife had a problem with his behavior. Before and after his marriage, James enjoyed the favors of several lovers, siring a total of eight royal bastards with four of them. He also had six legitimate children (four sons and two daughters) with Margaret over the course of what was said to be an affectionate marriage, despite his rampant infidelity. She did not become pregnant until she was sixteen, which still seems quite young to twenty-first-century sensibilities; yet in her era tongues wagged, wondering what was taking her so long to conceive. Unfortunately, of all her children only their third son (also named James after their firstborn James lived only one year) survived to adulthood. Margaret's childbirths were very difficult and she often remained very ill for weeks afterward.

During his reign James IV increased Scotland's navy and was a great patron of architecture for beauty's sake, as well as for military purposes, renovating his palaces and building castles in the west of the country to bolster his authority there. His court was also a seat of literary culture, where homegrown poets, clowns, and musicians flourished. Other patrons of the arts were frequent visitors. And in 1507, James licensed the first printing press in the realm to publish statutes, chronicles, laws, and Scottish liturgical works. His fascination with the sciences and medicine, particularly dentistry, purportedly led him to extract one of his courtier's teeth himself. He also sponsored an alchemist's quest for the elixir of life. James was a superb jouster and enjoyed hosting tournaments and other displays of chivalric culture. In the summer of 1508, he staged the "counterfutting of the round tabill of King Arthour of Ingland" in Edinburgh.

The following year, Margaret's father died and her only surviving brother ascended the throne as Henry VIII. Much as she hoped the two men would treat each other as family, things between Henry and Margaret's husband were bound to come to a head when Scotland sought to remain an ally of France, while England regarded the French as an enemy.

In the spring of 1513, Margaret asked the English ambassador to secure for her the significant bequest that her late brother Arthur had left her in his will, as well as the plate and jewels left to her by their paternal grandmother, Margaret Beaufort. But Henry VIII refused to hand over these treasures— which were described as "silverwork, goldenwork, rings, chains, precious stones and the other habillements pertaining to a prince"—unless Margaret extracted a promise from her husband to remain on peaceful terms with England. The queen begged James not to attack her homeland. And if her urging wasn't enough to put the fear of God (or at least Henry) in him, Pope Julius II issued letters from Rome ordering James's excommunication should he invade England. However, James's reasons for invasion were to redress specific wrongs perpetrated by the English: their border raids on the Scots, the slaying of the king's good friend (a sea captain whom the English claimed was a pirate), the taking of Scots prisoners and chaining them by their necks, and finally, the matter of Margaret's legacy, which Henry had often made written promises to deliver.

Confident that the Scots king would at least fear his maker, Henry sailed to France on June 30, preparing to invade. Yet north of his borders, war was popular; only two members of James's council spoke out against it.

The Scottish armies had mustered by August 22. After a prophetic nightmare in which she saw her husband dead on the battlefield, Margaret, now pregnant with her sixth child, warned James, Calpurnia-like, not to leave home. He dismissed her fears as folly, but the queen insisted, "It is no dream. Ye are to fight a mighty people."

In the English county of Northumberland, on September 9, 1513, the Scots and English forces met at the Battle of Flodden—a disaster for James's army. Some ten thousand Scots soldiers were killed, along with their forty-year-old king, who died excommunicate. As proof of James IV's demise, Henry VIII's queen, Katherine of Aragon, sent the king's bloodstained coat to Henry in France with the words, "In this your grace shall see how I can keep my promys, sending you for your banners a king's coat. I thought to send himself unto you, but our Englishmen's hearts would not suffer it."

Margaret was so certain her dream had come to fruition that she didn't even send a party to search the bloody battlefield. Lord Dacre, Henry VIII's chief representative in the Borders, who had known the Scots king well, identified James's body, which had been stripped naked like all the other fallen enemy soldiers; yet many were convinced it could not be his, because there was no metal chain about the waist. The corpse that was believed to be James's was brought to Berwick-upon-Tweed for embalming, and Henry VIII obtained a breve from the pope, permitting his late brother-in-law to be buried in consecrated ground at St. Paul's. However, for some reason, the body lay unburied for years at Sheen Priory in Surrey, and was eventually lost after the Reformation.

In his will, James had named his widow the regent for their

seventeen-month-old son, who was now King James V. However, there was one major provision to Margaret's regency: She could not remarry.

Margaret now had a delicate path to tread. Although she was the mother of Scotland's infant king, she remained the sister of an enemy sovereign. Soon, a council comprised of a quartet of pro-French nobles was assigned to "help" her govern, even as Henry VIII was attempting to pressure her from the south to be as pro-England as possible. Desperately seeking allies of her own, she made the fatal error of turning to the powerful Douglas clan, finding herself passionately drawn to the handsome and charismatic Archibald Douglas, 6th Earl of Angus. The same age as Margaret, Angus was the greatest Scottish magnate at the time, but even his own uncle, the poet and bishop Gavin Douglas, referred to Angus as a "young witless fool."

Angus, too, had been widowed in 1513; his first wife, Margaret Hepburn, daughter of the Earl of Bothwell, died in childbirth. Angus's father, George Douglas, oldest son of the 5th Earl of Angus, had also fallen at Flodden. Ironically, the 5th earl and Margaret's first husband, James IV, had shared a mistress, the old earl enjoying Janet Kennedy's favors before she became the king's lover.

It was an accepted tradition in the fifteenth and sixteenth centuries that a noblewoman's first marriage should be for dynastic or monetary reasons, but that her second union could be a love match. Margaret seemed to be following this convention, but it wasn't intended to apply to queens, who were always expected to make politically advantageous marriages. However, at the time she fell in love with Angus, Margaret was particularly vulnerable—probably hormonal, being postpartum—lonely, possibly even a bit frightened. Aware of the Douglases' power, she was also in need of a strong ally to help her push back against the nobles.

Angus took his seat on the council in March 1514, when Margaret was in her final trimester of pregnancy. According to Robert Lindsay of Pitscottie, whose *History and Chronicles of Scotland* were published in the early nineteenth century, Angus "haunted the court and was very lusty in the sight of the Queen," who loved him, "and thought him most able."

One can't imagine Margaret was placing the interests of her son first and foremost when she secretly wed the russet-bearded Angus in the parish church of Kinnoull on August 6, 1514, just a few months after the April 30 birth of her youngest child by James IV, Alexander, Duke of Ross.

Naturally, the word got out and soon spread. By remarrying, Margaret was viewed by the council as voluntarily forfeiting her regency. She had played right into the hands of the nobles, who wanted nothing more than to topple her from power. The council even demoted her with an insulting new title. Margaret, who was technically the dowager queen, was no longer to be styled "the Queen's Grace," but "My Lady the King's mother." Angus's maternal grandfather, old Lord Drummond, was so incensed the first time he heard the Lyon herald address the dowager queen by her new title that he boxed the man on his ears.

By marrying a scion of Scotland's most powerful family and then nominating him as her coregent, Margaret had angered her brother. Henry had automatically assumed the prerogative of choosing her next husband so he could forge a beneficial alliance for England. And by selecting one of their rivals, Margaret also alienated many of Scotland's other aristocratic houses. In reprisal, the nobility took up arms against Angus's family, the Red Douglases, and to pressure Margaret further, they stopped payment of her dower rents, which were her due as James IV's widow. Margaret and Angus retreated to Stirling Castle with her sons.

The Privy Council offered Margaret a deal: She could retain custody of the young king and his infant brother if she voluntarily relinquished the title of regent. However, unwilling to trust the dowager queen or her new husband, the council invited a cousin of James IV, John Stewart, Duke of Albany, who had grown up in France, to return to Scotland and act as regent until James V came of age. This would ensure a Francophilic, rather than a pro-Anglo, alliance. The Privy Council was convinced that Albany was the best man to defend the country against English aggression. In September 1514, Margaret was compelled to consent to his appointment.

The duke arrived in Scotland in May 1515, and was installed as regent in July. His first order of business was to separate Margaret from her sons, claiming it was politically necessary—to safeguard them from being kidnapped by their English uncle, Henry VIII. Pregnant at the time with Angus's child, Margaret at first refused to surrender her boys to Albany. On August 20, she did so under coercion, although her sworn statement was made to appear as if she had relented of her own volition. Much later, she would angrily reveal the truth.

> *[Albany] by reason of his might and power did take from me the King and Duke my said tender children. He removed and put me from out of my said castle [of Stirling] being my enfeoffment paid for by the King my father of most blessed memory . . . and by his crafty and subtle ways made me signify in writing to the Pope's Holiness and to my dearest brother the King of England and the King of France that I of my own mooting and free will did renounce my said office of tutrix and governess.*

Having lost her sons, her regency, and her revenues, and heavily pregnant with Angus's child, Margaret obtained permission to travel to Linlithgow Palace. From there she escaped without Angus across the border into England, arriving on the verge of collapse in the wild and dangerous Northumberland countryside around Harbottle Castle.

Henry then sent men to stage a coup and seize his nephews at Stirling Castle, but lost sixteen soldiers in the attempt. Soon afterward, on October 7, at Harbottle, Margaret gave birth two weeks prematurely to Angus's daughter, Margaret Douglas. Despite having only one parent of royal blood, because little Margaret was also a niece of Henry VIII, she was often styled Princess of Scotland.

Angus had not accompanied his wife on her desperate flight to England. He remained in Scotland, ostensibly tending to the business of managing his estates. On December 18, Margaret was still in Northumberland, in Morpeth, gravely ill with swelling in her right leg from sciatica, when her younger boy, Alexander, the little Duke of Ross, died in Albany's care. Now she had only one surviving son: the future king. Margaret was not given the dreadful news until the end of the month, for fear it would prove fatal to her. With little Alexander dead and the young king only three years old, the Duke of Albany—being the nephew of King James III and the closest surviving relation to James IV—was now the heir presumptive to the throne of Scotland.

Still determined to visit her brother in London, Margaret arrived with her infant daughter on May 3, 1516, and was welcomed with a month of tournaments and celebrations. It was the first time she'd seen Henry in thirteen years. Angus had not accompanied her, much to Henry's annoyance. "Done like a Scot," the English king sneered, when he'd heard that Angus had abandoned his sister and returned to Scotland. And Margaret did feel betrayed, especially after she had sacrificed the pomp and power of the regency in order to be his wife. But Scotland was the earl's seat of power, money, and influence, and in this era a Scots laird's first allegiance was to his family, not to his wife.

Yet Angus had another reason for returning to Scotland without Margaret. He had resumed an affair with his former fiancée, Lady Jane Stewart of Traquair, residing with Jane on Margaret's estate at Newark and living off the queen's money. He also took Margaret's rents from two of her properties, Methven and Ettrick Forest.

Living off Henry's largesse, as her dower rents were not forthcoming, Margaret spent a year in England. During this time, her marital separation caused a great deal of speculation. It was rumored that her union with Angus had been dissolved and that she intended to wed the Holy Roman Emperor. In some ways, a divorce was less difficult to obtain than it would become in later eras (for example, papal decrees that permitted cousins to wed each other were often issued in reverse when the same cousins sought a divorce, citing consanguinity!). However, the result of such dissolutions was that children of the marriage were retroactively declared illegitimate. Henry VIII was fond of his niece, little Margaret Douglas, and did not want to see her bastardized. He also had other, more selfish motives: Should the girl ever be delegitimized, her stock on the international marriage market would plummet, destroying Henry's chances of forging an important political alliance.

After Margaret returned home and discovered her husband's infidelity, as well as the baby daughter that was the result of it, she became determined to divorce him. In October 1518, she wrote to Henry, informing him, "I am sore troubled with my Lord of Angus since my last coming into Scotland, and every day more and more, so that we have not been together this half year," adding that Angus had done her "more evil . . . which is too long to write. . . . I am so minded that, an [if] I may by law of God and to my honour, to part with him, for I wit well he loves me not, as he shows me daily." She accepted full responsibility for choosing Angus in the first place, and never openly blamed him for taking a mistress, or, more accurately, returning to his former sweetheart, even as she continued to lament, "he loves me not."

It wasn't so much Angus's adultery that angered Margaret, nor his bastard baby, but that he had seized the rents from her two estates. Even with help from the council, Margaret was able to recover only two thousand of the nine thousand pounds that Angus had appropriated. Her second inglorious marriage had been ignominious indeed. Even though Angus was the adulterer, it was Margaret's reputation that was tarnished.

In 1519, she was so impoverished that she was pawning her jewelry and dismissing her household staff because she could not afford to pay them. Miserable over the woeful state of her marriage, her funds, and her inability to see her son, she begged Henry to allow her to revisit England, but he refused, urging her to return to her husband's arms instead. Ever the hypocrite, Henry, who was in the throes of an extramarital affair with Bessie Blount, lectured his sister on the sanctity of her wedding vows.

Rebuffed by her own brother, Margaret turned to the regent, Albany. In the mistaken belief that he had connections with the pope, she was now willing to throw her support to the duke, if he'd reach out to the pontiff on her behalf about obtaining a divorce.

Her situation dragged on for years. In 1521, Lord Dacre wrote to Margaret, urging her to re-ally herself with the Douglases, because the connection was more beneficial to England. On the eleventh of March, Margaret sharply replied that if Angus "had desired my company or my love," he would have been more kindly disposed to her. Instead, ". . . of late, when I came to Edinburgh to him, he took my house without my consent . . . withholding my ferms [rents] from me . . ."

Poor Margaret: She couldn't catch a break. Her shifting allegiances, born out of her wish to escape her unhappy marital circumstances, only brought her additional misery. Angus and his adherents spread malicious rumors that Albany was her lover and that he supported the dowager queen's divorce so he could wed her himself after it was granted. The vicious gossip had made its way to England as well. Henry accused Albany of "the dishonourable and damnable abusing of our sister, inciting and stirring her to be divorced from her lawful husband for what corrupt intent God knoweth." And in February 1522, Henry sent Margaret a "sharp and unkind letter," in which he told her that it was assumed she had become Albany's mistress.

The duke, supported by the Scottish estates, succeeded in banishing Angus to France. But Albany was merely a fair-weather friend to Margaret. He then prepared to invade England, and only his army's fear of a repetition of the Battle of Flodden held them back. At least Margaret was able to persuade Albany to sign a truce. Perhaps in retribution, when he appointed a new regency council, he excluded her from it, sailing for France himself on October 27, 1522.

Placing her son's interests ahead of everything, Margaret decided to cooperate with her brother the following summer in the hope that Henry would do something to dissolve or disband the regency council and thereby elevate James V to active rule on his own. Obviously this signified her desire to see Albany ousted as regent. But when Albany returned to Scotland on September 23, 1523, with several thousand French troops in tow, Margaret grew nervous. Fearing he might seek reprisals for her turning against him, she petitioned Henry for permission to come to England. Her brother refused her entreaties, sending her money instead, and ordering her to stay put in Scotland. Angus, meanwhile, had fled to France after Albany resumed his regency.

Albany devised a new system of rotating governorship for the young James V: A quartet of nobles would have custody of him for three months at a time. He also tried, but failed, to negotiate a three-way truce among England, Scotland, and France. Before departing for France again, he sought assurances from Margaret that she would do nothing in his absence to undermine his authority.

Margaret assented, but as soon as the wind was at Albany's back, she staged a coup with the aid of the powerful Hamilton family, led by the 2nd Earl of Arran. On July 26, 1524, twelve-year-old James V was invested with full royal authority, even though a Scots king did not attain his majority until the age of fourteen.

Margaret and Arran now headed the government, while she worked toward a beneficial Anglo-Scottish alliance, well funded by Henry VIII. Meanwhile, she endeavored to keep the adulterous Angus at bay. According to the 3rd Duke of Norfolk, Margaret had reason to put some distance between herself and Angus, beyond being a scorned wife. On September 19, 1524, Norfolk wrote to Thomas Wolsey, Henry VIII's Lord Chancellor, "The Queen is very unpopular for taking so much on herself, and being ruled only by Arran and Henry Steward [sic]; also for her ungodly living, in keeping Angus out of the realm when he is so beloved."

Henry Stewart was Margaret's treasurer. And Angus was perhaps "beloved" only to the English. Margaret's brother was funding the earl, providing him with "power, substance and counsaill" during his diplomatic efforts to destroy the Franco-Scottish alliance. Henry VIII also tried to bully his sister into returning to Angus, threatening to stop payment for her two hundred bodyguards and feigning outrage over her adulterous liaison with Henry Stewart, even though by then he'd sired a royal bastard of his own.

Unfortunately for Margaret, she was never a strong leader, even when she was finally able to grasp the reins of power. Perhaps she listened to the wrong advisers. Perhaps she was not a born governor. And she was hampered by her circumstances: an Englishwoman in Scotland, disliked by the Parliament and the people because of her gender and her nationality—less the mother of their king than the daughter and sister of an ancient enemy. And yet Henry viewed her as unreliable, flighty, and a complainer: always asking for more money and never delivering the goods. When she finally was able to topple Albany as regent, all she could manage to secure for England was a two-month truce.

The English were convinced that Margaret was willfully scheming to prolong her marital conflict. Angus returned to England, and Henry was eager to see him head north to rejoin Margaret. She still believed the earl to be as duplicitous in love as he was in politics, and made it clear to her brother and his advisers that Angus was unwelcome across the border. But Henry was less interested in what was good for Margaret than in what was good for Henry. Angus was useful to him.

Shortly after the opening of Scotland's Parliament, Angus scaled the stone walls of Edinburgh with four hundred followers in tow. They marched to Market Cross on the High Street and announced that they had come in peace as faithful subjects of King James and desired only as their forebears had done—to take their seats in Parliament.

In response, Margaret, who was at Holyroodhouse with her son, ordered four or five light cannons to be turned on Angus. Two of the lairds were shocked that she should attack her lawful husband in such a manner. One of the cannons was fired, killing a priest, a woman, and two merchants.

Margaret's regency was confirmed by Parliament, and Angus retreated to his fortified castle at Tantallon. Henry, not to mention the rest of Europe, was scandalized by his sister's behavior.

In February 1525, when Angus was able to secure a leading role in Scotland's government, his brother-in-law also agreed that he should take control of Margaret's property. But later that year, Angus showed his true colors to Henry as well. When his turn came and went in the rotation to take charge of James V, he refused to relinquish the thirteen-year-old king to the next group of governors, retaining custody of his stepson for three years, until 1528.

Throughout that time, Margaret endeavored to prize her son from her estranged husband's clutches. An attempt to free James, led by the 3rd Earl of Lennox, ended in disaster when the earl was killed during the effort. Margaret was also determined never to reconcile with Angus, but to obtain a divorce so that she could wed Henry Stewart. She was sure she'd found true love at last. To assuage her conscience for choosing the wrong guy the second time around, Margaret sought to sunder her marriage to Angus on the grounds that she had wed him when James IV might have still been alive. After the Battle of Flodden, numerous rumors of the king's survival had sprung up, because many people were convinced that James's corpse hadn't conclusively been identified. There were stories of sightings in the Holy Land, or in Kelso, where, three days after the battle, James had purportedly been seen staggering about. His Holiness, however, didn't buy into any of the folklore. The pope's basis for dissolving Margaret's second marriage was that Angus's previous relationship with his former fiancée (and current mistress), Lady Jane Stewart of Traquair, was tantamount to a precontract of marriage with Jane.

Margaret did not learn of Pope Clement VII's March 11, 1527, granting of her divorce petition until December of that year. That spring, unaware of the decree, Henry, who believed that his sister had disgraced the family by cohabiting with Henry Stewart while she was still married to Angus, confided in the French ambassador that it was "impossible for anyone to live a more shameful life than she did."

Margaret secretly married Stewart on March 3, 1528, and by the beginning of April was openly acknowledging him as her third husband. Stewart, a son of the 1st Lord Avondale, was a fourth cousin, twice removed, of Margaret's first husband, King James IV.

An enraged Angus ordered Stewart arrested and taken prisoner, on the grounds that he had wed the dowager queen without royal approval. Because the earl was controlling the king, who was still a minor, if Margaret wanted to reside with her new husband, she would have to remove her ex, Angus, from power. Finally, on May 28, 1528, after telling his minders that he intended to go hunting, James V escaped from Angus's aegis disguised as a yeoman, announced that he had attained his majority, and proclaimed himself king in his own right. On June 19, at his mother's urging, James ordered Angus and his relations, except for James's half sister, Margaret Douglas, not to come within seven miles of his person. He then created his new stepfather, Henry Stewart, Lord Methven, "for the great love he bore to his dearest mother." In September, James sentenced Angus and his associates to death for treason, albeit in absentia, because Angus had gotten the better of him—and

Margaret—once again, having fled with their daughter to England. Angus remained under Henry VIII's protection, working as an informer, for the next thirteen years. Margaret Douglas was raised at the English court with the Princess Mary, despite her mother's wishes to be reunited with her.

Margaret's allegiances were torn between her native England and Scotland—which was not only a perpetual enemy of her homeland, but was often allied with England's other perennial nemesis, France. At this stage in her life, she harbored high hopes of brokering a grand meeting between her brother and her son similar to France's spectacular Field of Cloth of Gold summit in 1520 between Henry and François I, spending a fortune to plan an opulent event that never materialized. Margaret also hoped to forge a marriage between James and Henry's daughter Mary Tudor, another nonstarter. After years of being micromanaged by regents and committees of governors, James V had no intentions of listening to anyone's advice but his own, even if it came from his mother.

By the mid-1530s, Margaret must have felt she couldn't win. She'd done everything within her power for a son who had no use for her. Her only child by Lord Methven, their daughter Dorothea Stewart, had died in infancy; and now he was stepping out on her as well, repeating the pattern her second husband had traced— taking a mistress, Lady Janet Stewart, and impregnating her. The adulterous pair was living off of Margaret's lands and revenues so irresponsibly that *she* was now eight thousand merks in debt.

In 1537, Margaret attempted to divorce Methven on the grounds that he had squandered her income, appealing to her son to sunder her marriage. Yet Methven somehow managed to lay the blame for their connubial woes on his wife, persuading James V that the real reason Margaret sought to dissolve their union was her desire to remarry Angus—who remained in self-imposed exile in England, with that pernicious death sentence still over his head. James, therefore, refused to give his consent to a divorce. In early October, Margaret tried to escape over the border to Berwick, but James had her intercepted, in case she really did plan to join her second husband. Beleaguered, Margaret wrote a pathetic letter to her brother, threatening to enter a convent if he didn't intercede for her.

"[W]yth owt I get remedy, I wol pas to some relygeous place, and byde wyth them. . . ."

For the remainder of her years, Margaret continued to beg Henry for funds for one thing or another, as her now-detested third husband remained in control of her revenues. It was Henry who begrudged her the cost of lavish garments for James V's marriages (to Madeleine of France in 1537, and the French-born Mary of Guise in 1538), so that she could appear at the weddings in style, every inch the dowager queen, as well as the mother of the bridegroom.

At the age of fifty-one, Margaret Tudor died of a stroke at Methven Castle on October 18, 1541—bitter, unloved, and unappreciated. After all, in three marriages, two of which had ostensibly been love, or at least lust, matches, she'd never had a faithful husband. In her final hours, Margaret sent for her son, who was at Falkland Palace, but James didn't arrive at his mother's deathbed in time. Among her last words to her confessors was a request that the king ". . . be good and gracious unto the Erell of Anguyshe, and [she] dyd extremely lament, and aske God mercy, that She had afendet unto the sayd Erell as She hade." As poorly as he had treated her, perhaps the Earl of Angus had been Margaret's grand passion after all. And maybe she regretted turning those cannons on him.

Margaret had not made a will, because she expected to recover from the attack of palsy that she had suffered four days prior to her death. But when she realized that the end was near, she had asked that her valuables be given to her only surviving daughter, Margaret Douglas. However, because his mother died intestate, James peevishly did not honor this bequest, and all of her property reverted to the crown. Margaret Tudor was buried at the Carthusian Priory of St. John in Perth, among the Scots kings. The abbey was destroyed during the Reformation.

The Earl of Angus remained in England until 1542 and was one of the first to hear of the December 14 death of James V of Scotland. James's infant daughter, Mary, was now queen, and her governor, the 2nd Earl of Arran, invited Angus to return home, promising to restore his forfeited estates.

Still loyal to Henry VIII, Angus spent the next couple of years in

Scotland as the head of a pro-Anglo, pro-Protestant party. On April 9, 1543, he wed his third wife, another Margaret, the daughter of Lord Maxwell. The earl became a renowned military commander as well, but by 1545, he had switched allegiances and was staunchly pro-Scotland. His victory at Drumlanrig in 1548 began the death knell of England's ambition to conquer Scotland, and by 1550, the wild land to the north was completely lost to them.

Angus spent the rest of his life in the law courts, fighting to reclaim the lands that James V had taken from him and given to others. He had resigned his earldom on August 31, 1547. With no aristocratic title anymore, known merely as Archibald Douglas, he died ten years later in January 1557, not on the battlefield, but in his bed at his beloved Tantallon Castle. He was buried in Perthshire in the collegiate church of Abernethy, of which he was a patron.

In May 1541, Margaret Tudor's third husband, Lord Methven, was appointed sheriff of Linlithgow. By 1545, *he* had taken a third spouse, Lady Janet Stewart, his mistress during the years he was married to Margaret. Methven and Janet had four children prior to their marriage; they were legitimized in 1551.

During the minority of Mary, Queen of Scots, Methven sat on the Privy Council and participated in her mother Mary of Guise's attempt to overthrow the Earl of Arran as the young queen's regent. Yet both Arran and Mary of Guise employed Methven as an ambassador to England in 1544 and 1545. Three years later, Methven was master of the artillery, playing a major role in the siege of Haddington, one of a series of sieges begun in 1543 comprising "the War of the Rough Wooing"—England's effort to literally force a marriage between Henry VIII's son Edward, Prince of Wales, and Mary, Queen of Scots. In Scotland, it was known as the "Eight" or "Nine Years' War." By Haddington, in the summer of 1548, the teenage prince had ascended the throne as Edward VI, and five-year-old Mary was pledged instead to the dauphin of France.

Not much is known about the end of Lord Methven's life, including his date of death or the particulars surrounding his demise. In June 1553, he was recorded as making a payment to the crown, but the following April the wardship of his heir was assigned to the archbishop of St. Andrews, meaning that Methven had already gone to his maker. Janet Stewart, Lady Methven, survived him.

If marital success is defined by one's legacy, two of Margaret's otherwise inglorious unions made an impact on world history. Her granddaughter—James V's daughter (by his second wife, Mary of Guise) was Mary, Queen of Scots. And the progeny of Margaret's second marriage—her only daughter, Margaret Douglas, Countess of Lennox—was the mother of Henry Stuart, Lord Darnley, who was the Scots' queen's fey, duplicitous, bisexual second husband. Darnley's strange murder in 1567 set the wheels in motion for Mary's imprisonment and judicial execution at the hands of her cousin, Queen Elizabeth I of England, the younger daughter of Henry VIII.

Because Elizabeth had no children, the Tudor dynasty ended after 118 years. Her successor, the first of the Stuart monarchs, was a double great-grandson of Margaret Tudor: James VI of Scotland, who became James I of England as well. *His* great-grandson would become George I, the first Hanoverian king of England. How ironic that it is through Margaret Tudor's decade-long union with James IV of Scotland and her subsequent rocky marriage to Archibald Douglas, 6th Earl of Angus, that the rest of England's royal family descends and—despite some of their own ignominious pairings over the centuries—continues to thrive so gloriously.

LADY JANE GREY

AND

GUILDFORD DUDLEY

MARRIED: 1553–1554

*L*ady Jane Grey and Guildford Dudley enjoyed the proverbial fifteen minutes of fame as Tudor teens, such footnotes to history that Jane is often omitted from lists of England's monarchs, although she reigned during a rare "year of three kings." There would not be another such year until 1936.

This young duo was yoked together in wedlock because their families were desperate for power and glory. But Jane and Guildford's inglorious marriage achieved the opposite result: dishonor and disgrace for all concerned. The pair were pawns on their parents' chessboard, but to understand how and why they ended up being manipulated about the field, we must return to the king's square in an earlier game.

Henry VIII had moved heaven and earth in his desperate desire to perpetuate the Tudor dynasty and guarantee the security of the realm with a male heir. He broke with the Church of Rome, because it had refused to invalidate his marriage to his first wife, the devoutly Catholic Spanish princess Katherine of Aragon. Katherine had given Henry a daughter, the Princess Mary, but it was commonly believed that a female did not possess the mind or character necessary to rule, even though Renaissance princesses were scholarly women. Moreover, it was a martial era, and a monarch was expected to lead his troops into battle.

While Henry appreciated the practical things the reformed religion could bring him—the concept that he could be head of the Church in his own kingdom and that the lands and revenues previously belonging to the Roman Church would now devolve to the crown—he had been a scholar of Catholic theology prior to his divorce from Katherine. Henry was never entirely comfortable with the new religion, slipping a bit backward when he wed his third and fifth wives, Jane Seymour and Kathryn Howard, who had both been raised Catholic.

Henry did a lot of politically expedient waffling. He had his daughter Mary declared a bastard after the birth of his daughter Elizabeth by Anne Boleyn. When Jane Seymour bore his only son, Edward, both princesses were retroactively made illegitimate, so that only Edward stood in line to inherit Henry's throne. Toward the end of his reign Henry was finally persuaded to restore his daughters to legitimacy and the succession. He ultimately stipulated in his will that Mary should succeed Edward "upon condition that she shall not marry without the written and sealed consent of a majority" of Edward's surviving Privy Council, and that Elizabeth should succeed *her.* But Henry played a bit fast and loose with genealogy, stating that after Elizabeth's eventual succession, the throne was to go to the heirs of his younger sister, Mary, rather than those of his older sister, Margaret, thereby eliminating Margaret's granddaughter, the Catholic Mary, Queen of Scots, from the succession.

On January 28, 1547, Henry died at the age of fifty-five, his numerous infirmities and morbid obesity finally gaining the better of him. His death was kept a secret for two days so that matters regarding the smooth succession of the nine-year-old Edward VI could be put in order. Although his late mother had been a Catholic, little Edward had been raised as a fervent evangelical Protestant by his governors. As king, he was a hard-liner, acting upon the advice of Archbishop Cranmer to cleanse the realm of the imagery and idolatry of the Catholic Church. By 1550, England's rich and colorful history of medieval Christianity had been whitewashed, painted over, or destroyed entirely. A new era of austerity was ushered in; even cultural frivolities like holy-day pageants and maypole dances were abolished.

So it could not have come as much of a surprise when the little prig of a king violated the terms of his father's will in 1553 and removed his half sisters from the succession, not only because they might marry foreign princes and undermine "the laws of this realm" as well as "his proceedings in religion," but because they also bore the "shame" of illegitimacy, despite the fact that their own father had officially removed that stigma before his death.

According to the interpretation Edward and his ministers, lawyers, and clerics placed on the laws and statutes governing the royal succession, a bastard could not inherit the crown. Henry's divorces from Katherine of Aragon and Anne Boleyn had been duly ratified by "divers acts of parliament remaining in full force." Therefore, argued Edward, it had been illegal for Henry to pass the crown to his daughters, whom his recognized divorces had rendered illegitimate; and his last will and testament could not override the law. Of course, the king's subjects didn't know that; nor would they understand the legal technicalities and loopholes.

Edward's new document, known as the "Devise" for the succession, went through a couple of iterations before it was finalized. Full of hypotheticals, as originally conceived, the crown would pass to Protestant males or, in their absence (and indeed there were none), to one of their mothers, who would rule as a governess of the realm, rather than as England's queen, in conjunction with an appointed council of twenty men. Then Edward reworked the draft of the Devise to specifically name as governess Frances, Duchess of Suffolk, the daughter of Henry VIII's younger sister, Mary Tudor, by Mary's second husband, Charles Brandon. Frances was the wife of the 1st Duke of Suffolk, Henry Grey. According to the terms of Edward's Devise, her accession would be followed by her three daughters according to age: Jane, Katherine, and Mary. Next in line after Mary Grey would be Mary Clifford, the daughter of Frances Grey's younger sister.

But as Edward grew more frail from the pulmonary infection that would eventually claim his young life, he revised his views on the most appropriate candidate to replace him, to concentrate solely on his cousin Jane Grey, his spiritual sister, indoctrinated in the "godly learning," as they called it, of the Cambridge-educated evangelicals. Only Jane Grey could be trusted to carry the banner of Edward's Reformation and continue to instill its precepts in their subjects.

Jane had been named after Edward's mother, Jane Seymour. For years it was commonly accepted that she was born in October 1537, the same month and year as Edward, because the announcement of her birth was eclipsed by the news of Henry's male heir; yet more recent scholarship posits that she may have been born sometime during the spring of that year. Jane's parents, Henry Grey, Marquess of Dorset (a grandson of Edward IV's queen Elizabeth Woodville by her first marriage), and the sturdy, florid, sporty, and self-important Frances, were both social climbers. Because of their daughters' royal lineage, they wanted the best for them, especially Jane. During her childhood, Jane had been "placed out," the term for children from middle-income families who were sent to live with members of the nobility, or the offspring of an aristocrat who were sent to the palace to learn the manners and customs of royalty, to better cement the family's social connections and pave the way for a spectacular marriage. In exchange, the child became a ward, page, or lady-in-waiting.

Jane Grey was placed out with the former queen, the evangelical Catherine Parr, and her husband, Thomas, Baron Seymour of Sudely, the younger brother of the late queen Jane Seymour. Dorset sold Jane's wardship to Sudely in the expectation that she would be married well. After the fizzling of a proposed match with the Protector Edward Seymour's eldest son, Lord Hertford, the assumption was that Jane would eventually wed Edward VI, her first cousin once removed.

Catherine Parr died on September 5, 1548, a few days after giving birth to a daughter. Jane, who at ten years old was her chief mourner, had been happy under the dowager queen's roof. The child's piety and thirst for learning were encouraged and admired there, whereas her parents clearly didn't appreciate or comprehend those passions. Far from being proud of Jane's intellectual accomplishments, the Greys mocked and punished her for preferring to sit home alone with her books and finding genuine rapture in study, instead of being like other little girls who loved to play outdoors. In the summer of 1550, Jane confided in a houseguest, the noted scholar Roger Ascham, who found her reading Plato in the original Greek instead of hunting in the park with the rest of her family,

"Alas! good folk, they never felt what true pleasure meant." Unless she was exaggerating in order to elicit his sympathy, which seems out of character for such a serious child, it's difficult not to sympathize with Jane when she went on to tell Ascham that her parents were physically cruel to her, and that she drew pleasure only from the gentle pedagogy of her tutor, Mr. Aylmer. "For when I am in presence either of father or mother, whether I speak, keep silence, sit, stand, or go, eat, drink, be merry or sad, be sewing, playing, dancing, or doing anything else, I must do it, as it were . . . even so perfectly, as God made the world, or else I am so sharply taunted, so cruelly threatened, yea, presently sometimes with pinches, nips and bobs and other ways (which I will not name for the honour I bear them) so without measure disordered, that I think myself in hell. . . ."

There is much to consider in this remark, although Ascham was writing about the event twenty years later, so it may have been colored by anything from hazy recollection to hyperbole. Jane was receiving the humanist education that was popular for noblewomen of the era, but she was beyond precocious, reading mostly theological tracts, and she spoke several languages. She was even learning Hebrew so that she could read the Old Testament in the original text. Jane's enormous intellect and remarkably rigid religious outlook for one so young must have seemed daunting to most adults, particularly to her less well-educated parents. Sparing the rod was not a staple of child rearing at the time. Nor were compliments and coddling, which were believed to engender too much independence, both in daughters and sons. Perhaps the exasperated Greys, who had sold Jane's wardship for several thousand pounds in anticipation of the ultimate prize, sought perfection in her behavior because they were grooming her to wed the king.

One thing that is often glossed over by scholars who seek to portray Jane as a bit of a drip is her referral to several enjoyable pursuits in the lament to Ascham. Despite her overwhelming passion for doctrine and theology, she did dance and play. There were days when she was merry. Although she was hardly frivolous, she was *not* an ascetic. Yet, according to her twentieth-century biographer Alison Plowden, Jane complained about the Greys' mistreatment of her to anyone who would listen, and there may have been some exaggeration in her insistence that her parents made her life a living hell. Perhaps every teenager feels that way at some point.

Known for her outspokenness, Jane was rather arrogant about her remarkable intellect; the recognition and praise from international theologians had gone to her head. Jane *did* believe she was *all that*, which had not only made her headstrong, but her dismayed tutor fretted that his prize brainiac was also displaying too many tendencies typical of adolescent girls, focusing undue attention on her hair and jewelry, clothes and music. A discussion ensued among the pedants on how to best rein in their pious little pupil before they lost her to the world of prideful vanity.

After the execution of Thomas Seymour, Baron Sudely, for treason and the subsequent fall of his older brother, the Lord Protector Edward Seymour, the aspirational Greys—as of 1551 elevated to the titles of Duke and Duchess of Suffolk—threw their support behind the king's new chief minister, John Dudley, Duke of Northumberland. The families' mutual ambitions would become a literal marriage of convenience as they jockeyed two of their children into position to claim the throne.

The king was at death's door now, and he had reordered the succession not only to eliminate his half sisters, but to leapfrog over Frances Grey, Henry VIII's niece, who was one genealogical step nearer the throne than her children, nominating instead her eldest daughter, Edward's kindred spirit Jane.

And so the Devise for the Succession was altered yet again, at first to favor "Jane's heirs masles" and finally reworded to give the crown directly to "Jane and her heirs male" after Edward's imminent demise. The rewrite had evidently taken place soon after Guildford Dudley was married to Jane on Whitsunday, May 21, 1553 (according to the Julian calendar). It bears noting that current scholarship reveals a discrepancy in their wedding date. Some sources list it as May 25, but in 1553 that date was a Thursday on the Julian calendar, and on the Gregorian calendar (which was not adopted in England until centuries later), May 25 falls on a Monday. So it would appear that the viable date for a Whitsunday wedding is May 21.

Fully aware that with Edward's death his role as the de facto king of England would end, and his input, if any, in the governance of the realm would be greatly reduced, the Duke of Northumberland had sought to retain his power in every way possible. If he could not control England's king, why not its next queen, who was also merely a teenager?

The extent to which Northumberland used, or perhaps abused, his position to influence Edward's decision to revise the Devise for the Succession has been debated for centuries. On the scaffold he admitted that he had "done wickedly . . . against the Queen's Highness," but added that he had not been "alone the original doer thereof," although he declined to name his confederates. Yet a pair of unimpeachable eyewitnesses confirmed the duke's role in the proceedings: Sir John Gosnold, solicitor-general of the court of augmentations, and Sir Edward Montagu, chief justice of the common pleas. On June 21, when King Edward was on his deathbed, Northumberland charged both men to personally authenticate the Devise under letters patent.

Crucial to the story of Jane and Guildford Dudley's marriage is the timing of the final revision. It was generally assumed that by the spring of 1553, the king was not going to live much longer. Although still in his minority, Edward was fifteen years old and mature enough to know his own mind and will. When the chief justice, Montagu, informed Edward on June 14, 1553, that he was flouting his late father's wishes and that "the execution of this device after the king's decease" would be treasonable, Edward "with sharp words and angry countenance" commanded him and the other judges to accept it. Covering his bases, Montagu agreed to ratify it only after first securing the dying king's pardon, aware that because Edward was still a minor he could not write a valid will, and that only Parliament could overturn Henry VIII's Third Succession Act of 1544. Men had been executed for worse, and Montagu wanted to make certain he would not end up hanged, burned, or beheaded after Edward's death for following the young king's orders.

Edward fervently believed he was saving the realm by nominating Lady Jane Grey to succeed him. But what benefits would the

Duke of Northumberland derive from the Devise? The answer was full control of the government. John Dudley could never be king himself, but perhaps he could be a king's *father*.

Most likely born in 1535, Guildford Dudley was one of thirteen children—the fifth surviving son of Northumberland and Jane Guildford. He was the closest in age to Jane Grey, as well as the Dudleys' only unmarried son in 1553. Described by the contemporary chronicler Richard Grafton, who actually knew the youth, as a "comely, virtuous and goodly gentleman," Guildford, too, had enjoyed the benefits of a humanist education, although he was hardly the studious and scholarly teen that his fiancée was.

Although Jane might not have objected to Guildford's physical appearance, she strenuously resisted the idea of marrying him, primarily because she regarded her parents' prior plans to bind her with the Earl of Hertford as a precontract of marriage, and therefore indissoluble. During this era, such a precontract was legally regarded as tantamount to the nuptials themselves. Jane had been fond of Hertford, the younger Edward Seymour. The Protector's son was handsome and serious, and she believed that she and the earl were well suited, embracing the idea of their match.

Beyond Jane's objections to a marriage with Guildford Dudley on technical grounds, she didn't like him personally, deeming him a mama's boy. He was indeed the duchess's favorite child, spoiled and cosseted. Jane also seems to have mistrusted his father, but the Duke of Northumberland was at the time the most powerful man in the kingdom, running the government for His (dying teenage) Majesty. And as far as the Greys were concerned, it was unthinkable that their chit of a daughter should flout their wishes, especially by holding fast to the terms of a mooted arrangement with the Earl of Hertford.

Jane's consent to the union with Guildford Dudley was literally coerced "by the urgency of her mother and the violence of her father," who tag-teamed her into submission with a torrent of verbal and physical abuse. Those nips and pinches the Greys gave her for refusing to play in the park were nothing compared to the blows she received at her father's hands for rejecting a match with the son of the de facto king.

The source for this crap-kicking episode is considered fairly reliable; however, it comes from the nineteenth-century authors Agnes and Elizabeth Strickland, who were translating a pirated edition of Raviglio Rosso's *History of Events in England*. Rosso was visiting England on a diplomatic mission for the Duke of Ferrara. His account, as well as that of the Venetian ambassador to the Spanish imperial court in Brussels, is based on hearsay, and the Italian travelers were notorious gossips. However, the beatings would be credible for the personalities of Frances and Henry Grey as Jane presents them, and for angry and exasperated parents in an era where corporal punishment of children was the norm—parents who were livid that their arrogant adolescent had dared to question their judgment and authority, especially in a situation when the stakes could not have been higher.

For such a special event as Jane's union with Guildford, it's surprising that it was transformed into a triple wedding. The Northumberlands hosted the nuptials on May 21, 1553, at their London residence, Durham House, an enormous mansion along the Thames riverside. Twelve-year-old Katherine, the middle Grey sister, was wed to Lord Herbert, the fifteen-year-old heir to the Earl of Pembroke, and Guildford's sister Katherine, also in her early teens, was united in wedlock with the eighteen-year-old Lord Hastings, heir to the Earl of Huntingdon. It was a rushed affair, planned in less time than usual, because both sets of parents were so keen to unite their families, and particularly to secure Guildford's connection with the heir presumptive to the throne. Nevertheless, the Northumberlands spared no expense. The nuptials were celebrated in splendor, not merely with a ceremony but with a festival featuring three days of jousting, masques, and games. Two theatrical companies, one male, one female, had been booked to perform. Northumberland had authorized the Master of the Wardrobe to release the finest textiles and gems from the royal stores so that the mothers of the respective brides and grooms could bedeck themselves with "certain parcels of cloth of gold and silver."

Among the distinguished wedding guests was the Venetian ambassador Giovanni Francesco Commendone (historians disagree as to whether the French envoy was also there), as well as "large numbers of the common people . . . and of the most principal of the realm," according to Commendone. Unfortunately for the egocentric Greys and Dudleys, none of the royals were in attendance. The king's half sisters were personae non grata, and Edward himself was too ill to put in an appearance.

Although Jane, freckled and small for her age, looked charming, her strawberry-blond hair braided with pearls, she hardly appeared in love with her bridegroom. It was no secret to anyone present that theirs was a purely dynastic alliance.

On June 21, 1553, the patent naming Jane as Edward's successor was signed. By the end of the month, it was endorsed, albeit reluctantly, by some troubled consciences—not only Sir Edward Montagu, but the king's godfather, Archbishop Cranmer; twenty-two peers of the realm; the Lord Mayor of London; the aldermen and sheriffs of Middlesex, Surrey, and Kent; the officers of the royal household; the privy counselors; and the secretaries of state.

Immediately after her wedding ceremony, instead of cohabiting with her new bridegroom, Jane returned to Suffolk Place, her parents' home at Westminster. Soon afterward, she went to their new country home, a renovated Carthusian monastery on the south bank of the Thames at Sheen. Now called Jane Dudley, although she'd had only limited contact with her new in-laws, she knew them enough to despise them. They must truly have been heinous if Jane preferred the company of her mother, as Frances Grey had never been particularly maternal, or even kind to her. The two mothers-in-law mightily disliked each other. The Duchess of Northumberland had made it quite clear to the Duchess of Suffolk that she found it not only ludicrous, but unacceptable for the newlyweds to live apart.

Jane, who never minced words, seems to have had no qualms about speaking disrespectfully to her mother-in-law. She told Lady Dudley just what she thought of her, sparking a ferocious row between the two duchesses. Guildford's mother accused Frances Grey of deliberately endeavoring to keep the young couple apart.

Toward the end of June, as Edward's condition steadily worsened, the Duchess of Northumberland advised Jane to prepare herself for an imminent summons to London, because the king had named her his heir. Evidently this was the first Jane had heard of both her royal cousin's illness and the change in succession, and frankly, she didn't believe it. She thought the old cow was "boasting," massaging her vanity in order to separate her from her mother.

Failing to gain any traction with an argument that should have filled Jane with excitement, the duchess changed tack. A woman's place was beside her husband, insisted Lady Dudley, so she practically force-marched Jane to Durham House to join Guildford. It is possible that the newlyweds finally consummated their marriage there—they certainly did, if the Dudleys had anything to do with it: They were all but pushing the teenagers' hips.

Jane remained only a few days at Durham House before falling ill, convinced, with her all-or-nothing adolescent temperament, that her in-laws were trying to kill her. As she was now heir to the throne, did they believe her demise would mean that Guildford would become king, with his father acting as regent? In Jane's view, that would be a wild misinterpretation of the new act.

In reality, the Dudleys needed Jane to remain healthy, to bear heirs with Guildford and perpetuate the Tudor dynasty, benefiting all of them. They sent her to convalesce at Chelsea, Catherine Parr's former home. There, on Sunday afternoon, July 9, Jane received a surprise visit from Guildford's oldest sister, Mary Sidney, requesting her immediate departure for Syon House.

The bewildered Jane complied, and was greeted at the Dudleys' residence by her father-in-law, acting in his capacity as president of the Privy Council, as well as her mother-in-law, her parents, and the earls of Arundel, Pembroke, Huntington, and the Marquess of Northampton. According to Jane, these distinguished personages welcomed her with "unwonted caresses and pleasantness"; and then, to her astonishment and embarrassment, knelt before her.

Northumberland informed her of Edward VI's death—the fifteen-year-old king had in fact died three days earlier, on July 6. He then told her about the Devise for the Succession, explaining how Edward had arrived at the determination that she should be his heir.

Jane collapsed in tears at the news of her beloved cousin's death. When she finally regained her composure, she protested, "The crown is not my right and pleases me not. The Lady Mary is the rightful heir," referring to Edward's oldest half sister, Mary Tudor, who had been stripped of her title as princess by their father upon the annulment of his marriage to Katherine of Aragon.

Many scholars find it hard to believe that the remarkably intelligent Jane was genuinely shocked by the news of her accession—that she had absolutely no inkling of the Machiavellian machinations that had been taking place behind the scenes, particularly where the unscrupulous Dudleys, especially the duke, were concerned. Why else had she been hastily married to Guildford while the king was dying?

Declaring herself insufficient for so great a responsibility, the sixteen-year-old Jane did not cheerfully embrace her new destiny. Rather, she had to be entreated to accept it by her parents, in-laws, the assembled nobles, and her husband, who attempted to convince her with "prayers and caresses." Finally, steeling her resolve, Jane then murmured her thanks to God, adding that if it was indeed her duty and her right to succeed her cousin on the throne, she prayed the Almighty would aid her in governing the realm to His glory. At this point, her father-in-law was surely thinking she would seek more terrestrial guidance.

Now that Jane had accepted the grave responsibilities of sovereignty, she was determined to perform them to the fullest.

The following day, Monday, July 10, 1553, wearing a green velvet gown stamped in gold with long flowing sleeves, a bejeweled close-fitting white headdress, and chopines—platform shoes—to make her appear taller, the new queen of England, Lady Jane Grey (although she was now Jane Dudley), was transported in state aboard a royal barge from Syon to Westminster. She likely stopped to dine at Durham House before the barge brought her to the Tower of London, where, by ancient custom, all English monarchs took possession of the realm and began their reigns.

A great and curious crowd had gathered to catch a glimpse of their new sovereign, purportedly among them a Genoese merchant, Baptista Spinola, who was close enough to Jane to describe her appearance. "This Jane is very short and thin, but prettily shaped and graceful. She has small features and a well-made nose, the mouth flexible and the lips red. The eyebrows are arched and darker than her hair, which is nearly red. Her eyes are sparkling and reddish brown in colour." Spinola was so close to the "gracious and animated figure" of Jane that he could spy her freckles, as well as her teeth when she smiled, which he noted were "white and sharp." Wherever she walked, a ceremonial canopy of state was held over her head. Beside her stood Guildford Dudley in a magnificent white-and-silver suit, "a very tall strong boy with light hair," who "paid her much attention."

This description of Jane and her husband has been handed down through the decades, presented as fact from one biography to another. However, it has been unmasked as historical fiction by Leanda de Lisle, a recent biographer of the three Grey sisters. She attributes it to a New York City journalist, Richard Davey, who penned the paragraph in 1909. Sixteenth-century eyewitnesses remarked only that Jane's mother carried her train, a striking reversal of the traditional familial roles, and that Guildford strode beside her, his cap in his hand as a sign of humility.

It was true, however, that Guildford was playing the devoted husband to the hilt that day, and it behooved him to maintain a pretense of affection for Jane where little, if any, existed. Married for less than two months, during which time Jane had returned to reside with her parents or been sick in bed, the teens scarcely had time to get to know each other, let alone overcome their initial, and mutual, dislike.

Comfortably ensconced in the royal apartments at the Tower, Jane was presented with an array of jewels by the Lord Treasurer, who instructed her to choose what pleased her. He also brought her the crown and insisted that she try it on. Although she had already started signing documents as *Jane the Quene*, Jane tried to refuse.

Altering the rules of succession and coups d'état is all fun and games until the crown actually hits the hairline. Then somebody's gonna get hurt. The crown itself, that symbol of majesty and power, wasn't some piece of costume jewelry, and all these old men weren't indulging Jane in a game of dress-up. The Lord Treasurer, the rather ancient Marquess of Winchester, mistook Jane's reluctance and distress. He thought she was declining to wear the crown because there was only one, so he hastily assured the poor girl that she needn't fear accepting it, because another one would be made for Guildford!

At this, everything suddenly became crystal clear, as Jane realized "with infinite grief and displeasure of heart" the extent of the Dudleys' manipulation of her—that the entire scheme to redraw the line of succession so that it pointed toward her had been designed to place Northumberland's son, a youth without a shred of royal blood in him, on the throne of England.

Adopting her most regal manner, Jane reminded the Lord Treasurer that nothing could be done without the consent of Parliament. Jane's Tudor ire was now up. She adamantly refused to make Guildford king, purportedly avowing that "the crown was not a plaything for boys and girls." At this, the Dudleys became infuriated. But after Jane had a conversation with Guildford, he "assented that if he were to be made king, he would be so by me, by act of parliament," acquiescing, at least, to her authority in the matter. Painfully aware that merely because he was her husband, by *law* he would have dominion over her, even if she were queen, Jane had no intention of awarding the undeserving Guildford the crown matrimonial.

To assuage him, Jane offered to make Guildford Duke of Clarence, but he petulantly refused the title, flatly stating, at his mother's prompting, that he wanted to be king, not a duke.

This declaration precipitated a huge contretemps between the young spouses. Guildford ran off to fetch his mommy, and then the pair of them laced into Jane, with the duchess screaming at her like a lunatic. After realizing that the new queen wasn't about to back down, the mother-in-law from hell announced that from now on, she was forbidding her son from sleeping with his ungrateful and unnatural wife. The pair stormed out in high dudgeon, but Jane had them detained by the earls of Pembroke and Arundel, mistrusting what the Dudleys might do outside her presence. She ordered Guildford to return to her side and remain there.

Jane won that round, but the prize was her twit of a husband. Guildford pouted about it, but obeyed. She lamented, "[A]nd thus, I was compelled to act as a woman who is obliged to live on good terms with her husband; nevertheless I was not only deluded by the Duke and the Council, but maltreated by my husband and his mother."

Meanwhile, throughout the streets Jane was proclaimed queen by London's sheriff, accompanied by a trio of heralds, but the announcement met with little excitement. The *Greyfriars Chronicle* observed, "few or none said God save her." And there were none of the usual celebrations—bonfires and bell ringing—to accompany the news.

Upon Jane's accession, the Duke of Northumberland had begun to shore up his power base, but he had been unsuccessful in ensnaring the Lady Mary, whom he'd tried to trick into traveling from Hunsdon to London. Mary had started on the journey, but a funny feeling in her gut compelled her to turn back. She was, understandably, peeved that the duke hadn't seen fit to inform her of "so weighty a matter" as her brother's death. Reminding Mary of all the acts of Parliament that had declared her illegitimacy, in case she had designs on the throne, Northumberland condescendingly warned her not to vex the loyal subjects of "our Sovereign Lady Queen Jane."

Yet Mary, who had her own network of spies, must have learned about the gravity of Edward's condition long before Jane was told of his demise, because she communicated with Jane's council on July 9, the same day Jane herself learned of her accession. Mary demanded that the council renounce her cousin and recognize her as their sovereign instead, in accordance with her father's will. Mary also made it abundantly clear that she was aware of the plot against her ". . . to undo the provisions made for our preferment . . ." exhorting the men of the Privy Council to display their loyalty to her. The reply she received the same day was insultingly addressed to "my Lady Mary," referring to her claim as "your supposed title which you judge yourself to have."

The council reiterated its support for Jane as the rightful queen, her authority enforced by the letters patent signed by the late Edward VI, and they began issuing commands over Jane's signature. Guildford was dispatching correspondence of his own to the English ambassador at the imperial court, instructing him to act on

his behalf, and the French ambassador was describing Guildford as "the new king." Jane's husband was even insisting that he be addressed as Your Majesty by anyone entering his presence.

Yet Mary's supporters were amassing in East Anglia, prepared to contest the new regime. The Dudley and Grey families hurriedly conferred, recognizing the importance of sending a force to suppress them, but Jane "with weeping tears, made request to the whole council that her father might tarry at home in her company." However, Robert Wingfield of Grantham, author of the *Vita Mariae Angliae Regina*, maintained that it was Jane's *mother* who became hysterical over the thought of Suffolk's deployment.

In any event, Northumberland was deputized, and, with an army of three thousand behind him, sometime between July 12 and July 14 he rode out to confront Mary. But as the days wore on, popular sentiment for Edward's half sister increased, and many of the duke's soldiers deserted him. Town after town began to declare its support for Mary; yet her rebellion might have failed had the ships Northumberland dispatched to blockade her not defected to her side.

Inside the Tower of London, Jane busily signed letters to local authorities to suppress Mary's rebellion, but on the eighteenth of July, several of the lords on the council quit the Tower like the proverbial rats fleeing a sinking ship. The following day, holed up at the Earl of Pembroke's residence, they insisted that Northumberland had bullied them into accepting the Devise for the Succession and that in their hearts they believed Mary to be Edward's true and rightful heir. In fact, they intended to proclaim her queen that very day in London!

Yet, on the morning of July 19, the lords were not at all prepared to depose Jane. As far as they were concerned, she would remain queen. However, between five and six that evening at the cross in Cheapside, the very site where ten days earlier Jane's accession had been announced, thirty-seven-year-old Mary Tudor was proclaimed the sovereign. Coins were thrown in the air; bonfires were lit. There was singing and dancing in the streets. The swiftness of the turnaround in public sentiment from being against Mary to supporting her was astonishing.

During her exceptionally brief reign, Jane and her handlers had viewed Mary's amassing of troops as a rebellion and Henry's bastardized daughter as a usurper, but Mary had always seen herself as the true queen, and many of her subjects agreed with her. Many more of them were less pro-Mary than they were anti-Northumberland. They hated the duke, knew he had controlled King Edward's government, and saw that they were in for more of the same with the underage Jane on the throne, especially because she was married to Northumberland's son. Mary was not necessarily beloved, but the Dudley family was detested. In the county of Kent on July 19, the day that Jane Grey was deposed and Mary proclaimed throughout the land as queen, a group of Johnny-come-lately noblemen hopped onto Mary's bandwagon, declaring that she was queen "as of right she is, as well as by descent of royal blood as by lawful succession granted, ratified and confirmed by the nobility and the whole realm"—a reference to the 1544 Act of Succession— at the same time denouncing Lady Jane Grey (curiously, they did not refer to her by her married name, Jane Dudley) as "a queen of new and pretty invention."

Jane may have heard the hoopla from the Tower and wondered what it was all about. Interrupting her supper, her own father broke the news: She had been deposed after only thirteen days on the throne, although she is known to posterity as the Nine Days' Queen because she did not learn of her accession until three days after Edward's death, and was not proclaimed queen until July 10.

The Duke of Suffolk himself helped dismantle the cloth of estate, the canopy denoting Jane's sovereignty, which hung above and behind her throne. Henry Grey then went out to Tower Green, where he vociferously proclaimed his support for Queen Mary before hastening home to Sheen.

The Tower was both a royal residence and a prison in those days, and Jane went from queen to inmate in a matter of minutes. The following day, the Lord Treasurer demanded all of the jewels and finery he had so obsequiously bestowed upon Jane not ten days earlier, then went through Jane and Guildford's possessions like a repo man. The wrangling over the whereabouts of a few items, including a box that once belonged to Henry VIII, containing, among

other things, thirteen pairs of old gloves and "a square coffer covered with fustian of Naples," would drag on into the autumn of 1553.

Courtiers were defecting left and right to Mary. On July 21, Northumberland was arrested for treason by his former pal, the Earl of Arundel. The duchess and all of Dudley's sons were placed under arrest as well, and confined to various quarters in the tower. Guildford's mother was released fairly quickly and tried to intercede for her men, but Mary was not in a forgiving mood.

Jane's father was arrested at Sheen and brought to the Tower. Because her mother was not only Mary's cousin, but her goddaughter, she was accorded a royal audience on July 30, and consequently, the Duke of Suffolk was incarcerated for only a few days. No record has been found of any effort by Frances Grey to request clemency for their daughter.

After Mary made her entrance into London amid great pomp and pageantry, Jane was moved to the Gentleman Gaoler's house. Guildford was confined with his brothers in the Beauchamp Tower.

On August 12, Jane and Guildford were indicted. Since everyone wanted to wash their hands of Jane as quickly as they had rallied around her on July 9, she was left to plead her own case to her cousin, referring to herself as "a wife who loves her husband." She admitted in her correspondence to Mary that accepting the crown had been a mistake, but that she had been persuaded to do so by older, wiser, and more experienced heads than her own, who had since proven themselves to be nothing of the kind. Jane acknowledged the gravity of her error, realizing that "but for the goodness and clemency of the Queen," she hardly expected to be pardoned. However, she denied ever being a willing party to Northumberland's conspiracy, explaining to Mary, "For whereas I might have taken upon me that of which I was not worthy, yet no one can ever say either that I sought it . . . or that I was pleased with it."

Mary believed her outspoken little cousin and was inclined to grant her clemency. She was less interested in avenging herself on the traitors than she was in reuniting a divided country under her sovereignty; however, her subjects would have to accept the fact that under her reign, Protestantism was out and Catholicism was back in.

Mary's most trusted confidant, Simon Renard, the imperial ambassador in England, tried to force her to remove the rose-colored glasses. According to Renard, "As to Jane of Suffolk, whom they tried to make Queen, she [Mary] could not be induced to consent that she should die." Mary was all the more firm in her conviction, Renard claimed, because she believed that Jane's marriage to Guildford Dudley was invalid, "as she was previously betrothed by a binding promise . . . to a servitor of the Bishop of Winchester."

Mary must have confused this mysterious fiancé for the Earl of Hertford, but in any event, this convenient legal loophole that could sever Jane from the traitorous Dudley family salved the queen's conscience. However, toward the end of the summer, Mary was being persuaded to change her mind about leniency. Her imposition of heavy fines instead of death sentences was viewed as weakness, and as England's first adult queen regnant (Jane had been a minor, and all other queens had been merely consorts), it was imperative to prove to her subjects that she was in control of her throne. Renard lamented, "Her authority has suffered from the pecuniary compositions for offences, and people have come to judge her actions so freely that they go so far as to laugh at them."

No one would laugh at what Mary did next. On September 19, she ordered "the four sons of the Duke of Northumberland, and Jane of Suffolk, to be tried and sentenced to receive capital punishment for the crimes they have committed."

Northumberland had already been executed for treason on August 22. Ten thousand people had gathered the day before to witness his dispatch, only to have the event delayed when Mary offered the condemned man the opportunity to recant his Protestant beliefs and embrace the old religion. What appalled Jane most about her father-in-law's demise was his deathbed conversion to popery, perhaps in the mistaken hope of a royal reprieve. "Should I, who am young and in my few years, forsake my faith for the love of life?" the evangelical teen had exclaimed in horror. She had nothing but contempt for the man who "hath brought me and my stock [family] in most miserable calamity and misery by his exceeding ambition . . . for what man is there living, I pray you, although he had been innocent, that would hope of life in that case; being in the field against the queen in person as general, and after his taking, so hated and evil spoken of by the commons? . . . Like as his life was wicked and full of dissimulation, so was his end thereafter."

In November 1553, Jane and Guildford stood trial for high treason, charged with taking possession of the Tower. Guildford was also convicted of conspiring to depose Mary by sending troops to his father and by proclaiming and honoring Jane as queen. Jane was also found guilty of having signed a number of documents with the signature *Jane the Queen*. They both pled guilty and were duly condemned, as expected—Guildford to be beheaded, and Jane to be "burned alive on Tower Hill or beheaded as the Queen should please." Yet Mary still remained inclined to spare them. And then Jane's own father, who had already hedged his bets by converting to Catholicism, did the most boneheaded thing imaginable, something that left Mary with no choice but to execute them all: He participated in Wyatt's Rebellion.

Mary Tudor was, of course, half Spanish, her mother being Katherine of Aragon, so she had always been close to the various Spanish ambassadors. At the time, the king of Spain, Charles V, was also the Holy Roman Emperor, and Mary harbored intentions of wedding his son, Philip.

In January 1554, Thomas Wyatt the Younger, whose father had been a poet and courtier in Henry VIII's court, led an uprising of a dozen or more aristocratic coconspirators to protest Mary's plans to wed Philip of Spain. They did not want England returned to Catholicism, nor a foreigner as their king. Although deposing Mary was not specified as part of their plot, their implied intention was to replace her with her Protestant half sister Elizabeth, daughter of Henry VIII and Anne Boleyn.

No one ever suggested that Jane Grey had any foreknowledge of Wyatt's plans or of her father's intention to take part in them, but she had been vehemently opposed to the sheeplike acceptance of Catholicism by the English in the wake of Mary's accession. Ever the fierce evangelical, even if her faith flew in the face of political pragmatism, what use, she fumed, was unity when it was the "unity of Satan and his members . . . thieves, murderers, conspirators, have their unity," Jane raged, reminding the true believers of the reformed religion that Christ had come "to set one against another," not to bring peace, but a sword. "Return, return again unto Christ's war," she urged. Therefore, Jane's very existence as a fulcrum for Protestant discontent made it impossible for Mary to remain merciful.

The executions of Guildford and Jane were originally scheduled for February 9, 1554, but Mary delayed them for three days in order to give her cousin a chance to convert to Catholicism in her final hours. If the queen couldn't save Jane's body, at least she could try to save her soul. Mary dispatched her chaplain, John Feckenham, to guide Jane from Protestantism to popery, but the queen should have known this was a lost cause; Jane's religious convictions were as firm as her own. However, the condemned girl and Feckenham enjoyed three days of spirited theological argument. While Jane refused to allow him to sway her principles, she developed so much respect for the cleric's intellect that she permitted him to accompany her to the scaffold.

There had been a good deal of preparation for Jane's appointment with her maker, perhaps more so than for her brief marriage. She had to choose her gown and select the witnesses to her execution, who would also be responsible for disposing of her body. She had written the requisite farewell letters, including one to her father, who had been returned to the Tower as a prisoner on February 10. Her note, written directly above Guildford's sincerely affectionate farewell to his father-in-law, was intended to be one of comfort, but the outspoken Jane hastened to remind the Duke of Suffolk that the need for writing the letter in the first place was only because, thanks to him "by whom my life should rather have been lengthened," her death was taking place sooner rather than later. Jane also sent a good-bye letter to her sister Katherine, written inside the pages of a Bible. None were penned to her mother and husband.

Many biographers of the couple state that Guildford sent Jane a message on the day before their executions, asking to see her one more time, but she refused, replying that as it "would only . . . increase their misery and pain, it was better to put it off . . . as they would meet shortly elsewhere, and live bound by indissoluble ties." Yet this may be a later imposition on their relationship. There never was any love or affection between these spouses, and it's unlikely that Guildford had any interest in a tearful adieu.

His turn to die came first. On the morning of February 12, he was taken from his rooms to the place of public execution on Tower Hill, where several gentlemen waited to shake hands with him. Jane watched the procession from the window. Guildford gave a brief, customary farewell speech to the crowd gathered about him, then knelt and prayed, looking up to God several times, asking the assembled witnesses to pray for him as well. One swift stroke of the ax and Guildford Dudley was dispatched. "Oh Guildford, Guildford!" Jane was heard to exclaim. She remained at the window until the straw-covered cart bearing her husband's headless corpse clattered toward the Tower's chapel of St. Peter ad Vincula.

Guildford was probably only eighteen years old. His body was interred in the chapel, where Jane's would soon lie. She had chosen the same black gown she had worn during her trial, and, dry-eyed and composed, an open prayer book in her hands, she was escorted from her quarters by the Lieutenant, Sir John Brydges. Following at a respectable pace were Jane's tearful attendants, Mrs. Ellen and Mistress Elizabeth Tylney.

Because of Jane's royal status, if not as a deposed queen, then as the granddaughter of a princess, her execution was not held on Tower Hill, but rather on Tower Green, within the precincts of the fortress's walls. It did not, however, take place indoors, as depicted in the famous nineteenth-century French painting by Paul Delaroche. Admitting in her speech to the witnesses that she had committed a crime against the queen's highness by accepting the crown, she also stated that she was innocent of desiring that which constituted her crime.

An eyewitness claimed that Jane "wrung her hands, in which she had her book," asked those assembled to attest to the fact that she had died a good Christian, and exhorted them to pray for her. She then fervently recited Psalm 51, the Miserere, in English, while Feckenham repeated it in Latin after she had finished speaking.

Jane handed her gloves and handkerchief to Mistress Tylney and offered the prayer book to Thomas Brydges, brother of the Tower's Lieutenant. Then, as she began to unlace her gown, the masked executioner stepped forward. Uncomprehending, modest, and terrified, Jane jumped back, urging him to leave her alone, unaware that his victims' outer garments were an executioner's perquisite.

Her ladies then removed her headdress and collar. The headsman asked her forgiveness, according to protocol, and Jane granted it, pleading, after seeing the straw and the block for the first time, "I pray you dispatch me quickly." Then, referring to her head, she asked fearfully, "Will you take it off before I lay me down?"

"No, madam," replied the executioner.

Jane blindfolded herself, but, her bearings lost, found herself groping for the block with her hands. "What shall I do? Where is it?" she cried, suddenly the frightened girl inside the fervent evangelical.

After invoking Jesus's last words according to Luke, "Lord, into thy hands I commend my spirit," Jane was beheaded. The witnesses were so close to her body that they were spattered with her blood. For some reason, her corpse was not immediately removed. Hours later, the former queen's headless body remained on the scaffold, the straw beneath it stained crimson with her blood. By the end of the day, Jane's corpse was cast into the same pit within the chapel where Guildford's body had been tossed. Their bones were eventually interred beneath the paving stones of St. Peter ad Vincula, between those of Anne Boleyn and Kathryn Howard, the two executed queens of Jane's great-uncle Henry VIII.

Her father, the Duke of Suffolk, was executed for treason eleven days later, on February 23, 1554. Jane's mother eventually remarried, wedding Adrian Stokes, her Master of the Horse, in March 1555.

There was no public outcry at Jane's death from Protestant evangelicals; Mary was now queen, and Tudor tempers were legendary. But not too much time passed before both Jane Grey and Guildford Dudley were regarded as martyrs and their executions as judicial murders.

In Grafton's *Abridgement of the Chronicles of England*, published in 1563 when the Protestant Elizabeth I was on the throne, the author, who had personally known the "comely" Guildford, insisted he "most innocently was executed, whom God had endowed with such virtues that even those that never before the time of his execution saw him, did with lamentable tears bewail his death."

Legend has it that after Jane's death the oak trees in Bradgate Park where she spent her childhood were pollarded, meaning that the top branches were lopped off to allow for dense new growth. It was a symbolic gesture of arboreal defiance, as well as mourning for the estate's native daughter. Also among the lore surrounding Jane's demise is the story that when word of her beheading reached Leicestershire, the judge who had sentenced her became barking mad. Convinced he could see her spirit floating about him, he died raving, "Take the Lady Jane from me! Take away the Lady Jane!"

What's wrong with this picture, mythology aside, is that Lady Jane Grey, the scholarly prodigy who had so impressed Roger Ascham and the learned Lutherans of Germany and Switzerland, did not suffer a religious martyr's death, burned alive in the center of a town square—although *she* may have viewed herself as a sacrifice on the altar of religion. Admitting she had done Mary a wrong, even though it had not been *her* idea to so transgress, the Nine Days' Queen died a *traitor's* death, beheaded at the pleasure of the sovereign whose place in the succession Jane had usurped, even though her accession had been neither of her making nor desire.

Had Jane not been the daughter of a duke and the grandniece of Henry VIII, and therefore worth something to her parents on the marriage market, and had she not been of value to her dying cousin Edward VI as the standard-bearer for the reformed religion, she might have enjoyed a quiet existence with her books and theological tracts, perhaps even refusing to wed, if she thought she could get away with it. Had Jane been a Catholic, she might have made a terrific nun. She was an ideologue to the last, her own faith unswerving.

Sir John Brydges, Lieutenant of the Tower of London, became the beneficiary of Jane's prayer book. At his behest, she had penned an inscription to him shortly before her execution.

". . . Live still to die," she wrote, "that by death you may purchase eternal life. . . . For, as the preacher sayeth, there is a time to be born and a time to die; and the day of death is better than the day of our birth. Yours, as the Lord knoweth as a friend, Jane Duddeley [sic]."

She may never have liked her husband. She certainly hadn't loved him. And his parents, the parties most responsible for her mismatched union to their dull and petulant mama's boy, had brought her nothing but trouble. But when all is said and done, from the day they were united in wedlock to the day of their deaths, the girl the world knew then and still remembers only as Lady Jane Grey, acknowledging the legal and holy ties that, like it or not, bound them till their last breaths, referred to *herself* as Guildford's wife, Jane Dudley.

♔

MARY I

AND

PHILIP II OF SPAIN

MARRIED: 1554–1558

*F*ew royal marriages are as inglorious as Mary Tudor's. Wed relatively late in life, she was in many ways as naive as her teenage counterparts who hoped for a love match filled with bouncing babies to continue the dynasty—only to be disappointed by a husband who secretly mocked her, found her physically repellent, and couldn't get away from her fast enough, rendering her an international laughingstock. Might Mary have enjoyed a happier future without Philip of Spain?

The first prospective marriage of Mary Tudor, the only surviving child of Henry VIII and his first wife, Katherine of Aragon, was arranged when the gray-eyed, golden-haired princess was barely potty-trained. Henry betrothed this apple of his eye to the dauphin of France, the first son of his rival François I, when Mary was only two years old.

But political bedfellows changed over the years, so her father sought to shore up different international alliances as time went on. In 1522, when Mary was six, she was betrothed to her Spanish first cousin, Charles V, the Holy Roman Emperor. However, the lantern-jawed Charles, the son of her mother's madly unhappy elder sister, known as "Juana la Loca"—was twenty-one years old at the time; he had no interest in waiting for a little girl to grow up before he could marry.

Over the next few years, Henry would consider hitching young Mary to her Scottish first cousin James V, the son of his elder sister, Margaret, yoking his daughter to other French princes; or uniting her with the Duke of Milan, Francesco Sforza. All of it came to naught. Of course, back then, Henry assumed he would have sons to inherit his own throne, and that Mary's marriage would merely be another necessary international alliance—a peace treaty, really—with one of England's enemies.

That was before Henry's passion for Anne Boleyn led to his break with the Church of Rome over their refusal to nullify his marriage to Katherine, rendering Mary retroactively illegitimate. Mary's own royal household was dismissed. She was stripped of her royal title, to be known henceforth only as the Lady Mary, and was compelled to dance attendance on her infant half sister, Anne's daughter Elizabeth, whom she ever after resented. At her own peril, risking a charge of high treason, and her father's immense and very public displeasure, Mary consistently denied the English clerics' verdict that her mother had always lived in sin with her father and was not the true queen of England. Moreover, she refused to repudiate the Roman Church. Her "Spanish blood"—another dig at her beloved mother's lineage, was blamed for her obstinacy. It was only under threat of death that Mary signed a confession on June 22, 1536, betraying her mother and torturing her soul with the admission that her father was the supreme head of the Church in England.

The stress of obeying the dictates of her conscience nearly overwhelmed her. In midadolescence Mary had been a precious and precocious child, proficient in several languages as well as music and dance, who loved to hawk and hunt and was as passionate about jewelry and fine clothes as she was fond of gambling. By the time she reached her maturity, she was a frail and fragile young woman, small for her age and plagued with health problems, including violent headaches, stomach complaints, and irregular—and very painful—menses. Her self-esteem was permanently stunted. In nearly everything but her rock-solid faith in Catholicism, she was riddled with doubt.

Although Henry had disinherited his daughters, his Third Succession Act of 1544 restored them to the line of succession: Their reigns would follow, in order of their birth, after the death of his only son, Edward. But when fifteen-year-old Edward was dying, he reordered the succession to favor their Protestant cousin Lady Jane Grey. After Jane succeeded Edward on July 9, 1553, Mary quickly mobilized her adherents, and within ten days Jane was deposed and Mary claimed her rightful place in the succession—and the crown.

However, Mary did not make her formal entry into London until seven p.m. on August 3. Petite, woefully nearsighted, and missing many of her teeth, England's first true queen regnant, a thirty-seven-year-old virgin, was resplendent in a gown of violet velvet and kirtle of purple satin "all thicke sett with gouldsmiths worke and great pearle," according to a contemporary account. She wore ". . . a rich baldrick of gold pearl and stones about her neck, and a rich billement of stones and great pearl upon her head." Her trailing sleeves and skirts were also embroidered with gold. Even her palfrey was trapped in a full-length cloth of gold caparison. Mary led a magnificent procession of nobles and courtiers to the Tower of London, where she laid claim to it as queen amid "a terrible and great shott of guns . . . lyk to an earthquake." Following the celebratory cannonade, she released the political and religious prisoners that had long been held there, including her kinsman Edward Courtenay, a great-grandson of King Edward IV.

Mary had a strong personality, and from the outset she intended to take an active role in the governance of her realm. Contrary to centuries of Protestant propaganda, she worked very well with her councilors and did not take her marching orders from Spain and her cousin Charles V and his emissaries. But winning the populace to her side as their new sovereign would be an uphill battle in every way. Becoming England's first adult queen in her own right was difficult enough. In addition, Mary Tudor still clung piously to the Roman religion during a time of fervent evangelism. And, being half Spanish, she had indeed always been most comfortable around her mother's Iberian attendants; the Spanish ambassadors to England had become her chief confidants, although they did not dictate her policies. Loyal to a fault, Mary also surrounded herself with trusted friends. Among them was the beloved cousin who had been raised in her household, Margaret Lennox, the daughter of her aunt Margaret Tudor from her marriage to Archibald Douglas. The Countess of Lennox became one of the most favored persons in the realm, the recipient of substantial largesse in the form of real estate and material goods.

Mary's coronation was an unprecedented event that was weeks

in the making. On September 27, she and the Princess Elizabeth arrived at the Tower of London by barge escorted by a spectacular flotilla. For the September 30, 1553, journey from the Tower to Westminster Abbey, with the canopy of state above her head, Mary rode in a chariot covered in cloth of gold, preceded by a parade of barons, knights, judges, bishops, and councilors. Everyone was arrayed in sumptuous finery, a grand display of colorful silks, velvets, and cloth of silver and gold. Pageants were staged in her honor along the route. Mary wore a blue velvet gown trimmed with powdered ermine, although the grandeur of the image was somewhat marred when she had to clasp her headgear throughout the journey because the gold trelliswork cap and gilded garland studded with pearls and precious gemstones were too heavy for her small frame.

Edward VI's 1552 Act of Uniformity, parliamentary legislation designed to make England a more Protestant country, still remained in force, and Mary was about to be crowned as the supreme head of the Church. However, she had obtained absolution for her coronation to proceed as a full Catholic Mass from the papal legate, her kinsman Reginald Pole. Wearing the traditional crimson velvet mantle in the manner of male monarchs, on October 1, 1553, Mary was crowned by her old friend Stephen Gardiner, Bishop of Winchester and Lord Chancellor. As she had refused to be anointed with oil that had been consecrated by one of Edward VI's evangelical clerics, she had secretly secured specially consecrated oil from the bishop of Arras in Brussels. The vial arrived from the Low Countries in the nick of time.

Mary's coronation made history, because in a way, the participants were winging it: There was no existing precedent to crown a queen regnant of England. The five-hundred-year-old ceremony followed the same ritual for male rulers, investing Mary with all the powers granted to her predecessors. She adopted the royal motto "*Veritas Temporis Filia*"—"Truth Is the Daughter of Time"— meaning, perhaps, that in the fullness of time, she had been able to restore the truth about the legitimacy of her parents' marriage, and by extension, *her* legitimacy as Henry and Katherine's daughter, and as England's rightful monarch.

Unsurprisingly, Mary's first Parliament reinforced the terms of the Third Succession Act and upheld the legality of her parents' union. The next step was the repeal of all of Edward VI's religious legislation, turning back the clock to 1539, although here Mary was compelled to compromise. Those landowners who had profited from the dissolution of the monasteries during the Reformation, receiving swaths of Church properties, were not inclined to hand them back. Mary would need their support for her ambition to restore England to the Roman fold.

Although history paints her as more of a religious tyrant than her younger brother, the Catholic Mary and her council initially did no more than the Protestant Edward and his ministers had done with regard to making and enforcing new laws and strictures governing the practice of religion. Yet many of her subjects weren't keen to embrace the preaching of papists, no matter how learned. One Sunday morning, a Catholic chaplain, Gilbert Bourne, preached outdoors at St. Paul's Cross, the same site where a Protestant cleric had spoken the previous week. An angry crowd gathered below began to murmur that Bourne's words were an abomination, and soon shouts of "[T]hou lyest" and "Kill him! kill him!" filled the air. A dagger whizzed past his head, bouncing off the side post of the pulpit. Ushered to safety, Bourne was lucky to escape with his life.

The queen was able to form a council comprised of men who had always remained loyal to her, with holdovers from Edward VI's reign. It would seem at first glance that, with different religious agendas, they might be at odds. But what the councilors shared in common was years of government experience and the fact that they were loyal and devoted servants to the crown, no matter which Tudor wore it.

Even before Mary's coronation had taken place, ministers began raising the subject of her marriage; naturally, these men assumed that a *femme sole*, in the formal parlance, could not efficiently govern the realm, and that she needed a husband to do it for her. Mary, too, was an old-fashioned girl, sharing the popular belief that a woman was incapable of ruling alone. Besides, she knew very well that she needed an heir to continue the succession. She did not get along with Elizabeth and despaired of her Protestant half sister ruling the realm, which she would do, in accordance with Henry VIII's will, if Mary died childless.

However, Mary's choice of a bridegroom shocked and appalled her ministers and subjects. And yet it should not have been remotely surprising. To wed the queen of England, of course the man would have to be of royal blood. And a good Catholic. At the suggestion of her cousin Charles V, who was the Spanish king as well as the Holy Roman Emperor, Mary set her cap at his oldest, not to mention his only legitimate son: the heir to Charles's Spanish throne, her handsome cousin Philip. Both Mary and Philip were also descendants of John of Gaunt, the third son of Edward III, who was quite the prolific sire over the course of three marriages.

Because Charles had enough to govern, Philip had been acting as king of Spain since 1543, although he hadn't formally inherited the crown. Therefore, he already had years of experience as a ruler—yet another feather in his cap. Philip had also been married as a teenager to another cousin, the infanta Maria Manuela of Portugal, who had died in childbirth. Their son, Don Carlos, was now nine years old.

As part of the marriage negotiations, a portrait of the prospective groom, painted by Titian, was sent to Mary in September 1553. Eleven years younger, Philip was a genealogical generation removed from Mary, being a great-grandchild of that royal power couple Ferdinand and Isabella, whereas Mary was one of their grandchildren. Because of their age difference, Philip had always referred to her not only as his cousin, but, somewhat embarrassingly, as his *cara y muy amada tía*—his dear and beloved aunt.

Mary had zero experience in the ways of men. And while she knew perfectly well that she was obligated to choose a husband for dynastic and political reasons, like her father before her she, too, hoped to marry for love, desiring a man with whom she could live in harmony and who would be a constant presence in her life. Yes, it was a wildly romantic notion, and by and large an unrealistic one, but given the upheaval of her girlhood and her parents' unhappy marriage, she certainly had a right to expect something more. When it came to Philip, Mary became a teenage girl all over again, her untested heart experiencing the pangs of emotion for the first time. Through Philip's paternal line, the Flemish Hapsburgs of Burgundy, he had inherited their strikingly pale complexion, large jaw, and fleshy lips—a combination that Mary found particularly alluring. Titian's portrait showed a trim figure of middling height with finely shaped calves. In a word, Philip of Spain was dreamy. And because Spain was a Catholic country, Mary's marriage to Philip would help her accomplish the number one item on her agenda: to restore England to the bosom of the Roman religion.

Well—a foreign match would have been all very well and good for Mary when she was just a princess whose father, or a long-lived brother, wore England's crown, but that was not the scenario. *Her* prospective union to a Spanish prince was not remotely the same as Henry VIII wedding a Spanish infanta. Mary's mother had been merely a consort. Under the English common law doctrine known as *jure uxoris*, upon her marriage a woman's property and titles held in her own right became her husband's as well. Therefore, it was not a stretch of the imagination to fear that any man Mary married would become king of England in fact as well as in name. Under the terms of *their* marriage treaty, Mary's maternal grandparents, Ferdinand of Aragon and Isabella of Castile, remained sovereigns of their respective realms after they wed. But the laws of Spain were vastly different from those of England.

As for the twenty-six-year-old Philip, back in Spain, he had been in negotiations for a match with the current infanta of Portugal when his father communicated his desire for the English union. Dutiful son that he was, Philip had replied, "All I have to say about the English affair is that I am rejoiced to hear that my aunt has come to the throne . . . as well as out of natural feeling . . . because of the advantages mentioned by your Majesty where France and the Low Countries are concerned." A Spaniard on England's throne checkmated their mutual enemy, France, from considering invasion. And with a single stroke of the pen on a marriage treaty, a potential King Philip of England would be transformed from a foreign oppressor of the Dutch (as Spain possessed the Netherlands, which chafed under their rule) to their valuable trading partner (because England had an economic relationship with the Low Countries). Philip then added, "As your Majesty feels as you say about the match for me, you know that I am so obedient a son that I have no will other than yours, especially in a matter of such high import."

However, the Spanish ambassador Simon Renard was concerned about the "common rumour" that Mary intended to wed a fellow Englishman instead—her kinsman Edward Courtenay, the Earl of Devon. The queen adamantly assured Renard that she "knew no one in England with whom she would wish to ally herself." Not only would an English marriage create factions among the courtiers, but Courtenay had behaved in a debauched manner since his release from the Tower upon Mary's accession, and for that reason alone was not husband material.

So, on October 10, on behalf of Charles, his imperial sovereign, Renard formally offered Mary his son Philip's hand in marriage. Over the moon, Mary called it a "greater match than she deserved," although she admitted that "she did not know how the people of England would take it." Then, although the queen knew that the main purpose of a royal marriage was to beget an heir, she expressed a bit of squeamishness in that regard, even as she privately found Philip extremely attractive. "If he were disposed to be amorous, such was not her desire, for she was of the age your Majesty knew of [thirty-seven, considered middle-aged at the time], and had never harboured thoughts of love." This remark may have been merely a bit of self-preservation, preparing herself for a situation where Philip might not find her physically attractive, given their difference in ages. Nonetheless, she would "wholly love and obey him to whom she had given herself, following the divine commandment and would do nothing against his will." Then, fearing that her remark might have been misleading, she emphatically added that if Philip desired to "encroach in the government of the kingdom, she would be unable to permit it, nor [would she allow it] if he attempted to fill posts and offices with strangers [foreigners], for the country itself would never stand such interference." Just as her maternal grandmother Isabella of Castile had done, Mary would compartmentalize her roles as a wife and as a queen.

Mary's councilors, as well as her subjects, had a massive problem with her selection of Philip. They believed that no matter what she intended, at the end of the day the man she married would master and govern her and, by extension, England. But if an English queen wed a *foreigner*, he might seek to conquer England, absorbing the realm into his own empire through their marriage treaty. Arguing against the match, Sir Francis Englefield reminded Mary that Philip had a kingdom of his own to rule, which he was unlikely to quit to dwell in England. Moreover, his own subjects spoke ill of him. Another courtier, Edward Waldegrave, tried to scare Mary out of the prospective union with Philip by suggesting that it would provoke a war with France.

Aware that her courtiers and ministers had their own personal and religious agendas for wishing her to espouse an English subject, Mary defended her choice. The kingdom needed to checkmate French plots, and the contracted marriage of the dauphin to Mary, Queen of Scots, would strategically unite two of England's greatest enemies. How would Mary Tudor's kingdom benefit if she wed Edward Courtenay? And how might it profit by an alliance with Philip of Spain!

On November 16, 1553, a parliamentary delegation requested that Mary marry within the realm. John Pollard, the Speaker of the Commons, was a trained lawyer and judge. He launched into a long-winded, xenophobic, and condescending diatribe about the perils and pitfalls inherent in the queen's selection of a foreign husband. Such a man would displease her subjects. He would deplete England of money and arms. "Out of husbandly tyranny" he might even dare to remove the queen from her own country. If Mary left him a widower with young children, he might even attempt to usurp the crown. When Pollard finally had the nerve to lecture the monarch as if he were speaking to an ignorant schoolgirl, rather than to his sovereign, insisting that "it would be better for the queen to marry a subject of hers," Mary finally lost her patience.

She rose to address the assembly of men. Controlling her temper, she informed them that a search of histories and chronicles would reveal that no one—*no one*—had ever used such disrespectful language to a king of England, and that even when kings had been children, their advisers had given them liberty in matters of marriage.

Mary was just warming up. She did not appreciate the notion of Parliament choosing "a companion" for her "conjugal bed," declaring in her reportedly deep and booming voice, "I now rule over you by the best right possible, and being a free woman, if any man or woman of the people of our realm is free, I have full right and sufficient years to discern a suitable partner in love." Her Tudor dander up, she continued: It was "entirely vain for you to nominate a prospective husband for me from your own fancy, but rather let it be my free choice to select a worthy husband for my bridal bed—one who will not only join with me in mutual love, but will be able with his own resources to prevent an enemy attack, from his native land."

According to the Spanish ambassador, Mary resolutely insisted that "if she were married against her will she would not live three months and she would have no children. . . . [A]nd so, Mr. Speaker, you will defeat your own ends." Her selection of a husband would be divinely inspired; only prayer and guidance from the Almighty would lead to the correct choice "who would be beneficial to the kingdom and agreeable to herself . . . for she always thought of the welfare of her kingdom, as a good princess and mistress should."

Her reply rendered Pollard and his delegation dumbstruck, and they departed in silence.

But Mary wasn't finished. Suspecting that her Lord Chancellor, the Bishop of Winchester, had prompted the visit from the parliamentary delegation, she confronted Gardiner directly. She would "never marry Courtenay," Mary told him angrily. "Is it suitable, that I should be forced to marry a man because a bishop made friends with him in prison?"

Gardiner backed down, and Mary's Parliament and council begrudgingly accepted the monarch's choice of bridegroom. Her subjects, however, were not so easily appeased. Spanish negotiators, arriving in mid-January 1554 to discuss the terms of the impending marriage treaty, were pelted with snowballs by London apprentices.

The Spaniards favored the match for precisely the reason the English were so fervently against it. The tiny, auburn-haired Mary, already physically shriveled and looking older than her years, with her poor fashion sense—abundant jewelry, and garish textiles in every shade of red—was herself not the prize: It was control of England. Moreover, any child of their union would inherit not only Mary's England, but Spanish Hapsburg territories as well: the Low

Countries and, under certain circumstances, Spain. As Philip's father Charles V wrote, "I trust [the marriage] will prove a factor of weight in our endeavours to serve God and guard and increase our dominions."

However, Charles was fully aware of Mary's age. Her poor health was no secret, and although she'd always been fond of young children and had dreamed of motherhood, her childbearing days were numbered. The emperor hoped for the best from his son's marriage treaty, but the terms overwhelmingly favored England. Mary's team leveraged Parliament's opposition to negotiate a contract that would preserve all of her rights as queen and keep Spanish power and influence in England to a minimum, regardless of the law of *jure uxoris*. Looking ahead to any children of Mary and Philip's union, according to the marriage treaty their oldest son would inherit England, as well as Philip's lands in southern Germany and Burgundy. Don Carlos, Philip's son from his first marriage, would inherit Spain and the Hapsburg territories in Italy; those lands would, however, come under English dominion if Mary and Philip had children and Don Carlos eventually had no offspring of his own. By the terms of the marriage contract, Philip was prohibited from removing Mary and their children from England without the approval of Parliament. Should the couple have no children and Mary predecease Philip, not only would he have no rights of succession to her kingdom, but he was forbidden from influencing it. Although Philip could style himself king of England, he would really be no more than a glorified subject. The provisions of their marriage contract denied him any actual regal power, although he was permitted to assist Mary in the administrative governance of the realm. Even the attendants in his household were to be English. Finally, England was not to be dragged into any of the Hapsburgs' foreign wars, whether instigated by the Spanish branch of the family or the Burgundian Hapsburgs.

However, favorable as the terms were for England, they failed to assuage the fear of foreign domination. Moreover, the details of the marriage treaty were not common knowledge, even to the members of Parliament.

England remained a powder keg of discontent, riven with ruinous poverty due to bad harvests and rampant greed among the wealthy, as well as the ongoing religious dissent. Little was needed to spark an explosion.

Philip of Spain was a match in more ways than one. Mary's choice of bridegroom remained so odious to her countrymen that during the early months of 1554, a handful of aristocrats fomented a four-pronged revolt, comprised of uprisings in Devon, Hereford, Leicestershire, and Kent. Their plan was to depose Mary, replacing her on the throne with Elizabeth. When the conspiracy was uncovered in January, Mary's council acted swiftly and the Devon and Hereford plans fizzled. Jane Grey's father joined up with the Leicestershire plotters, and Thomas Wyatt the Younger spearheaded the Kentish revolt, with a force of twenty-five hundred to three thousand men.

Thanks to his father, Philip of Spain had his own spies and uncovered the plot. Most of the rebels never made it as far as London, but Wyatt and his men successfully reached the capital. Overriding the advice of her ministers to flee, Mary stood her ground instead, insisting that "she would tarry to see the uttermost," proving her Tudor mettle by confronting the rebels unflinchingly. She denounced Wyatt as a traitor to the crown, and, declaring that she was "already married to this Common Weal and the faithful members of the same," vowed to remain and shed her own royal blood, if need be, to defend her loyal subjects.

Wyatt and his followers were tried and executed.

Rather than see her impending Spanish marriage as the catalyst for her kingdom's unrest, Mary chose to view the union as the only way of smothering it. Only Spanish Catholic orthodoxy could stamp out Protestant heresy, and only an alliance with Spain could keep the French wolf from England's back door, and scare off any Scottish plans to invade as well.

But that winter, Mary had other bad news to contend with. No longer able to swallow his discontent, on January 4, Philip had openly disavowed their marriage treaty, insisting that he could not be bound by a contract that had been negotiated without his knowledge. Nevertheless, cognizant of the importance of their union to both their realms, he agreed to sign the document, aware that he had no other choice, "but by no means in order to bind himself or his heirs to observe the articles, especially any that might burden his conscience."

Ultimately, Philip sucked it up and made no protest, sending England his assent to their formal betrothal by proxy on March 6, 1554. However, as a passive-aggressive way of registering his ongoing disenchantment with the terms, he churlishly sent Mary no wedding gift, or even so much as a personal letter accompanying his official consent. The ring didn't even come from Philip; it was sent by his father. Nor did he prove the eager bridegroom. Although Philip assured his father, "My own happiness and dearest hopes hang upon the result. . . . If the queen wishes me to go soon I will start without loss of time," he did not quit his homeland until July 13, 1554.

Anxious that his son's attitude might botch things for Spain and the Hapsburgs, Charles V wrote to the Duke of Alva, who was assigned to accompany Philip to England: "For the love of God, see to it that my son behaves in the right manner; for otherwise I tell you I would rather never have taken the matter in hand at all."

"Notes for Prince Philip's Guidance in England" had been prepared by the Spanish ambassador Simon Renard in the hope of engendering mutually good relations from the outset. The suggestions included:

> Item: when his Highness enters the kingdom, he will be well advised to . . . be affable, show himself often to the people, prove that he wishes to take no share in the administration, but leave it all to the Council . . . caress the nobles, talk with them on occasion, take them out to hunt with them. If he does so, there is no doubt whatever that they will not only love his Highness, but will adore him.

> Item: it will be well to show a benign countenance to the people and lead them to look for kindness, justice and liberty.

> Item: as his Highness knows no English it will be well to select an interpreter and have him among his attendants so that he may converse with the English. And let his Highness learn a few words in order to be able to salute them. . . .

Item: no soldiers from the ships must be allowed to land here, in order not to confirm the suspicion inculcated by the French, that his Highness wishes to conquer the realm by force.

Accompanied by a flotilla of eighty large ships and more than a hundred smaller ones, Philip sailed into Southampton amid torrents of rain on Friday, July 20. Before the royal spouses-to-be met in person, gifts were exchanged by their emissaries. Each gave the other a diamond, although the gem that Philip presented to his bride was considerably smaller than the one she had sent to him. Mary also invested Philip with the Order of the Garter and sent him "a very richly wrought poignard [a dagger], studded with gems, and two robes, one of them as rich and beautiful as could be imagined." A fine white horse, handsomely caparisoned in crimson velvet, was waiting for him when he disembarked—yet another wedding gift from the generous Mary.

On July 23, Philip finally set off for Winchester Cathedral, where he would greet his bride. The rain had never subsided. Late that evening, at long last, he met Mary, making her acquaintance in a candlelit long gallery, a grand room suitable for dancing or entertaining. Unless Philip had changed his attire beforehand, the first impression he made on his bride-to-be may have been of a drowned rat. His "rich coat embroidered with gold, his doublet hosen and hat suite-like," with its once-jaunty plume, were sodden with rainwater. The yellow-bearded Philip saw a diminutive, russet-haired woman endeavoring to appear younger than her years, wearing a flamboyant black velvet gown heavily embellished with jewels and an underskirt of frosted silver. Mary was so fair-skinned that she appeared to have no eyebrows, and she had an unusually masculine voice.

If Mary and Philip had been comic strip characters with thought bubbles floating above their heads, their initial impressions would have revealed the greatest royal mismatch since Henry VIII and Anne of Cleves. Mary was smitten by Philip's blond hair, his gray-blue eyes, and his fine, courtly manners (which he employed to successfully conceal his revulsion for her). The thought bubble for Philip, who spoke no English (the pair communicated in fractured

Spanish, French, and Latin), might very well have been a universally understood "Ugh," "Bleh," or "Ick."

While Mary's ladies sweetly serenaded them on musical instru-
ments, the couple enjoyed a pleasant meeting, with much hand
kissing in the Spanish fashion. Philip even kissed Mary on the
mouth, which was an English custom. They did not dine together
on the night before their nuptials, further reducing their opportunity to become acquainted before they were joined together for all
eternity.

To place Philip on an equal social footing with his bride before
their marriage, Charles V conferred upon his son the kingdom of
Naples, as well as his own claim to the kingdom of Jerusalem. This
made Philip an actual king, rather than merely an acting sovereign
and prince.

The royal wedding was held at Winchester Cathedral, the bish-
opric of Stephen Gardiner, on a rainy July 25, the feast day of Saint
James, the patron saint of Spain. Another reason Winchester was
chosen was because there had been seditious rumblings in London,
and Mary felt it wise to remove the event from the capital.

Accompanied by a number of Spanish knights, the twenty-seven-
year old groom arrived first, resplendent in a white satin doublet
embroidered with gemstones and a mantle of fluted cloth of gold
(another gift from Mary), that was equally embellished with jewels.
Philip wore the Order of the Garter about his neck, in addition to
priceless jewels of Castile. The bride reached the cathedral a half
hour later, wearing an ensemble that matched Philip's, which
"blazed with jewels to an extent that dazzled those who gazed upon
her." Her purple satin gown, according to her wardrobe books, was
made of "rich tissue with a border and wide sleeves, embroidered
upon purple satin, set with pearls of our store, lined with purple
taffeta." The style of gown was called a partlet, a skirt with a high-
collared, matching sleeveless jacket covering the chest. Mary's white
satin kirtle was embroidered with gold and silver threads. At her
breast she wore a piece of jewelry known as "La Peregrina," a pair
of large diamonds set together with an enormous pear-shaped pearl,
a gift from Philip and Mary's father-in-law. Centuries later, after
the piece endured several peregrinations, the actor Richard Burton

would purchase "La Peregrina"—which means "The Wanderer"—for his wife, the glamorous Elizabeth Taylor.

The banns were read in English and in Latin, and Mary, lacking a male relative to stand up for her at the altar, was given away by four of her councilors, who were peers of the realm.

Before Gardiner and the six other bishops who were officiating at the royal nuptials continued with the ceremony, the Bishop of Winchester made a speech to the assembled guests about the marriage treaty and announced Charles V's gift to Philip of the kingdom of Naples.

The couple exchanged vows in Latin and English, Mary pledging "from henceforth to be compliant and obedient . . . as much in mind as in body"—against Gardiner's wishes, because he had insisted that Philip remain her subject as one of the terms of the marriage contract. Mary then vowed to endow Philip with all her "worldly goods," although Philip promised only to endow his bride with all his "moveable goods." According to a contemporary account, Mary's wedding band "was a round hoop of gold without any stone, which was her desire, for she said she would be married as maidens were in the old time, and so she was."

However, even at the postceremonial banquet, one little detail revealed that it had not been a wedding of equals. Mary was served on gold dishes; Philip's food was served on silver ones. After the formal feast, the bridal couple and their guests adjourned to an adjoining hall for more revelry. A letter from one John Elder gives another contemporary description of the reception—"such triumphing, banqueting, singing, masking and dancing, as was never seen in England heretofore, by the report of all men."

And no one nowadays thinks of Mary I as a party girl! Truth is, she was falling in love with her husband and, at thirty-eight, was finally beginning to sense what it must be like to be a complete woman. Almost. There was still the wedding night and the forfeiture of her virginity to come. As one of Philip's gentlemen wrote soon after the festivities wound down, "the Bishop of Winchester blessed the bed, and they remained alone. What happened that night only they know. If they give us a son, our joy will be complete."

But Mary's warm and fuzzy feelings for Philip were not reciprocated. He was not merely unattracted to his wife; he found her physically distasteful. Four days after the wedding, his longtime adviser Ruy Gómez de Silva confided to a colleague in Brussels, "to speak frankly with you, it will take a great God to drink this cup [but] . . . the king realises that the marriage was concluded for no fleshly consideration, but in order to remedy the disorders of this kingdom and to preserve the Low Countries." Philip did not have the guts to reveal to Mary that the Spanish—and most of all himself—viewed their union as purely political and that his father had counseled him to tarry in England for no more than five or six days after the wedding ceremony. After that, he had the business of Spain and the rest of the Hapsburg Empire to contend with, depending upon the assignment he received from the emperor.

Too craven to confront Mary with the truth, Philip remained in England. Scholars posit that one reason he stayed was because Charles V, or his ministers, no longer saw the need for Philip to journey to the Netherlands to set up a satellite court there.

The newlyweds honeymooned in Winchester for ten days and then headed toward London, stopping at Windsor and Richmond before making their grand entry into the capital.

Philip was now not merely king of England, and Mary the queen of Naples. Eventually the couple would be jointly styled as Philip and Mary by the Grace of God King and Queen of England and Spain, France, Jerusalem, both the Sicilies and Ireland, Defenders of the Faith, Archdukes of Austria, Dukes of Burgundy, Milan and Brabant, Counts of Hapsburg, Flanders and Tyrol. In 1555, Pope Paul issued a papal bull recognizing Philip and Mary as the rightful sovereigns of Ireland, and the following year, Philip ascended the Spanish throne in his own right, making Mary queen of Spain.

Over their first few months of marriage, Mary and Philip settled down—but had separate households, as was the royal custom at the time. Within their various royal residences, because Mary was England's reigning sovereign she dwelled in the more lavish king's apartments, while Philip resided in the rooms designated for the consort. Meanwhile, the mood in the London streets was often unpleasant. The xenophobic English were spoiling for a fight with any Spaniard, whom they insisted outnumbered them four to one, loudly proclaiming the queen's preference for Spaniards and bishops over her own countrymen.

However, according to at least one (unnamed) Spanish courtier, the monarchs themselves could not have been more delighted with each other. The courtier wrote to a friend in Salamanca, "Their Majesties are the happiest couple in the world, and more in love than words can say. His Highness never leaves her, and when they are on the road he is ever by her side, helping her to mount and dismount. They sometimes dine together in public, and go to mass together on holidays."

This verbiage was merely propaganda designed to make their woeful mismatch appear to be a great success. Philip was doing his best to put a good face on it because the stakes were so high, but he never loved his wife. Helping her on and off her horse was a chivalrous gesture that only the self-deluded Mary could mistake for love; a stable groom would have done as much. But she certainly had feelings for Philip, naively inflating his courteousness into affection, even as their communication was hampered by language barriers. Philip spoke to Mary in Spanish; she replied in French. Sometimes they would both converse in Latin. Philip, as counseled, did learn a few words and phrases of English, but not enough to hold a conversation, and never enough to comprehend any government proceedings, which were translated into Latin for him.

The same Iberian courtier damned Mary with faint praise in his letter to Salamanca. ". . . the Queen . . . is not at all beautiful: small, and rather flabby than fat [this contradicts all reports of her as being thin and frail-looking], she is of white complexion and fair, and has no eyebrows. She is a perfect saint and dresses badly. All the women here wear petticoats of coloured cloth without admixture of silk, and above come coloured robes of damask, satin or velvet, very badly cut."

French fashions were all the rage in England at the time; even Mary and Philip's wedding garments had been cut in the chic French style. But the Spanish, who hated all things French, were duty-bound to declare the silhouettes hideous and unflattering.

In September 1554, new coinage was issued depicting the profiles of both sovereigns with a crown floating between them. What irked many of Mary's subjects was that Philip's head was placed on the dominant left-hand side of the coin, the position reserved for monarchs, not consorts.

By the middle of the month, the kingdom had something to cheer about when Mary stopped menstruating. As the weeks went by, she gradually gained weight and exhibited other signs of pregnancy such as morning sickness. The entire court, from the ladies of her privy chamber to her physicians, was certain she was pregnant. By November, Te Deums were sung and the news was proclaimed across Europe. The various foreign ambassadors scrutinized and reported every detail of the queen's medical condition to their respective sovereigns. Because Mary's heir stood to inherit so much by the terms of her marriage treaty, her pregnancy was a matter of international importance.

Yet not everyone was thrilled with the news. A conspiracy to kill both sovereigns was scheduled to take place during a demonstration of Spanish cane-play that Philip organized, and in which he was set to participate. The mock tournament had three rounds, and luckily (for Philip) the hideous weather and the English spectators' utter incomprehension of the rules of play led to the abrupt cancellation of the event after the second round. Consequently, the plans for a number of heavily armed men to arrive during the third round and murder the royal couple were serendipitously thwarted.

The following spring, all the ducks were lined up in preparation for the royal baby's imminent arrival. Mary's due date was projected to be May 9, 1555, give or take a few days. To allay any fears the queen might have about bearing a child at her advanced age, she was shown a set of beautiful infant triplets born to a mother of similar years and physical stature, who had come through the dangers of childbirth and remained healthy and strong.

Summoned to witness the birth in late April, Elizabeth Tudor was released from the Tower, where she had been imprisoned after Wyatt's rebellion, suspected of some form of tacit cooperation, although nothing had ever been proved against her. Should Mary die in childbirth, a very real possibility in this era, a provision was made for Philip to become guardian of the realm during their child's minority, although he would have no other regal authority.

On Tuesday, April 30, the church bells tolled the great news. The sixteenth-century English clothier and diarist Henry Machyn recorded, "the Queen's grace was delivered of a prince, and so there was great ringing through London and divers places, Te Deum laudamus sung." Evidently, Her Majesty had borne a son "with little pain and no danger" shortly after midnight. By May 2, the imperial court had received the good news and was reported to be "rejoicing out of measure."

But the announcement of Mary's successful delivery turned out either to be a false alarm, or political spin-doctoring that got out of control, because there was no baby. At first everyone believed that it had just been a mathematical error, that Mary's due date had been miscalculated.

Then nasty rumors began to circulate that someone else's child would be substituted and passed off as the queen's, or that the birth on April 30 had been a lapdog or pet monkey, or that Mary had been delivered of "a mole or lump of flesh and was in great peril of death." And the Venetian ambassador Giovanni Michieli scoffed that the episode was more likely to "end in wind rather than anything else." Sadly, he was closest to the truth. As the summer months wore on, Mary, horribly melancholy, curled herself into a ball with her knees drawn into her chest, something no pregnant woman could do without enduring extreme discomfort. It seems most probable that, rather than ever having been pregnant and suffering a miscarriage somewhere along the way, news that surely would have been chronicled or reported, she must have had a phantom pregnancy—all of the genuine symptoms, with no fetus in her womb. Mary's mother had experienced the same tragedy.

In July 1555, the queen's swollen abdomen receded as mysteriously as it had enlarged. There never had been a baby. If Mary had experienced a phantom or hysterical pregnancy, also known as pseudocyesis, her condition could have been purely psychological, or it could have been the result of changes in her endocrine system. She would have begun secreting hormones, leading to physical changes in her body that mimic those of an actual pregnancy.

Mary, heartbroken, fell into a profound depression. Philip now saw no reason to remain much longer in England. The queen was equally disconsolate over the idea of her husband's departure. She truly loved him; she believed they made a good couple. It was Philip who had been most instrumental in restoring England's relationship with the papacy, approaching the issue in a more diplomatic manner than Mary did. He believed that the better and more successful way to restore the kingdom to the Roman religion was not through coercion and punishment, but by increments, which in the course of time would become accepted and embraced by their English subjects.

In the month after her accession to the throne Mary had issued a proclamation to the effect that she would not compel any of her subjects to follow her religion, but things hadn't really worked out that way. By the end of 1554, Philip had persuaded Parliament to repeal the Protestant religious laws passed by Mary's father, returning the English Church to Roman Catholic jurisdiction. The couple's greatest concession to the wealthy and influential evangelicals was the agreement not to confiscate the Church lands they had gained during the Reformation. Pope Julius gave the deal his imprimatur by the end of 1554, and the Heresy Acts were revived.

So much for Mary's religious tolerance. Under the Heresy Acts, dissenters were executed in what were known as the Marian Persecutions, which began in early February 1555. Not that it lessens the impact or import of her deeds, but "only" 283 "heretics" (as religious dissenters were referred to then) were consigned to the flames. Most of them were laborers from the working classes. However, a few marquee names went up in smoke, most notably Archbishop Thomas Cranmer, in 1556. Mary finally was avenged on the man who had pronounced her parents' marriage null and void on May 23, 1533. Many more evangelicals, such as John Foxe, whose writings during the Elizabethan era would be among the first to refer to the sovereign as "Bloody Mary," chose exile over martyrdom. Evidently Mary, and her papal legate, her kinsman Reginald Pole, had not expected to burn so many dissenters; they desired the heretics to be reconciled to the Roman religion instead, and had wanted the public burnings to be carried out judiciously, and not seen to be vindictive. Yet how could they have imagined these executions as anything other than Church- and state-sanctioned murder? And how could they not have reckoned that the Protestants' faith was as unshakable as their own?

Protestantism was increasingly associated with resistance to Spanish domination, and Philip took the heat for the burnings; it had been a popular punishment for heretics in Spain ever since Mary's grandparents inaugurated the Inquisition in the third quarter of the fifteenth century. In fact, Philip took no active or direct role in the Marian Persecutions. However, he did not speak out against them. Philip had been advised by Simon Renard, the Spanish ambassador, to avoid being too hasty in religious matters. It was Mary who wanted the burnings. And so they continued. But they were exceptionally unpopular, even then.

By the time Philip was prepared to depart England's shores in the late summer of 1555, the Catholic restoration had been achieved. When it appeared quite clear by July that Mary was not pregnant, he gave up all hope of fathering an heir with her, and prepared to abandon her as well. Mary was heartsick when he left in late August. She had wanted to accompany him to Dover, but Philip insisted it would delay his departure too much, so the queen went only as far as Greenwich.

Michieli, the Venetian ambassador, wrote a detailed and poignant report of their leave-taking. Mary had retained her composure through the customary kissing of hands. ". . . But when she returned to her own rooms, she lent on her elbows at a window overlooking the river, and there, thinking she was not observed, she gave scope to her grief in floods of tears. She did not stir from the spot until she had seen the king embark and depart; not till the last sight of him; he mounted on a raised and open part of the barge, so as to be better visible as long as he was in sight of the window, kept on raising his hat and making salutes with the most affectionate gestures."

Mary began to miss her husband as soon as she lost sight of him. According to Michieli, "the Queen not content with having sent two of her chief chamberlains in the King's company for the purpose of being acquainted with all that takes place, writes to him daily in her own hand, and despatches courtiers, demonstrating in every way her great desire."

But Philip replied to Mary's frequent correspondence less and less. On September 13, she told Michieli "very passionately with tears in her eyes, that for a week she had had no letters from him." The ambassador's informant reported that Mary mourned the absence of her husband "as may be imagined with regard to a person extraordinarily in love."

Philip allowed his ecclesiastical household to remain behind for several months. His Spanish and Flemish guards stayed in England as well. It had been suggested to him that he let Mary down lightly. Departing by degrees would be less traumatic for his wife than removing every last stitch of his household in one fell swoop. This way, perhaps she might anticipate his eventual return one day. Or slowly accustom herself to his absence. It didn't work. Mary felt abandoned and alone.

In January 1556, Charles V abdicated the crowns of Aragon and Castile, making Philip the true, rather than nominal, king of Spain. The emperor also resigned his lordship of the Netherlands to his son. Nonetheless, Philip increasingly desired to wear the crown of England as a king regnant and not as a consort. He evidently intimated to Mary that he might be tempted to return to English soil, should she begin making plans for his coronation. But as saddened as Mary was by their separation, she was a pragmatic ruler who knew the minds of her subjects and her ministers. After she informed Philip that Parliament would never stand for his being crowned, he did not press the matter any further.

Philip would have to pick his battles, so to speak, because he would soon need his wife's consent to violate one of the cornerstones of their marriage treaty: England would be drawn into one of Spain's foreign conflicts.

When Philip ascended his father's throne, he inherited the kingdom's mounting tensions with France. Mary recognized that any proposal to commit England's scant resources to a Spanish invasion of France during difficult economic times for her kingdom would be just as unpopular with her Parliament as suggesting that Philip be crowned king. Moreover, she'd heard rumors that Philip had been unfaithful to her while he'd been abroad, and although she had no way of confirming them, she had already begun to despair of his ever returning to her arms. On December 30, 1555, the French ambassador, Antoine de Noailles, had reported that Mary had "told her ladies, that she had done all possible to induce her husband to return, and as she found he would not, she meant to withdraw utterly from men, and live quietly, as she had done the chief part of her life before she married."

Then the marriage of someone else became a source of tension in Mary and Philip's relationship. He was pressing for a match between the Princess Elizabeth and one of his cousins, Emmanuel Philibert, Prince of Piedmont and titular Duke of Savoy. Such a union would preserve Philip's interests in England and the Catholic restoration, no matter what happened to Mary. For once, the half sisters were on the same page; they were both against the match, although for different reasons. Mary didn't want to place Elizabeth in any position where she could become too powerful or influential. However, the queen didn't have to worry about Philip strong-arming Elizabeth into a marriage. Anne Boleyn's daughter, not only in 1556 and ever after, but from the time she was eight years old, had no interest in a husband.

Mary had always been an avid cardplayer. What she really wanted was her husband back. Keen not to reveal her hand with regard to her position on the Elizabeth-Philibert match, she merely told Philip that it would be impossible to arrange such a marriage in his absence. He would have to come to England so that the two of them could jointly pray to God, "who has the direction of the hearts of kings in his hand."

Philip returned, but it was not so much to push Parliament to sanction Elizabeth's marriage. It was to request a declaration of war against France, and the money, ships, and men to invade her. A thirty-two-gun salute greeted his return to Greenwich Palace at five p.m. on March 20, 1557. The following day, the church bells pealed in celebration and the next few days were spent in a round of festivities—"a warmed over honeymoon," in the words of one diplomat.

Predictably, Mary's councilors refused to openly declare war on France; they would approve financial and naval support for Philip's endeavor, but would go no further, reminding the queen of the terms of her marriage treaty. Mary angrily demanded a new verdict that would "satisfy her and her husband," summoning each of the councilors to meet with her individually on April 13, 1557. She threatened "some with death, others with the loss of their goods and estates, if they did not consent to the will of her husband." Even at this, Mary's Privy Council stood their ground. Money and troops was as far as they would go. Philip remained displeased. The sole acceptable response was the council's sanction of an open declaration of war.

Only a genuine provocation could sway them. They got it on April 23, 1557, when an expatriate English Protestant, Sir Thomas Stafford, landed on the Yorkshire coast at Scarborough with two French ships and a force of a hundred men comprised of English and French rebels. Seizing Scarborough Castle, their ultimate aim was to depose Mary for marrying a Spaniard. Stafford was tried, condemned, and executed for treason by the end of the month. On June 7, Mary's heralds proclaimed that the kingdom was at war with France. This time, the queen did accompany her husband to Dover, where on July 6, as he prepared to sail for France, Philip said his last good byes to England and to his loving wife.

Less than half a year later, in early January 1558, Calais, England's only remaining continental territory, fell to France. Gone was a centuries-long legacy of English dominion on at least some part of French soil. It was Mary, not Philip, who was forever blamed for her kingdom's loss of Calais. Ultimately, as the English sought an explanation for the defeat, they accused Lord Thomas Wentworth, the Lord Deputy Governor of Calais, and John Highfield, Master of the Ordnance, of selling the English stronghold to the French. The men were not tried until after Mary's death. Due to inconclusive proof, they were acquitted, although that did not necessarily render them innocent of the charges leveled against them.

By the early months of 1558, Mary believed herself pregnant again. From the Continent, Philip expressed his delight, replying to Cardinal Pole's correspondence containing the happy announcement that "The news of the Queen, my beloved wife . . . has given me greater joy than I can express to you, as it is the one thing in the world I have most desired and which is of the greatest importance for the cause of religion and the care and welfare of our realm." Philip added that it had "gone far to lighten the sorrow I have felt for the loss of Calais."

But once again, it was wishful thinking. Unfortunately, Mary was not pregnant, but suffering from a lingering illness. Her health had been steadily deteriorating during the past year. The Venetian Giovanni Michieli, who had left England in 1557, when his ambassadorial duties came to an end, noted then that the forty-one-year-old monarch appeared "very grave," her "wrinkles . . . caused more by anxieties than by age, which make her appear some years older." Michieli admired Mary's "wonderful grandeur and dignity," and thought her "valiant" and "brave," but attributed much of her "deep melancholy" to "suffocation of the matrix [womb]," which was believed to be caused by retention of menstrual fluids, a medical condition that had plagued Mary for decades. According to Michieli, "the remedy of tears and weeping . . . which from childhood she has been accustomed, and still often used by her," was now insufficient, requiring the queen to be "blooded either from the foot or elsewhere, which keeps her always pale and emaciated." The Venetian also attributed Mary's bitter and lachrymose disposition to her unhappiness in love and marriage, and her resentment toward, and jealousy of, Elizabeth.

At the end of March, still believing herself to be pregnant, the queen wrote her will. The assumption that her kingdom would be left to the heir she carried within her was more than a refusal to accept reality; it was a legal document intended to keep Elizabeth off the throne.

But the spring came and a baby didn't. By the end of May, Philip's letters to England no longer mentioned the prospect of imminent fatherhood. Over the summer of 1558, Mary grew progressively weaker. Ultimately accepting that she was not pregnant and needed to name a successor, she added a codicil to her will stating that if God did not grant her an heir from the fruits of her body, then she would be "succeeded by my next heir and successor by the Laws and Statutes of this realm." The codicil did not name Elizabeth, but Mary acknowledged that by those same laws and statutes Elizabeth was the rightful heir to her throne.

Having bequeathed a number of gifts to her husband in her will, including the "table diamond" that Charles V had sent her upon their betrothal, urging Philip to keep it as a memento, Mary also exhorted him to protect and care for England after her eventual demise "as a father in his care, as a brother in his love and favour . . .

and a most assured and undoubted friend to her country and sub-jects." Despite this entreaty, within thirty years, Philip II, king of Spain would be England's deadliest enemy.

In accordance with Mary and Philip's marriage treaty, all of his prerogatives in England would cease with her death. By the begin-ning of November 1558, Mary was the likely victim of an influenza epidemic that was ravaging the country, and in pain from her other ailments and conditions, including, quite possibly, uterine cancer and/or ovarian cysts, and she did not have long to live. A parlia-mentary delegation visited her on the sixth of the month and, for the sake of the realm, pressed her to name an heir. No coyness, no vagueness; misunderstandings and miscommunications could lead to civil unrest, or worse. Accepting the inevitable, Mary agreed to nominate Elizabeth as her successor. Aware even as she said the words that they were spoken in futility, she asked that Elizabeth discharge her debts after her demise and keep the Catholic religion as it had been established.

On November 17, 1558, at St. James's Palace, the forty-two-year-old Mary I died during a final Mass at her bedside. Philip was in Brussels at the time, mourning the death of his father. He in-formed his sister Juana in Spain of the event, writing unemotion-ally, "my wife is dead. May God have received her into his glory. I felt a reasonable regret for her death."

However, Philip did hold a proxy funeral for Mary in Brussels at the end of November. The chief mourner was Emmanuel Phili-bert of Savoy, the man Philip had hoped would wed his former sister-in-law, Elizabeth. A riderless black horse with a crown perched upon its saddle represented the late queen.

Mary's body lay in state in a lead coffin in the Privy Chamber of St. James's Palace for three weeks. In accordance with royal tradi-tion, her heart and viscera were removed and her belly slit open, the cavity filled with sweet-smelling herbs and spices. Respecting the Catholic traditions, Elizabeth made sure that Masses were said 'round the clock and the room was illuminated with candles. Mary had wanted to be interred beside her mother, who reposes at Peter-borough Abbey, or to have Katherine of Aragon's remains removed to Westminster, but she was not granted her final wish.

On December 10, her coffin was carried to the Chapel Royal.

Three days later, the funeral cortege made its slow and somber procession to Westminster Abbey, where Mary was laid to rest with great pomp and majesty in a traditional Catholic funeral. No expense was spared. The new queen had insisted that the details laid down in their father's "funeral book" be followed to the letter.

Ironically, the half sisters, more often at odds than not, would eventually share a tomb in Westminster Abbey, although the monument to Elizabeth, erected by her successor James I in 1603, all but eclipses Mary's grave. The half siblings shared a royal motto as well. For all of the Virgin Queen's grand innovations, she cribbed her older sister's *"Veritas Temporis Filia"*—"Truth Is the Daughter of Time."

Elizabeth did not pay Mary's debts; nor, of course, did she maintain England's ties to the Church of Rome. During her reign she would burn Catholics for heresy, but was never blackened with the sobriquet "Bloody Elizabeth."

Elizabeth and Philip tried at first to maintain amicable relations between their respective realms, but it became impossible. Philip was prepared to commit himself to the Ridolfi plot in 1571 that would overthrow Elizabeth, replacing her with Mary, Queen of Scots—yet he did not condone Elizabeth's assassination. Although Mary's execution in 1587 ended Philip's hopes of placing a Catholic monarch on England's throne, he was not prepared to mend fences with Elizabeth. In his view, she was sanctioning piracy on Spanish vessels bearing treasure from his territories in the New World.

In 1588, their ships met in one of history's most famous naval battles. Spain's purportedly invincible armada proved otherwise, substantially aided by Mother Nature, who churned up a massive storm in the English Channel, causing many of the Spanish fleet to lose their bearings. Under fire, the Spanish losses were significant enough to force them to retreat. Undeterred by the defeat of his grand armada, Philip would send two more armadas to England, in 1596 and 1597, and a third, in 1599, which ended up being diverted to the Canary Islands and the Azores for defensive purposes there. The Anglo-Spanish War would continue until both Elizabeth and Philip were dead.

After Mary's death, Philip married twice more. In 1559, the year after Mary's demise, he wed Elisabeth of Valois, the oldest daughter of the French king Henri II and Catherine de Medici. They had five children, although only two of them survived to adulthood, but Elisabeth died hours after suffering a miscarriage in 1568. In 1570, Philip took a fourth wife, Anna of Austria. Anna was not only his niece, but was a cousin of her own stepdaughter, Catherine Michelle of Spain. The Spanish Hapsburg inbreeding, one of three uncle-niece marriages in the line of Philip II, would ultimately destroy the dynasty: physical abnormalities, deformities, and mental illness eventually resulted in sterility and early deaths. Nonetheless, by all accounts, Philip and Anna enjoyed a happy marriage, producing eight children (four of each), although most of them died young. Anna passed away after giving birth to their daughter Maria in 1580.

Philip's oldest child, his son Don Carlos by his first wife, Maria Manuela, Princess of Portugal, died without issue in 1568.

Philip's own end was agonizing. Suffering from cancer exacerbated by a high fever, gout, and a horrifically painful attack of dropsy (edema or swelling in the joints), he lay in extremis for fifty-two days, steadily deteriorating. Because he was in too much agony to be bathed, a hole was cut in his mattress for the release of bodily fluids. The seventy-one-year-old Philip died on September 13, 1598, in El Escorial near Madrid, the historic residence of kings of Spain. He was buried there the following day. Philip was succeeded by his twenty-year-old son Philip III, whose mother had been Anna of Austria.

Philip II's thirty-two-year reign in Spain had witnessed the blossoming of a cultural renaissance. It was the Golden Age in literature, music, and the visual arts; the era of Cervantes, and of El Greco and the Mannerists.

Also known as the Spanish Tudor, Mary I has gone down in history as one of England's worst sovereigns, further tarred with the nickname "Bloody Mary" for her highly unpopular executions of Protestant evangelical dissenters.

Where history has glorified her half sister and successor, Elizabeth, Mary has been vilified. Then and ever since, this incomplete and jaded image of Mary was created by a largely Protestant body of scholars who, by burnishing Elizabeth's achievements, sought to tarnish or diminish the accomplishments of her Catholic predecessor. As a result, we are not left with a true or full picture of England's first queen regnant. During the sixteenth century, the writings of the Scottish reformer John Knox and the Elizabethan-era evangelical John Foxe, through his 1563 *Actes and Monuments* (more commonly known as the *Book of Martyrs*), which graphically depicts "the horrible and bloudy time of Queene Mary," helped to cement her image as a tyrant. By 1600, Catholicism itself was viewed as foreign and un-English. Had Mary lived longer or reigned for even half as many years as Elizabeth, her efforts to solidify a Catholic restoration might have been largely successful. She had many coreligionists, even if she had very few supporters for her methods of stamping out heresy.

Yet Mary provided both a vital role model and an object lesson for her younger sister. Elizabeth, whose reign was nine times longer, reaped many of the benefits from reforms and programs that Mary had sown during her brief five years on the throne. Hardworking, conscientious, and diligent, Mary literally burned the midnight oil, devoting long days to the governance of the realm. On her ascendance she inherited more problems than a deep religious schism, which would have been enough trouble to contend with on its own. England was plagued at the time with a massive amount of debt that Mary sought to bring under control with plans for currency reform (which Elizabeth I was ultimately able to achieve), and the search for new commercial markets for England's exports. Mary granted a royal charter to the Muscovy Company, commissioned a world atlas, and sanctioned exploration to the coast of Africa.

During her last two years on the throne, Mary and her council worked to provide disaster relief to families afflicted by poor harvests and health epidemics. Her government also passed a Militia Act in 1558, which gave the lord lieutenants in England's respective counties the responsibility for raising troops and mustering commissions. Mary overhauled the administration and finances of the navy and ensured that her ships were in good repair. Those vessels aided Philip by clearing French shipping from the English Channel during his ill-advised war with France in 1557. Nevertheless, Mary's reputation remains marred by this military defeat, and for centuries, biographers repeated the—likely apocryphal—incident recorded in Holinshed's Chronicles that Mary lamented after the debacle, "When I am dead and opened you will find Calais lying in my heart."

How ironic that the robust navy Elizabeth inherited from Mary, and was able to strengthen even further, would in 1588 engage in the mother of all sea battles with Mary's husband's Spanish Armada, solidifying England's dominance of the waves and shaming Philip of Spain.

Without intending to do so, Mary's marital actions and decisions, as well as the unintended consequences of an inglorious union, had also taught her sister a key life lesson. Mary's overt desperation for a husband who did not reciprocate her passion was the talk of her own court and was snickered about in foreign dispatches. Her insistence on wedding Philip in the first place nearly discredited her sovereignty and derailed her fragile monarchy. As for Philip, he was on a different page from the outset, never viewing their marriage as anything more than a treaty; from the moment the bridal couple left the altar, the Spanish courtiers gossiped about his effort to master his revulsion for her body.

By the time Elizabeth ascended the throne, she had seen all too well what happened—and not merely politically—when a queen of England wed a foreign sovereign. The public and private price that Mary paid in emotional, physical, and psychological currency, appearing the fool by giving her heart so freely to an undeserving man who hardly mirrored her affection, could never yield a reward that would outweigh the risk.

ISABELLA ROMOLA
de MEDICI
AND
PAOLO d'ORSINI,
DUKE OF BRACCIANO

....

MARRIED: 1558–1576

&

ELEONORA di GARZIA
di TOLEDO
AND
PIETRO de MEDICI

....

MARRIED: 1571–1576

"*I*nglorious" can also mean "dishonorable" and "scandalous," but the union of Isabella Romola de Medici and Paolo d'Orsini as well as that of Eleonora di Garzia di Toledo and Pietro de Medici are the only inglorious marriages profiled here that also qualify for the pages of a true-crime compendium, culminating as they did in a shocking pair of "honor killings" that even the likes of Al Capone might not have contemplated.

Perhaps even more horrifying than the lurid details of the assassination of a pair of beautiful cousins at the hands of their husbands—the quartet as high-living as they were highborn, yet none of them a faithful spouse—was that the men literally got away with murder. Where these two married couples were concerned, the

Medici motto, *"Semper,"* meaning "forever," with its attendant connotations of loyalty, did not apply.

In the sixteenth century, Italy was comprised of several city-states and kingdoms. While the Spanish Hapsburgs ruled the kingdom of Naples in the south, powerful families such as the Este, Ferrara, Sforza, Orsini, and Medici vied for domination of Rome and the northern cities.

The House of Medici gained prominence in Florence in the late fourteenth century, becoming wealthy from the textile trade—which led to myriad slurs against them as merchants, no matter how high they rose socially. Although their beginnings were humbler, ultimately their international influence was gained through banking. By making canny political and social connections, the Medici bank eventually became the largest and most respected financial institution in Renaissance Europe, and over the next few generations its family members gained immense political power in Tuscany and beyond, producing four Medici popes. In 1532, under Hapsburg auspices, the Medici became the hereditary dukes of Florence; the title was elevated to Grand Duke of Tuscany in 1569. However, the family would always be considered Italian citizens rather than royalty, a distinction often made by the bridegroom's relatives whenever one of the family's upwardly mobile heiresses married a social superior, including the union of Catherine de Medici to the future Henri II of France.

The Medici had strong ties to the Spanish Hapsburgs. In 1539, the daughter of the Spanish Viceroy of Naples, Eleonora di Toledo, wed the duke of Florence, Cosimo I de Medici, in a love match. Such an illustrious marriage also helped legitimize the powerful Florentine family's ducal title.

Their romance is practically biblical. Cosimo had fallen in love with Eleonora, who was the younger daughter of Pedro Álvarez di Toledo, yet the Viceroy of Naples was unwilling to let her leave the family without a struggle. He tried to convince Cosimo to wed his older, less beautiful daughter Isabella instead—a Leah-for-Rachel scenario. Cosimo stood fast. He wanted the lovely Eleonora, not her elder sister, but Álvarez made him pay for the pleasure; Eleonora's dowry would be fifty thousand *scudi* less than he was prepared to give Cosimo if he took Isabella off his hands.

The fertile Eleonora was known as "La Fecundissima." She and Cosimo, who was elevated from Duke of Florence to the first Grand Duke of Tuscany by the king of Spain and Hapsburg Holy Roman Emperor Charles V, became the proud parents of eleven children. Cosimo particularly doted on the older girls, Maria, Lucrezia, and Isabella.

Isabella Romola de Medici, Eleonora and Cosimo's third daughter, was born shortly after the death of his beloved illegitimate daughter Bia, a golden-haired six-year-old angel. Pampered as a child, and always her *babbo*, or daddy's, favorite, Isabella was, in her father's eyes, the reincarnation of Bia, and Cosimo showered all the love upon her that he had once bestowed on his precious bastard daughter. Death had taken Bia, but if Cosimo had anything to say about it, he was never going to let Isabella part from him. And that was perfectly all right with her!

In Cosimo's opulent Florentine court, his large Medici brood was raised together, flouting the custom of giving sons and daughters of the nobility separate, and different, upbringings. All of Cosimo's children were afforded the same advantages of a sophisticated humanist education; however, accepting the perceived wisdom of the era that female children should learn to sew and spin, an effort was made to school Isabella in these womanly arts. As a home-economics student, she was a disaster. She hated girly-girl activities, and did not excel at them. Yet she had been passionate about dancing since she was a toddler, and was a superb equestrienne and huntress, raising and training her own hounds.

There was no stigma attached to her being considered an intellectual. As a child, Isabella was familiar with Virgil and Homer. By the time she was a teenager she spoke several languages impeccably, and was a gifted lute player and the author of numerous madrigals, talented enough to have been a professional musician and composer. Isabella was specifically renowned for her *poesia per musica*, patently hedonistic, erotic verses filled with double entendres.

By the time she reached her mid-teens, Isabella was an acknowledged beauty—tall and slender, with curling reddish-brown hair, dark eyes with arched brows, a high, domed forehead, a patrician, aquiline nose, and a sensual mouth. She was as renowned for her beauty and vivacity as she was for her erudition in philosophy.

Isabella also had a flair for fine fashion that extended beyond representing the Medici in their family colors of red, white, and green. She was painted numerous times, beginning in her girlhood. Each canvas was an advertisement for her desirability, fecundity, and family wealth and connections; the intention was to attract an equally suitable husband. Although the Medici were not related to any royal family by blood, their sons and daughters were considered princes and princesses whose marriages would be negotiated for political gain.

The lucky candidate was chosen when Isabella was only ten. On July 11, 1553, she was formally betrothed to the twelve-year-old scion of an ancient Roman family, Paolo Giordano I Orsini of Bracciano. Paolo's family tree boasted a dubious distinction: Both of his grandmothers were the illegitimate daughters of popes. Cosimo had no interest in whether his adored daughter liked, let alone could ever love, her future husband. He chose Paolo because the union provided territorial acquisition and consolidation of power for the Medici.

Cosimo stated, "We have chosen to make such a match for these reasons: This Lord has, with his estate, many beautiful and important lands close to our own; the other is the antiquity of the relationship between his house and ours in making other matches."

On hearing of his good fortune, Paolo expressed his appreciation in a thank-you note that was probably composed by one of his elders, and to which he did nothing but sign his name. "When I learned this morning of the match which has been made between your daughter and myself, I thought a grave mistake had been made, and I am very much in your debt, and these few lines cannot do sufficient reverence to Your Excellency."

Prophetic words. There would soon come a time when Paolo was literally in Cosimo's debt—to the tune of hundreds of thousands of *scudi*.

Because the Orsini family had suffered tremendous losses and damage to their property during the sack of Rome by Charles V's armies in 1527, in a way, Isabella was marrying down. Paolo's father, Girolamo Orsini, had also been sentenced to death for murdering his own half brother, and the Medici pope Clement VII had confiscated his lands. Paolo's mother, Felice, had successfully petitioned for a stay of execution and raised enough money to pay a whopping fine, getting the Orsini estates restored to the family. Nonetheless, the Orsini were not exactly squeaky clean. Very few families in Renaissance Italy were free of violent vendettas, whether the feud was with another powerful family or within their own house.

Cosimo promised Isabella a spectacular dowry—more than generous, at fifty thousand gold *scudi*, plus five thousand *scudi* worth of jewels from his purse. The total dowry had a value of approximately twenty million in 2007 dollars, as estimated by Gabrielle Langdon, author of *Medici Women: Portraits of Power, Love, and Betrayal*, a comprehensive study of the Medici women through their portraiture.

Paolo was the Renaissance equivalent of a playboy, preferring wild parties, fast horses, and fast women. He was no stranger to brothels and gambling dens. Isabella's Florentine society was more conservative, but in Rome, as in Venice, prostitution was institutionalized. Paolo grew up in a world where noblemen and clergy routinely mingled with lowlifes—pimps and bawds, cardsharps and thieves. The Eternal City had a more popular sobriquet then: It was nicknamed the "city of whores." By 1559, Paolo himself would be intimate with a pair of rivals known as Pasqua the courtesan and Camilla the Skinny, a common prostitute.

Although it was customary for the betrothed couple to correspond before they wed so they might get to know each other better, sex seems to have been on Paolo's mind when he wrote to his fourteen-year-old fiancée: "Every hour, I would give a thousand years to find myself sleeping one night with you. I desire you so much. The first thing I desire is to speak with you of many things, the second, I do not wish to say, but I will leave it with a smile to you, and I kiss both your hands, and your mouth."

In this era, a letter was rarely a private document. To begin with, it was usually dictated to, and written by, a third party, such as a secretary or a tutor. If Paolo wrote an erotic letter like this to Isabella, it surely would have been read at the Medici court by some adult in a parental or otherwise supervisory capacity who no doubt would have deemed it indecent; consequently, the note probably never reached her.

Not only did the tone of Paolo's letters to his virginal bride-to-be raise a red flag regarding his uncouthness, but the Medici already had issues with their future son-in-law over financial matters. The teenage Orsini was a profligate, spending *scudi* like *acqua* on horses, coaches, and costly equestrian trappings, and hunting and hawking paraphernalia, including the falcons—not only for himself, but for his entire entourage. By the time Paolo was sixteen years old, he was up to his armpits in debt, indiscreetly boasting that he was leveraging the enormous dowry he'd eventually receive from his fiancée against his expenses—sums he intended to repay after his marriage, just as soon as he got his hands on the money.

Cosimo had already made his bed as far as arranging Isabella's match with Paolo. But he didn't have to lie in it. He sent the youth a raft of stern warnings, cautioning him that if he continued to be a spendthrift, he should not expect Isabella's dowry as a matter of course.

"You are a ship blown about on the winds, on the brink of being broken on the rocks, and the winds are those unloving servants of yours, who are consuming you little by little, the rocks are your creditors, who will break you up with the interest they are charging you." Cosimo instructed Paolo to downsize his entourage. "You do not need more than four gentlemen companions, of which one should be a cavalier, four gentlemen of the bed chamber, four or six pages, and four footmen." But the duke was just warming up. Finally he delivered his coup de grâce: "I have heard that you have promised my daughter's dowry to the merchants. . . . Do not think that you will be able to take care of your affairs and escape debt in such a way. I do not want to consign my daughter's dowry to you, because spending and frittering away everything, you will then condemn Donna Isabella to bartering with merchants. . . . When I see that you do not wish to ruin yourself, and wish to attend to your well-being, I will not fail to help you in any way that I can that is not damaging to my daughter. You are of an age to know right from wrong, and truth from falsehood."

Paolo himself was a putz, but the Orsini family had its merits. Cosimo wanted to ensure the security of his southern boundaries and therefore needed the connection to a venerated Roman family. Additionally, the Medici needed a man inside the Vatican, and Paolo's uncle, Cardinal Sforza, had become their go-to guy whenever Cosimo needed a favor from the Holy See.

Isabella's father made it clear to Paolo that although he was tall and well built, Cosimo knew he was no prize, and was perfectly aware of his weaknesses. Cosimo was also fully prepared to exploit Paolo's flaws, when necessary, for Medici ends. He was in no haste to rush his daughter to the altar. Not only was Isabella his favorite girl, but her betrothal had been negotiated when she was still a child.

Additionally, Cosimo didn't feel that it was necessary to make a grand demonstration of Medici excess by pulling out all the stops to throw Isabella a lavish wedding. But he did commission poems and songs in her honor. In June 1558, Filippo di Monte, a Flemish émigré, composed a madrigal in honor of the bridal couple. Chockfull of hyperbole, between the lines the verse really pays homage to the powerful houses of Medici and Orsini. Di Monte, a composer who was patronized by the younger Medici family members as well as the courts of London and Vienna, wanted to keep his clients happy and his palm greased for future commissions.

> *The strongest of Rome*
> *Flora's wisest and most beautiful*
> *[Are] Paolo and Isabella.*

Cosimo also made sure his favorite daughter would look spectacular on her wedding day, authorizing the purchase of nearly thirteen meters of white damask, satin, taffeta, and velvet. A few months before the ceremony, Isabella posed for the celebrated painter Bronzino, who did her wedding portrait; draped over her arm was the bejeweled pelt of a *zibellino*, a type of weasel that was considered a fertility talisman.

Isabella and Paolo finally celebrated their nuptials in a semiprivate ceremony at the Villa Medici in Poggio a Caiano on September 3, 1558, four days after Isabella turned sixteen. Music composed specially for the occasion welcomed the Orsinis into the Medici family—a reversal of tradition, because the bride was customarily welcomed into the groom's house. The famed Florentine goldsmith Benvenuto Cellini designed the wedding jewelry for the stepmother of the groom, employing eight people working around the clock to create priceless bracelets, buttons, belts, and rings.

The madrigal performers sang in Latin, "Oh, Paolo, pinnacle and glory of the Orsini Family, favourite and son-in-law of the magnanimous Cosimo [who had hired the singers]. You who practise with unbeatable strength, and retain in your mind the arts of both powerful Mars and chaste Pallas [Athena]. Rejoice immensely now that a bride is given to you, for nowhere is there anyone more beautiful or better than she. And promptly beget numerous offspring like yourself to rule over Latium and the land of the Tiber."

Like any royal marriage, the pair's primary duty was to produce an heir. And, because of their exalted stature, nothing they did in private could be expected to remain a secret. Although the wedding was held a few miles from Florence, soon the entire city knew that on "Saturday evening, Lord Paolo Orsini, son-in-law to Duke Cosimo, consummated his marriage with the Lady Isabella. The next day he rode back to Rome, and they say that he will go . . . to the court of Philip II, the King of Spain."

So much for setting up house together as man and wife. But right from the start, Isabella's marriage to Paolo was unorthodox. Because he departed for Rome immediately after consummating their union, there was no honeymoon. And the couple remained apart— to the delight of all concerned. By dispatching Paolo to Spain, Cosimo was not only shoring up Medici allegiance to Philip, but letting Philip foot the bill for Paolo's sojourn at the Spanish court, rather than paying Paolo's expenses out of his own pocket. In this way, Cosimo was able to hold on to both Isabella's dowry for the time being, *and* Isabella—who was elated to remain in Florence at her father's side. The duke had decreed that Paolo would live by himself in Rome, and if he wanted to see his wife, he could travel north to Florence. If Isabella went to Rome, her dowry went with her, and Cosimo did not trust Paolo to be a prudent financial manager. Paolo could register no objections to Cosimo's directives, because he was dependent upon his father-in-law's largesse. Given Paolo's predilection for prostitutes, he probably preferred to be left to his own devices anyway.

Cosimo bestowed numerous gifts of real estate upon the young couple, including the Antinori Palace, the old Medici Palace, Villa Baroncelli (also known as Poggio Imperiale), and a property at Pisa. Paolo and Isabella established opulent households in each location, in which they perpetually lived beyond their means and relied upon the duke to bail them out after every shortfall, but most of the time the pair lived apart. Paolo was made the first duke of Bracciano in 1560, and dwelled either at his castle there or at home in Rome with the Orsini family, and Isabella's father had accorded her the exceptionally rare permission to remain in his household after her marriage. Isabella's greatest wedding present of all was her independence. The freedom from her husband's authority and dominance was worth more than all the gold in the Medici bank.

In December 1560, eighteen-year-old Isabella saw her husband's castle at Bracciano for the first time; the gloomy, urban, high-walled fortress was the antithesis of the Medicis' Tuscan villas surrounded by olive groves and cultivated, rolling hills. Her sojourn at Bracciano also marked the first time in their marriage that the couple was together on Paolo's turf. Isabella was miserable. Bracciano was cold and damp; everyone spoke the unfamiliar Lazio dialect. Isabella had been in Rome for less than two months when she realized how her husband spent the better part of his time: giving free rein to his other sexual pursuits. Her parents' loving marriage had been a touchstone; her own was a joke. Paolo saw her only as a conduit to her father's bankbook. He was not even terribly upset when she suffered a miscarriage; there would surely be more pregnancies and the opportunity to beget an Orsini heir.

Despite their antipathy for each other, and the fact that Isabella always considered herself a Medici by birth before she thought of herself as an Orsini by marriage, it was necessary to maintain the outward appearance of a happy couple. Nothing they did was totally private. Even their correspondence was read by others. Consequently, it was written for public consumption—filled with loving thoughts and expressions of longing during their lengthy absences. There were too many enemies, including other powerful families, and members of anti-Medici factions who had received refuge from the French, who would be delighted to make use of the knowledge that things were less than perfect between the Duke and Duchess of Bracciano.

By the middle of January 1561, Isabella and Paolo were on their way back to Florence. Isabella hoped that she would never have to set foot in Bracciano again. Surely her father would require her presence at his court while he focused his attentions on his latest project, and the one that would define Cosimo's reign: the costly construction of the Palazzo degli Uffizi Magistratura, the palace of the office of the magistrates, or as everyone called it then and since—the Uffizi.

After her mother died of tuberculosis and malarial fever in 1562, nineteen-year-old Isabella became the de facto first lady of Florence, assuming Eleonora's duties as her father's hostess. Dressing in phenomenally costly garments to throw opulent parties and stage extravagant events in the furtherance of her family's interests was right up Isabella's alley; as the new doyenne of court society, she also assumed the responsibility of arranging good marriages for the daughters of Medici courtiers.

In addition to her own sparkle, she brought a cultural luster to Cosimo's court. His goal was to promote Florence, the birthplace of Dante, as Italy's cultural capital. With Isabella herself as its leading intellectual light, under her aegis her father's court became a grand salon where the great minds of the day met and were lavishly entertained. Isabella's salon attracted philosophers and statesmen, architects and artists, musicians and poets. Clerics, ambassadors, rhetoricians, and magistrates came from as near as the northern Italian courts of Urbino and Ferrara, and from as far as the court of Spain.

After the death of Eleonora, although Isabella had no interest in becoming a surrogate mother to her younger siblings, she remained close to those who had been her playfellows, but the dynamics of their relationship changed. The Medici children grew up quickly; by their mid-teens, engaging in very adult behavior, they were one another's confidants and erstwhile partners in crime. Isabella had always been closest to her brother Giovanni, two years younger, who, because he was a Medici, had been made a cardinal by Pope Pius IV in 1560 at the tender age of seventeen. Apart from Isabella's enormous devotion to her father, Giovanni was her one great love. Many people believed that Giovanni acted as a system of checks and balances for his older sister's wild ways, and that if he had not died of malarial fever less than a month before their mother passed away, Isabella might not have acted so promiscuously. She had never loved Paolo, but when Giovanni was alive, there was room for no one else in her heart.

Isabella had never been close to their oldest brother Francesco. They didn't understand each other's temperaments. Francesco cheated on his wife, the sister of the Holy Roman Emperor, and in general behaved like a nasty, conniving, contrariwise, melancholy jerk to everyone except his lover, Bianca Cappello. In 1562, when Cosimo sent Francesco to the Spanish court as the Medici family's representative, instead of considering it an honor, Francesco deemed it a punishment, intimating that his father had banished him.

The exceptionally close relationship between Cosimo and Isabella, and her clear preference for her father's companionship over her husband's, sparked plenty of rumors, especially after the death of Isabella's favorite brother, Giovanni, on November 20, 1562. Father and daughter began to enjoy private hunting excursions, inviting a good deal of catty speculation regarding what the two of them were doing all alone. A rumor spread that Isabella was "loved by the Duke Cosimo in a way that some voices say is carnal." Another story circulated that the painter Giorgio Vasari had witnessed them in a compromising embrace, while he was painting the hall of the ducal palace. Titillating though it was, it was nonetheless a complete fiction that was repeated through the centuries, even making its way into English guidebooks for aristocrats on the Grand Tour. The intimation that Isabella and Cosimo were incestuous is found in the eighteenth-century curate Mark Noble's *Mem-*

oirs of the Illustrious House of Medici, and Alexandre Dumas also added more than a whiff of sex in his history of the Medici.

During her lifetime, this closeness to Cosimo raised eyebrows. Why should he want to keep Isabella in Florence, away from her husband? Why did she lack the desire to join Paolo and properly fulfill her marital obligations? Parallels were drawn to the sinister relationship between Lucrezia Borgia and her father, Roderigo, Pope Alexander VI. To the tongue-wagging gossips, Isabella was clearly just as unnatural. "This is what happens when a woman goes about without her husband," they concluded.

In 1563, Isabella and Paolo began to maintain separate residences in Florence, although Paolo usually remained in Rome or Bracciano. Superintended by Isabella, the Palazzo Medici underwent substantial and costly renovations, including an aquatic system, whereby water was brought in from the Arno for her daily baths.

Unsurprisingly, Paolo and Isabella soon racked up stratospheric expenses. They had vast staffs, but labor was cheap, especially when some of their servants were slaves. However, it cost a small fortune to keep up appearances if you were a Medici. The *"spesa d'arme,"* or weapons expenses, included those items needed to defend their establishment: swords, crossbows, harquebuses, and lances. The wardrobe expenses, or *"spesa di vestire,"* included not only the opulent garments and accessories that "His Illustrious Lordship" purchased for his own use, but the household's extravagant liveries of red and yellow silk and velvet, and red taffeta shot with yellow, as well as the numerous page boys' blue velvet ensembles. The fancier a servant's livery, the more prestigious a household would appear to the outside world. Like the sentimental contents of their correspondence, Paolo and Isabella's domestic sphere presented the outward show of a harmonious and financially healthy marriage.

Isabella used Orsini funds for the custom of almsgiving, the *"spese di limosine."* She and Paolo didn't seem to give too much to charity, but they spent an awful lot on the upkeep of their stables and their hunting expenses. Another costly line item in the Medici-Orsini household was the purchase and upkeep of the fashionable new conveyances that every rich young noble wanted to gad about in—coaches. Paolo and Isabella were the first on their block to obtain one, but the expense was such that Cosimo had to advance his son-in-law 105 *scudi* just for the upgrade to the red leather upholstery. The cost to gild the frame, adding accents of red trim, was an additional expense, as was Isabella's perfectly matched quartet of pure white horses.

The maintenance of the old Palazzo Medici, one of the marital properties that had been a wedding gift from Isabella's father, fell to Paolo. Yet he continued to demonstrate an utter incapability of living within his means. To pay his creditors he shamelessly sold some of his mother's jewelry, resorted to patronizing Jewish moneylenders, and, without compunction, he even sold off some of his lands. Meanwhile, his servants often went hungry so that he could afford to go hunting or host jousting tournaments. And Paolo continued to purchase horses the way Titian bought paintbrushes.

Isabella was no thriftier. She would borrow money from the Medicis' own bank, the Monte di Pietà, and could always count on her *babbo* to discharge her vast debts to the silk and velvet merchants and to the furriers. She also breezed through the allowance Cosimo gave her, frequently requesting a loan against the next installment. When her father agreed to advance her the sum of four thousand *scudi*, she trilled to Paolo, "I can pay my debts, and then I can live like a queen."

The primary reason that Cosimo had united his favorite daughter with Paolo Giordano Orsini was to safeguard Medici property in the south. But that plan would go south if, in order to satisfy his myriad creditors, his son-in-law started selling off the territory that was intended to be Cosimo's buffer zone. So in February 1563, the duke decided to loan Paolo a whopping thirty thousand *scudi* to pay off his debts in exchange for the rights to the estate's income. A year later, he bought back two more Orsini fiefdoms from a pair of Paolo's creditors. Cosimo placed them irreversibly in Isabella's name so that she could derive an income from the property even if her husband continued down his path toward financial ruin.

And continue Paolo did. Cosimo's thirty thousand *scudi* became a drop in the bucket. By 1568, the Duke of Bracciano had his hand out again. The initial loan from the Monte di Pietà was so large that it had to be divided into smaller accounts. The recipient's name was supposed to be a secret, but the initials on the forty-thousand-*scudi* loan would have been recognizable to anyone in the know: PGO.

In 1566, Pope Pius V nominated Paolo governor general of the Catholic Church, which meant that he was in charge of papal troops. He wrote to Isabella to inform her that the new job had encouraged him to turn over a new leaf. ". . . every morning I hear Mass, have the table blessed and overall I live like a Christian whereas before I was a dissolute and a wretch."

At least he admitted it. But Isabella was not convinced that he was capable of such a transformation, replying sarcastically, "So now that you have become a good Christian . . . may God let you persevere, as Our Lord commands that you wish only for one wife, and you do not desire the women of others, and I would be the happiest woman in the world if you were to observe these two things. . . ."

Paolo tried to convince Isabella to come down to Rome to live with him, because his new exalted position demanded an attentive wife. But Isabella wasn't having any of it, and Paolo's boasting about his new employment opportunity, particularly to the French ambassador, so offended the pontiff that he rescinded the offer.

Writing to Isabella, Paolo revealed that he thought he'd lost the governor generalship because the Spanish ambassador had maligned him, and that he had acted as a servant of Spain only due to the "dependence and relationship" he had with her father. The Orsini had always been supporters of the French, and now he intended to offer his services to them.

Annoyed with her husband's shortsightedness, Isabella curtly reminded him that the French "will promise you oceans and mountains, and you will get absolutely nothing. . . . In times of peace, King Philip has given more to you than any other Italian cavalier, and if you wait he will give you more. . . . Give caresses to every one, but know the difference between those who are your real friends and those that would do you damage." Then, larding her letters with wifely subservience, she assured Paolo, "If you wish to be French, then I will be French, if you are Imperial, then I am Imperial. You being much more wise than I, I will leave you to decide for yourself." Paolo chose Spain.

Isabella did the best she could at managing her husband, but he had ways of gaining the upper hand, physically and psychologically. She was already aware of Paolo's infidelity, but when she taunted him on one occasion about the House of Orsini's social inferiority to the Medici, he had slapped her. This episode of abuse had not been unique. In February 1565, Isabella wrote to Paolo ". . . I was, and with reason, of the . . . opinion that first I should tell the duke my lord [Cosimo] of the injuries I have received from you, but I am now resolved that it is better for us if I do not speak of this to anyone as it is so very prejudicial. . . ."

If Paolo, so deeply in debt to his father-in-law, had struck Isabella, it was a spectacularly stupid thing to do. His wife might not have been able to physically defend herself, but she had a more powerful weapon: her *babbo*.

In the mid-1560s, Isabella and Francesco engaged in a tug-of-war over the Baroncelli, a villa on the outskirts of Tuscany that had been confiscated from a rival family. "Give it to her," declared Cosimo, and Isabella became the owner of the very first real estate that was entirely hers. At the Baroncelli, as well as at her Florentine residences, occasionally in the company of Paolo, she hosted banquets, parties, and—in her husband's absence—girls' nights. There was always plenty of music and dancing, and even though the guest lists boasted the crème de la crème of society, their rowdiness routinely kept the neighborhood awake, because ". . . at around 2 a.m. Signora Isabella would be departing with her four coaches, singing, shouting, carousing because she was young, and without any mind for the scandal she was creating, knowing full well that in her company were some of the most dissolute young men in Florence."

During her wild soirées, Isabella and her guests enjoyed a variety of parlor games. Some were fairly innocuous, where they had to imitate animal sounds, or the male guests had to extol the beauty of the females, using the language of the popular poets Ariosto and Petrarch. Secrets were revealed in "the game of misfortunes," where the players related an amorous misadventure.

However, they also enjoyed less wholesome games: participants of both sexes were "sold" into bondage in "the game of slaves" and the "game of servants"; and in "the game of madness" those who claimed to be suffering from unrequited love would be "locked up" in an asylum. Indulging in gleeful sacrilege, they also would dress up as nuns and monks and enact mock religious rites.

While she might have presided over a rather staid and prestigious salon at Cosimo's court, left to her own devices Isabella offered the "sweetest temptations," according to the Ferrarese ambassador, her friend Ridolfo Conegrano. Her party games were designed for hookups; men and women were encouraged to choose the most appealing partner.

Isabella knew full well that Paolo was no stranger to the brothels of Rome as well as the charms of other women. "Would you do me the favour of sending me your portrait engraved on a ring, just the same as you gave that woman?" she wrote to him once, a gentle reminder that she was aware of his infidelities. On another occasion, after Paolo dared to accuse her of being less than true to him by making music with Signor Mario, a gentleman who remains unidentified, Isabella immediately fired back a lengthy salvo regarding her extramarital conduct—and Paolo's. "I am not that big a fool, having heard of the deeds, that I would believe the words, and I do not believe that you could imagine I would. . . . I am at the Baroncelli because I can better pass my miseries there than in Florence, and I wish to God that the music you claim I am making with Signor Mario would be often enough to distract my imagination from the little love you bear me."

But even though she often signed her letters, "Your wife, who sleeps alone in her bed," *did* she indulge in those "sweetest temptations" available at her own entertainments? By this time Paolo would hardly have been an alluring bedfellow. He had grown nearly as wide as he was tall, too heavy to sit on a normal-size horse, and was patronizing thermal baths in an effort to lose weight. Isabella affectionately nicknamed him *"il mio grassotto"*—my big fat one—and, punning on his surname, *"il mio orso"*—my bear.

Despite their mutual distaste, the ducal couple nonetheless understood their dynastic duty. Although they lived apart for most of their marriage, Paolo and Isabella reunited often enough for her to become pregnant, which she did with some regularity, although only two of their children survived to adulthood. A daughter born in 1564 died in childhood, as did one possibly named Francesca, born in 1568. The couple would also lose a girl born around 1576. Because they had been married for so many years without conceiving a son, by 1569 Paolo had begun to grow concerned about his lack of an heir, especially when Isabella perpetually made excuses not to join him in Rome. Another daughter, Francesca Eleonora, named for both their mothers, but nicknamed Nora, was born in 1571. Their son Virginio, conceived while Paolo was home in Florence on furlough after the Battle of Lepanto, was born on September 13, 1572.

But it was in 1564 that Isabella, then twenty-three, unhappily wed, and possessed of too blithe and passionate a nature to remain unfulfilled, is presumed to have taken a lover. The man was Paolo's dashing cousin, Troilo Orsini de Monterotondo.

Due in large part to Cosimo I de Medici's largesse, Paolo Giordano Orsini was the most privileged member of his house, the man with the most estates, pensions, and benefits. But his other family members had to distinguish themselves through their actions.

Troilo was a genuine Renaissance man, a lover and a soldier who, in addition to his horse and dog, brought his violin on military campaigns so that his comrades wouldn't lack for a little cultural entertainment. A portrait of him in three-quarter profile bowing before Catherine de Medici depicts a dashing cavalier with dark curly hair and a trim beard who dresses like a fashion plate. This heartthrob was described by one of his contemporaries as ". . . a man who was elegant in all his endeavours, extremely handsome, a great entertainer, a true courtier, [and] the friend of all the ladies and gentlemen."

Whereas Paolo had had everything handed to him, the charismatic Troilo was determined to succeed on his own merits. As his looks alone would not cover his expenses, he made a name for himself as a soldier, but in peacetime there was no work. So he became a hanger-on in the Orsini household, with a foot in the

Medici camp as well, ever on the alert for an opportunity from Cosimo.

Troilo knew perfectly well that his cousin's wife should have been sexually off-limits to him—*intoccabile*, or untouchable. But their extramarital affair lasted for a dozen years, creating an immense public scandal that would finally become too much for the respective Medici and Orsini family honor to bear.

Isabella and Troilo were passionately in love. They both enjoyed practical jokes and would roam the streets of Florence together in the wee hours of the morning, Isabella aping the manner of Venetian courtesans by cross-dressing as a man—shocking behavior for a Medici princess. Troilo was her most trusted confidant, and if anyone desired a favor from Isabella de Medici, they soon learned that first they had to persuade Troilo Orsini of its merits.

The poetry that Isabella commissioned at this time contained coded messages of love for Troilo. Even if some members of their inner circle were aware of their romantic liaison, she could acknowledge nothing publicly, nor sign her name to anything that would incriminate either of them.

Nonetheless, their correspondence, although not florid, certainly reflects their ardor. Often, the duchess would sign her letters, *"Schiava in perpetuo"*—"Your Lordship's slave forever." The notes also disparage Paolo, referring to her husband in one of them as "that animal," and Isabella reveals plenty of ill will for her brother Francesco, who was acting as Cosimo's regent in Florence. "I feel as if I've been knocked over into kneeling at the feet of the prince . . . it is so evident that everybody sees his miserable ways from morning 'til night."

Isabella's liaison with Troilo was even riskier because they spoke different languages, and their letters were either composed by a third party or written with Isabella's limited knowledge of the southern Lazio dialect and Troilo's scant abilities to communicate in Toscano.

More than their correspondence required the utmost discretion. Isabella may have borne Troilo two children who were housed as orphans or abandoned children in the Ospedale degli Innocenti. Given her fecundity, it would hardly be surprising if she hadn't become pregnant and carried to term over the course of a twelve-year love affair, but the subject is never comprehensively discussed by her biographers.

Cosimo was aware of his daughter's relationship with Troilo, and, being a sexual libertine himself, he took full advantage of his authority as a concerned, if indulgent parent to mitigate any damages to the family honor, without ever demanding that Isabella terminate her extramarital romance. However, to remove Troilo from temptation, he dispatched him on protracted, though prestigious assignments abroad. Troilo became the Medicis' representative in Germany, Mantua, and France, where he was made welcome at the court of Cosimo's widowed cousin, Catherine de Medici.

But after Cosimo's death in April 1574, Isabella no longer had a champion and protector and could not go running to her *babbo* every time she needed a favor. Cosimo's successor, his oldest son, Francesco, was an adulterer as well, but he was more discreet about it. Besides, the rules were different for girls. A sexually voracious man was a stud; a woman, a slut, and Isabella's activities had become the target of public gossip. She had done more than admit a man (or more than one) to her bedchamber; she had invited a male outsider—Troilo Orsini—regardless of his family connection, into her circle of power and trust. It was not merely her own honor she was impugning by her actions, but that of the entire House of Medici.

Cosimo's corpse was barely cold when Francesco sent Troilo on a pair of international assignments, first to Poland and then to France. Isabella's brother further betrayed her by reneging on an agreement she had made with Cosimo to provide for her children. Knowing that Paolo would fritter away their funds, leaving little for Nora and Virginio's inheritance, she had intended to secure their future before her father passed on, a plan in which "Signor Paolo donates to his son all of his possessions before he destroys them completely." However, documents in the Florentine archive reveal that after Isabella signed her name below this agreement, Francesco had the text altered.

Isabella's lifestyle changed dramatically after Cosimo's death. No longer required to play hostess at his court, she had run out of excuses for not permanently joining her husband in Rome and inventing delays for visiting him or welcoming him to Florence. Her days of freedom were over. She despaired of ending up a housewife stuck at home with the kids, while Paolo continued to patronize the bordellos and consort with his low-life friends in the Eternal City, embracing the popular expression *"In Roma vale più la puttana che la moglie"*—"In Rome, the whore is worth more than the wife."

In July of 1574, Isabella wrote to Paolo telling him she'd lost her looks, perhaps in an effort to convince him that he wouldn't want her to come to Rome after all. "The beauty that caused you to fall in love with me is no more because it has gone with the years. [She was about to turn thirty-two.] However, I congratulate myself that you love me with that love that exists between husband and wife."

Yet Isabella was still breaking hearts. That December, Troilo killed one of her brother Pietro de Medici's gentlemen of the bedchamber, twenty-year-old Torello de' Nobili da Fermo, "because of the Lady Isabella de' Medici, with whom both men were in love," according to the contemporary diarist Giuliano de' Ricci. Troilo's hotheaded murder of a pup who was scarcely a rival drew attention to his affair with Isabella at a time when they needed to be discreet. Rather than arrest him right away, Francesco bided his time and continued to send Troilo on international assignments as a Medici envoy.

Meanwhile, Isabella continued to avoid Paolo, side-skirting his requests to come to Rome. On September 3, 1575, he wrote, "I have sent you six letters and not had a response to one. I've heard about Nora's illness and that she has been quarantined, and it displeases me that I should have to learn that my daughter has been at death's door from others. Madam, I beg you to remember that I am your husband, and if myself or my letters bother you I will write no more."

Isabella replied to the letter on the seventeenth of the month, pleading ill health and assuring him that she was scoping out an architect for renovations he planned for his properties. ". . . I desire nothing more than to serve you, so order from me the things you want."

Francesco then began to close in on Troilo, arresting two of his servants on suspicion of their involvement in another murder. As city officials had rarely intervened in the rash of homicides that had taken place in Florence since Cosimo's death, Troilo correctly sensed that his turn was coming. He bade farewell to Isabella and spurred his horse for Bologna. Eventually he would find sanctuary in Paris, having always been a favorite of Catherine de Medici.

Troilo had a good reason for not going south to Rome and the bosom of his Orsini family. Sleeping with the wife of their most powerful family member for nearly a dozen years would not have made him terribly popular there.

On September 22, a warrant for Troilo's arrest was posted in the Florentine piazzas. He and his servants were accused of harboring murderers and for killing Torello de' Nobili da Fermo. In February 1576, a notice was issued stating that Troilo and his accomplices were condemned to banishment and all of their property was to be confiscated; this would include any of his love letters to Isabella. The crimes for which Troilo Orsini was condemned, apart from the stabbing of a nobody, were ordinarily considered misdemeanors. The real reason Francesco wanted Troilo arrested was because the man was his sister's lover. Now he was an outlaw. If Troilo returned to Florence, and Isabella's arms, he faced execution.

In May of 1576, Isabella quietly retreated to the Medici property at Cafaggiolo, a renovated fourteenth-century villa with castellated crenellations fifteen miles north of Florence. Ercole Cortile, the Ferrarese ambassador, speculated in his report of May 13 that "Lady Isabella has been these past five days staying at Cafaggiolo, and there are some saying that a previous time when she went, it was to let her body swell, and that it will be like that other time, when she was healthy again after nine months."

Cortile's speculation may have been merely the regurgitation of a rumor. Or not. Isabella and Troilo probably did enjoy a passionate final encounter, knowing they would likely never see each other again. However, there is no firm proof that Isabella was concealing a pregnancy, and if so, how far along she might have been. Troilo had fled Florence in September. She had not seen Paolo since the end of October and, pleading genuine sickness at the time, probably would have kicked her husband out of her bed.

He arrived in Florence during the first week of July 1576. Cortile reported, "Signor Paolo Giordano Orsini . . . is coming to take the Lady Isabella back to Bracciano, if he can. But it is believed that he's not going to be able to, because the aforesaid lady does not want to leave here for anything." Isabella's horror of losing her freedom and leaving her beloved home for her husband's gloomy castle and overbearing companionship was now a matter of national curiosity.

Paolo fetched his wife from Florence, but he did not take her all the way to Bracciano. Instead, he brought her to the isolated Medici villa at Cerreto Guidi. On July 16, 1576, Isabella died under suspicious circumstances. She was thirty-four.

Paolo offered a number of explanations for his wife's death. His story changed a few times: that she suffered an epileptic fit (although Isabella was not an epileptic), or had a sudden heart attack during a planned hunting expedition, or that she had struck her head on a basin while she was washing her hair. In his letter to Francesco informing him of Isabella's demise, Paolo used the word "repentantly," intimating that Isabella might have had time to receive last rites, but Francesco's public statements, issued after he learned of the sad event, indicated that she had been found dead and all attempts to revive her had been unsuccessful.

Yet rumors quickly spread that Isabella's husband had killed her because of her adulterous affair with his cousin. It wasn't too long before those stories reached Philip II's court in Spain.

On the day of Isabella's murder, Francesco sent Paolo Orsini a letter. He did not even deign to console his brother-in-law himself. The coldhearted note, which evinced no shock at Isabella's demise, was penned by his secretary.

> *With so much sorrow I have heard in your letter about the death of the Lady Isabella, your wife and my sister. You can judge it so, because this lady remained the last of this house, and was loved by me so tenderly. I believe you did not lack any diligence or remedy in attempting to save her from the accident which took her life, and if Your*

*Excellency has any need of anything at this time,
I will send whatever I have in store. . . . You can
have her brought tomorrow morning or the next
in a box to outside the Porta San Frediano, where
the monastery of Monticello or of Monte Olivero
will take care of all the formalities for taking her
to bury her in San Lorenzo with the honours that
merit such a lady. . . .*

Given his calculated reply to Paolo, Francesco already knew
more about his sister's untimely demise than he was willing to reveal in a letter written on his behalf by an employee.

Paolo's lies weren't believed for long. Isabella's servants had been
present, and soon the truth about her death was revealed. Ercole
Cortile described her final moments in lurid detail to his patron, the
Duke of Ferrara, Alfonso II d'Este.

*The Lady Isabella was strangled, having been
called by Lord Paolo when she, the poor woman,
was in bed. She arose immediately, and as she was
in a nightgown, drew a robe about her, and went
to his room, passing through a room in which the
priest known as Elicona was with several other
servants; they say that her face and the set of her
shoulders told that she may have known what was
in store for her. Morgante [her dwarf] and his wife
were in his chamber, and Lord Paolo hunted them
out and bolted the door with great fury. Hidden
under the bed was a Roman Knight of Malta,
Massimo, who helped to kill the lady. He did not
remain more than a quarter of an hour locked in
the room before Paolo called for a woman, Donna
Lucrezia Frescobaldi, telling her to bring vinegar
because the lady had fainted. Once she had entered, followed immediately by Morgante, she saw
the poor lady on the ground and propped against
the bed, and overcome by her love for her, said,*

"Oh, you have killed her! What need have you of vinegar or anything else?" *Lord Paolo threatened her and [urged her to] hold her tongue or he would kill her. . . . [T]he lady was placed in a coffin already prepared for this purpose, and this was taken at night to Florence and placed in the Church of the Carmine and was forced open for anyone who wished to see. And it was said that there was never seen a more ugly monster. Her head was swollen beyond measure, the lips thickened and black like two sausages, the eyes open [and] bulging like two wounds, the breasts swollen and one completely split, it is said because of the weight [of] Lord Paolo who threw himself on her to kill her as quickly as possible. And the stench was so great that no one could go close. She was black from the middle up and completely white below, according to what Niccolò of Ferrara told me, who had lifted the covers, as others had done to see her. She was buried the following night in San Lorenzo.*

So much for Francesco honoring his sister's corpse. What really happened is that he left it out to stink and become putrid, a tacit warning to other wayward wives. The diarist Agostino Lapini wrote of the once beautiful Isabella, "She appeared to those who saw her like a monster, so black and ugly."

Yet rather than be horrified by the brutality of Isabella's death and the stunning revelation that it was her husband who had been complicit in her murder, it was the Medici princess who suffered the blame for tarnishing the family honor. Isabella's brother Francesco, who became the head of the family after their father died, had long accused her of sullying the Medici name, even as he had hypocritically enjoyed the favors of a mistress for years. He had already attempted to eliminate Isabella's lover Troilo Orsini. It was not a big leap for the unscrupulous Francesco to be complicit in the death of his own sister if he thought she was causing trouble for the family. And he was so powerful—and ruthless—that he may even have ordered it. Her husband, however, was the executioner.

The tension between Isabella and Paolo was known to some insiders. Their living apart demeaned Paolo's masculinity, which was so much a part of his Italian character. Ercole Cortile described Isabella as Paolo's *"moglie tanto odiato"*—his "wife so hated."

But the public knowledge of their dirty linen had been too much for him to bear. Paolo no longer needed Isabella after she'd given him a healthy heir, Virginio, four years earlier, in 1572. And with her powerful father dead and buried and her dour, misanthropic, vegetarian brother Francesco now Grand Duke, Isabella no longer had an ally and protector in the family. If Francesco asked Paolo to squash Isabella like a bug, he would do just that—literally, by restraining her with his massive bulk, crushing her to death as he choked her.

On September 1, 1576, Cortile reported to the Duke of Ferrara that Isabella had died intestate, meaning without a will, and that in order to pay off her debts, all of her possessions were being sold—at least those items that were not being appropriated instead by Francesco's greedy longtime mistress Bianca Cappello. According to Cortile, "They have given the Lady Duchess [Francesco's wife Johanna] guardianship of the children of the Lady Isabella. It has been said that Signor Paolo does not want them, claiming that they are not his children, although I have not had confirmation of this."

Paolo had washed his murderous hands of his wife. Citing his vast debts, he wrote to Francesco trying to beg off paying for her tomb. But he had just derailed his gravy train of his own accord. His wife wasn't around anymore to keep sending him money.

Isabella's twenty-first-century biographer Caroline P. Murphy cogently notes that, metaphorically speaking, while it was an Orsini sword that slew Isabella, it was a Medici hand on the hilt, meaning that Paolo would not have acted so rashly without Francesco's approval. And while Paolo was immediately ready to disavow everything about Isabella, including their children, insisting for the first time after her murder that his only son and heir (as well as their daughter) were not his kids, it was Francesco who was prepared to pursue his vengeance even further before her corpse grew cold. Blaming her even in death for dishonoring the House of Medici, he targeted those in her circle of acquaintances, confidants, and servants, rounding them up, detaining them, and in some cases ordering their executions. More than a year after his sister's demise, the duke was still hunting down his quarry.

Through a third party, he hired Ambrogio Tremazzi, a contract killer, to track down Troilo, who had been living in Paris. After bargaining the price up from two hundred *scudi* to three hundred because of the duration and complexity of the job, Tremazzi had to forfeit his twelve-year-old son as a hostage; the boy would be returned safely to him upon the successful completion of his mission.

After stalking Troilo's movements for several weeks, on November 30, 1577, Tremazzi finally got a clear enough bead on him to accomplish the purpose of his errand. According to the detailed account written by the assassin himself, "I took my harquebus from my side, and fired it with as much force as I could." The bullet hit its target, knocking Troilo from his horse. As he fell to the ground, "he uttered nothing other than oh, oh."

The formidable Queen Mother of France, Catherine de Medici, expressed her fury at Troilo's assassination, an emotion that remained unabated four years after the fact. In 1581, when Francesco continued to be unmoved by her anger, Catherine declared, "The Grand Duke does not take account of me, as to the displeasure of myself and the king [her son Henri III], and in front of our very eyes he had Signor Troilo Orsini and others killed."

Francesco's reply, which resulted in an utter breakdown of diplomatic relations between Florence and France, was, "Even if the lives of Signor Troilo and others were taken in your kingdom, what they had done meant they did not deserve life."

Five years after Isabella's murder, Paolo d'Orsini, Duke of Bracciano, took a mistress, the very married Vittoria Accoramboni. Vittoria's husband, Francesco Peretti, had initially turned a blind eye to her adulterous affair with Paolo, because it gained him entrée into the powerful Orsini circle. But when the duke decided he wanted to marry Vittoria, Peretti became an inconvenience, and so Paolo had him murdered. This little shenanigan mightily displeased the Medici family, who were looking forward to a long and spectacular career for their only legitimate heir, Virginio—Paolo's son by the late Isabella. The last thing the Medici wanted was for Paolo to remarry and father more *bambini* by a non-Medici wife. Well connected with Pope Gregory XIII, the Medici were able to have His Holiness prohibit the new Orsini marriage.

Nevertheless, Paolo recklessly went ahead with it, wedding Vittoria on April 20, 1585, ten days after the death of Gregory XIII. But the pope's successor was even worse news for Paolo: Pope Sixtus V Peretti was the uncle of Vittoria's murdered husband, Francesco.

The newlyweds fled, splitting up—Vittoria to Padua, and Paolo to Venice, then to Albano, and Salò, where he died on November 13. Vittoria was stabbed to death in December 1585 in Padua by Prince Lodovico Orsini, who had been sent there to settle her affairs under the terms of Paolo's will. John Addington Symonds, in his *Renaissance in Italy: The Catholic Reaction*, explains that Vittoria's murder arose out of a dispute over the distribution of property. Additionally, Lodovico believed that his kinsman had married beneath him and couldn't accept the idea of Paolo's low-class widow receiving his worldly goods. Yet another source claims that Lodovico was a member of the Monterotondo branch of the Orsini family, as was Isabella de Medici's lover Troilo, and had killed Vittoria in a vendetta because Paolo had been responsible for Lodovico's brother's death, as the result of a family feud in which Paolo had somehow been involved.

But Lodovico was not able to take the money and run. He was imprisoned for murder and strangled while incarcerated. Having eaten their own, the House of Orsini's power and authority was entirely debased by the scandal, ending its dominance over Roman affairs.

John Webster's highly fictionalized 1612 revenge tragedy *The White Devil* was loosely based on the death of Vittoria Accoramboni and the ensuing vendettas. In the nineteenth century, the lurid events of her demise and the sordid behavior within one of Renaissance Italy's most notorious families would inspire both Stendhal and Dumas *père* to take up their pens, the former with his novel *Vittoria Accoramboni* as well as his three *Italian Chronicles*, and the latter with *Les Médicis*.

Paolo's lands and dukedom were inherited by his son, Virginio. In the late autumn of 1600, Virginio arrived in England for an extended stay at the court of Elizabeth I, and soon became very popular there. On January 6, 1601, the queen's players aptly performed William Shakespeare's *Twelfth Night*, which had been composed as the entertainment for the Epiphany feast. A principal character, the love-struck Duke Orsino, who yearns to be surfeited with music, if it be the food of love, was most likely named in honor of Her Majesty's Florentine guest.

Isabella and Paolo's daughter, Nora, became an accomplished composer. Wed to her cousin Alessandro Sforza for two decades, she did not enjoy a happy marriage and eventually retired to a convent she had founded.

The death of the faithless Isabella at the hands of her equally philandering husband, and the murder of her lover at the behest of her brother Francesco, immediately entered the realm of legend. The eighteenth-century curate Mark Noble deemed Isabella "one of the most profligate princesses that ever disgraced the Christian profession."

And then she disappeared for centuries, her genuine accomplishments obscured or obliterated entirely by a code of silence known as a *damnatio memoriae*, condemning the display of any memories of her. Thus, Isabella's achievements with regard to music, and the furtherance of the Tuscan language and scholarship, went unheralded because she had soiled the family honor with her adultery. Her love poetry and celebrated musical compositions, including the madrigals, have disappeared without a trace. Even the miniature portraits of her, which would have been included in a set painted of the entire Medici family, are gone, as if they had been willfully removed.

While little is known about Isabella's life compared to many of the other women profiled in this volume, even less is known about her first cousin and sister-in-law, Eleonora di Garzia di Toledo. She enjoyed a brief resurgence as a sentimental tragic heroine in the nineteenth century, but then disappeared under the waves again. No major English-language biography has been written about her. Her story is inextricably linked to Isabella Romola de Medici's, and mirrors it almost completely.

Eleonora di Garzia di Toledo was named for her father's sister, Isabella's mother. The junior Eleonora, nicknamed both "Leonora" and "Dianora," was half Spanish and half Italian. Her father was a Spanish grandee, or nobleman, García Álvarez de Toledo y Oso-rio, the 4th Marquis of Villafranca del Bierzo as well as Duke of Fernandina. Her mother was Vittoria d'Ascanio Colonna. Eleven years younger than Isabella, Leonora had been born at the Floren-tine court because her father had been assigned to oversee the cas-tles of Valdichiana. On behalf of Philip II, king of Spain, García Álvarez subsequently became Viceroy of Catalonia, and later Vice-roy of Sicily. In October 1571, García would distinguish himself as Philip's commander at the Battle of Lepanto, a major maritime conflict off the coast of Greece that pitted a fleet of the Holy League (a coalition of Catholic allies, all of which were southern European maritime states) against the navy of the Ottoman Empire.

Leonora was left in the care of her aunt Eleonora and uncle Cosimo to be raised in the Medici court as a *menina*, a girl groomed to be a professional courtier in the Spanish tradition of courtly fostering, similar to the outplacing enjoyed by Lady Jane Grey and English girls of her social status. But Eleonora's death on December 17, 1562, left Leonora motherless again, and the independent-minded Isabella took her young cousin under her wing.

Like Isabella, when Leonora grew up she too became a patroness of art and culture. By the time she was twenty-two in 1575, Le-onora was the only female patron of the Accademia degli Alterati, a literary academy to promote the elevation of discourse and works of verse, drama, comedy, and prose in the Tuscan language.

Cosimo remained utterly enchanted by Leonora, impressed by her vivacious personality and her athletic skills. Tall, slender, and graceful, with auburn hair and the vigor of a tomboy, she was a skilled equestrienne who excelled in feats of arms, and who re-ceived the occasional scolding from her indulgent uncle to conduct herself more like a proper Florentine lady.

Leonora was also more or less under Cosimo's wardship, and it was important for him to make a fine marriage for her that would mutually benefit the Toledo family and the House of Medici. Owing to the families' already close ties, it seemed a no-brainer for the duke to unite Leonora with his youngest son, Prince Pietro. The two cousins had been raised together, so it stands to reason that they would have had ample time to get to know each other and would have made a perfect match, being childhood companions, although Leonora was fifteen months older than her prospective spouse. But there was something wrong with Pietro, and Cosimo knew it. The emotionally disturbed youth had a cruel and violent streak, and had always displayed an unstable temperament that had troubled his parents. Cosimo was aware that it would be difficult to find a match for Pietro, and that few foreign brides would deem him acceptable after their families discovered his history. He assumed that Leonora would be able to handle Pietro because she was already familiar with his idiosyncrasies. Nevertheless, political expedience and the perennial necessity for a legitimate Medici heir to perpetuate the dynasty trumped Cosimo's concern for Leonora's welfare.

With the approval of Philip II of Spain, the couple was betrothed in 1568 when Leonora was only fifteen. Her father provided a substantial dowry of forty thousand gold ducats. Yet the teenagers were not married for another three years.

In April 1571, eighteen-year-old Leonora, and Pietro, not yet seventeen, were wed at the Palazzo Vecchio in Florence. The marriage was a disaster from the start. According to the Ferrarese ambassador, it was not consummated until April 1572, a year after the wedding had taken place, and even then the ambassador to Urbino wrote that the eighteen-year-old Pietro "had to be forced to penetrate" Leonora.

Pietro had an eye for the ladies, and evidently had no difficulty fornicating with other women at court; the reason for his refusal, or inability, to consummate his marriage remains unknown. However, the young prince's mistreatment of his beautiful and high-spirited wife soon became common knowledge at the Medici court. In January 1575, at a lively party hosted by her cousin (and now sister-in-law) Isabella, Leonora unwisely, and tearfully, confided her misery to the Ferrarese ambassador Ercole Cortile, who of course reported it to his boss. "[S]he is very unhappy, and the reason is her husband.

He will not sleep with her, he attends only to whores and matters of vice. . . . [S]he really is the most unfortunate and unhappy princess who ever lived, especially for being one so beautiful and accomplished."

At least Isabella was aware that other eyes were on her, especially those of foreign ambassadors, and made certain that in her correspondence to Paolo she appeared to be nothing but a loving wife who missed him. But Leonora was never that restrained. Airing her dirty linen to a foreign ambassador was a potentially fatal indiscretion.

Leonora became embroiled in an even more dangerous game during the summer of 1575. On July 25, Ercole Cortile reported to the Duke of Ferrara, "Pierino Ridolfi has been accused of plotting to kill Don Pietro when he was in a whorehouse, to murder his son and poison Cardinal Ferdinando [another Medici brother]. He is in the service of Donna Leonora and the duke [Francesco de Medici] is in a great rage with her for having given Pierino a necklace worth 200 *scudi* and a horse on which to escape."

Like Isabella, Leonora was never at a loss for male admirers, even if her own husband demonstrated little attraction to her. Bastiano Arditi, a Florentine diarist of the era, claimed that Pietro had caught "the French disease [syphilis] . . . from cavorting with so many whores in Florence, when he had the most beautiful girl in the city for a wife!"

And there were occasions when a cavalier's interest in Leonora was reciprocated. Bernardino Antinori was a poet, hero of Lepanto, and a Knight of the order of San Stefano who "appeared frequently as a courtier in the Lady Leonora's coach," where they were seen flirting with each other. She hid his love letters and poems in her footstool.

Born in 1537, Antinori was no saint. The last location from which he composed passionate love poetry to Leonora was a prison cell in Elba, where, after being invited to dine with a local count, he had been jailed for repeated brawling.

Nonetheless, Antinori rhapsodized about his inamorata's "alabaster throat," her "polished ivory" hands, and the thrill of gazing into her eyes.

Oh what perfect joy! oh what bliss!
Oh what pleasure, to see two trusting lovers
as each, intent on the other's eyes
sees there his own image!
Oh what sweet oblivion of all torment,
when the holy spirits of sight go out
And with a miracle so rare and so welcome
transform the lover into the beloved!

But thick stone walls and iron bars could not keep him from the long arm of Medici justice. At five a.m. on July 9, 1576, Antinori was strangled to death in Elba's prison, presumably because of his illicit relationship with Leonora.

The shame that the flirtatious Leonora brought upon the House of Medici and her dishonor of Pietro's name (even though he had done plenty to stain it himself) was too much for him to bear. During the second week in July, the spouses traveled to the Medici villa at Cafaggiolo. On July 10, 1576, Pietro de Medici strangled his twenty-three-year-old wife to death with a dog collar.

Unsurprisingly, he attempted a cover-up. On July 11, the morning after Leonora's death, he scrawled a hasty note to his brother Francesco, stating (as if he had not been present when the tragedy had taken place), "Last night at six hours an accident occurred to my wife and she died. Therefore, Your Highness be at peace and write me what I should do. . . ."

Of course, Leonora's death was hardly an accident.

The diarist Agostino Lapini, who knew Leonora personally, eulogized her in his datebook, recording that she was "beautiful, gracious, genteel, becoming, charming, affable, and above all had two eyes in her head which were like two stars in their beauty; everyone said that she was murdered . . . she was buried with rites in S. Lorenzo."

However, Bastiano Arditi recorded that she was "deposited, in a box, in San Lorenzo, without any other ceremonies." No Mass had been said. Given the lack of respect the Medici had for Leonora, it would not be surprising if they interred her without the dignity of a proper funeral Mass. Arditi's account of her postmortem is probably the more accurate one.

Isabella had been Leonora's closest friend and confidante. Yet she was not directly informed of her sister-in-law's death, leading one to conclude that plans for her own murder may have already been set in motion. Suspiciously, it was Paolo Giordano to whom Francesco had addressed the information about Leonora's death. Replying to the not-so-shocking news, Paolo told Francesco in an oddly worded note soaked with crocodile tears: "I learned with extreme sorrow, as Your Excellency rightfully supposed, in the letter it pleased you to write to me, of the strange and unexpected accident that Donna Leonora has suffered. The Lady Isabella has suffered no less sorrow. If pain could restore the loss we would grieve to the heart to bring her back . . . as it is we shall console and comfort ourselves that it is Divine vocation."

The official Medici lie was that Leonora, young and beautiful, had expired of a heart attack. Pietro had the nerve to tell his brother Cardinal Ferdinando in Rome that she had been found in bed suffocated, already fudging the time they had discovered her corpse to approximately five p.m.

Knowing that she was miserably married, Leonora's Spanish family with its Hapsburg connections had been hoping to spirit her away from Pietro "to take care of her in Naples." Ironically, at the time they began making plans to perform their intervention, they were unaware of her death.

But the truth managed to reach Spain with lightning speed. Medici law was absolute in Florence, and the victim would receive no justice, because the perpetrator had been a Medici prince. However, because Leonora came from one of Spain's highest-ranking noble families, Duke Francesco de Medici, who had ultimately been given the real story, had to confess it to Philip II. He said that his younger brother had in fact killed Leonora, but that Pietro felt justified in doing so "because of the treason she had committed through behaviour unbecoming to a lady . . ." Francesco assured the king of Spain that he would soon be sent relevant documents (Antinori's amorous letters and poems) "so that he should know with what just cause Lord Pietro was moved to act." The duke expected Philip to understand and fully accept the Medicis' contention that uxoricide (the murder of a wife by her husband) was a justifiable response to Leonora's infidelity.

On July 29, 1576, the Ferrarese ambassador Ercolo Cortile reported the true events of Leonora's death in graphic detail to his boss, Duke Alfonso II Este, writing:

I advise Your Excellency of the announcement of the death of Lady Isabella [16 July] of which I heard as soon as I arrived in Bologna, [and] has displeased as many as had the Lady Leonora's; both ladies were strangled, one at Cafaggiolo and the other at Ceretto [Guidi]. Lady Leonora was strangled on Tuesday night; having danced until two o'clock, and having gone to bed, she was surprised by Lord Pietro [with] a dog leash at her throat, and after much struggle to save herself, finally expired. And the same Lord Pietro bears the sign, having two fingers of his hand injured by [them being] bitten by the lady. And if he had not called for help to two wretches from Romagna, who claim to have been summoned there precisely for this purpose, he would perhaps have fared worse. The poor lady, as far as we can understand, made a very strong defence, as was seen by the bed, which was found all convulsed, and by the voices which were heard by the entire household. As soon as she died, she was placed in a coffin prepared there for this event, and taken to Florence in a litter at six o'clock [in the morning], led by those from the villa, and accompanied with eight white tapers [carried] by six brothers and four priests; she was interred as if she were a commoner.

Leonora's murder had preceded Isabella Romola de Medici's homicide by six days.

Pietro and Leonora's only child, their son Cosimino, died of dysentery at the age of three in August 1576, a few weeks after his mother was murdered. Although there were rumors that Pietro had poisoned him, nothing was proven. Cosimino's body was later buried near his mother's in the Cappella dei Principi (Chapel of the Princes) mausoleum in San Lorenzo.

On September 11, the Florentine ambassador to France urged Francesco to put to rest Catherine de Medici's "false impressions" that Leonora and Isabella had met their ends by violent means. "She evidently marvels at how these strange accidents could cumulate together in such a way, and the greater marvel is that Your Highness has not sent her any account of the incidents. I would have willingly avoided writing such things, increasing the infinite sorrow that I am certain accompanies such disgrace. . . ."

Leonora had corresponded so often with her brother Pedro di Toledo about Pietro's cruelty to her that in April 1577, Pedro declared her assassination reprehensible. Yet Pietro de Medici claimed to possess enough samples of Leonora's "treason" to condemn *her* for infidelity, rather than indict *him* for uxoricide, so the Spanish Hapsburg court not only absolved him, but was prepared to accept him as a courtier and permit him to stand as godfather to King Philip II's infant heir.

However, this assignment was intended to be a punishment. Pietro was being exiled to the rigid Spanish court by his disgusted big brother Francesco "to see if he makes [of himself] a man of this house and rises above the indolence that vainly consumes the best years of his youth."

But Pietro was incapable of cleaning up his act. He behaved just as recklessly in Spain, his temperament no different, and his manners and behavior described by witnesses as *"fastidioso"*—repugnant. On April 3, 1578, Prospero Colonna reported that Pietro's entourage was filled with scoundrels.

Making only the occasional return to Florence to beg his family for more money, Pietro de Medici lived out his remaining years as a Spanish grandee, squandering every *scudo* his relatives handed him—perpetually in debt, primarily from his gambling losses. On his death in 1604, his creditors swarmed about his corpse even before the flies had a chance to land. Some of Florence's most prominent names appeared on a list of his creditors dated June 13, 1605, demanding a total of 148,374 *scudi*, which in 2007 translated to between $30 and $40 million. Ironically, one of the items demanded as compensation for their unpaid loans was a miniature of Leonora set in a frame studded with gemstones that she had probably commissioned around the time of their betrothal, or even before their marriage. It was the frame that was of value.

In Italy during the high Renaissance, a double standard for men and women was firmly in place. Paolo Giordano Orsini's infidelities, including his well-known whoring in the brothels of Rome, were not a blot on the family escutcheon. Husbands were expected to stray, whether they took highborn mistresses or went slumming in the city's stews. It was the rare man who did not have at least one lover during the course of his marriage. But wives were supposed to remain faithful, no matter how miserable they were. Cosimo I de Medici, himself a ladies' man, had turned a blind eye to his favorite daughter's indulgences. But after he was dead and gone, her cruel and humorless older brother Francesco inherited the dukedom and became the titular head of the Medici family. He had no tolerance for Isabella's independent streak, especially when it manifested itself in adultery.

Francesco undoubtedly blamed his sister for Leonora's wildness, as the younger woman had looked up to and emulated Isabella. Both cousins had become the target of pasquinades, the ribald, scurrilous poems posted around the statue of Pasquino near Rome's Piazza Navona, where people gathered for the latest gossip. Paolo Giordano d'Orsini and Pietro de Medici had been able to tolerate their respective wives' wild ways as long as the women were fairly discreet (despite the fact that their own love affairs were an open secret within the court).

Not only was the family honor to remain untarnished, but the bloodline was to remain pure and untainted as well. If a wife was unfaithful, there was always the chance that any child she bore might not be her husband's, thereby threatening the dynasty. The rules were unspoken, but simple: A man could raise hell with impunity, but a wife had to practice chastity within her marriage and remain above suspicion at all times. Isabella's wild parties, at which Leonora was surely a guest, her girls' nights and bawdy games, and her dozen-year love affair with her husband's cousin—as well as the many casual illicit liaisons she'd enjoyed before she met Troilo Orsini—broke every rule. Strictly speaking, Leonora's alleged adultery may not have been provable beyond a shadow of a doubt, but she did not behave chastely as a good Renaissance wife should, and that was all Pietro needed to convince himself she needed killing.

In sixteenth-century Florence, the deaths of Isabella Romola de Medici and Eleonora di Garzia di Toledo were referred to as *delitti d'onore*—"honor" uxoricides. Men routinely punished their cheating wives, even immuring them in convents for violating their marriage vows. But Paolo d'Orsini and Pietro de Medici, serial adulterers themselves, *killed* their wives with impunity—and got away with it. Crime paid, if you were rich, powerful, and your family was at the top of the political and ecclesiastical food chain.

But for these two noblewomen, Isabella and Leonora, beautiful, intelligent, vivacious, and desperately unhappy, their marriages were more than a vow made till death us do part; in fact, the vow had a sinister connotation. Theirs was a life-ending lesson in rough justice that makes the clear and present dangers of being "married to the mob" look tame by comparison.

LOUIS XIII

AND

ANNE OF AUSTRIA

···

MARRIED: 1615–1643

*M*ost people are more familiar with the fictional reign of Louis XIII and Anne of Austria than the factual one. In the mid-nineteenth century, Alexandre Dumas *père* immortalized the monarchs in *The Three Musketeers* and his subsequent novels of the swashbuckling swordsmen, led by another historical figure—the noble and dashing d'Artagnan. These high-booted cavaliers protected Dumas' ineffectual and effeminate king, whose realm was actually being governed by the Machiavellian Cardinal Richelieu, while the unhappily wed but clever Anne of Austria was clandestinely cavorting with the English envoy, the Duke of Buckingham.

Dumas wove a few elements of the truth into a sumptuous brocade of historical fiction. If he'd written the real story, it might not have been sexier, but it certainly would have been stranger. Although Louis was not the fop portrayed in the numerous cinematic adaptations of the Dumas classic, he did have male favorites, known as *mignons*, on whom he bestowed titles, offices, and estates. Yet he was passionately attached to a couple of young women as well, although he probably never slept with any of his favorites of either gender. And while the minister-cardinal Richelieu did wield a tremendous amount of power, Louis was no ineffectual, mincing ignoramus who let others run his government. His policies, both foreign and domestic, were his own, and had been formed long before Richelieu became a force to be reckoned with.

The real story begins with Louis' unusual upbringing. He was the eldest of six children born to the first Bourbon king of France,

Henri IV, and the Florentine Marie de Medici. Louis XIII's maternal grandfather was Francesco I de Medici, Grand Duke of Tuscany. Francesco was the brother of both Isabella Romola de Medici, who died at her husband Paolo d'Orsini's hands, and Pietro de Medici, who murdered his wife, Eleonora di Garzia di Toledo.

In his lifetime, Louis XIII would come to be known both as Louis the Just and Louis the Chaste. Both nicknames were apt, though not necessarily compliments.

From his infancy, Louis' personal physician Jean Héroard kept an anally detailed log of his charge's every waking moment, chronicling everything from the boy's bowel movements and urinations (or any notable lack thereof) to each and every accomplishment and conversation. From this journal a picture emerges of a child who by twenty-first-century standards would be considered sexually abused—diddled by his own father, by his nurse, and by the king's mistress, among others—all in an effort to instill the infant with a healthy sexual appetite and pride of penis, as well as a fearlessness to consummate his eventual royal marriage. It didn't work.

Told from the cradle that he would marry his distant cousin, the Infanta of Spain, Louis was quizzed by Héroard as if it were a catechism: "Where is the infanta's darling?" According to the physician's journals, the fourteen-month-old baby "puts his hand on his cock." At the age of three, Louis lay in bed, "crosses his legs, asking, 'Will the infanta do this?'" A lady-in-waiting answered him, "Sir, when you go to bed together she will put her legs in that position." Louis replied "promptly and cheerfully, 'And I, I will put them like *that*!' spreading his legs apart with his hands."

At least the birds and the bees had been explained to the boy, albeit somewhat early on. Some biographers believe that Louis had witnessed adults having sex when he was barely a toddler. One day he informed Héroard that the infanta "will sleep with me and I'll make a little baby for her." Of course, he was also repeating the information his parents had given him from the time he was old enough to sit up.

"Sir, how will you do that?" his doctor inquired.

"With my cock," the little prince replied shyly.

"Sir, will you kiss her a lot?"

"Yes, like that," he told Héroard, and flung his body on top of the bolster with wild abandon.

Suiting the word to the deed would be decades away, however.

Louis XIII's twentieth-century biographer Elizabeth Wirth Marvick puts her subject on the couch, tracing his crippling stutter and his charmless, quick-tempered, impatient, backbiting, vengeful, and suspicious personality to the sex games his father would play with him when he was barely old enough to walk. She places Louis in bed with his infant sister, noting that the servants were allowed to frighten him into behaving well by telling him that if he didn't do so, his penis would be chopped off. The child was also encouraged to treat adult women as sex objects, suckling and spanking them and making overt references to their genitalia, which he was inappropriately permitted to observe. The notions of sexuality and pain were introduced to the boy simultaneously, with unsurprisingly unhealthy results. Beginning when Louis was two years old, if he misbehaved, the king permitted certain persons at court to take a switch made of twigs to his bottom, a punishment the dauphin began to anticipate with a perverse sort of pleasure, referring to it as "my darling."

The court of Henri IV was a spectacularly dysfunctional place to raise an emotionally stable heir. No wonder Louis XIII's eventual marriage was wildly unsuccessful. The king shamelessly impregnated the queen and his mistress-of-the-moment during the same time period. Louis found himself competing for his mother's attention, and the court's respect and recognition, with his own father and his bastard half siblings, who had been raised within the royal household, as well as with Marie de Medici's favorite child, Gaston, Louis' younger brother by nearly seven years. This could explain his jealousy of anyone he thought might be taking something that he believed was rightfully his. He even hated the name Louis, wishing he had been named after his father, or else for his grandfather Gaston, a favorite, ancestral name that was instead bestowed on his baby brother.

Portraits of Louis as a youth depict him with a heart-shaped face and a mass of curly dark hair. But he had two congenital impediments that made it taxing for him to speak. According to the English ambassador to Paris, Edward Herbert, 1st Baron Herbert of Cherbury, who presented his credentials to Louis in 1619, ". . . his words were never many, as being so extream [sic] a stutterer that he wou'd sometimes hold his tongue out of his mouth a good while before he cou'd speak so much as one word; he had besides a double row of teeth, and was observed seldom or never to spit or blow his nose, or to sweat much, 'tho he were very laborious, and almost indefatigable in his exercises of hunting and hawking, to which he was much addicted. . . ."

Héroard described Louis as a muscular, large-boned, and well-proportioned boy, with brown eyes, small lips that turned up, and large hands and feet. Oil portraits of an older Louis do depict his chubby cheeks, but already reveal elements of his psyche: a suspicious cast to his eyes, and narrow, pursed lips. As an adult, he sported the mustache and Vandyke beard of the cavaliers.

According to his physician, Louis was a stubborn child, prone to temperamental outbursts. He alternately worshiped his father and was insanely jealous of him. Louis was also compelled to grow up too fast, learning far too much at an age when he was too young to process it. His father would brag about his sexual prowess, pointing out a beautiful woman to his young son, then boasting that he had made a baby with her. And who wouldn't love the king? Despite his rampant philandering, Henri was seductive, popular, charming, affable, and moreover, a courageous and visionary ruler who had earned the admiration and respect of his subjects, including the poorest among them.

And then Louis lost him. On May 14, 1610, while Henri IV was enjoying an afternoon carriage ride near the Louvre, François Ravillac hopped onto the coach and stabbed the "tyrant" king in the chest three times, assassinating the monarch for trying to wage war on fellow Catholics, as Henri had been involved in military conflicts with Spain and Italy. Eight-and-a-half-year-old Louis was now king of France. After a period of mourning for his father—whose tragic death had immediately martyred Henri in the eyes of his former subjects—Louis XIII was crowned at Reims on October 17.

Upon Louis' accession, because he was a minor, his mother acted as his regent in concert with a number of advisers, some of whom

had been his father's ministers. One of the most pressing issues facing France was that the kingdom was fractured along religious
lines; however, the matter was far more complex than the traditional tension between Catholics and Huguenots, the French Protestants whose freedom of worship Henri IV had protected through
his Edict of Nantes. Within the Catholics were ultramontanist factions that wanted to look over the mountains to the pope for guidance in all things. On the other side were the *bon Français*, or
Gallican elements, who were often more secular and might nowadays be viewed as jingoist: These latter factions were Frenchmen
first, last, and always, and never wanted their government's policies
to be directed or dictated by His Holiness in Rome. The concept
that a French king ruled by *divine* right, raised during the 1614–
1615 meeting of the Estates General (a convocation of the three
orders of France's society—the clergy, nobility, and bourgeoisie),
was France's clever way of declaring that their sovereign was not
now, nor ever would be, beholden to the pope.

Added to the religious friction Louis inherited was the anxiety
of the Huguenots, in large part because his coronation ritual included an oath to extirpate Protestantism from his realm. So they
began amassing a military defense. Their aim was to transform
France into a Protestant pseudo-republic modeled on the Dutch
Netherlands, which was enemy Hapsburg territory.

Louis formally came of age on his thirteenth birthday, but his
mother continued to act as his regent while the young king developed crushes on handsome male courtiers and continued to practice his childhood pursuits. He built mechanical devices like clocks
and working models of toy cannons and miniature forts, shod
horses, and whipped up omelets and fancy desserts, becoming quite
the respected little chef.

However, as time went on, Marie de Medici began to surround
herself with Italian-born men, who were vastly disliked by the populace because they were foreigners. Louis developed a favorite of
his own, the court's gentle, middle-aged falconer, Charles d'Albert.
As Marie's fortunes fell at court, d'Albert's star rose until he became the monarch's chief adviser.

Despite his innate prejudice against Spaniards (for one thing, they were "papa's enemies"), Louis XIII had been betrothed since the age of eleven to the eldest daughter of Philip III of Spain, the Hapsburg princess Anne of Austria, who was just five days Louis' junior. There had been protests against the match from within the Bourbon family, most notably from the prince de Condé, who argued that not only were the two kingdoms inveterate enemies, but that such an alliance was a reversal of Henri IV's anti-Spanish foreign policy, and therefore *any* union between the French and their neighbors to the south was, ipso facto, inglorious. A Franco-Spanish marriage had been proposed for Louis during Henri's lifetime, but the monarch had dismissed the notion as ". . . a step impolitic, and likely totally to alienate the crowns; for, as the grandeur of France is the humiliation of Spain, no concord is possible. . . ."

However, the Louis-Anne match continued a tradition of political alliances between France and Spain that had begun with the marriage of King Philip II to Elisabeth of Valois, the daughter of Henri II of France and Catherine de Medici. Born in the Escorial in Madrid, the pretty, blond Anne was raised according to her parents' strict religious beliefs. Her mother was Margaret of Austria, so although Anne was the infanta of Spain and Portugal as well as an archduchess of Austria, her title derived from her mother's lineage and the House of Hapsburg.

Philip III provided his daughter with a dowry of half a million gold écus, augmented by numerous jewels worth fifty thousand écus. Anne's fiancé and his mother also promised her a twenty-thousand-écu annuity. Yet the fear that Louis might die young prompted the Spanish court to negotiate France's return of Anne's dowry, wardrobe, and jewelry upon her eventual widowhood. Prior to her marriage Anne also had to renounce all succession rights to Spain, not only for herself but for her descendants by Louis, in order to prevent France from making any claims to the Spanish throne. However, should Louis leave Anne a childless widow, by the terms of the marriage contract her rights of Spanish succession would be restored.

Anne carried more into France than a load of cash and jewelry, enough silver in her trousseau to equip several households, and a massive wardrobe that included fine batiste underpinnings, ruffs and other collars, and lavishly embroidered and embellished gowns, sleeves, bodices, and skirts of watered silk, taffeta, satin, and velvet, in every conceivable hue. Many of her garments were richly studded with gold and silver spangles, pearls, and other gems. Anne also had the weight of her father's expectations on her shoulders, his hope that she would be able to influence Louis' foreign policy.

She traveled from Spain with a vast entourage that would become a subject of contention long before she reached the altar; it was too small by Spanish standards and too large for the French, who had wanted her to enter the kingdom with a retinue of only fifty-three. Although more than two hundred attendants departed Spain with Anne, only half that number crossed the border into France.

The final weeks of November 1615 saw the proxy marriages and the formal nuptials of Anne and Louis, both only fourteen years old, as well as the union of their respective siblings. Anne's brother, Philip IV of Spain, only ten, was married by proxy in Bordeaux to Louis' thirteen-year-old sister, Elizabeth.

As Anne neared Bordeaux on November 21, in the manner of courtly lovers Louis approached her carriage incognito, in order to glimpse her before their wedding day. What he saw was an adolescent girl with full cheeks, a slightly fleshy nose, and a somewhat prominent lower lip. In a mash-up of their native tongues, Louis loudly cried out from the window of his coach, *"Yo son incognito, yo son incognito! Touche, cocher, touche!"*

The next few days were filled with festivities leading up to their nuptials. The court was enchanted by the couple's gestures of affection: On November 22, Louis personally visited the royal kitchens to order Anne's breakfast, and then called on her when she was making her toilette. When she indicated that she needed a feather for her headdress, he gallantly offered the queen a plume from his cap and asked for one of her hair bows in return.

Anne and Louis' two-hour wedding ceremony in the cathedral of Bordeaux took place on November 25, 1615, Saint Catherine's Day. Anne was clothed in a flowing gown of royal purple velvet trimmed with ermine and embellished with gold fleurs-de-lis. The crown was so heavy she had to steady it with her hand to keep it balanced atop her head.

Louis wore white satin brocade embroidered with gold and embellished with precious gems; a huge ruff encircled his neck. The adolescent bride, described by one of the Spanish onlookers as more beautiful than an angel, was "weighted down with robes and diamonds" and visibly dripping enormous drops of sweat, but she managed to smile at her groom throughout the ceremony. Their nearly identical looks were much remarked upon, although Louis had tousled dark hair and Anne was blond.

After the nuptial Mass, the newlyweds dined separately and Marie de Medici undertook the ritual of preparing the marital bed for her son and daughter-in-law. During Louis' supper, his courtiers entertained him with bawdy stories to put him in the mood for love before his mother arrived to escort him to Anne's chamber. The marriage bed was blessed and the curtains drawn about the teens, leaving them to follow nature's course.

Hours later, Louis brashly confided the details to Héroard, and when his physician inquired whether the queen had enjoyed herself, Louis boasted, "She liked it; I did it twice." It was a lie. The king had returned to his own bedchamber at about eleven that evening, as much a virgin as he had been the night before.

However, *something* had happened on his wedding night: a good deal of effort. Louis retired to his own bed with, in Héroard's words, a *glande rouge*. The young king had rubbed himself sore attempting to do his duty. Unfortunately, all that grinding or masturbation wasn't going to result in an heir, leaving both teenage spouses frustrated and Louis' failure on the linens.

Yet the official lie had to be that the marriage had been consummated, in order to prevent naysayers like the prince de Condé from seeking a reason to annul it. Marie de Medici had the nerve to display the dirty bedsheets the following morning. Louis was humiliated. Although he continued to pay ritual visits to Anne during the day, just as he called upon his mother, and bade the queen a brief good night before turning in, it would be six months before he ate dinner with Anne again, and four long years before they repeated the effort to consummate their marriage. Modern biographers attribute this difficulty to the damage Héroard caused to Louis' psyche by publicly chronicling and analyzing his every bodily function from the time the youth was born.

While fourteen was not a particularly unusual age for royalty to wed in this era, it was considered unhealthy for a couple that young to regularly cohabitate as man and wife, because they were physically and emotionally too undeveloped. Louis himself admitted to his confessor that he felt he was too immature for sexual intercourse, and feared he might suffer physical harm from engaging in it.

And yet France expected an heir from their barely adolescent sovereigns. Nowadays, kids that young qualify as jailbait, and forcing them to play house together would constitute child abuse.

At the outset of the royal marriage there was widespread enthusiasm for its success—which really meant a future dauphin. Soon after the wedding, a popular pamphlet, dripping with hope and hyperbole, made the rounds:

> *Rejoice, France, for after this happy night, so much desired by these two lovers and all their people, heaven and this princess promise you a succession of kings and princes and you shall see her as fertile as a vine, bearing fruit in abundance and in all seasons.*

During the queen's official entry into Paris on May 16, the provost of the merchants greeted her on his knees with a panegyric larded with erotic double-entendre. "May we thus, Madame, see the lilies of France flower in the golden fleece of Spain in a happy lineage, for which we implore Heaven."

If only it had been so. Although they shared a few of the same hobbies, such as hunting, Louis otherwise demonstrated little interest in his bride. Anne of Austria was queen of France and yet her husband had reduced her to a mere cipher at court. Her mother-in-law, the formidable dowager queen Marie de Medici, was given precedence on public occasions and had more actual power and authority. True, Marie had the benefits of age and experience, but Anne should have been treated with the appropriate deference as queen consort.

Undoubtedly homesick at first, Anne surrounded herself with her Spanish ladies-in-waiting, taking refuge in the familiar. She continued to abide by her native court etiquette rather than trying to assimilate into her adopted homeland, and by continuing to converse with the members of her satellite court in their own tongue, she did not improve her French.

A coded message from the Venetian ambassador to France noted the *froideur* between the spouses. "No great inclination toward his wife is shown by him, and he abhors all those close to her who belong to the Spanish nation," the envoy wrote of Louis. "While during earlier months they tried to keep him from making himself his wife's slave in everything [there is no proof of this in Héroard's diaries], now they have to work at preventing him from showing how little he cares about her." The next month, the Venetian ambassador reported an incident where Louis had spitefully locked up Anne's Spanish ladies-in-waiting for having taken the keys to some chests from his nurse's daughter. Although Louis began to mature as a monarch, as a person he remained emotionally stunted, hampered by his embarrassing stammer, repressing his feelings, obsessed with minutiae no matter the subject and, even at the age of eighteen, building miniature toys.

While the king was incapable of connecting with his wife physically or emotionally, when Anne arrived in France at the age of fourteen, she, too, had been derided for her perceived emotional immaturity, viewed by some as flighty and frivolous. The insult is absurd. How sober and staid could she have been at that age? Anne had a refreshing candor and zest for life. But she also had an innate pride and stubbornness that she had to work on in order not to sound too pro-Spanish. In an effort to please her husband she finally began to assimilate, learning Louis' language and ditching her native silhouettes for French fashions, insisting that her Iberian entourage do the same. But that gesture made no impact on Louis; he dismissed Anne's Spanish ladies-in-waiting for being too strong an influence on her.

Consequently, Anne had no friends at court. Her mother-in-law, who had been acting as Louis' regent ever since the death of his father in 1610, treated her as a supernumerary rather than as the new queen of France, and behaved as though she were still Henri's queen consort.

In November 1616, a member of the petty nobility, Armand-Jean du Plessis, Seigneur de Richelieu, the former bishop of Luçon, became secretary of state for foreign affairs. He was bright, energetic, and ambitious, and his rise to prominence at court was swift. The king soon came to rely upon Richelieu, and time and time again he would choose the cardinal's advice over that of his domineering mother.

At the age of fifteen, Louis finally kicked Marie de Medici to the curb after her continued meddling in state affairs threatened to subvert his own authority. In 1617, the king conspired with Charles d'Albert, the Grand Falconer of France, who had become his favorite and chief confidant, to stage a palace coup. Marie de Medici was exiled to Blois. The man she had elevated to the titles of Marshal and Marquis of Ancre, the Italian Concino Concini, her arrogant chief adviser and possible lover—according to numerous scurrilous pamphlets—was judicially assassinated. Concini's wife, caught in the metaphorical cross fire, was charged with witchcraft. To reward d'Albert, Louis created him the first duc de Luynes. In the French court, which had a rigid hierarchy, one's place in the social order, and his or her degree of proximity to the sovereign, was of paramount importance, because it was directly related to his sphere of influence. Charles de Luynes soon became the most unpopular man in France, perceived as monopolizing and controlling the king to the same degree Marshal Ancre had once controlled Marie de Medici's government. Soon the former falconer had the important role of sealing state documents.

It is a hallmark of Louis' reign that he perpetually sought someone strong to lean on, usually an older man, whether it was de Luynes or Richelieu. It's hardly surprising that the king was looking for another father figure, having been only eight years old when he lost his biological parent. During his preadolescent years, however, the king had relied primarily upon his mother, despite their dysfunctional relationship.

Marie de Medici effected a dramatic flight from Blois on February 22, 1619, escaping from the château via a swinging ladder suspended along the façade. She quickly assembled a cadre of malcontents and began spreading propaganda about her own son's governance, sparking what would come to be known as the "Wars of the Mother and Son." No shots were fired in these battles, despite Marie's efforts to stage a coup.

Meanwhile, the royal spouses weren't getting along any better, as Louis continued to avoid Anne's bed. In 1619, his younger sister Christine was engaged to the Duke of Savoy, and his illegitimate half sister Catherine Henriette de Bourbon, known as Mademoiselle de Vendôme, wed Charles de Lorraine, duc d'Elbeuf. Louis became sexually aroused while he witnessed the consummation of the latter couple's nuptials—not as a voyeur, but as part of the court ritual!

Hopping out of bed, the freshly postcoital new duchesse announced to the king, "Sire! You do the same thing with the queen, and you will do well." By this time, the court was fully aware that the royal marriage was celibate, but no one was considering an annulment. An heir had to be conceived for the sake of the realm—and the sooner the better.

The following week, on January 25, 1619, the duc de Luynes physically grabbed his boss as the king was on his way to his own bedchamber and force-marched the sobbing monarch into his wife's boudoir, depositing him onto Anne's bed. Leaving a servant in the room to verify the couple's activities, Luynes departed, locking the door behind him. The following day, Héroard reported the consummation of the royal marriage—at long last—in his journal. The *Mercure Français* also published the good news, and the foreign ambassadors disseminated the intelligence to their respective sovereigns.

Louis awoke and swore his undying love and fidelity to Anne, then informed the Spanish ambassador that he loved her more than anything in the world, a sentiment the king began to share with anyone he encountered.

The discovery of sex was a revelation to the sovereigns. After four years of celibacy, suddenly they experienced a honeymoon of sorts. Anne was no longer queen in name only. The normally suspicious-looking Louis appeared radiant. Naturally, Héroard chronicled the monarchs' nocturnal comings and goings in his journals, inventing a system of symbols to refer to when and how often the pair made love. For example the letter "r" or "n" to the second power or degree would indicate copulation twice in one night. Louis became so delighted with this whole lovemaking thing that he began to linger for hours in Anne's bedchamber every night and started to forgo his habit of rising early in the morning. Fretting that the king might literally wear himself out, his household urged him to take breaks of a fortnight between his connubial exertions with the queen.

Unfortunately, despite all that sex, Anne was unable to bear a child. Toward the end of 1619, she suffered a miscarriage, becoming so ill and weak that the court despaired for her life. Louis devotedly remained by her side during her illness, agreeing with the doctors, who felt it would be dangerous to bleed her any further.

Although there was no dauphin, Anne did at least earn Louis' devotion. Written in 1620 from his army camp, one of his notes to the queen survives, containing the romantic declaration: "I passionately want to see you." He took her with him on his summer military campaigns, left her in charge of the government when she stayed home (although Anne was not expected to make any major decisions on her own), and vowed never to touch another woman. While there were periods of ardent crushes on young ladies of the court, Louis never did commit adultery with them.

The sovereigns' honeymoon lasted all the way through 1621. But in 1622, Anne chose to stay behind, because she was two months pregnant. However, on March 22, encouraged by two of her ladies, Anne playfully raced through the halls of the Louvre, tripped, and tumbled down a staircase. Two days later, she miscarried.

Louis learned of the incident a week later, and from that moment his attitude toward Anne shifted. The little love notes ceased. Not only had she lost his baby, she had also lost his trust, and so had the duchesse de Chevreuse (the now-remarried widow of the duc de Luynes), who had not just urged her to dash along the corridors, but had been feeding Anne a steady diet of libertine love poems, which the king believed were far too provocative for his wife to be reading. From then on, Louis would visit Anne's bedchamber solely out of duty, most often during a time of political crisis, or when he had the queen in his complete control and she was utterly subservient to his will.

Anne's father died on March 31, 1621. When the news reached France, she was inconsolable. She felt even lonelier without a family of her own to comfort her.

The Spanish delegation at the Bourbon court blamed Louis for Anne's continued failure to produce an heir, but one of them reported to their new sovereign, Anne's brother Philip IV, "The king comes seldom or never to sleep with the queen since her illness, and it is believed [he thinks] if he has sons, however young they are, they will be the cause of civil war in his kingdom. Whenever the queen is thought to be pregnant he shows much regret. It is to be feared that the interests of the queen are in danger from this disposition of the king."

The prudish Louis was never amused by sexually suggestive jokes; Anne, on the other hand, enjoyed a bit of risqué humor, even when it hit close to home. An epigram published in *Le Cabinet satyrique*, a bawdy magazine that the duchesse de Luynes often encouraged her to read, suggested:

> *Get married, it's an honorable thing to do,*
> *I shall never be sorry to see it:*
> *But don't ever be so foolish*
> *As to marry your husband.*

To punish Anne for enjoying herself at the expense of the realm, Louis dismissed Marie de Rohan, Madame de Luynes. He refused to entertain his wife's pleas to restore her entourage and to hear her side of the story regarding the events surrounding her miscarriage. The king still blamed her for the tragedy, but he would not even speak to her face-to-face. For weeks, communications flew back and forth as the monarch insisted that his orders had been issued for Anne's own good.

The year before Anne's accident on the staircase, Louis and Marie de Medici were formally reconciled. But during a military campaign to crush a rebellion fomented by the Huguenots, the duc de Luynes had succumbed to an epidemic of camp fever, ending his influence and opening the door for Richelieu to put his stamp on the government.

Louis' reign would continue to be marked by conflicts with family members: His younger—and only legitimate—brother, Gaston, attempted more than one coup; plus the king had to contend with France's two primary nemeses—the Protestant Huguenots on the domestic front and the Catholic Hapsburgs on the foreign one. Louis was often in the position of reassuring his subjects that he was not undermining France's Catholic interests by going to war against other Catholic rulers. During his reign, France was surrounded on all sides by Hapsburg territory: Hapsburg rulers included the king of Spain, and the Holy Roman Emperor, who controlled central Europe as well as Belgium, the Netherlands and Germany, Northern Italy, and what is now the Grand Duchy of Luxembourg. Being a Hapsburg herself, it had to have been extremely difficult for Anne of Austria to hear her family derided as the enemy and to know that her husband was contemplating a declaration of war. After all, their marriage, and that of her brother to Louis' sister, had really been peace treaties designed to preserve amity between the Spanish Hapsburgs and the French. When Louis was conflicted about aiding the Holy Roman Emperor Ferdinand II of Germany, a Catholic Hapsburg, because it would strengthen Ferdinand's secular power, Anne went to bat for her family. But Louis curtly put the kibosh on his wife's lobbying with the tart remark, "Madame, be satisfied with being Queen of France."

Anne had been trying her damnedest to be a good queen of France. She had already suffered three miscarriages, in December 1619, March 1622, and in 1626, and would endure the trauma of a fourth spontaneous abortion in April 1631. Unfortunately, the queen's continued barrenness further increased the tension between the monarchs.

By 1623, Anne's lady-in-waiting, the fun-loving duchesse de Chevreuse, had returned to court, although Louis refused to reinstate her in the queen's household. At the time, the duchesse's lover was Lord Holland, the English ambassador to Paris, and the pair of them decided that the poor unloved queen was in need of a handsome man to appreciate her. Holland was close to the tall, charming, bisexual George Villiers, Duke of Buckingham, whose reputation preceded him as both the favorite of James I and one of

England's greatest rakes. The ambassador sang Anne's praises to the duke, while Madame de Chevreuse rhapsodized about Buckingham to the queen and importuned her to receive him cordially when he arrived in France, hinting that Villiers was already a little bit in love with her.

Louis had not been keen on entertaining Villiers at his court because of the duke's reputation as a hothead. Buckingham and Charles, Prince of Wales, the son of James I of England, arrived in France in 1623, pausing at the Bourbon court on their way to Spain to discuss the possibility of a marriage between Prince Charles and the infanta. Those hopes were dashed, so they returned to France to negotiate a marriage between Charles and Louis' sister Henrietta Maria. While they were there, the French king feared that Buckingham might do or say something rude that would ruin the deal.

During his first visit to France in 1623, onlookers noticed the mutual attraction between Buckingham and the queen, and the pair fell into an easy rapport. But Anne failed to recognize that the Englishman's discourse went beyond the limits of courtly flirtation; his passion was in earnest. And she was a virtuous woman who, while flattered, had no intention of breaking her marriage vows.

Accompanied by an extravagantly equipped and attired entourage, in 1625, the duke returned to Paris to escort Charles's bride, Henrietta Maria, to the English Channel. Once again, Anne permitted herself to be flattered by his attentions, tremendously fascinated by the most dashing, charming, and witty of England's cavaliers, if the princesse de Conti is to be believed when she stated that she could vouch for Anne's fidelity from the waist down, but could not say as much for the part from the waist up.

At the time, Anne was considered to be at the height of her beauty and voluptuousness. According to her cloak bearer, La Porte, the blond Duke of Buckingham, who was then in his mid-thirties, was "the best built and the best looking man in the world." It's no surprise that the unhappily married Anne was susceptible to his skilled, smooth flirtation. And although she may not have committed adultery, the queen did behave indiscreetly.

The royal family comprised a small party to accompany Henrietta Maria to Calais. Anne had been eager to be among the delegation that would see her sister-in-law safely escorted to the seacoast by Buckingham. The journey was filled with parties, entertainments, and dances. In Louis' absence, Anne and the duke enjoyed a romantic interlude, although, evidently, they had different ideas about their relationship.

En route to Calais the delegation stopped in Amiens, where Anne was lodged in a house with a large garden facing the banks of the Somme. One evening, Buckingham spied the queen walking alone in her garden and purportedly tried to press his attentions upon her. Anne shrieked and her entourage came running before anything could happen. On another occasion, the duke managed to slip away from the English delegation. He insisted upon seeing Anne, but she had retired early and instructed her attendants to deny him admittance to her rooms. The duke persisted. Finally Anne sent a message to her mother-in-law, asking her how to handle the situation. Marie de Medici advised the queen to receive Buckingham from her bed, since she had done the same thing in her day. Bursting into Anne's bedchamber, in the presence of her ladies, Villiers fell to his knees and declared his love for her: She was his ideal woman—never mind that they were both married. Shocked, the queen had him ejected from her rooms.

As a consequence of this nocturnal hullabaloo, a furious, jealous, and scandalized Louis declared that Anne was no longer permitted to entertain any man in her quarters unless he himself was present. Although Marie de Medici argued on her daughter-in-law's behalf, insisting that good women were not responsible for the ardor they inspired in men, and admitting that she had admirers in her youth as well, Louis would not hear reason. He dismissed the ladies-in-waiting who permitted the bedchamber event to transpire, as well as Anne's cloak bearer, La Porte. But he tactlessly chose to give Anne the news while she was recovering from an epileptic seizure, and did not even deliver the message himself: He sent his mother to scold her. Louis' secretary wrote in his private journal that he was appalled the king lacked the kindness to speak to Anne gently about the new protocol. Instead, Louis' efforts to micromanage his wife's life, and his insistence on dictating any changes in her household staff and on keeping a tight rein on her purse strings, were insults that served only to widen the rift between them.

Yet Anne's purported betrayal was not limited to her behavior with the Duke of Buckingham. Louis also believed that his queen, along with Madame de Chevreuse, who was something of an *intrigante*, had acted in concert with his brother Gaston to overthrow him. In the wake of the prince's failed coup of 1626, the conspirators claimed that according to their plot, after Louis was removed from the throne, Anne was to wed Gaston.

Anne was questioned as to what she knew of Gaston's plans and whether she indeed harbored intentions to marry her brother-in-law, enduring the humiliation of an interrogation before the royal council without being offered the chair that should have been given to a woman of her rank. Fighting to retain her dignity in the face of such an insult, the queen denied all knowledge of the plot to dethrone her husband and replied that she "would have gained too little from the exchange to wish to blacken herself by such a crime for so paltry stakes."

Despite Anne's vehement disavowal of any involvement in the conspiracy or any desire to wed her brother-in-law after the overthrow of Louis, documents stored in the Archivo General de Simancas (AGS), an official state archive located within the castle of Simancas in Valladolid, Spain, reveal a different story: that Anne had full knowledge of the complete plot, and had assented to it. Throughout her reign, Anne maintained a correspondence with her brother, and whatever she may have written to Philip IV on the subject of Gaston's conspiracy would have been classified as a state document and filed accordingly. Yet if Anne was complicit in Gaston's conspiracy, her reasons for it are unclear. True, she would not have gained much by swapping one Bourbon brother for the other. Had she been hoping that Gaston and his cohorts, Louis' illegitimate brothers, promised a strong Franco-Spanish foreign policy?

Louis never forgave his wife for her perceived betrayal; nor, till his dying day, did he believe her protestations of innocence. Gaston surrendered—for the time being—and permitted himself to be hastily married off to Mademoiselle de Montpensier, who would die in childbirth the following year. As a wedding gift, he received the duchies of Orléans and Blois. For her suspected complicity in the conspiracy, Madame de Chevreuse was exiled to Blois. Instead, she managed to flee to Lorraine, where her husband's cousin, the duc de Lorraine, gave her sanctuary.

Meanwhile, the communication between Anne and the Duke of Buckingham had continued. For Buckingham, the queen became a passion bordering on obsession. For the next three years he looked for reasons to be sent to France. He exchanged messages with Anne in the hope of being invited back in some sort of diplomatic role, kept a portrait of her, and publicly toasted her health at his own sovereign's banquets.

For her part, Anne once confided to a friend that if it were possible for a virtuous woman to be in love with a man other than her husband, the Duke of Buckingham would be that man.

In 1626, having asked Lord Holland to assure Anne of his love, and discover whether it was reciprocated, Buckingham received Holland's reply: "I have been a careful spy to observe intentions and affections towards you. . . . I find many things to be feared, and none to be assured of a safe and real welcome. For the [king] continues in his suspects . . . and is willing to hear villains say that [the queen] hath infinite affections, you may imagine which way."

As for Anne's feelings, Holland continued, "You are the most unhappy man alive, for [the queen] is beyond imagination . . . and would do things to destroy her fortune rather than want satisfaction in her mind." The ambassador's words seemed to encourage Buckingham to find a reasonable excuse for crossing the Channel. Yet later that year, he told his friend, "Do what you will, I dare not advise you. To come is dangerous. Not to come is unfortunate." All too aware of Louis' jealousy, and perhaps of the powerful Richelieu's opinion that he was a madman, Buckingham chose to remain in England.

Although Louis continued to accuse Anne of treasonous thoughts, at least he recognized that they had to secure his succession. If the queen did not bear him a son, Gaston would not need to stage a coup to gain the throne; he would inherit it by law. In 1626, Anne became pregnant, although she lost the fetus. For the next decade, until 1637, she dwelled under a cloud of suspicion, primarily blaming Richelieu for her unhappiness, as it was the cardinal-minister, and not Louis, who was now selecting the members of her retinue.

The year 1628 was a banner year for Louis, but a dismal one for Anne. On August 23, 1628, the Duke of Buckingham was assassinated, stabbed to death by a naval officer named John Felton who was angry that the duke had passed him over for promotion. Buckingham had been responsible for England's latest military failure: leading the campaign in the summer of 1627 to aid the beleaguered Huguenots of La Rochelle. Even then, Villiers had harbored the illusion of seeing his beloved French queen again! His cabin on board his ship was draped in Anne's colors of yellow and black, her cipher was on prominent display, and a life-size portrait of her hung at one end of the cabin, backed by a drape of cloth of gold and surrounded by candelabra bearing flickering tapers. Even as he was sailing to aid her husband's enemies, the Duke of Buckingham had created a shrine to Anne of Austria and didn't care who saw it.

In November of 1628, starved by Louis' siege, the city of La Rochelle opened its gates to his army, setting the stage for the king's eradication of the last holdout of the Protestant "state within the state." Although Louis had secured a major victory and demonstrated his capability to achieve his domestic policy agenda, his own family members continued to create problems for him. They were like bad pennies, continually turning up again after they had been turned out. Marie de Medici evidently learned nothing from her exile of 1617, or from the king's willingness to allow her to return to court. In 1630, she orchestrated yet another coup against her own son and his chief minister, intending to have Richelieu murdered and replaced with a member of the council and keeper of the seals, Michel de Marillac, brother to the cardinal's potential assassin.

But Louis discovered the plot in the nick of time. On November 11, in what would henceforth be known as the Day of the Dupes, or Fool's Day, the king turned the tables on the conspirators. They were caught and punished. Forced to choose between loyalty to his mother or to Richelieu, the twenty-nine-year-old king chose the cardinal. Louis sneaked off to Versailles that day and never saw Marie de Medici again. She fled to Hapsburg territory, at first residing closely monitored in the Spanish Netherlands. She then traveled to London, and finally to Holland and to Cologne, where she died in obscurity on July 4, 1642, a few months before Louis met his own end. Over the years, Marie begged her son for permission to return to France, but as she was unrepentant, it would have been foolish and dangerous for him to relent.

With a mother who consistently betrayed him at the highest level, no wonder Louis didn't trust women—including his wife. He expected Anne to respect and heed those who had gained his favor, and to shun and despise those who had lost it, even when those opinions were to be applied to the same person. For years she had to defer to her mother-in-law because Louis wished her to do so, but when Marie de Medici's star at court fell, the king demanded that his wife reverse her feelings as well. Anne didn't comprehend Louis' caprices, his mood swings, and his coldness. Royal marriages were invariably political alliances, but Anne had optimistically hoped for less hostility and less disappointment from *her* union. Her suffering was not even private. Although the glowing notices in the *Gazette de France* in the early 1630s stated, "The affection their majesties have for one another is such that they can bear to be separated only when the king goes to make foreign conquests, and even then the queen wants to see them from the frontiers," the newsletter's readers, eager to catch up on the latest court gossip about the sovereigns, began to get the sense that all was not right with their marriage.

And by the mid-1630s, France still had no heir. Instead, Louis focused his attentions on his war against the Huguenots and spent an increasing amount of time in the company of his primary adviser, Cardinal Richelieu, who was made the king's First Minister in 1624. In time, Anne came to view Richelieu as her political enemy. She allowed herself to be influenced by the factions at court that were opposed to his policies, and drawn into the intrigues against the minister-cardinal that were organized by the duchesse de Chevreuse, who continued to correspond with Anne in secret from her sanctuary in Tours.

Although the purpose of Anne and Louis' marriage had been to solidify the alliance between Spain and France, to the king's dismay, in the intervening years Spain had begun to ally itself with disenfranchised French Protestants. Yet Spain was also currently embroiled in conflicts with Germany's Protestant princes. If Anne's brother prevailed, the Hapsburg hegemony in Europe would be even more powerful. As it was, France was surrounded on all sides by Hapsburg territory. On May 19, 1635, when Louis declared war on Spain—a conflict that would end up lasting twenty-five years—Anne was placed in a hopeless position, caught between her allegiance to her homeland and that of her husband. She chose the former, secretly corresponding with her brother Philip IV of Spain. Cardinal Richelieu kept his eye on her. On August 17, 1637, having intercepted a file of letters written in Anne's hand, he dared to force the queen of France to sign covenants regarding her correspondence, which from then on was subject to inspection.

The documents that Richelieu presented to Anne for her signature were in Louis' handwriting. One was titled "Memoir of Things I Wish of the Queen." Anne agreed to cease her clandestine communications and confessed her "bad conduct," first, for hoping against an Anglo-French amity (obviously she desired a Hispano-French political alliance), and second, for corresponding with the enemy—her relations. The queen was also compelled to admit information she had previously denied—that a coup to depose and assassinate Louis would lead to her marriage with his brother Gaston, who would then become king. Anne further promised never to relapse into similar faults and to henceforth live with the king as someone who wished to have no interest other than in his person and in his State.

Louis penned a formal response to Anne's confession, accepting it even as he forbade her any further communication with her usual correspondents, as well as any visits to convents, which had also been her custom. He coldly agreed to put the matter behind him, stating that he wished to live with the queen as a good king and a good husband. Countersigned by France's secretary of state, it was as formal a treaty as their marriage contract.

With Anne in the role of the penitent and Louis the Just in the morally superior role of the forgiver, the king was finally in the mood to visit her bedchamber. Louis was happiest when he had his thumb on someone.

As with most royal marriages, what was good for the gander was not acceptable behavior for the goose. Although he might have had crushes on courtiers of both genders, the king expected complete fidelity from Anne, even in her heart, and even though her own infatuation for the Duke of Buckingham had gone no further than a courtly flirtation. In *his* romantic life, Louis XIII was an utter hypocrite. "Do as I say, not as I do," would have been an apt catchphrase for this autocrat. Although his own passionate attachments engendered plenty of embarrassment, his wife was not permitted to degrade herself and dishonor him—and the House of Bourbon—with her *affaires du coeur*.

Throughout the 1630s, before, during, and after Anne's pregnancies, Louis devoted himself to a string of royal favorites. De Luynes had been the first, a father figure and adviser, training wheels for the king's political relationship with Cardinal Richelieu, but it's unlikely there was any physical attraction between them.

However, in the spring of 1630, the king became utterly beguiled by a spirited fourteen-year-old named Marie de Hautefort. Louis sorely needed distraction, and was soon asking his mother for permission to visit the rosy-cheeked, blue-eyed, yellow-haired Marie. Anne, however, was humiliated when her husband dressed up like a young gallant in brightly colored garments dripping with ribbons and bows, in a desperate attempt to secure Mademoiselle de Hautefort's love. And yet he was too afraid to actually touch the girl. An anecdote handed down through history has Anne pinning Marie by the shoulders after they had hidden a note in her bosom, taunting the king to fetch it. Fearing any physical contact with Marie's flesh, Louis tried to retrieve the note with a pair of silver tongs. The story is likely untrue, since it's nearly impossible to imagine the maritally neglected Anne of Austria actively encouraging her husband to plunge his hands down the bodice of an adolescent girl with whom he was wildly infatuated. But it does serve to illustrate Louis' discomfort with female sexuality. Nevertheless, Marie de Hautefort was not the only virginal girl to captivate him. He also fell for another teenager at his court, Louise Angélique de La Fayette, a dark-haired, blue-eyed angel. But he never had an adulterous relationship with either of them. Louise was so virtuous that she despaired of being in the same room with a man, let alone hearing the bawdy talk that was de rigueur at court.

Ultimately, Louis felt ashamed of the way he courted the incorruptible Louise. On May 9, 1637, with both of them in tears, the young lady-in-waiting parted from the monarch, leaving the dry-eyed queen's chambers for a carriage that would convey her to the Vistadine convent at Chaillot, where she took the veil.

Before thus exiting stage left, Louise had long encouraged the sovereign to make an heir, for his own happiness and that of the realm. Louis may not have tried too hard during his infatuation with Mademoiselle de La Fayette because he was too focused on himself and on the notion of being in love with someone. After Louise joined the Sisters of the Visitation, on June 4, 1637, Louis replied to Richelieu's reminder that, for the comfort of his soul, he needed a special friend like her in his life. The king wrote, "If I must love someone, I would rather try to get back with Hotefort [sic] than with any other girl at court. However it is not my intention to get involved with anyone . . . also because I have promised this to la Faiette (to whom I have never gone back on my word nor she to me). . . . I will try to live the best I can on earth in order at the end to win Paradise, which is the sole goal one should have in this world. . . . You should know that since I have been here [at Fontainebleau], I haven't spoken to any woman or girl except the queen."

The king did attempt to rekindle his passion for Marie de Hautefort, but the spark was no longer there. For the remainder of the year, Louis availed himself of every opportunity to visit Louise. He saw her for the last time on December 5, 1637. Right around that time, the king was persuaded by Louise and his male companions to sleep with Anne. He was fortuitously compelled to accept her hospitality when, caught far from home during a hunting expedition, a torrid rainstorm obliged him to abide for the night with the queen at Saint Germain. Nine months later—after twenty-three years of marriage—on September 5, 1638, at the remarkably old age of thirty-seven, Anne gave birth to a son, the dauphin Louis.

So much time had passed, especially considering the sovereigns' long-standing cool relations, that the dauphin's birth was considered a divine miracle. Consequently, Louis would forever be nicknamed *"le Dieudonné"*—the God-given. The miracle baby had arrived seven months after Louis XIII had vowed to place "our person, our estate, our crown, and our subjects" under the special protection of the Virgin Mary. However, not everyone was impressed with Louis' dedication. The abbé de Saint-Cyran considered it a highly cynical gesture, stating, "There is nothing more capable of offending God than causing religion and piety to serve politics."

France rejoiced in its heir. In the capital the cannon thundered, carillon bells pealed, and fireworks illuminated the night skies for days. Extravagant pageants were held throughout the provinces. Strangers greeted one another in the street with the exclamation, *"Vive le Prince Dauphin, l'attente de la France"*—"Long live the Prince-Dauphin, the expectation of France!"

And yet, the subject of the dauphin's birth immediately became a scandal. French queens delivered their babies in the presence of a roomful of nobles, eyewitnesses who could attest to the infants' legitimacy. Yet the king himself had not been present; nor had Cardinal Richelieu. And Marie de Medici did not appear to be overjoyed at the little boy's arrival into the world. This information was enough for the pamphleteers to spin more than one fanciful tale about the birth of the dauphin. One popular story held that little Louis was one of a set of twins, and the other twin had mysteriously disappeared (a fiction that would inspire the film *The Man in the Iron Mask*, based on Dumas' final installment of *The Three Musketeers*). Another rumor circulated that the dauphin could not possibly be the son of Louis XIII, for certain reasons that were well known to many. Even if these hints at Louis' relationships with his *mignons* were meant to suggest that he was too fond of men to successfully perform his marital obligations, the king knew his duty (and had been equally fond of some of the young women at court). Moreover, he never disavowed his heir, nor gave the slightest doubt that the dauphin was not his son.

Anne was a devoted mother, often visiting the nursery to see her little boy, rare behavior for a royal in any era. In early April 1639, one of her attendants wrote, "The queen hardly leaves him. She takes great pleasure in playing with him and taking him out in her carriage whenever the weather is fine; it is the whole of her amusement."

On Christmas night, 1639, Louis paid Anne another rare conjugal visit. The following year, on September 21, at Saint-Germain-en-Laye, little Louis got a baby brother, Philippe, the duc d'Anjou. In 1661, Philippe would be given the title of duc d'Orléans; he was the founder of this cadet branch of the Bourbons (a "cadet" branch being a male line established by the younger sons of a monarch).

The *Gazette de France* reported that ". . . three years ago it would have been difficult to persuade their majesties of what we see today: namely, that they would give us two princes like so many columns to assure our conquests. . . ."

Although Louis had seemed even more joyful at the birth of his second son—perhaps because the proverbial "spare" provided a bit of insurance if something befell the dauphin—Philippe's birth failed to reconcile the royal couple. Instead, Louis continued to devote his romantic attentions to a series of young male courtiers. For all his prudishness around the young women who had previously captivated him, the king threw himself at these *mignons*, who were often in their teens when they became the objects of royal favor. At the time, because the Church accepted that royalty was divinely anointed and therefore more highly evolved than other mortals, clerics did not become as scandalized over same-sex attractions among kings and their *mignons* as one might imagine.

Back in 1624, Louis had become so smitten with François de Barradat that in order to retain the king's good graces, Cardinal Richelieu was writing groveling letters to the new *favori*. Although his allegations could not be proven, Tallemant des Réaux, the king's near contemporary, wrote that Louis loved this young man "violently; one accused him of committing a hundred indecencies [*ordures*] with him." And yet, as starry-eyed as he could be over a courtier's face and form, Louis was clear-eyed when it came to the governance of his realm. In 1626, when Barradat tried to meddle in politics, he was banished from court.

Three weeks later, Louis fell for another teen. His infatuation for

Claude de Saint-Simon was a form of slumming, as Claude was not a sophisticated youth, but short and homely, with salty language and a way with horses. Claude's relationship with the king was intriguing; the monarch invented a coded language in which the pair could send romantic correspondence. Evidently, after Louis involved Claude in a love triangle with Marie de Hautefort, the boy urged his sovereign to just go ahead and bed the lovely young girl. As with Barradat, there is no concrete proof of any physical sexual affair between Louis and Claude de Saint-Simon, who was heterosexual, and was often seen slipping away from Louis' quarters in 1634 to rendezvous with one of his "wenches," as Claude's casual liaisons were described. Louis was just as jealous of his male favorites' attachments to someone else as he was of the idea of Marie de Hautefort marrying anyone. At least Louise de La Fayette had become a bride of Christ—a different sort of rival for Louis' love. The king remained enamored of Saint-Simon for a decade. As the years passed, he elevated him from a gentleman of the bedchamber to honorary councilor of state to governor of the town of Blaye in 1630 (the same year Louis fell in love with Marie de Hautefort), and in 1635, he made Saint-Simon a duke and a peer.

Until that year, the king had managed to retain a sense of perspective where his crushes were concerned; he never gave them too much power when they were still adolescents. However, the last of Louis' *mignons*, Henri Coiffier de Ruzé—the handsome marquis de Cinq Mars who didn't have a brain in his curly golden-haired head—bit the hand that fed him harder than anyone could have imagined.

It was Cardinal Richelieu who had first become captivated by the fifteen-year-old son of his deceased colleague Marshal Effiat. When war with Spain erupted that year, Louis made Henri d'Effiat, marquis de Cinq Mars, the commander of one of his new companies of bodyguards. Over the next four years Cinq Mars, who had been made grand equerry, the master of the royal stables, assumed a seat on Louis' council. He rose through the military ranks, fighting alongside the king in 1639 at the northeastern front. By the end of the year, the thirty-eight-year-old monarch admitted to Marie de Hautefort that his heart now belonged to the nineteen-year-old marquis.

During the period between the births of the sovereigns' two sons, while Cinq Mars set the fashions at court, and Louis (as well as all the women) fawned over the oh-so-handsome nobleman with the melodious singing voice, Anne resided at St. Germain with the dauphin. She preferred to be alone with her much-cherished son, rather than face daily humiliation at her husband's court.

Louis saw in Cinq Mars what he wanted to see: the youth's handsome face and long, blond, perfumed curls, rather than his arrogance, ostentation, and promiscuity. Courtiers who had so recently witnessed their sovereign utterly moonstruck over young Marie de Hautefort, as well as his very public attractions to other ladies in his wife's retinue, were astonished at Louis' passionate volte-face for a young man, although the monarch's infatuation with Cinq Mars in fact marked a return to his preference during the mid-1620s for male *favoris*. One of Gaston's servants claimed that the king loved Cinq Mars *"ardemment"*—ardently. In his *Historiettes*, Gédéon Tallemant des Réaux wrote that Louis *"l'aimait esperdument,"* meaning that Louis loved him to distraction. Although none of his stories were confirmed, Tallemant wrote extensively about the king's ardor for Cinq Mars, mentioning a lovers' tryst between the pair, stating that one day someone interrupted the king's *mignon* in the act of rubbing jasmine oil all over his body, and a moment later, His Majesty appeared at the door. Tallemant refers to another incident where the marquis arrived for a rendezvous with the monarch "adorned like a wife"—whatever that means—and Louis, his garments in disarray, "started kissing his hands almost before this minion got [in bed with him]."

Unless Tallemant de Réaux's statement was pure gossip, it would appear that, at least with Cinq Mars (if not possibly with Barradat several years earlier in 1624), Louis' flirtations may have finally crossed the line into adultery. Otherwise, the king appears to have been faithful to Anne, in body, if not in his heart.

Tallemant was a bourgeois who "married up," wedding his wealthy cousin Elisabeth de Rambouillet. Elizabeth fed him many scurrilous stories of the reigns of Henri IV and Louis XIII. However, she was no fan of either king. Consequently, her husband's anecdotes are most likely little more than spurious invention, but they have enough of a whiff of truth about them that they were given credit at the time—perhaps because so many of Louis' private letters to Richelieu, as well as the king's diaries, are extant. In them, the monarch complains of the poor treatment he has received from his favorite, every "dirty look" Cinq Mars gives him, every act of arrogance and haughtiness, until His Majesty is beside himself with misery. Louis and his *favori* bickered like an old married couple, much to the embarrassment of the court. And whatever Cinq Mars's pleasure, the sovereign granted it.

In the early spring of 1642, after the dauphin burst into tears one evening at the strange and unfamiliar sight of the king in his funny-looking nightcap—which the toddler must have found somewhat frightening—Louis made the decision to separate Anne from their sons, claiming that she was raising them to hate their father. He forbade her to leave St. Germain during his absence, even for her customary visits to the convents of the Carmelites and Val-de-Grâce. The queen was humiliated enough by these restrictions, but was completely devastated by the loss of her children.

That June, Richelieu anonymously received a draft copy of a treaty with the Spanish, revealing Cinq Mars's participation in a plot to conspire with Gaston and a handful of prominent courtiers to assassinate the cardinal-minister, laying the groundwork for their own regime by opening negotiations with Anne's brother. The cardinal shared the information with Louis, who promptly ordered Cinq Mars's arrest. Because the treaty was with the Spanish, the king also suspected Anne of being involved, although she vehemently denied it. She may in fact have been in her husband's corner, as the anonymous source who forwarded the duplicitous treaty to Richelieu. It has been speculated that Anne may have done so because she desperately wanted her sons returned to her, and recognized that the proper conduit for these negotiations would be the all-powerful cardinal-minister. Neither Gaston nor Cinq Mars ever suspected Anne of betraying them to the crown, if indeed she had done so.

Cinq Mars begged the king's pardon, but Louis' heart had hardened against him. When the request reached the king, he had been boiling sugar and treacle in a pan. Louis took the pan from the fire, rolled the contents about, and showed the caramelized sugar and molasses to the messenger, declaring that Cinq Mars's soul was as black as the bottom of the pan. From then on, Louis openly averred that he had never liked the marquis, calling Cinq Mars an irreligious boy who had never said a *pater* in his life and whose idleness made him vomit.

Found guilty of treason, on September 12, 1642, the marquis de Cinq Mars was beheaded. Although the king had made a fool of himself over the young man, he displayed no emotion over the marquis' execution, remarking instead that he would have liked to have seen the grimace Cinq Mars made on the scaffold.

In February 1643, Louis fell ill while he was staying at his boyhood residence of St. Germain. He never recovered, instead growing steadily worse throughout the winter and spring. His intestines were ulcerated and inflamed, he had lost control of his bowels, and his body was racked with tuberculosis, which by then had spread to his lungs. A popular anecdote about Louis XIII's final hours has been handed down through the centuries, published by generations of biographers as fact, although the story has been revealed to be apocryphal. When the king was on his deathbed suffering from complications due to intestinal tuberculosis, the queen brought the dauphin to see his papa for the last time. Asking his heir if he knew who he was, the four-year-old child replied that he was Louis the Fourteenth.

Still clinging to life, the forty-one-year-old monarch is said to have responded, *"Pas encore, mon fils, pas encore!"*—"Not yet, my son, not yet!"

He appointed Anne as regent for their son, and Gaston lieutenant general of the kingdom, but the pair of them were to be assisted by an entire council of nobles who had the real authority when it came to governing. Anne's role was merely nominal; Louis had not permitted her a scintilla of power. And yet, while she saw her husband slip away, remaining by his bedside day and night—even as she quietly, if not covertly, prepared for her future—she was surprised by the intensity of her grief. According to the memoirs of Madame de Motteville, whose mother was Anne's private secretary, and who herself became a courtier, the queen had often admitted after Louis passed that as she'd watched him dying she'd felt as though her heart were being torn from her body.

Louis XIII died on May 14, 1643, the thirty-third anniversary of the assassination of his father. Ever parsimonious when it came to his own expenses, his request for a minimal amount of extravagance at his funeral was heeded. Louis' embalmed body was encased in a lead casket covered with a velvet drape embellished only with a white satin cross and his coats of arms embroidered in golden thread. A team of six horses conveyed his hearse to his sepulcher at Saint Denis. The funeral procession was so long, it took a full day to arrive there.

During his reign Louis earned the sobriquet "the Just"—not because he was a fair and wise ruler, but because he firmly believed in justice being served, dispensing it when he thought the punishment fit the crime. Louis XIII presided over more judicial murders than any other French monarch, starting in April 1617 when his mother's pet minister Concini was executed because he had become too powerful and posed a potential threat to the king's authority. Nor did he hesitate to behead his own favorite, the marquis de Cinq Mars.

Contrary to the fictional depictions, Louis XIII was hardly a weakling who lacked courage; in 1617, he expelled his mother from the court, and he destroyed the Huguenot Protestant "state within the state" that culminated with his successful siege at La Rochelle in 1629; a few months later, he led an army of thirty-five thousand infantry and three thousand cavalry across the Alps in the dead of winter to combat the combined forces of Savoy, the German emperor, and Spain, and he eventually declared war on Spain, his wife's homeland.

Louis consistently placed principle above his personal feelings. He permitted the Huguenots to worship in peace as long as they did not attempt to revolt—but showed no mercy when they did, waging nearly annual military campaigns against them from 1620 to 1629, which effectively plunged the kingdom into civil war. These were his own policies, as was his desire to curb the growing power of the Hapsburgs, whose territory bordered that of France, so that his kingdom would not become one of their satellites.

Although Louis placed no personal stamp on France's science, art, and culture as his son, the Sun King, would do, his reign marked the dawn of France's golden age and did boast luminaries such as René Descartes, and the great dramatist Corneille.

Cardinal Richelieu, who had died of lung disease in September 1642, made a gift to Louis of his opulent mansion, the Palais Cardinal, in 1636, but the king had never resided there. After her husband's death, Anne of Austria installed herself in the château with her two sons, renaming it the Palais Royal. Thwarting the late Louis' plans to deny her the regency because he always considered her a Spaniard at heart, Anne connived to have the Parlement of Paris, the capital's judicial body, revoke his will. Louis XIV affixed his signature to the document awarding his mother the regency, attesting that it was executed with his full consent.

Anne then filled the position of chief minister with the Italian-born Cardinal Jules Mazarin, turning over the reins of government to him. She'd first met Mazarin in 1634, when he was a protégé of Cardinal Richelieu. Her nemesis introduced the pair of them with the sly and indiscreet remark, "He will please you, Madame, he is much like Buckingham."

Fast-forward to her widowhood, and before long tongues were wagging, suggesting that Mazarin and the queen mother were lovers. Some believed that they had secretly wed. The cardinal was not an ordained priest and therefore could have married within the Church, although his role as Louis XIV's godfather made him off-limits by canonical law; a union with Anne would have been considered incest. However, Anne confided to her friend Madame de Brienne that the kind of love she bore for Mazarin was a spiritual and not a sexual one. Later in their relationship the pair would exchange coded correspondence that could be interpreted as highly romantic or sentimental, but there is no conclusive proof of any formal union between Mazarin and the dowager queen.

Anne of Austria became as formidable a regent for her son as Marie de Medici had been before her. During Louis XIV's minority, with the aid of Cardinal Mazarin, Anne fended off the two-pronged civil revolt known as the Fronde. During the Fronde, both Anne and Mazarin were savaged by her son's subjects in vicious, bawdy poems known as Mazarinades that quite graphically accused the pair of fornication.

For some reason, during Louis XIV's upbringing, Anne deliberately suppressed any mention of his father's methods of governance, so he grew up mistakenly believing that Richelieu had ruled not only France but had controlled Louis XIII as well. Anne's regency formally ended when the young king came of age in 1651, although she retained considerable power and influence until Mazarin's death a decade later.

France's protracted war with Spain had finally ended in 1659; the following year, Anne celebrated her son's wedding to her niece, the infanta Maria Theresa of Spain. Unlike his parents, Louis XIV and his bride, whose name had been francofied to Marie-Thérèse, didn't dawdle when it came to consummating their marriage. Anne's first grandchild, a boy, Louis de France, was born in November 1661. That March 31, the bisexual Philippe, duc d'Orléans, had married his first cousin Henriette-Anne, the daughter of his aunt Henrietta Maria and Charles I of England.

In the spring of 1663, soon after the Easter celebrations, Anne fell ill. Her arms became weak, and she developed a fever, nausea, and pain in her legs. The queen mother was bled so often that she fainted from the loss of it. She eventually recovered after a slow convalescence, but in May 1664, she began to feel pain in her left breast. Anne had detected a nodule, but told no one of it and was determined to endure the agony. When her family noticed how ill she looked and insisted that the royal physicians be consulted, the doctors confirmed the worst. Seventeenth-century French surgeons knew little about cancer; they did not cut into the tissue. Instead, Anne was treated with bloodletting, emetics, and topical ointments. Obviously these remedies were useless.

In September of 1665, Anne of Austria was transported to the convent of Val-de-Grâce, built on land she had acquired for the nuns of Valprofond on May 7, 1621. She had wanted to die in peace there, but both the king and her doctors found the location too inconvenient for them to properly care for her. Louis XIV personally fetched his mother from Val-de-Grâce and brought her back to the Louvre, where she died of breast cancer on January 20, 1666, with her son Philippe at her bedside. Her body reposes in the Basilica of Saint Denis, the final resting place for France's monarchs. After so many decades of celibacy within their marriage, the oft-neglected Anne of Austria and the suspicious and insensitive Louis XIII now sleep together for all eternity.

PHILIPPE OF FRANCE, DUC d'ORLÉANS

AND

HENRIETTE-ANNE OF ENGLAND

....

MARRIED: 1661–1670

AND

ELISABETH CHARLOTTE von der PFALZ, PRINCESS PALATINE

....

MARRIED: 1671–1701

*E*veryone loved "Minette," except her own husband. *What a waste!* is probably the first phrase that sprang to mind regarding the mismatched union between the younger son of Louis XIII and Anne of Austria, and his first cousin—the eighth and last child of Charles I of England and Philippe's aunt Henrietta Maria.

Perhaps they were too much alike—both so fine boned and physically beautiful, so enamored of sumptuous fashion and lavish jewels. Both of them outrageous flirts. And both so attractive—and attracted—to men.

Anne of Austria learned a valuable lesson during her husband's reign: Louis XIII's younger brother Gaston had attempted more than one coup d'état. Consequently, she was determined to raise her own younger son in a way that would present no threat to his elder brother Louis XIV's government or throne. Like seventeenth-century royal daughters, "Monsieur" (as a king's next-youngest brother was styled) received lessons in decorum, music, and dancing, but he was deliberately not taught the skills necessary to rule France. This tactic seems absurd, given the high infant mortality rate and the likelihood of Monsieur inheriting the throne himself, but Philippe was consciously denied any education in statecraft, history, or the humanities. Moreover, he possessed only the rudimentary fundamentals of grammar and spelling in his own tongue, and was unskilled in other languages as well—a far cry from Renaissance-era princes. Monsieur's penmanship remained so poor throughout his life that he could barely decipher it himself.

Given the title of duc d'Anjou at his birth, Philippe spent his earliest years in his mother's household among her attendants. He performed many of the activities that a daughter would have done under the same circumstances, such as accompanying the queen mother on her visits to convents—where the nuns made as much of a fuss over him as did her ladies-in-waiting. Anne often referred to him as "my little girl." Always petite and dainty, a delicate boy with dark eyes, a profusion of long brown curls, and the same swarthy complexion as his older brother, Philippe was the darling of Anne's entourage. He became fascinated at a tender age by their colorful, extravagant gowns and accessories, and particularly by their makeup and jewelry. If it glittered, Philippe loved it. According to Madame de Motteville, whose mother was the private secretary to Anne of Austria, and whose own memoirs paint an indelible picture of the Bourbon court, Monsieur enjoyed the company of women and girls and loved to style them—delighting in dressing their hair, and offering makeup tips. When Philippe did play with other little boys, his usual companion was François-Timoléon de Choisy, the future abbé (and transsexual), whose mother was raising him as a girl. François-Timoléon had pierced ears, was dotted with decorative *mouches,* and dripping with diamonds, and when Monsieur came over to hang out, the children played dress-up in women's clothes.

As a young man, the prince enjoyed attending parties and balls in female attire, although it was the notion of flamboyance, no matter the disguise, that most intrigued him. Philippe was as notorious for his shepherdess costume as he was for his exotic regalia as the king of Persia.

Monsieur was raised to defer to his older brother in all things. Although they played together, Philippe was always supposed to lose to Louis. Only through his complete obeisance to the king, who was clearly their mother's favorite, could Monsieur earn her love. Unlike his athletic brother, he was also averse to any physical exercise. Small wonder, since he was not permitted to outperform Louis on the tennis court or in the saddle. His second wife, Elisabeth Charlotte of the Palatinate (Liselotte), once wrote, "Were it not for war, [Monsieur] never in his life would have mounted a horse." Philippe's penchant for cross-dressing and his homosexual affairs did not impact his bravery on the battlefield or his skill as a military strategist. He literally dressed to kill, dripping with diamonds and silken ribbons, his face painted and powdered, and he forswore a hat when he rode into the fray because it would crush his wig. In 1667, Philippe distinguished himself in the War of Devolution, in which Louis' armies overran those of the Hapsburg-controlled Spanish Netherlands and the Franche-Comté region. Louis claimed a right to those territories on behalf of his queen, because Marie-Thérèse's renunciation of the Spanish throne prior to their marriage had been contingent upon a dowry that had never been paid.

And in 1677, Philippe would lead an army of thirty thousand to defeat William III of Orange at the Battle of Cassel, proving that he was hardly craven or inept in the field. Although Monsieur had participated in other campaigns, Cassel was the only time Louis permitted his brother to cover himself in military glory; jealous of Philippe's success, the king kept him home during subsequent expeditions.

Excessively vain and fastidious about his toilette throughout his life, Monsieur would spend hours at his dressing table, deliberating over which rosette or plume should adorn his hat, and he hated to soil his clothes or expose his skin to the sun. Philippe was also fascinated by the details and distinctions of protocol and etiquette, which his brother had transformed from an issue of common courtesy into a political strategy. Louis XIV had learned much from the ramifications of the Fronde and from the reign of his father, whose own relatives committed high treason by fomenting rebellion.

Never again would the nobility, let alone the royal family, have the opportunity to stage a coup. If they desired Louis' favor, they would have to remain at court, where he could keep an eye on them, and they would be too busy arguing over the arcana of Louis' new protocols to raise an army.

Nevertheless, Philippe always expected special treatment from his older brother. He was primarily dependent upon Louis' largesse to support his extravagant lifestyle; yet the king didn't mind footing Philippe's bills, because he preferred that everyone at court focus all their time and spend all their money on inconsequential pastimes. Monsieur appreciated the subsidy, and enjoyed his untold hours of leisure, but resented his exclusion from matters of state and international diplomacy. Because he feared that history would repeat itself, the monarch never awarded his younger brother a governorship nor permitted him a meaningful role in the military. From Louis' perspective, Philippe need only look to him for his happiness; and so Monsieur was kept idle, leaving him (and everyone else at the Bourbon court) with plenty of time for his morals to stray into all manner of indulgence. According to Cardinal Mazarin, "Monsieur does nothing [and] knows nothing."

Scholars of previous generations have posited that Anne and her chief minister, Cardinal Mazarin, deliberately encouraged Philippe's effeminate tendencies, as if an interest in frippery and diamonds would somehow neutralize him politically, or check any machismo outbursts of sibling rivalry, such as plotting to depose his brother. But this argument fails to acknowledge that until Louis XIV fathered a son—and the king's marriage would not take place until 1660—Philippe was the heir apparent. Not only that, during Monsieur's adolescence, he evinced an attraction to certain ladies of the court; in 1658, he even had a mistress. Also, in an cra where little boys traditionally wore dresses until they were between the ages of four and six, and where men's attire was just as elegant as women's, where males *also* painted their faces and enjoyed the playful application of *mouches* or decorative patches to disguise the lingering scars of small pox, the young prince's passion for fashion would not have been viewed as particularly outré. Until, of course, it *did* become a subject of discussion—but only because it was connected to his disruptively flamboyant behavior with a clique of gay men at court and it began to affect the success of his marriage.

When his cousin "Mademoiselle," Anne Marie Louise d'Orléans, duchesse de Montpensier, returned to court in 1657 after an absence of some years, she was shocked to find Monsieur had changed little in the years she'd been gone. While Louis had matured, Philippe was still pranking his mother's ladies-in-waiting and splashing about in the river with them like one of the girls.

Monsieur's interest in women's clothing and accoutrements notwithstanding, the issue of his sexuality became apparent around 1658, when he was seventeen or eighteen years old and had his first homosexual encounter. Rumors spread through the Bourbon court that Cardinal Mazarin had introduced the prince to his own nephew, Jules Mancini, duc de Nevers. Mazarin's family were native Italians, and in France homosexuality was nicknamed the "Italian vice," as well as *le goût abominable* (the abominable preference). Homosexuality was also considered a sin and a crime punishable by death, but because this "vice" was believed to be confined to France's first two Estates (the clergy and the nobility), whose social privileges were sacrosanct, the death penalty for sodomy was rarely invoked.

Although no hookup between Monsieur and the duc de Nevers can be confirmed, the prince may have had some form of a sexual relationship with the duc de Candale, and he did commence a lifelong attachment in 1658 with an avowed homosexual, Philippe de Lorraine-Armagnac. A member of the House of Guise, the Chevalier de Lorraine held the rank of *prince étranger* (foreign prince) at the French court, because his cousin was the duc de Lorraine. The chevalier's lofty status enabled Monsieur to promote him within his household and retain him in his entourage without creating a scandal or offending anyone's sensibilities regarding the court's rigid protocol as to who was permitted to wait upon a prince of the blood.

At the Bourbon court, Monsieur became known as "one whose heart could never be won by woman." Instead he was the queen bee of a coterie of gay and bisexual noblemen that also included Armand de Gramont; the arrogant and Machiavellian comte de

Guiche; and the marquis d'Effiat, Antoine Coiffier, who began his service in Philippe's household as his captain of the chase and remained a cherished member of his entourage until Monsieur's death in 1701. The marquis d'Effiat was a relation of Henri Coiffier de Ruzé, marquis de Cinq Mars, the *mignon* who had been Philippe's father's *favori*, and who was executed for treason in 1642. The degree to which Philippe was ruled by his *mignons* became an embarrassment. The haughty and charismatic comte de Guiche not only palled about with Monsieur, he literally pushed him around, on one occasion shoving him in the middle of a ball, in the presence of the entire court.

In 1658, Monsieur also began indulging in another of his passions: that of home improvement. That year, he purchased the Château de Saint-Cloud, ten kilometers west of Paris. He immediately undertook the transformation of what had been a small villa into the grand palace that would become his favorite residence, eventually employing Mansart and Le Nôtre, two of the geniuses who redesigned the château and gardens of Versailles for his brother.

Until the death in 1660 of his uncle Gaston, Philippe was technically styled as "le Petit Monsieur." And with no surviving male heirs to inherit the dukedom of Orléans, which was traditionally the birthright of the oldest of the king's younger brothers, Gaston's demise meant not only that Philippe would henceforth be called Monsieur, but also that he would inherit his uncle's title as duc d'Orléans. Upon Gaston's death, Philippe also inherited the subsidiary titles of duc de Valois and duc de Chartres—which during his lifetime would be bestowed upon his sons—as well as the lordship of Montargis. However, the appanage—a title's real estate and revenues granted by the king—was not customarily awarded until the time of the appanagist's marriage. Louis was a stickler for etiquette. And Monsieur had no bride on the horizon. No wife, no income, although His Majesty did permit Monsieur to assume their late uncle's titles before he was formally entitled to acquire Gaston's appanage.

Philippe was quite the eligible bachelor, but Anne of Austria's first priority was to marry off his older brother. Henrietta Maria, the exiled queen of England and sister of Louis XIII, who had fled her adopted homeland during the civil war and received sanctuary from the French court, had dropped numerous hints about wedding her youngest child, Henriette-Anne, to Louis XIV, but Louis had never looked upon his cousin as anything more than a scrawny poor relation. The king was then a cocky seventeen-year-old, and was not only uninterested in his skinny, impoverished cousin who could (at the time) offer nothing to France, but he haughtily dismissed her as a little girl. With the six-year age gap, he had a point; she was barely eleven.

In any event, the queen mother had her eye and heart on a Spanish match instead, hoping to unite her son with her own niece, the daughter of Philip IV and Elisabeth of France. On June 9, 1660, the king of France wed his first cousin on both sides, Maria Theresa, the infanta of Spain, a pious flaxen blonde. Marie-Thérèse, as she was called thereafter, would never manage to become proficient in French and would eventually bear Louis six children, only one of whom survived to adulthood.

With Louis successfully married, it was Philippe's turn to be sacrificed on the altar of matrimony. A match with Gaston's daughter, his formidable first cousin, styled at court as "Mademoiselle," was a nonstarter. Several years his senior, the immensely wealthy Anne Marie Louise d'Orléans had initially viewed herself as *Louis'* intended bride, when the king was little more than a boy. But she had supported the rebels during the Fronde. On July 6, 1652, she ordered the Bastille's cannons to be fired upon the army of Turenne (which at that time guarded Paris on behalf of the crown), in order for the rebellious prince de Condé to enter the capital. All hope of wedding the monarch died with the sound of the explosion. Cardinal Mazarin was said to have remarked, "With that cannon, Mademoiselle has shot her husband."

Even though the Fronde had ended in 1653, why the cardinal and Anne of Austria still believed that Mademoiselle might make a good wife for the queen mother's younger son defies logic. In any event, Mademoiselle declined the offer, stating that Philippe was too much of a mama's boy. The more she saw of him, the more she realized he wouldn't care for anything but his own beauty and his glamorous wardrobe; nor would he ever distinguish himself as a leader of men.

So Anne of Austria went to plan B and approached her sister-in-law. The exiled English queen had failed in her effort to unite her daughter with Louis XIV, but the king's younger brother would be an excellent consolation prize! And given Henriette-Anne's background and prospects, Monsieur was likely the best the princess could do.

Fought between 1642 and 1651, the English Civil War pitted the crown and its royalist, or cavalier, sympathizers against the "Roundheads," or Parliamentarians, who sought to give Parliament control over the sovereign's administration of the realm. The war had torn apart the English royal family when Henrietta, as she was called then, was only a toddler.

In 1644, shortly after Henrietta's baptism into the Anglican faith at Exeter Cathedral, leaving her under the care of her governess, Lady Dalkeith, her mother fled to France, receiving sanctuary from her nephew Louis XIV. The following year, when Exeter surrendered to the besieging Roundheads, Lady Dalkeith brought Henrietta to Oatlands Palace in Surrey. They remained there, despite orders from the Commons (as the House of Commons was then known), to bring the little girl to St. James's Palace in London to join her siblings Henry and Elizabeth.

On July 25, 1646, Lady Dalkeith bravely donned a disguise as a humpbacked ragamuffin. She sneaked her charge (resentfully dressed as an urchin boy named Pierre) out of Oatlands, sailing with little Henrietta for France, so that the princess could be reunited with her mother. The exiled queen of England, a Roman Catholic, became determined to raise little Henriette d'Angleterre, as the French called her, in her own religion. With Charles I then a prisoner of the Scots, he could not prevent it. Soon after her arrival in Paris, the child was also given a middle name. As a compliment to the French king's mother, Anne of Austria, the English princess would now be known as Henriette-Anne, although nearly everyone who was close to her would call her by the affectionate nickname Minette.

She and her mother still had to contend with deprivations, because the Fronde was sapping the Bourbon treasury as well; Louis XIII's niece, Mademoiselle, described the hardships that befell even the royal family: lack of bed hangings, linens, clothes, and food.

Nonetheless, Minette was a darling of the French court, charming her Bourbon cousins and their vast entourages when, as a nine-year-old, she made her maiden appearance as Erato, the Muse of Love and Poetry, in a ballet to celebrate the carnival of 1653. Even then, Monsieur, who was four years her senior, enjoyed dressing up as a girl and painting his face with makeup and *mouches*. At one court ball the pair of them wore identical costumes as *paysannes de Bresses*, in silver tissue skirts trimmed with rose-colored ribbons, black velvet stomachers, and hats adorned with pink, black, and white plumes.

Already admired for her endearing charm and sweet disposition, by the time Minette came of age, she was also an acknowledged beauty, with a complexion described as roses-and-jasmine, an enviably tall and slender figure, chestnut-colored hair, cornflower-blue eyes, rosy lips, and a dazzling smile that revealed a mouth full of small, straight white teeth in an era of horrendous dentistry. Minette's perfection was marred only by a slightly long face, and a minor spinal deformity that she was able to conceal with the cut of her garments: one shoulder was higher than the other and she walked with a slight limp.

Her sloped shoulder wasn't what made Henriette-Anne less marriageable. Her father had been executed by Oliver Cromwell and her oldest brother, Charles, the putative sovereign of England and Scotland, had been on the run for years, living on the Continent in exile and penury and fighting to reclaim his crown, a king without a kingdom.

However, rumors swirled about the French court that there was some interest in wedding Minette, both from the Grand Prince of Tuscany and from Charles Emmanuel, the Duke of Savoy. Nothing came of either prospect, due to her own status as an exile.

Finally, in the spring of 1660, the Convention Parliament proclaimed Charles II England's lawful monarch dating from the time of his father's execution on January 30, 1649, and the House of Stuart was restored to the throne. Suddenly, at sixteen, Minette was a very eligible princess.

Louis XIV began to taunt his brother on his haste to "wed the bones of the Holy Innocent," a reference to their cousin's extreme thinness. But before Monsieur's appanage was on the horizon—despite his protests of love for Minette—he had not thought much of her. Two years earlier, after Mazarin scolded him for insulting Henriette-Anne over a matter of royal precedence, Philippe had retorted, "We have come to a fine state of affairs when people like that, who owe their bread to us, go in before us. Why don't they go live somewhere else?"

On November 22, 1660, Minette was in England visiting her brothers and her sister, Mary, the Princess of Orange, widow of the ruler of the Dutch Republic. Charles had not seen his youngest sister for years and was astonished by her beauty, poise, and sweet solicitousness for his welfare. Charles II fell madly in love with her, and although their relationship never crossed the border into incest, their mutual feelings ran exceptionally deep. As their correspondence reflects, the bond was much stronger than an ordinary fraternal one. Although Charles would never be faithful to his own wife, and would have passionate, and lengthy, extramarital affairs, as well as countless one-night stands, many believe the great love of his life was his sister Minette. She was the woman who understood him best, and whom he most wanted to cherish and protect. Charles openly admitted that he could deny his sister nothing.

Their mother had made the journey to England as well, in an effort to prevent the Duke of York from announcing his marriage to one of Mary's former ladies-in-waiting, a commoner named Anne Hyde, who was the daughter of Charles's chancellor. While they were across the Channel, Minette received France's official request for her hand on behalf of Philippe, duc d'Anjou (Louis XIV would not *formally* grant Monsieur the title of duc d'Orléans until May 10, 1661).

Anne of Austria was delighted with Monsieur's choice, declaring that nothing made her happier than to see her younger son wed so well, especially to the sweet, gentle princess she loved like a daughter. Henrietta Maria was thrilled; she had shared every day of Minette's life since their reunion, and now her child need never leave France.

If his sister was pleased by it, then Charles II was happy about the match, too. But their cousin, Prince Rupert of the Rhine, who was also a grandson of England's James I, proposed a union with the Holy Roman Emperor instead. Tempting, certainly, but Charles believed that a marriage between Minette and Monsieur was the alliance that was in the best interests for both kingdoms.

However, because the cousins were related within the proscribed degree of consanguinity, Henriette-Anne and Philippe had to wait for the necessary papal dispensation. Consequently, they did not sign their marriage contract until March 30, 1661, formalizing the document at the Palais Royal, which would become their primary residence as a married couple, with Philippe's beloved Saint-Cloud as their countryside retreat. Charles II promised his sister an enormous dowry of eight hundred and forty thousand pounds, plus an additional twenty thousand pounds for wedding expenses. The princess was also awarded an annuity of forty thousand livres from Louis XIV, plus the Château de Montargis for use as a private residence. For a girl who had relied upon the charity of her Bourbon cousins for much of her childhood, her marriage might not have guaranteed her happiness, but it gave her three homes.

The royal wedding took place at noon inside Henrietta Maria's chapel at the Palais Royal on March 31, 1661. It was an intimate affair; only select members of the Bourbon court witnessed the cousins exchange their marriage vows as sixteen-year-old Henriette d'Angleterre became Madame, la duchesse d'Orléans. The modest ceremony was hardly the flamboyant spectacle one might have expected from the twenty-year-old bridegroom. That evening, the newlyweds dined with the sovereigns and their respective mothers. The wedding was announced to the public with the usual hyperbole in poetry and song, uniting the lilies of France with England's rose. The noted fabulist Jean de La Fontaine penned a paean to the nuptial couple, expressing the hope that the marriage would be blissful and last forever. The poem would turn out to be as fanciful as "The Grasshopper and the Ant."

When Philippe was younger, Anne of Austria had worried about his dissolute friends, avowed homosexuals or bisexuals, led by his vain and manipulative boon companion, Guy Armand de Gramont, the comte de Guiche. These *mignons* had the malleable Philippe wrapped around their fingers, certain that if he ever rose to power, they would be able to dominate him for personal, financial, and material gain. Concerned that the relationship between her son and de Guiche was bound to end in scandal, the queen mother ordered that under no circumstances was Monsieur permitted to give the comte a private audience. But issuing a directive to her son's household and enforcing it were two different things. The two men continued to enjoy a liaison.

Anne had hoped that marriage to a beautiful, high-spirited young wife would cure Philippe of his homosexual proclivities. But what neither Monsieur nor his mother could have imagined was that it was *Henriette-Anne* who would eventually embark upon an extramarital flirtation with the devilishly handsome de Guiche! Even before Minette's marriage, the 2nd Duke of Buckingham had prophesied that the comte would fall in love with her, although for the longest time she remained utterly clueless, despite de Guiche's hints, that *she* was the woman for whom he hopelessly pined in secret. Gallant, brave, studly, and supremely confident, the comte was one of the Bourbon court's greatest playboys—among the most licentious bees within a hive of promiscuity.

To the relief of their mothers, the royal marriage between Henriette-Anne and Philippe started out fairly well. The couple did share common interests. They were both passionate about fine art, amassing an impressive and prestigious collection of paintings. Both the duc and duchesse enjoyed designing formal gardens; Philippe oversaw Le Nôtre's improvements at Saint-Cloud, and Minette created a water garden at the Palais Royal. During the early weeks of their marriage, their satellite court became known as *the* place to have a good time without restraint—at banquets, supper parties, musical entertainments, gambling, and balls. At first, Monsieur was proud of the way everyone at court admired his wife for her beauty, wit, discriminating taste, and sparkling conversation.

His former childhood playmate, the abbé de Choisy, rhapsodized, "Never was there a Princess so fascinating, and so ready to please all who approached her. . . . Her whole person seemed full of charm. You felt interested in her, you loved her without being able to help yourself. . . . She had all the wit necessary to make a woman charming, and . . . all the talent necessary for conducting important affairs. . . . But at the Court of our young King in those days, pleasure was the order of the day, and to be charming was enough."

During the early 1660s, Louis XIV's court was filled with glamorous and giddy young people who had little to do but have fun, partaking in the lavish entertainments, and indulging in flirtations and sexual intrigues. Some of these liaisons were harmless—little more than gallantries, or courtly role-playing. Other seductions were high-stakes extramarital flings, involving the biggest player in the realm: the Sun King himself.

No one could have guessed this kind of trouble was brewing from watching Louis and Minette interact in years past. In fact, years earlier, Louis had publicly insulted Minette, refusing to lead her out for the first dance at a ball, and stubbornly insisting that he didn't dance with little girls. To the mortification of the respective queen mothers, the king chose instead to dance with one of Cardinal Mazarin's beautiful nieces.

Fast-forward several years from that embarrassing evening. During the summer of 1661, just a few months after the wedding of Philippe and Henriette-Anne, while the court was at Fontainebleau, the duchesse d'Orléans commenced a flirtation with her own brother-in-law. At the time, Louis' queen, Marie-Thérèse, was pregnant, shunning the delights of the court—which she had never really participated in to begin with. Conservative, devoutly religious, and not fluent in French, Marie-Thérèse always preferred to remain in her rooms praying or playing cards with her dwarves, attendants in her Spanish retinue who had amused her since childhood, and with whom she was more comfortable than the frankly sexual French courtiers. Now that Her Majesty was carrying the hopes of France within her womb, there was no thought of her dancing till dawn, or partaking of jouncing carriage rides, or joining her husband's hunting excursions.

Consequently, Minette, being the second-highest lady in the kingdom, became the ranking woman at court functions. Madame's natural beauty, her grace and enthusiasm, and her love of dancing, music, theater, and adventure made her the ideal person to lead the gaiety.

Flattered by all the attention she received, the vivacious Henriette-Anne was often surrounded by the queen's ladies-in-waiting as well as her own attendants—known as her "flower garden"—attracting a swarm of gallant cavaliers. Madame was soon collecting hearts like trophies.

And the most fascinated man of all was the king. He became smitten with his teenage cousin/sister-in-law. Louis' partiality for Minette was abundantly clear: He visited her daily, he invited her to lead the dances with him at formal balls, and soon they were taking long walks together and enjoying lengthy nocturnal carriage rides in his vast park. A fearless equestrienne, Minette shared the king's hunts. She sat beside him during moonlit gondola rides on the canal, accompanied only by the sweet strains of Jean-Baptiste Lully's violin serenades. They planned and costarred in fetes, balls, and masquerades. Louis and his sister-in-law exchanged meaningful looks, furtive whispers, and indiscreet notes. Courtiers shook their heads in regret that His Majesty hadn't noticed that Minette had blossomed before fettering himself to the Spanish infanta, with whom he shared so little in common. He and Minette might both have been spared far from perfect marriages.

The attraction was not only mutual, it could not be concealed from their respective spouses. Monsieur was openly insulted by what looked like Madame's public cuckoldry of him, but his reprimands fell on deaf ears. Minette was simply enjoying herself, just like everyone else at court was doing, including Monsieur. She was young, beautiful, and popular. Marie-Thérèse was especially wounded by the king's flirtation with Minette. Sadly, the queen was in love with her husband, even though her affection was not returned. And the duchesse d'Orléans was too naive or self-absorbed or unhappy in her own marriage to empathize with her sister-in-law.

Both Marie-Thérèse and Philippe complained to Anne of Austria about the relationship between the king and Minette. Had it blossomed from flirtation into indiscretion? Whether or not the pair had taken the leap into adultery was almost beside the point, because their friendship had the appearance of impropriety, and their behavior had already hurt, humiliated, and angered their spouses.

And in the seventeenth century, when someone married into a family, their sibling-in-law was called brother or sister; the notion of enjoying a full-blown extramarital affair with them was considered as incestuous as sleeping with their own blood sister or brother. If Louis and Minette had crossed the line, it would become an unfathomable scandal.

Within four months of their wedding ceremony, the Orléans marriage was in a shambles. Minette's *affaire du coeur* with the comte de Guiche, which she began later in 1661, after the king lost interest in her and she was smarting from the rebuff, was carried out in full view of the court. Her liaison with Louis was just as indiscreet, intensifying Monsieur's jealousy of the king, and tipping his bisexuality further onto the homosexual spectrum. Was his overtly flamboyant behavior an act of revenge on his wife and his brother, or was Philippe merely seeking solace in the arms of his manipulative *mignons*?

The queen mother postponed her thoughts of retiring to the convent of Val-de-Grâce. For the sake of the queen and the duc d'Orléans, someone had to keep a watchful eye on Louis and Minette. At first Anne of Austria had not taken Marie-Thérèse's complaints too seriously, but when Anne herself began to fear that the king had become intimate with his sister-in-law, or was about to, she scolded the pair of them, warning of the scandal that would come crashing down upon the entire family if they allowed their hormones to do the thinking.

Neither Louis nor Minette heeded Anne's warning to stop behaving as though they were lovers. The cousins were having too much fun and adored each other's company. Louis arrogantly reminded his mother that as he was king in his majority, he no longer needed to obey her. Madame ignored her mother-in-law's urging to modify her conduct. Anne even raised the matter with Minette's mother, asking Henrietta Maria to talk some sense into the girl.

The last thing Anne of Austria needed was for her niece the queen to write to her father, the king of Spain, complaining about her husband's insensitivity and potentially adulterous conduct. Finally, Anne changed tack. If she couldn't compel Louis and Minette to nip their blossoming romance in the bud, she could at least attempt to screen it. From then on, Louis' visits to Madame would be made in the guise of paying court to one of her maids of honor, a lovely, sixteen-year-old blond naïf, Louise de La Vallière.

The plan worked better than the queen mother had hoped. Sort of. Louis fell madly in love with little Louise within days of meeting her, and in 1661, he made her his first *maîtresse en titre*, or official royal mistress, a formal position at the French court. Having been thrown over for Louise, and jealous of her own maid to the point of vindictiveness, Madame now understood what it felt like to wear the queen's shoes; both she and Marie-Thérèse were brokenhearted by the king's new infatuation. And yet, Her Majesty naively continued to believe that her sister-in-law was her true rival, unaware that the king's dalliance with Minette of only a few months' duration had been overtaken by his passion for Louise.

When she matched Minette with Philippe, Anne of Austria had been right about one thing: At least Henriette-Anne was stylish and attractive enough to encourage her younger son to perform his marital duty, even if he was also sleeping with his *mignons*. In March 1662, Madame bore the first of four children, a girl who was baptized Marie Louise. In the pain of childbirth, sorely disappointed by the baby's gender, Minette is said to have exclaimed, "[T]hrow her into the river!" Marie Louise would always be her papa's favorite, despite the rumors swirling about the court that the duc d'Orléans could not possibly have fathered the child—and that Marie Louise's paternity was a result of the efforts of either the comte de Guiche or the king himself. However, not only was the infatuation between Minette and the king long over and her flirtation with de Guiche probably never consummated, but Philippe never disavowed Marie Louise.

That summer, Monsieur and Madame, with his retinue of a thousand and hers of only forty-three, moved from the Tuileries to their permanent residence at the vast Palais Royal, which from then on would be the seat of the Orléans dynasty. Philippe's popularity in the capital made Louis—who distrusted the Parisians—nervous.

With the queen *enceinte* once more and in voluntary seclusion from the social whirl, Madame resumed her place as the cynosure of the court; parties, excursions, dances—everyone yearned to be in Minette's orbit. Too pleased with herself and by the admiration she excited among courtiers of both sexes (incurring Monsieur's extreme jealousy), she formed a clique of mean girls (and guys) who skewered the queen and queen mother with their disrespect. Where was the sweet-tempered girl who had captivated her own brother Charles only three years earlier? Anne of Austria expressed her regrets to her niece, Mademoiselle, about wedding Philippe to such a flibbertigibbet as Minette. If only Mlle. de Montpensier had agreed to marry Monsieur instead, "[Y]ou would have lived on better terms with me, and my son would have been only too fortunate to have a wife as sensible as you are."

As the months and years wore on, Philippe sought to punish his wayward wife for her perceived infidelities, especially with the AC/DC de Guiche, who previously had been Monsieur's bosom buddy. After the king began to indulge his passion for Louise de La Vallière in the summer of 1661, the flirtation between Madame and the comte de Guiche heated up. He once disguised himself as a fortune-teller in order to be able to visit Minette's sickbed without being turned away. She was immensely entertained, and all the more amused when she realized that she was the only one who was clever enough to penetrate his disguise. Unfortunately for Madame's reputation and Monsieur's ego, Minette and de Guiche's names were linked in popular songs and satires that spread well beyond the walls of the court. It didn't matter to people whether the pair had really committed adultery; their mutual infatuation was indiscreet enough to warrant speculation.

Despite his behaving even more indiscreetly with handsome young courtiers, Monsieur retaliated for his wife's flirtation with the comte de Guiche. One by one, Philippe began depriving Minette of her confidantes until she became horribly lonely. He visited her bed infrequently, but often enough to impregnate her eight times in nine years. She suffered a number of miscarriages but bore a son in July 1664, who was given the title of duc de Valois. Tragically for the *famille* Orléans, the little duc succumbed to convulsions in 1666, just hours after his baptism. The court was already in mourning for Anne of Austria, who had died that January, but Henriette-Anne was completely devastated by her son's death. It must have stung when Philippe's greatest lament over the demise of his heir was the loss of the hundred-and-fifty-thousand-livre allowance the child had received from the king, a sum that Monsieur was eager to maintain.

Monsieur's biographer Nancy Nichols Barker mentions that *both* parents appeared to have recovered from their son's death with remarkable velocity, as their own court soon resumed its whirlwind of entertainments. But they should not be condemned too quickly. During the seventeenth century, the philosophy regarding the deaths of young children was different. With the prevalence of disease and poor hygienic conditions, *survival* was the exception, and it was always hoped that more children would be conceived to replace those who had died too soon. Additionally, Louis XIV forbade death to hang over his court. Only immediate members of the royal family were permitted to expire within its precincts, and afterward, the usual amusements were to resume as quickly as possible.

Throughout the first half of the 1660s, the Orléans spouses continued to practice their separate infidelities. De Guiche's liaison with Minette lasted for the better part of four years, ending only when the comte was banished from the court in 1665 for offending the king. Even so, the following year, a pamphlet titled *Amours de Madame et du comte de Guiche* was disseminated in Holland. Daniel de Cosnac, bishop of Valence and a member of Madame's household, endeavored to buy up every copy, but Monsieur somehow managed to see one anyway, and the predictable marital fireworks erupted.

Meanwhile, Philippe hypocritically indulged in his own adulterous betrayals, mortifying Minette with his flamboyant passion for the penniless Chevalier de Lorraine, the younger son of the former grand *écuyer* of France, an office equivalent to England's master of the horse. A contemporary described the chevalier, a confirmed bachelor who became formally attached to the Orléans household in 1666, as *"Séduisant, brutal et dénué de scrupules"*—"seductive, brutal, and devoid of scruples." The duc was growing increasingly self-indulgent in every aspect of his life. Despite his victorious campaigns, Monsieur eventually grew bored with soldiering and sieges and became more interested in decorating his tent. While he was away on a military campaign, Henriette-Anne suffered a miscarriage at Saint-Cloud that nearly killed her. Hearing how ill she was, Philippe sped to her side and remained with her until she recuperated. Once Minette was safely out of danger, he returned to the front, where he cast off his malaise and proved his merit at the Siege of Lille in the summer of 1667.

Although Philippe's solicitousness for Henriette-Anne was admirable, to her chagrin he resumed his extramarital relations with the Chevalier de Lorraine. Lorraine preferred women sexually, but had no qualms about gratifying any of Monsieur's pleasures in exchange for influence and largesse.

The Palais Royal became the scene of two warring camps, with each spouse intent upon inflicting the maximum embarrassment on the other. Monsieur dressed in full drag during Mardi Gras balls and offered the chevalier his hand to lead him onto the parquet. When the dance was over, he took his seat with the ladies of the court. Philippe had become the stereotype painted by the eighteenth-century courtier and diarist, the duc de Saint-Simon, of "[a] little man propped up on heels like stilts; gotten up like a woman with rings, bracelets, and jewels; a long wig, black and powdered, spread out before; ribbons wherever he could put them; and exuding perfumes of all kinds."

On August 9, 1668, Charles II sent his sister a letter by private courier, stating, "I thinke you have taken a very good resolution not to live so with [Lorraine], but that, when there offers a good occasion, you may ease your selfe of such a rival, and by the carracter I have of him, there is hopes he will find out the occasion himselfe, which, for M^r's sake, I wish may be quickly." Minette was in the process of obtaining her husband's compromising correspondence with the chevalier. In the autumn of 1669, she would ultimately present the letters to Louis with the hope of discrediting Monsieur in his brother's eyes.

Minette and Philippe's last child, Anne Marie, was born on August 23, 1669, and baptized the following year. Yet each pregnancy, the miscarriages as well as those the duchesse was able to carry to term, took a tremendous toll on Madame's health. Her figure was always as delicate as a doll's, but she was now growing even thinner and becoming frail. And since 1667, Minette had complained of an intermittent, intense pain on her left side. Her emotional well-being plummeted in the late summer of 1669, after her mother was found dead on September 10 at the Château de Colombes, her residence since Henriette-Anne's wedding to Monsieur. Henrietta Maria had been suffering from a fever and insomnia for several weeks, but that was not what killed her. Instead, it was the treatment offered to her by her physicians, who insisted she ingest what turned out to be an overdose of opiates. As if Minette didn't need enough reasons to resent her husband, Philippe immediately rushed to claim Henrietta Maria's possessions under French law. Thanks to the intervention of Charles II, he received nothing.

In January 1670, the duchesse d'Orléans was finally able to prevail upon Louis XIV to imprison the greatest thorn in her side, Philippe's grasping and manipulative lover. Monsieur had cajoled Louis for too many favors on Lorraine's behalf. He even had the nerve to ask his brother to grant the chevalier the rents from a pair of abbeys that had fallen vacant. On January 30, the king had his captain of the guards burst into Monsieur's apartments in the palace of Saint-Germain, seize the Chevalier de Lorraine, and escort him to the prison of Pierre-Encise near Lyons. Livid over Louis' mistreatment of his *mignon*, Monsieur vented his wrath on Madame, publicly cursing her out, and vindictively hauling her off to his country estate at Villers-Cotterêts. During their twenty-five-day enforced exile from court, Philippe continued to berate his wife, especially after he learned that Louis had asked Minette what she intended to do about her untenable situation. To Monsieur, his brother's question sounded like encouragement to neglect her marital responsibilities, a suggestion perhaps to abandon Philippe because even an estrangement would be preferable to a living hell.

The chevalier's absence created a new source of marital tension between the battling Orléans spouses. According to Mademoiselle, they had daily rows over it. She was so appalled at the violence of Monsieur's rage that she was compelled to remind her cousin that these vicious arguments were detrimental to his children.

Insisting that the chevalier had always been devoted to Louis,

Monsieur refused to return to court until the Sun King permitted Lorraine to brighten his doorstep again. Instead, the king dispatched the chevalier to a *more* impenetrable location, the infamous Château d'If, a Mediterranean island-fortress (where Dumas would later imprison his fictional Count of Monte Cristo), forbidding him to communicate with Monsieur. Louis finally banished the chevalier to Rome, after he boasted that he could convince his lover to divorce Madame.

The rupture between the two Bourbon brothers over Philippe's favorite became a subject of international gossip. Madame was viewed with universal sympathy as the injured party. After an especially painful scene where Monsieur dredged up Minette's previous indiscretions, she told her friend Madame de Saint-Chaumont, "So if in the past I made some mistake, why did he not go ahead and strangle me then when he claimed I was deceiving him? To suffer like this now, and for nothing, I cannot stand it." She confided that Monsieur continued to blame her for the chevalier's banishment, and remained petulant over the king's refusal to grant Lorraine the pensions he'd sought for him.

Louis temporarily reconciled the battling spouses, but then Monsieur eventually found another way to disrupt his wife's happiness.

Henriette-Anne had always been a cultured woman, numbering some of France's finest literary minds—La Fontaine, Voltaire, Racine—among her correspondents. Racine, who dedicated his play *Andromaque* to Minette, complimented her intelligence and thanked her for patronizing the arts, stating, "The court regards you as the arbiter of all that is delightful."

Madame also wrote often to her brother, and communicated as well with several high-ranking members of Charles's court, including the Earl of Arlington and the Villiers cousins, Charles's mistress Barbara Palmer and the 2nd Duke of Buckingham—the son of the 1st duke, George Villiers, who had become so passionately attached to Minette's mother-in-law, Anne of Austria. Although Henriette-Anne was born an English princess, she was raised in France and was barely able to read and write in her native tongue, communicating instead in fluent French. Many of Madame's letters, especially those to her brother and to the English ambassador Ralph Montagu, complain of her husband's preference for the Chevalier de Lorraine, whom she describes as "the man who is the cause of all my sorrows, past and present." She enumerates Philippe's cruel treatment of her, and his frequent humiliations of her in public. In 1669, Montagu confided to a colleague that Monsieur "takes pleasure in crossing his wife in everything."

That wife was a "woman of parts," as it was said then of intelligent, multitalented females. For years, her brother had hoped to broker an alliance with France, a kingdom that had so often been England's great nemesis. Charles acknowledged that Minette, whom Louis XIV also appreciated and loved for her brains as well as her beauty, was a better ambassador for both sides than any minister from either country.

Not only were the two kings first cousins, but Charles viewed the French as natural allies against one of England's other enemies— the Dutch. Of course, at the time, many of the European royals were interrelated. The provinces within the Dutch Republic known as the Spanish Netherlands (corresponding to present-day Belgium and Luxembourg) were ruled by Hapsburgs. Louis XIV's mother, Anne of Austria, who died in 1666, had been a Hapsburg. Charles and Minette's sister, Mary, who died of smallpox in 1660, had married the Protestant William II of Orange, the stadtholder, or ruling prince, of the Netherlands.

Nevertheless, economics was always thicker than blood. The Sun King viewed the Dutch as less of a threat than the English to his ambitions in the Spanish Netherlands, so he'd signed a defensive treaty with them in 1662.

The amity between Louis and Charles had cooled over issues of money, protocol, and sovereignty in the waters known as the narrow seas or Straits of Dover. And when Louis was obliged by the terms of this 1662 treaty to declare war on England, Charles went to war against the Dutch in 1665. Three years later, feeling no allegiance to Louis, even though their enemy had become his enemy, the Dutch signed the Triple Alliance. This 1668 pact between Holland, England, and Sweden was designed to limit French gains in the Spanish Netherlands. Louis was furious, but felt personally betrayed by Charles, because the English sovereign had pledged to conclude no treaties within the next twelve months without first informing him of his plans. So when Charles expressed an interest that same year to form an alliance with Louis, the French monarch was reluctant to trust him.

Enter Madame, the perfect minister without portfolio. Beginning in the autumn of 1668, brother and sister had begun to correspond, often in cipher. They kept the details of a prospective treaty between England and France such a secret that neither Colbert de Croissy, who was assigned to a special diplomatic mission at the Court of Saint James's, nor Ralph Montagu, the English envoy in Paris, was informed of them.

The initial bargaining chips that formed the basis for the treaty were thus: In exchange for helping Louis conquer the Dutch Republic, which the Sun King wished to claim for his Spanish Hapsburg queen as part of her unpaid dowry, Charles would abandon the Triple Alliance he had signed in 1668. If Louis' conquest was successful, Charles was to receive in return a number of profitable seaports that lay along one of Holland's major rivers.

Charles would also convert to Roman Catholicism—at a later, unspecified date—and would return his entire realm to the papal fold. The due date was characterized only with the spectacularly vague phrase "as soon as the welfare of the kingdom will permit," but the treaty did specify that the conversion would be done in exchange for two million crowns from Louis, a sum that would enable Charles to defray his military expenses and pay off some of his debts. The English monarch got the better end of this clause, receiving a huge payment from the French up front without having to name a specific date for his religious conversion.

Minette saw the treaty as a way to unite her brother and brother-in-law. And in the spring of 1670, when the sovereigns' negotiations reached a sticking point as to which would come first—Charles's announcement of his conversion to popery or Louis' declaration of war against the Dutch—the Sun King proposed that the surest way to settle things was for Madame to appeal to Charles in person.

At this, Monsieur threw a violent tantrum, asserting all the rights of a husband by refusing to allow Minette to travel to

England without his permission. He was also peeved because he had not been made privy—nor would he be—to the diplomatic secrets between his wife and their respective sovereign brothers. Louis must have exerted a considerable amount of pressure on Philippe, because he finally relented—to a point. He insisted somewhat spitefully that she could go only as far as Dover—and limited the duration of her visit to no more than a few days. It was pure retaliation for Madame's insistence on the Chevalier de Lorraine's banishment.

Meanwhile, even as he endeavored to forestall her journey to London, Philippe insisted on a quid pro quo from his wife, urging her to request favors from Louis on the chevalier's behalf. By this point, Madame was complaining to one of her confidantes that "Monsieur now refuses to come near me, and hardly ever speaks to me, which, in all the quarrels we have had, has never happened before." Minette added that only Louis' gift of some additional revenues was able to mollify her husband's choler. She had begged the king never to permit the Chevalier de Lorraine to return to France, because things would only become worse for her.

In Lorraine's absence, Monsieur had begun to surround himself with a new coterie of vicious young *mignons*, even as he kept up the pressure on his brother and his wife to restore the chevalier to him. In April of 1670, Minette wrote to one of her frequent correspondents, Madame de Saint-Chaumont, that Monsieur even had the temerity to suggest that he "cannot love me, unless his favourite is allowed to form a third in our union. Since then, I have made him understand that, however much I might desire the Chevalier's return, it would be impossible to obtain it, and he has given up the idea, but, by making a noise about my journey to England, he hopes to show that he is master, and can treat me as ill in the Chevalier's absence as in his presence. This being his policy, he began to speak openly of our quarrels, refused to enter my room, and pretended to show that he could revenge himself for having been left in ignorance of these affairs, and make me suffer for what he calls the faults of the two Kings."

In an effort to make up for Philippe's hellacious behavior, including his efforts to prevent Madame from traveling to see her brother,

Louis gave Minette a massive sum of money for her household's travel expenses. Monsieur then insisted on accompanying her, although the French royal family journeyed with Minette no farther than Lille, but along the way he verbally abused his wife every chance they got, transforming their carriage rides into nightmares. On one occasion, during a conversation on astrology, Philippe declared viciously, "I have been told that I should have several wives; and given the condition Madame is in, I can well believe it."

On May 16, 1670, Henriette-Anne arrived on the English seacoast. Acting as France's emissary, on June 1 she formally completed the terms of what would come to be known as the Treaty of Dover (or the Secret Treaty of Dover—as the details of this pact were not revealed until long after the death of all parties involved). It was signed by Croissy, the French diplomat, and, on England's behalf, lords Arundel, Arlington, and Clifford, as well as Sir Richard Bellings.

The Secret Treaty contained details that enabled Charles II to remain, theoretically, faithful to the Triple Alliance, and also allowed him to retain his fidelity to the Treaty of Aix-la-Chapelle that he had recently signed with Spain, which more or less permitted him to have his cake and eat it, too. However, a second, very similarly worded treaty was negotiated as well—by the 2nd Duke of Buckingham, through traditional diplomatic channels. The later treaty, and not the one with which Minette was involved, was the instrument that would be made public. The second treaty, signed in December 1670, was a cover-up, a phony deal negotiated with France that specified the terms of the Anglo-French alliance against the Dutch, down to the number of ships and soldiers to be supplied by each side. Aware that this capitulation would infuriate his subjects, the lords deliberately omitted any mention of Charles's eventual conversion to Roman Catholicism from this document.

After the formalities of the Secret Treaty of Dover were concluded in May of 1670, Charles took the opportunity to squeeze as many celebrations as possible (including that of his fortieth birthday) into what remained of his sister's holiday. Minette finally had the opportunity to meet Charles's queen, the diminutive Catherine of Braganza, whose infertility issues her brother had chronicled in his letters across the Channel. Describing her sister-in-law to Mademoiselle, Minette found her "a very good woman, not handsome, but so kind and excellent that it was impossible not to love her."

At the end of her visit, Charles was loath to say farewell to his beloved sibling. Visibly weeping at her departure, he loaded her down with gifts, and flirtatiously begged one little jewel from her in exchange, angling for the person of Henriette-Anne's maid of honor Louise de Kéroualle, a doe-eyed virgin with a complexion like milk and a halo of dark curls. But Minette knew her brother was a rake and had promised Louise's family that she would look after their daughter. Pimping her out to the king of England was not what the Kéroualles had in mind.

(Or was it? After Minette's death, Louise would indeed end up at Charles's court—and, after much wrangling, in his bed—sent as a gift from Louis XIV, who all but planted the girl at Whitehall with the seventeenth-century equivalent of a wiretapping device between her legs. If the Secret Treaty of Dover couldn't compel King Charles to become a Catholic, Louise was the last weapon in France's arsenal. Many of the Francophobic English were certain that Louise de Kéroualle was a French spy. They were right. But whatever she learned at Charles's court had no impact on English foreign or domestic policy. He eventually made her Duchess of Portsmouth and ennobled their bastard son, creating him Duke of Richmond and Lennox in 1675.)

Although she'd tried to conceal her ailments from her brother, Minette had not been well during her sojourn in England. In April 1670, she'd begun to suffer from digestive problems that were so severe she could ingest nothing but milk. Right after her return to France, on June 26, she and Monsieur went to Saint-Cloud, where she complained of stomach pains and an ache in her side. The following day, she wrote her first letter in English to Thomas Clifford, the "C" in Charles II's C.A.B.A.L. of advisers, apologizing for her dreadful spelling and syntax. It was also the *last* letter she would pen in her native language. For the next few days Minette was ailing and so restless she took moonlit baths in the river to help her sleep.

On June 29, after drinking a glass of iced chicory water, Henriette-Anne suffered a sharp pain in her side. She cried out in anguish, immediately assuming that she must have been poisoned by her husband's lovers, the Chevalier de Lorraine and the marquis d'Effiat. She demanded an antidote for poison and asked that the chicory water be examined. The doctors treated her with their remedies for colic and poison (probably purgatives), but to no avail. They bled her from the foot, a traditional remedy for just about everything in those days, but that only made her worse.

As soon as the royal family heard the news of Madame's collapse, they rushed to her bedside at Saint-Cloud. Bishop Bossuet administered the last rites. On her deathbed, Henriette-Anne was said to have told her husband, "Alas! Monsieur, it is long since you have loved me; but that is unjust: I have never been unfaithful to you," while she assured Louis as they embraced, both weeping, "You are losing the truest servant you ever had."

According to Ralph Montagu, the English ambassador, Minette's final thoughts were of her brother, as she whispered to the envoy, "I have loved him better than life itself and now my only regret in dying is to be leaving him."

Only twenty-six years old, Henriette-Anne died between the hours of two and three in the morning on June 30, 1670. To dispel the myriad rumors that she had been poisoned, Louis XIV ordered her autopsy to be performed in public by a team of French and English physicians in the presence of at least a hundred onlookers. The doctors' formal report stated that the cause of death was "cholera morbus [gastroenteritis] caused by heated bile," the autopsy having revealed an abscess on her liver. Her stomach cavity was filled with "fermented bile," and her vital organs were gangrenous. Modern medical forensics suggest that the duchesse d'Orléans was felled by an acute infection causing peritonitis, following the perforation of a duodenal ulcer. Her lungs were also diseased, suggesting tuberculosis, the illness that killed her brother Henry, Duke of Gloucester, in 1660.

But at the time of Madame's death, many people disagreed with the physicians' findings. According to Louis XIV's nineteenth-century biographer John Abbott, the doctors had been bribed to sign the autopsy report. However, other accounts state that both the English and French doctors agreed with the findings, but believed that the autopsy had been so badly botched, it seemed "as if the surgeon's business were rather to hide the truth than to reveal it."

Abbott is the only biographer to mention the arrest of Monsieur Pernon, the controller of Minette's household. Louis XIV questioned him privately, offering him immunity if he revealed the sources of the poison that had killed Madame. Of course, a man who believes he may be executed for murder might say anything to absolve himself, so Pernon's statements should be taken with several grains of salt. He described a roundabout route that began with the Chevalier de Lorraine and the marquis d'Effiat, who had employed country gentlemen as unwitting intermediaries and mules to transport the poison to confederates of the marquis at Saint-Cloud. According to Pernon, it was the marquis d'Effiat who rubbed it along the inside of Minette's favorite drinking cup. Pernon assured the king that Monsieur himself knew nothing of the plot. According to Abbott, the interrogation went no further. Pernon was released. No one else was questioned or punished.

However, the anecdotes regarding a poison conspiracy were written years after the fact by those with no connection to the events or to the participants. And the chicory water that Madame ingested was mixed by her closest and most trusted servant, who also tested it by drinking from the same cup. But some of the English still believed the rumors of poisoning, including the Duke of Buckingham, who was all for declaring war on France.

Henriette-Anne was interred among the royalty of France at the Basilica of Saint Denis—by decree of Louis XIV, with all the pomp due to a crowned head. Ironically, Minette's burial ceremony was more extravagant than her wedding; it was attended by the highest clergy and nobility in France, as well as by several mourners from the general public. There were torches, candles, and incense. The Mass was chanted by the king's own musicians, a performance organized by the famous court composer Jean-Baptiste Lully. Minette's coffin was covered in cloth of gold edged with ermine and embroidered with the arms of her native and adopted kingdoms.

Her heart was removed to the convent of Val-de-Grâce and her entrails brought to the Church of the Celestins, according to the custom of burying a royal's viscera and vital organs separately. Henriette-Anne's body was taken by torchlight from Saint-Cloud to Saint Denis and laid alongside that of her mother in the crypt of Saint-Louis. Monsieur's guards watched over it night and day, and monks chanted Masses around the clock.

Charles II was disconsolate at the news of his beloved sister's demise. In a rare display of emotion, he shut himself into his bedroom for days, prostrate with grief. The great wit of the Stuart Restoration court, the Earl of Rochester, remarked that Henriette-Anne had died the most lamented person in both England and France, then quipped, "Since which time dying has been the fashion."

Louis' court lost some of its innocence after Minette's death. The years of her fey, cultivated presence corresponded to the lighthearted spring of the Sun King's reign. But once she was gone, it entered its sultry summer of soulless, vulgar dissipation—the era of the voluptuary, his mistress Athénais de Montespan. Louis never again danced in a court ballet, and for the next ten years these entertainments were abandoned entirely.

Monsieur clad himself in extravagant mourning attire, but according to eyewitnesses, he did not appear to be grieving the loss of his wife. The tears he'd shed during her final hours were soon dried. Upon Minette's death, Philippe seized her letters and the money that was supposed to have been distributed among her servants, fleeing with it to Paris. Such was the behavior of the man known as the founder of the House of Orléans, among the richest, if not the single wealthiest family in France. Because he is the ancestor of most modern Catholic royals, Philippe d'Orléans has also been called "the grandfather of Europe."

At the urging of Louis XIV, who was eager for his brother to father a male heir to continue the Orléans line, Monsieur remarried in 1671. His new bride was a nineteen-year-old Protestant German, Elisabeth Charlotte of the Palatinate—chosen after the duchesse de Montpensier, now styled as la Grande Mademoiselle, rejected him a second time. But Louis had raised the subject by inquiring of la Grande Mademoiselle whether she was interested in filling the "vacancy" created by the death of the former Madame, so it's little wonder she'd refused Monsieur.

Louis had rejected a number of other potential brides until he and Philippe settled on Liselotte, as the Palatine princess was known within her family. She was ultimately chosen by the king, and not by Monsieur, because Louis had wanted to secure the reversion of the elector's rights on the Palatinate.

Born in Heidelberg in 1652, Liselotte was the only daughter of the Elector Palatine, Charles I Louis, and his estranged wife, Charlotte of Hesse-Kassel. The child of a broken home, Liselotte was a short, dumpy blonde with a take-no-prisoners personality. Her mother had refused to recognize her father's divorce by fiat, and consequently would not move out of the family residence. Meanwhile, her father insisted on dwelling there with his morganatic second wife, a former lady-in-waiting to his first one. Luckily, Liselotte escaped some of this craziness by spending four formative years of her girlhood at the court of her aunt Sophia of Hanover, mother of the future King George I of England. She remained close to Sophia throughout her life, penning some fifty thousand letters to her from the French court.

On November 16, 1671, Liselotte was wed to Monsieur by proxy in the cathedral at Metz with the marshal Plessis-Praslin standing in for the groom. When she exited the cathedral, she was already the duchesse d'Orléans, although she had yet to see her husband. Monsieur rode forth from Paris to greet her, meeting her in his usual glittering splendor on the road between Châlons and Bellay. Stunned by his new bride's homeliness, Philippe is said to have lamented, "[H]ow shall I ever be able to sleep with her?"

On her arrival at the Bourbon court, Liselotte received a wedding gift from the sovereigns worth as much as her father collected in a year's revenue as Elector Palatine. Monsieur, too, received a large brevet, or financial gift, from Louis for the maintenance of the new Madame's household.

Liselotte, who converted to Catholicism upon her marriage, was a tremendous correspondent, and as such was a terrific chronicler of her age and of her brother-in-law's court. Although French was not her native tongue and she never lost her German accent, Liselotte was already fluent by the time she became Madame, and she spoke and wrote French better than many at the Bourbon court, including her husband. An earthy tomboy with a coarse sense of humor, she was known for her passion for hunting, her disdain for dancing, her brusque demeanor, and her snarkiness, never fearing to say to someone's face what others might only whisper behind his or her back, even when she was talking about—or to—the king's *maîtresses en titre*. Devoid of vanity, she described her appearance in self-deprecating terms: small eyes set in a broad face and a heavy jaw, the physiognomy of a "badger-cat-monkey," her nose a "badger's snout," and her weather-beaten complexion as "red as a crayfish" from the exertions of so much horseback riding outdoors. Liselotte was also highly unfashionable, another faux pas at the French court. She had no taste in clothes, and even less interest in them, an immense contrast to the first Madame, the oh-so-chic Minette. Nor did Liselotte care what people said about her appearance. "All my life I have made fun of my ugliness," she declared, beating other, potentially crueler tormenters to the punch, noting that even her own father and late brother would remark on her unattractiveness. "I laughed it off and never cared one bit."

What a pair they made—the fragile, graceful, feminine, and diminutive Philippe, who was nearly a dozen years older than the tactless, dowdy, ungainly, and butch Liselotte. Only by hanging holy medals from his genitalia did he successfully perform his marital obligations. When Liselotte discovered her husband's noisy secret, at first he denied it, but one night she yanked the covers back and, shining a light on his privates, burst out laughing. The mirth was contagious, and finally Monsieur insisted that the medals of the Virgin and other relics guaranteed the success of everything they touched. Hysterical with amusement, Liselotte replied that he could never convince her he was respecting the Virgin by "parading her image over those parts made to destroy her virginity." Still laughing, Monsieur swore his wife to secrecy. Nevertheless, she recorded the event in her memoirs.

Surprisingly, the spouses were more compatible than many might have predicted. Soon after her arrival at court, Liselotte had written to her aunt Sophia, "I will tell you one thing about Monsieur: he is the best man in the world, and we get on very well together. He does not resemble any of his portraits in the least." Nine months later, Sophia wrote to Liselotte's father, "I am assured that there is a very perfect love and friendship between Monsieur and Madame." Three months after this letter came the news of Liselotte's first pregnancy. The expectant mother's only disappointment about her condition was the prohibition against horseback riding.

In time, the new Madame made peace with Monsieur's blatant homosexuality and overt affairs, except when his behavior led to her own humiliation. Her marriage to Philippe got off to a good start, perhaps because the Chevalier de Lorraine was in Italy at the time and did not return to France until 1673. However, Liselotte was unshakable in her conviction that her husband had poisoned his first wife, and would freely share this opinion whenever Monsieur incurred her ire.

Liselotte and Philippe had three children, although their first-born son, given the title of duc de Valois, died before he reached his third birthday. Born in 1674, their second son, Philippe II, duc d'Orléans, styled as the duc de Chartres until he inherited his father's title, grew up to be quite the rake and dissipate. After a horoscope that was cast for him when he was a baby predicted that he would one day become a pope, with her snarky sense of humor firmly in place Liselotte quipped prophetically, "I am very much afraid that he is more likely to be the Antichrist." Her son's morals would eventually leave a lot to be desired; however, as regent for Louis XIV's successor, the king's five-year-old great-grandson, Louis XV, he was an extremely capable administrator.

Liselotte gave birth to her last child, a daughter, Élisabeth Charlotte, in 1676. After that, by mutual agreement, the spouses agreed to sleep in separate beds. Although she had little to do with her husband after her usefulness as a broodmare was over, and had "never liked the business of making babies" to begin with, Liselotte was an excellent mother to their children and was also very fond of Minette's daughters.

But with the physical separation of individual bedrooms came emotional estrangement as well. Monsieur had always gotten along better with the second Madame because they did not have competing interests. Liselotte could never become the charming and sylph-like coquette Henriette-Anne had been; whereas Minette's heightened femininity only served to further humiliate her effeminate husband, Liselotte's masculinity seemed to complement it.

In the mid-1670s, Philippe distinguished himself on the battlefield against William III of Orange, the future king of England. For the next several years he focused on improvements to his estates and art collections. The Palais Royal reached its zenith as a social mecca during the 1690s, and throughout the 1680s and 1690s, Monsieur also continued to indulge his mania for precious gems. Liselotte often joked that it was a good thing she had no interest in jewelry, or she and her husband would always be competing to wear the choicest pieces.

But no woman's ego could withstand the indignities of Monsieur's infatuations for his *mignons*. By 1682, everyone at court knew that the honeymoon was long over for Philippe and Liselotte, and that they were living "like cat and dog."

Moreover, Liselotte had begun to lose the king's favor, principally due to his new relationship with Madame de Maintenon, the former governess to his royal bastards. La Maintenon found Liselotte coarse and grotesque. The distaste was mutual. After the queen died in 1683, Louis may have secretly married Maintenon. He certainly expected the court to treat her as his uncrowned queen. Liselotte, a genuine princess, who harbored a bit of a crush on the king, was disgusted at having to kowtow to the woman she referred to in her correspondence as the old whore.

Her relationship with Monsieur reached a new low when he wished to appoint his *favori* of the early 1680s, the marquis d'Effiat—"the sodomist" Liselotte also referred to as her "worst enemy" and the "most debauched fellow in the world"—as their son's governor. Only her most vehement protest blocked Effiat's assignment.

For the remainder of the 1680s and all through the 1690s, Monsieur's health finally began to show the effects of decades of debauchery and indolence. He was as much of a gourmand as Madame, although he had a sweet tooth, whereas her tastes still ran to heavy German fare. The pair of them grew morbidly obese, their complexions florid. Philippe never exercised, but once consumed eighty oysters in one sitting. Madame still loved to ride, but now had trouble finding a hunter that could support her weight.

As time went on, their shared bitterness at being perpetual underdogs at court reunited them, so that during Monsieur's final years, he mellowed to the point of being able to laugh about his flaws with Madame. He no longer allowed people to tell lies about her and attack her in his presence. They even enjoyed fart jokes together. Liselotte had become convinced that ". . . if Monsieur were not so weak and did not permit himself to be bamboozled . . . , he would be the best husband in the world; therefore he is to be pitied more than to be hated when he does one a bad turn."

On June 8, 1701, Philippe and Louis XIV met at the Château de Marly to discuss Philippe's son's conduct. Louis scolded his brother for not reprimanding his son; the duc de Chartres had been obnoxiously parading his mistress, Mademoiselle de Séry, in front of his wife (who happened to be one of Louis' illegitimate daughters). Monsieur then dared to call the king a hypocrite for doing exactly the same thing with his own mistresses. For years, Chartres' mother-in-law, Louis' most glamorous and alluring *maîtresse en titre*, Athénaïs de Montespan, had been such a prominent fixture at court that people called her the "real queen of France," while the *real* queen, Louis' wife, Marie-Thérèse, looked on in mortification, or retreated to her rooms, humiliated. Monsieur also alluded to his own sexual debauchery over the decades, retorting that fathers who have led certain lives are in no position to lecture their sons on morals.

Louis was shocked to be spoken to with such disrespect, even by Philippe. That evening, Monsieur returned to Saint-Cloud to dine with his son. The following day, June 9, 1701, he suffered a fatal stroke, collapsing into Chartres' arms. Liselotte remained by his bedside throughout his final hours, from ten p.m. until five a.m., when he slipped into oblivion.

Madame genuinely mourned her husband. Finally, her dignity had been restored and she was "on the point of becoming truly happy when our Lord God saw fit to remove my poor husband from life and I saw vanish in an instant the result of all the trouble and pains I had taken over thirty years to become happy."

The news of Monsieur's death hit the king very hard. "I don't know how to accept the fact that I shall never see my brother again,"

Louis murmured. In keeping with the tradition of burying a royal's body and viscera separately, on June 14, Philippe's heart was taken to Val-de-Grâce, while his corpse was interred at Saint Denis.

After his death, Liselotte defied conventional protocol, sneaking into theatrical performances incognito, rather than observing the customary two-year waiting period before enjoying herself. And she vociferously refused to retire from court to a convent, despite this retreat from the world being one of the terms of her marriage contract. Nevertheless, she was extremely kind to Monsieur's memory, stating, "I've been through all his things and found all the letters that his *mignons* wrote to him, and I burned them all, without reading them, to stop them falling into other hands. . . ."— although she also insisted that the heady violet scent he had used to perfume his correspondence nauseated her. Philippe's grand passion, the Chevalier de Lorraine, whose liaison with their husband had humiliated both Madames, died of an apoplectic attack at the gaming table in 1702, having proudly refused the pension offered to him by Monsieur's son, the new duc d'Orléans.

Liselotte had assumed that Monsieur had gambled away most of his fortune and left her with next to nothing, his appanage going to their son upon his death. But in fact his investments had been in farsighted, revenue-producing entities such as canals. Founding the House of Orléans, his enormous wealth enabled the family to become independent power players in France's history.

Through Louis' generosity, the widowed Liselotte was permitted to retain her rank and remain at court, spending the rest of her life in splendor and luxury. In 1722, at the age of seventy, she died at Saint-Cloud and was buried at Saint Denis.

As for the children of Monsieur's marriages, Philippe and Minette's older daughter, Marie Louise, became queen of Spain, wedding the literally imbecilic Carlos II, the progeny of one of the Spanish Hapsburgs' uncle-niece marriages—this one between Anne of Austria's brother Philip IV and his other sister's daughter. Miserable at her adopted court, Marie Louise died childless in 1689 at the age of twenty-six, the same age her mother was when she passed away. Her symptoms were so similar to Henriette-Anne's that she was also believed to have been poisoned, although there was no merit to this theory. Marie-Louise was most likely a victim of acute appendicitis. When Carlos II died, Louis XIV went to war with the Hapsburgs to claim the Spanish throne for his grandson Philippe, duc d'Anjou, who became Philip V of Spain.

In 1684, Anne Marie, Minette and Monsieur's younger daughter, married Victor Amadeus II, the Duke of Savoy, and became queen of Sardinia upon the death of her father-in-law. She and her husband had eight children. In 1697, the oldest, Princess Marie Adélaïde of Savoy, wed her cousin, Louis XIV's grandson, the Duke of Burgundy, and became the mother of Louis XV of France. Anne Marie also died at the age of twenty-six.

Élisabeth Charlotte, the daughter of Philippe and Liselotte, married Leopold, duc de Lorraine. They had five children, one of whom, Francis I, Holy Roman Emperor, would become the founder of the Hapsburg-Lorraine dynasty and the father of sixteen children, including Marie Antoinette and her older sister Maria Carolina, the future queen of Naples.

In 1692, Philippe and Liselotte's son, the duc de Chartres, married his first cousin, Françoise Marie de Bourbon, the legitimized daughter of Louis XIV and his mistress Madame de Montespan. Liselotte had been vehemently against the match from the start, viewing the bride as no better than the parvenue daughter of a prostitute, despite the fact that Montespan was herself the daughter of a duke and came from a tremendously wealthy and established family of nobles. After Liselotte discovered that her son had, at the king's insistence, agreed to the match, she slapped the duc's face in front of the entire court. She later admitted in her memoirs that she would willingly have shed her own blood to prevent the marriage. The union between the duc de Chartres and Mademoiselle de Blois signified a formal rupture in Monsieur and Madame's own marriage. Liselotte refused to forgive her husband, even after he admitted his regret at consenting to the match.

In October 1793, the Bourbon tombs housing the bodies of Minette and her mother were desecrated by a mob of French Revolutionaries. Their remains were tossed along with those of their ancestors and descendants into what the rebels called the cemetery of the Valois, a trench on the north side of the Basilica of Saint

Denis. Not until the restoration of the monarchy was Minette permitted to rest again in peace. On the night of January 20, 1817, the twenty-fourth anniversary of the execution of Louis XVI, in the presence of the French royal family, Henriette-Anne, her mother, and the ashes of their relations were reinterred in the vault beneath the church. A black marble tablet inscribed with their names marks the consecrated ground where the young woman beloved of two superpower sovereigns lies. Monsieur's tomb was also among those that were desecrated when the basilica was ransacked.

As the son of one seventeenth-century king and the younger brother of another, a few breaths away from the throne of France himself, Monsieur had been duty-bound to produce an heir, not only for the sake of the Orléans branch of the Bourbon dynasty, but for the kingdom. He finally did so, but with his second wife, a woman who was his complete opposite—who strode through the court in tall boots, wielding a riding crop, while he minced about in high heels, fluttering a fan. Ironically, Amazonian or tomboyish caricature that she was, it was Liselotte who was the natural mother, the nurturer that Minette never was, not only for her own three children, but for her predecessor's daughters as well.

Tragically for her marriage, and for Louis XIV's union as well, Henriette-Anne, the queen of hearts at the French court, married the wrong brother. With her personality and attributes, her glamour and good taste, her sense and sensibilities, and her tremendous rapport with Louis, she might have made a terrific queen of France, while Marie-Thérèse, the woman who did become the king's consort, and who never really left Spain behind, would have been happier as queen of her own homeland. But none of that was going to happen. Louis rejected the notion of wedding Minette when he had the chance; he had no idea she'd grow up to be such a beauty, and so *sympatique*. By that time, an alliance with Spain was more politically advantageous than one with England, and his mother was pushing him to marry into her side of the family. Who knows— perhaps if they *had* wed, Louis never would have been tempted to stray from Minette's bed. Then again, she was always sickly, and would have died young anyway. If she hadn't given Louis a son or two, whom might he have married after her demise?

Minette also had no prospects as a little girl, a half orphan with a father assassinated by the will of his people, a mother residing at the French court on charity, and her eldest brother living in exile and fighting for the throne he might never gain. There was nothing she could bring to the table, and royal marriages were not love matches; they were treaties. The timing was always off for Minette and Louis, and so she had to settle for second-best—his younger brother, Philippe. Mutual happiness might have been too much to expect from their marriage, but Minette and Monsieur never seemed to have enjoyed so much as mutual contentment or respect for more than the first few weeks of their union.

The man Henriette-Anne admired head and shoulders above all others was the one who literally stood that tall. But he was also the one man she could never, ever wed, despite an affection bordering on true love: her brother Charles.

CHARLES II

AND

CATHERINE OF BRAGANZA

....

MARRIED: 1662–1685

*B*y the time Charles II was restored to the throne, triumphantly entering London on his thirtieth birthday, May 29, 1660, perhaps he felt he'd earned a measure of merriment before settling down to matrimony.

After joining his father on campaign during the 1640s, and later leading his own forces, he had witnessed Charles I's defeat and eventual execution at Whitehall on January 30, 1649—the climax of England's civil war between the Royalists and the Roundheads, or Parliamentarians. This judicial murder severed England from its monarchy and ushered in the puritanical era known as the Interregnum, in which Oliver Cromwell, and for a brief period his son Richard, governed the realm as Lord Protector.

The eldest surviving son of Charles I and Henrietta Maria (a sister of France's Louis XIII), Charles II spent the Interregnum fighting to regain the English throne. Although Scotland had proclaimed him king, Charles was outnumbered by Cromwell's forces and suffered resounding defeats. From the Continent, where he lived in impoverished exile, he raised armies and funds, suffering a major setback when the Dutch Republic reversed its acknowledgment of his sovereignty to recognize Cromwell's Protectorate instead. Not until both Oliver and Richard Cromwell had died did a new Parliament re-form itself and invite Charles to return to England as king.

It was as though the sunlight finally emerged after more than a decade of darkness. Charles, a bachelor, who was nicknamed the Black Boy for his swarthy looks, sailed back to England with a glamorous mistress—a tempestuous (and married) brunette named Barbara Palmer. The kingdom cast off the pall of Cromwellian puritanism and began to party like it was 1639—in the days before the civil war. Charles reopened the theaters that the protector had shuttered, and for the first time actresses were permitted to tread the boards, playing the roles that had previously been performed by boys too young to shave and grown men dressed *en travesti*. The new king lavished gifts upon his favorites—those who had loyally stood by him during his exile and fought alongside him to retake his throne.

But England was broke. And she had enemies—namely Holland and Spain—with formidable navies that jeopardized her economic security by posing threats to international trade. Sooner or later Parliament was bound to urge Charles to do something about it. The solution to both problems could be found in one word: marriage.

The right bride was needed to make the perfect political alliance. She also had to bring a massive dowry that would replenish England's coffers. Last but not least, the ideal bride would bear a passel of children to secure the succession of the Stuart dynasty.

The third requirement was particularly important, because people didn't like the heir presumptive, Charles's brother James, the Duke of York, with his sour disposition and his papist proclivities. Charles needed to make babies. Well, on one hand Charles made babies just fine. In 1649, while he was living in exile in The Hague, Lucy Walter, aka Lucy Barlow, a Welsh-born courtesan, bore him a son, James Scott. But James didn't count. Charles needed legitimate sons.

At one point during their continental exile, Charles's mother hoped to unite him with Louis XIII's niece, styled at the Bourbon court as Mademoiselle. But Charles's imperious cousin had little use for an impoverished youth with no crown.

Another potential bride during these dismal years turned out to be a nonstarter as well. Charles had a fling with Hortense Mancini, Cardinal Mazarin's gorgeous and exceptionally wealthy niece. He would have been delighted to wed her, but Mazarin refused to waste Europe's greatest heiress on a kid with no future.

As soon as Charles was invited by England's Parliament to re-claim his crown in 1660, both Mazarin and Mademoiselle were kicking themselves, mightily regretting their respective mistakes. Both sought to reopen marriage negotiations with the new king, but Charles had no interest in wedding anyone who had snubbed him in his adversity.

Charles II wished to emulate his parents' marriage, which had been a model of conjugal fidelity and set a high moral tone. But he was not his father, and women found him irresistible long before he could claim that it was his power that was the aphrodisiac. "Odd's fish, I am an ugly fellow," he would later remark with self-deprecation to court painter Peter Lely. Of course, being a king, in addition to being charming, fun-loving, curious, and exciting, he hardly had a problem attracting women. Yet, tall, dark, and hand-some Charles's saturnine looks and luxurious black hair, which (to hide the strands of gray) he covered with a wig by the time he was thirty-three, were actually not his era's beau ideal, which still fa-vored fair-skinned blonds. Nor was his height, well above average at six-two or six-three. And his very large feet sparked Charles's lifelong passion for shoes.

At his April 23, 1660, coronation, Charles wore golden sandals with high heels and a suit of crimson satin. Even his hose were crimson. His royal mantles were fashioned from crimson velvet trimmed and lined with ermine. Charles's horse was no less osten-tatiously caparisoned. The saddle was embroidered with gold and pearls, crowned by an enormous oriental ruby; the stirrups and bosses were studded with an additional twelve thousand stones.

During the Restoration, a person's rank was demonstrated by his or her outward appearance. Wealth was flaunted on one's person—in clothes, jewels, and, well, shoes. Charles had begun spending lavishly on the trappings of kingship as soon as he ascended the throne, and his expenditures quickly outpaced the income voted to him by Parliament.

With a reign that began in need of money, his search for a bride was guided by the size of her dowry. Despite England's fear of Catholic monarchs, all things considered, the most strategically beneficial alliance was with Portugal.

Seven years Charles's junior, Catarina Henriqueta de Brangança was the eldest child of João (John), Duke of Braganza, as the English spelled it, and his wife, Luiza Maria, daughter of the 8th Duke of Medina Sidonia. In 1640, when the Portuguese established their independence from Spain, the duke had led the rebellion. It was therefore no surprise that the family of Braganza claimed the Portuguese throne. Aware that an Anglo-Portuguese alliance would create a formidable nemesis for Spain, João had suggested a marriage between Catherine and Charles II when his daughter was only seven years old and the Prince of Wales just fourteen, but nothing came of it. João died in 1656, and Catherine's mother was appointed regent for their son Afonso. Meanwhile, raising her daughter like a nun instead of a princess, Luiza Maria kept Catherine immured in a convent throughout her youth. Courtiers recalled seeing the infanta no more than ten times inside the royal palace in Lisbon. How would such a sheltered upbringing prepare Catherine to eventually become queen of a foreign land?

After a year of international negotiations—with the Spanish vehemently opposed to a match between Catherine and Charles II, and the French supporting it—at the opening of Parliament on May 8, 1661, Charles announced his intention to wed the Portuguese infanta. The Spanish felt betrayed; Philip IV, the brother of Anne of Austria, claimed that the union violated a previous Anglo-Spanish agreement and hastily proposed alternative candidates. Charles rejected the two wealthy Hapsburg princesses of Parma after hearing that they were both exceedingly homely, then conveyed the message to Philip of Spain that he would wed whoever he bloody well pleased, doubting that his selection of a Portuguese bride would bring England and Spain to the brink of war. Sucking on the proverbial sour grapes, the Spanish ambassador quipped that the Portuguese infanta was barren anyway. Although his comment was uttered in spite, it would prove prophetic.

No one could quibble at the size and scope of Catherine's dowry: a massive two million cruzados (approximately three hundred and sixty thousand pounds), the trading ports of Tangier on the Barbary Coast in North Africa, and Bombay in India, the license to trade freely in the East Indies and Brazil, and costly goods in kind—sugar and Brazilian wood. In return, England pledged military assistance to help protect Portugal from Spain and to give Catherine an income of thirty thousand pounds. Most important to the bride, she would be permitted to worship freely as a Catholic, practicing her religion in a private chapel at any palace where she might reside. Part of Catherine's dowry was to be paid on the day she departed her homeland, and the rest would be remitted in installments.

The Earl of Clarendon, England's Lord Chancellor (and the father-in-law of Charles's brother, James), assured the Portuguese ambassador that the king had chosen Catherine for her "piety, virtue and comeliness." Charles had yet to see her in person, although he had been sent a miniature, in which the infanta appeared to be an attractive brunette with meltingly soft eyes.

The fiancés began to correspond in Spanish. Although Charles continued to spend his nights in the arms of the luscious Barbara Palmer, who bore their first child, a daughter, that February, his love letters to Catherine were signed by "[t]he very faithful husband of Your Majesty, whose hand he kisses." Sadly, not only was Charles unfaithful even as he penned his billets-doux, but he would remain so throughout their twenty-three-year marriage. Yet his letters assured Catherine that she could make him wondrously content. By the time she learned of his deprivations during the civil war, her empathetic heart was already in love with him.

As early as September 1661, eight months before she set foot on English soil, Catherine's dowry was already being pledged as security for loans. And when the payments weren't made quickly enough, the man in charge of administering them, a *converso* named Eduarte Da Silva, was sent to the Tower of London.

The pope had refused to recognized Portugal's independence from Spain; therefore, if Catherine were to have the customary proxy wedding in her own country before leaving for England, His Holiness would have considered her merely the daughter of a duke, rather than the progeny of the king of Portugal. Consequently, the House of Braganza requested no proxy ceremony from Rome, and Catherine would not be officially wed until she reached Charles's homeland, although she was styled as queen of England while she remained in Lisbon waiting to depart.

Catherine had no idea that her mother had committed an amount to her dowry that was more than the Portuguese treasury held, having spent the money raising troops against the threat of Spanish invasion. She also didn't know that the English had discovered the dowry they were being given was only half the sum originally promised, and that instead of its being paid in gold, it was being sent in other commodities—spices, sugar, and jewels.

The Earl of Sandwich, admiral of the British fleet, who had come to escort Catherine to her new homeland, was in a quandary: Should he accept Charles's bride with less than what had been agreed upon—which would be an embarrassment to England—or should he just leave the infanta in Lisbon for failure to provide her full dowry? As none of this situation was of Catherine's making, and as the English had already taken possession of Tangier and begun to garrison the port, the earl continued with the original plan.

On May 13, 1662, Catherine's ship finally dropped anchor in Portsmouth. But Charles was not there to welcome her. His mistress, whose husband he had ennobled with an Irish earldom in December 1661, making Barbara Countess of Castlemaine, threw a temper tantrum. She insisted on being relocated to a house in Richmond, where she could create the maximum amount of trouble for Charles during his honeymoon at the nearby palace of Hampton Court. Enduring a difficult pregnancy with their second child, she threatened to kill herself if Charles left her. The king tended to be sympathetic to a woman in physical distress, and Barbara easily twisted him about her finger. He succumbed to Barbara's emotional blackmail and chose his mistress over his wife. It wouldn't be the last time he would make that decision.

A week after Catherine landed at Portsmouth, Charles finally arrived there and was greeted with the news that his spouse was ailing. Although still bedridden, she was recuperating. He sat by her side, trying to get a good look at his queen above the profusion of bedclothes. The portrait he had been sent hadn't lied about Catherine's expressive eyes, nor her mass of dark curls framing a tiny face. As for the rest of his bride, all he could see was a delicate, slender hand.

One of the first things Catherine had done upon setting foot in England was to request a cup of tea, a very popular beverage among the nobility in Portugal. It would become one of the most important things she ever did. Tea drinking was rare in England at the time, their brew of choice being ale; however, a glass of hops was hardly what Catherine had craved. A "cuppa" is now an Englishman or -woman's quintessential remedy for everything from the common cold to a broken heart, but Catherine of Braganza was responsible for reshaping their culture into a nation of tea drinkers, thanks to her popularization of the beverage during the reign of Charles II. In 1680, the poet Edmund Waller would praise "the best of queens" and "the best of herbs," writing,

> Venus her myrtle, Phoebus has his bays,
> Tea both excels which she vouchsafes to praise.

But passively "converting" the English from their preferred brew to Portugal's was the extent of the queen's influence on her adopted subjects. Although Catherine of Braganza was a devout Catholic, she was no religious proselytizer. She made no effort to impose her deeply personal faith on others. Therefore, because "[s]he will do that [which] is necessary for herself and her children," as Clarendon informed Charles, the queen had no problem agreeing to the Protestant wedding ceremony. But to assuage Catherine's conscience, Charles consented to a second—secret and brief—Catholic ceremony, in the privacy of her own rooms. It was conducted by her chief almoner, Ludovic Stuart, Lord d'Aubigny.

In the Great Chamber of the Governor of Portsmouth's residence, on May 21, 1662, Catherine of Braganza and Charles II were united in wedlock in a simple Protestant ceremony conducted by Bishop Gilbert Sheldon. Charles was just eight days shy of his thirty-second birthday. The event was hardly lavish, although the bridal couple sat on a throne that had been constructed especially for the occasion and placed safely behind a rail intended to keep the spectators at bay. The twenty-three-year-old Catherine was considered ancient for a seventeenth-century bride—forty in English years, as one wag quipped. Tudor roses formed the pattern of her lace veil, and she wore a rose-colored gown trimmed with blue ribbons fashioned into lover's knots. Unfortunately for Catherine, the dress, with its Iberian-style farthingales, was far too outmoded and unfashionable for English tastes, even though it was the Duke of York who had talked her into choosing it, instead of wearing an English gown. Catherine's abundant dark hair had also been arranged in the Portuguese style—tightly curled on either side of her head into two unflattering wings that fell to her slender shoulders.

Of the hideous hairdo, and perhaps also referring to her "swarthy" complexion and "sticking-out teeth," as the Restoration-era diarist John Evelyn described her appearance, Charles is said to have remarked to a friend, "At first sight, I thought they had brought me a bat instead of a woman." Yet historian Antonia Fraser, who has written copiously on the life and times of Charles II, does not believe he uttered that insult, because he was brought up to be chivalrous to women. In addition, the king is known to have told his chancellor on the day after the wedding that "Her face is not so exact as to be called a beauty, though her eyes are excellent good, and not anything in her face that in the least degree can shock one. On the contrary she has as much agreeableness in her looks altogether, as ever I saw. And if I have any skill in physiognomy, which I think I have, she must be as good a woman as ever was born." So either Charles was indeed being chivalrous about his wife's appearance, or else Catherine's detractors were then, and remain to this day, successful in discrediting her.

After the vows were exchanged, Catherine was compelled to stand still while, in a postceremonial ritual, the lover's knots were snipped from her dress and gleefully distributed to wedding guests as favors. Still recovering from a fever, the hapless bride allowed her dress to be despoiled by a bunch of screaming, rosy-cheeked foreigners, led by the Countess of Suffolk, her first lady of the bedchamber. There was a mad scramble to retrieve one of these precious tokens, which were scooped up so quickly that Catherine was unable to secure a single knot as a souvenir of her own nuptials.

The wedding night got off to a rocky start as well. Some scholars have stated that Catherine had her period, preventing her groom from consummating their marriage. Others posit that she was still feeling unwell, or that Charles's terribly uncomfortable coach ride down to Portsmouth had left him in no mood for sex (which is hard to believe, since he was incapable of keeping his hands off Barbara). Charles confided to his beloved sister Minette that it was probably for the best, as "matters would have gone stupidly." It's difficult to imagine that a king with the nickname Old Rowley (after one of his stud stallions) feared the inability to please his wife on their wedding night because of a jouncing carriage ride. Nonetheless, referring to her homosexual husband, Philippe d'Orléans, Charles remarked to Minette, "Yet I hope I shall entertain her at least better than he did you."

To his chancellor, the Earl of Clarendon, the king wrote, "I cannot easily tell you how happy I think myself; and I must be the worst man living, which I hope I am not, if I am not a good husband. I am confident never two humours were better fitted together than ours are. . . ."

The royal newlyweds arrived for their honeymoon at Hampton Court on May 29, and the following day they were greeted by crowds of curious Londoners who had come down the Thames to catch a glimpse of the rakish king and their new queen dining in public. But Catherine was so overwhelmed by the crush of onlookers that she rushed from the hall, her makeup "about to run off with sweat," according to an eyewitness, William Schellinks.

Apart from this little incident, their first several days of marriage seemed quite happy. The king was charmed by Catherine's soft and musical speaking voice, which was equally praised by Lord Chesterfield, although she had yet to become fluent in English. As the spouses came to know each other, Charles began to admire his little wife for her wit, a virtue prized as greatly as beauty at the Restoration court. According to a contemporary, during those halcyon days the king was "extremely fond, and spends all his time with her," finding the queen "of extraordinary piety, full of sweetness and goodnese." However, Catherine did appear concerned with the extreme frivolity of the ladies of the court, who seemed to "spend soe much time in dressing themselves, she feares they bestow but little on God Almighty, and in housewivry."

The queen took the terms of her marriage contract seriously, particularly the clause that permitted her the free exercise of her Catholic religion. The entourage she brought to England from Portugal was comprised of more than a hundred musty, black-robed priests, and a half dozen ladies-in-waiting that the Stuart court nicknamed the "six frights." These *dueñas* incurred both the mockery and the enmity of their adopted country for their outdated, square-silhouetted farthingales that made the wearers appear as though they had been stuck waist-deep inside a shoe box. These skirts were so wide that they kept the women a safe distance from others, especially men, hence their nickname, *gardas Infantas*. The queen had also hired "Portugall cooks," so that she did not have to subsist on the English staples of capon, roasted beef, and mutton joints.

Catherine had religious, linguistic, and cultural barriers to overcome before she could comfortably assimilate at the Stuart court. Surrounding herself with other Portuguese didn't ease the transition. Yet Charles was not doing his wife any favors when he presented her with a list of female courtiers to be appointed to positions within her household.

Everyone at court knew that the sloe-eyed seductress Barbara Villiers Palmer, now Countess of Castlemaine, was the merry monarch's official mistress, that she was carrying her second child by him, and that her husband, Roger Palmer, had finally grown tired of being publicly cuckolded by the king and had abandoned her. Many also knew that only Barbara arrogantly refused to light a fire in front of her residence to welcome the queen to England, although the rest of London had done so with good cheer. Barbara, who had been Charles's lover and the de facto hostess of his glamorous court for the first two years of his reign, was damned if she was supposed to share him with his homely little foreign wife—a woman described by the poet Andrew Marvell (who, it should be said, liked none of the royal family) as an "[i]ll natured little goblin . . . designed / For nothing but to dance and vex mankind."

Two months after the royal wedding, Barbara gave birth. She had wanted to do so at Hampton Court Palace, right under everyone's nose, which would have truly humiliated the queen. It was the one time Charles put his foot down and refused her whim. At his denial of her absurd request, the temperamental Barbara became hysterical. To calm her, Charles offered her an ill-thought-out carrot: He would appoint her a lady of the bedchamber to the queen, the highest rank a female could have at court. He placed Lady Castlemaine's name on the list of prospective attendants and gave it to Catherine, but the queen, whose mother had told her about the infamous countess and her illicit relationship with the king, struck Barbara's name from the list. Sheltered as Catherine had been, she wasn't born yesterday, and she was aware of the huge insult being perpetrated upon her by the very notion of insinuating the king's mistress—the mother of his bastard children—into her retinue. How dared her husband daily rub her nose in his adulterous affair and in his paramour's fecundity!

Peeved at Catherine's reaction, Charles simply readded Barbara's name to the list. Catherine crossed it off again. This little game of tit-for-tat was repeated a few more times. But the queen had yet to meet her nemesis in person. At Hampton Court, during a presentation of a number of ladies to the queen, Charles approached Catherine with a stunning brunette on his arm. The queen was entranced by the woman's beauty and hoped they might become friends. Then Charles dropped the bomb, introducing the gorgeous creature as Lady Castlemaine. The mention of her name sent Catherine into shock. Numerous eyewitnesses, including the chancellor, saw Her Majesty reel and grow pale; her nose began to spontaneously bleed, her eyes filled with tears, and she fell backward into a dead faint.

Barbara was incensed that she should be treated so poorly! Charles was mortified on his lover's behalf and left the servants to carry the prostrate queen into an adjoining chamber, where they tried to revive her. So much for chivalry. It was Barbara who claimed the king's attention—and received it—while his wife was given all the consideration of a sack of dirty linen.

After escorting Lady Castlemaine to her coach, Charles rebuked Catherine. How could she behave so uncivilly to Barbara—an old and dear friend whose father had fought beside *his* father and laid down his life for the royalist cause in the civil war? For that alone, he owed much to Lady Castlemaine. "I have undone this lady, and ruined her reputation, which was fair and untainted till her friendship with me, and I am obliged in conscience and honor to repair her to the utmost of my power," he insisted disingenuously. Charles's sense of honor seems misplaced, as he claims to have been discharging a debt to one lady by insulting another who was his wife and queen.

The king felt ill at ease with appearing "ridiculous to the world" if he did not triumph over Catherine in what had come to be known as the Bedchamber Crisis. His authority was not to be questioned, even by his wife. Exasperated with her, Charles dispatched Clarendon to explain the rules of the game: A queen-consort was expected to put up and shut up and bear the heir. The earl was placed in an uncomfortable position. Clarendon reminded Charles how strongly he'd once condemned Louis XIV for insisting that Minette retain his new mistress Louise de La Vallière in her retinue, and for parading about with Louise in the presence of his queen. At the time, Charles had even said, ". . . if ever he could be guilty of keeping a mistress after he had a wife, she should never come where his wife was."

Her temper finally up, Catherine hotly defended herself. Wasn't Charles making *her* appear ridiculous, degraded, a mere cipher or doormat to accept this one request? The queen told the chancellor, "The King's insistence upon that particular can proceed from no other ground but his hatred of my person. He wishes to expose me to the contempt of the world. And the world will think me deserving of such an affront if I submitted to it. Before I do that I will put myself on board any little vessel and so be transported to Lisbon." To accept Barbara in her bedchamber was not only to accept the humiliation, it was to condone the countess's sin with her husband, something that Catherine, as a devout Catholic, was unwilling to do.

Throughout the summer of 1662, the stalemate between the royal spouses continued. Barbara's name was added to, and vigorously crossed off, the list of prospective ladies of the queen's bedchamber, and Catherine continued to threaten to board the next ship weighing anchor for Lisbon. Clarendon warned her that unless she complied, Charles would recall his fleet from the Mediterranean, where it protected Portugal from the Spanish aggressors.

Finally, the only woman Charles ever truly heeded and respected, his sister, Minette, wrote to him from France on July 22 to inform him that the Bedchamber Crisis had become the subject of much gossip at the French court. "[I]t is said here that she [Catherine] is grieved beyond measure, and to speak frankly I think it is with reason."

Nevertheless, as the weeks dragged on, Charles made his preference extremely clear, and the court followed suit. He moved Lady Castlemaine to a suite of rooms directly above his own at Hampton Court and openly dined with her, laughing and joking and flirting, while Catherine was shunned. People didn't want to be seen talking to Her Majesty because it would give the impression that they had taken her side in the Bedchamber Crisis. When she left the hall to go to bed, courtiers showed so little respect for their own queen that they made insulting jokes about her.

By the end of the summer, Catherine had been worn down, relenting in August just before she traveled by barge to Whitehall, amid a spectacular flotilla on the Thames, entering London on the twenty-third of the month for a massive celebration in her honor. Among the crowd eager to catch a glimpse of England's new queen was Samuel Pepys, who saw Catherine again at Somerset House, the queen mother's residence, on September 7. Afterward, he wrote in his diary, "[T]hough she be not very charming, yet she hath a good modest and innocent look."

Her Majesty might not have given off a very charming vibe because she was still smarting from the recent resolution of the Bedchamber Crisis. The last straw for Catherine had been when her husband threatened to send her Portuguese entourage home.

Yet by the early autumn of 1662, she began to acknowledge that unless you were gorgeous and highly sexed, throwing a tantrum was not the way to get what you wanted out of Charles II. So she began to play to her own strengths: patience, goodness, understanding, and compassion. And while Charles never gave up his mistresses—in fact, he kept acquiring more of them—Catherine ultimately earned his love, trust, respect, and affection. And there were certain aspects of the king's life that he shared with no other woman but her.

Passionate about science and naval technology, Charles permitted only Catherine to visit his laboratory, where he and his cousin, Prince Rupert of the Rhine, would conduct various experiments in whatever scientific subjects had captured the king's interest. And when he purchased a new type of coach that was all the rage and Barbara insisted that she be the first one to have the glory of riding beside him, Charles awarded that honor to the queen instead. Although Catherine was also the queen of patience and forbearance, she quietly exulted, enjoying this, and her other infrequent triumphs over her husband's inamoratas. Yet she would never conquer her jealousy of them, and no matter how long she and Charles were married, she would not become inured to his infidelities, compelled to accept the unpleasant fact that he was incapable of being true to her.

Catherine has earned a reputation for remaining in the background, eclipsed by her husband's glamorous mistresses, a wren among macaws. In some measure this is true, but she and Charles also shared a number of common interests. At Hampton Court the queen would cheerfully awaken at five a.m. to go fishing with the king, "a recreation in which" she took "much pleasure." The royal spouses enjoyed picnics together, and Catherine was also quite an archery expert, becoming patroness of the Honourable Fraternity of Bowmen. A fan of Italian opera, Catherine, like Charles, was also the patron of a theater company. The queen had her comedians and her husband had the King's Players at the Theatre Royal, Drury Lane.

Drinking tea was not the only trend she began at court. Catherine set the fashion for cross-dressing in men's breeches, coats, and hose—velvet trouser suits and caps with ribbons—displaying her short, slight figure, shapely legs, and dainty ankles. The more zaftig ladies of the court were none too thrilled by it, as the style hardly flattered them. Catherine also loved to play dress-up, especially in the guise of a village maiden, a look that Samuel Pepys saw fit to chronicle. A year after her marriage, Pepys wrote that the queen looked "mighty pretty in her white-laced waistcoat and crimson short petticoat," with her hair dressed in studied disarray "*à la negligence.*" Catherine also loved to dance, and excelled at it, and in an era where grace and elegance were prized, although she was not the most beautiful woman at court, she might give that illusion on the dance floor.

Nevertheless, even as Catherine endured malicious charges of extravagance from her detractors, her apartments at Whitehall were practically Spartan, furnished with only the meager belongings she had been permitted to bring from Portugal. By comparison, Lady Castlemaine's rooms were lavishly appointed with wall hangings, jewel-framed miniatures, and expensive tchotchkes.

By 1663, Catherine's tact and restraint were serving her well. Madly in love with Charles, she made every effort to stifle her wounded feelings when he paraded his paramours about the court with a blithe lack of sensitivity. As her husband's chancellor had reminded her, her business was to not mind *his*, and to bear children. So far, she hadn't done her job, although the royal spouses enjoyed regular conjugal visits. Rumors had spread around court the previous December that she was barren.

In July 1663, Catherine began taking the waters at Tunbridge Wells and Bath, the first of several annual summer visits, in the hope that it would increase her fertility. She always suffered from dysfunctional uterine bleeding; an Italian visitor to the Stuart court in 1668 heard that "the extraordinary frequency and abundance of her menses" would make it unlikely for her to have children, and the English diarist Sir John Reresby recorded that the queen had "a constant flux upon her." In September 1662, Charles had joked to his mother that Catherine was pregnant; the queen's reply, "[Y]ou lye," was chronicled by Pepys.

In October 1663, after returning from Bath to Whitehall, Catherine became gravely ill, having miscarried for the second time. Charles remained by her bedside even as her fever spiked. In her delirium, she imagined they had three children, including a girl who very much resembled the king, and that she had given birth to twins—but the boy was so ugly, she feared that Charles could never grow to love him. "No, it's a pretty boy," he assured Catherine.

"If it be like you, it is a fine boy indeed," she finally agreed. But if he failed as her husband, Charles succeeded as her nurse. In her peril now, he was as solicitous as possible, preferring to stay by Catherine's side day and night, despite the fact that if anyone had thought her homely before, she was no oil portrait now. The priests insisted that her head, which had been shaved for health reasons, be covered with a tight cap believed to possess miraculous powers.

The queen was also deathly pale from numerous bleedings. Scandalizing the team of physicians, Charles ordered all the windows to be opened, unsealing the fetid chamber in which his wife would surely die if she did not receive fresh air and better care. He ejected the doctors and personally fed her orange juice by the spoonful, helping her own attendants give her wasted little body sponge baths and change her soiled bed linens. Days later, still gravely ill, when Catherine asked Charles, "How do the children?" he gently humored her, fearing that to disabuse her then might kill her.

A master of amorous multitasking, Charles tried to impregnate his wife while simultaneously juggling his passions for his many mistresses. By 1663, he had fallen for one of Catherine's teenage maids of honor, the exceptionally beautiful but childlike and maddeningly virtuous Frances Stuart. Meanwhile, he also maintained an on-again/off-again relationship with Holland. During the summer of 1664, the English defeated the Dutch in North America. Charles wrote to Minette to inform her that his forces had captured a "very good town, but we have got the better of it and 'tis now called New York."

The conquered city was named for Charles's brother, James, Duke of York. Three of the five boroughs that comprise New York City were also named for members of the royal family. Brooklyn is formally called Kings County—for Charles. Queens honors Catherine of Braganza, and from time to time local politicians discuss placing a statue somewhere in the borough to honor her. However, it hasn't happened yet because of her father's participation in the slave trade. The borough of Staten Island, officially known as the county of Richmond, would eventually be named for the 1st Duke of Richmond and Lennox, Charles's royal bastard by his French mistress Louise de Kéroualle.

Charles's subjects seemed to be spoiling for a fight with Holland, but the royal treasury was almost empty. Charles was on the fence, because he was never keen about going to war. Yet he was envious that the Dutch dominated shipping and trade, and wanted a piece of it. He was also obsessed with sailing and all things naval, and was eager for England to surpass the Netherlands' famous light, fast fleet.

So in February 1665, he declared war on them in what was known as the Second Dutch War. One of Charles's conditions of peace was that the States of Holland improve the position of his nephew William. He was being excluded from inheriting the title of stadtholder after the death of his father, Prince William II of Orange.

It was a terrible year. Not only was England at war, but there were rumors that Charles was planning to divorce the childless Catherine so that he might marry Frances Stuart. The king was so madly in love with Frances that Lady Castlemaine staged a mock wedding in an effort to convince her to become Charles's next official mistress. Nonetheless, Frances is said to have preserved her chastity, continuing to resist the king's efforts to seduce her.

The first signs of plague appeared in early May. The heat wave of June spread the disease, and while Londoners were decimated, by the summer of 1665 the court had decamped to the more healthful air of Oxford. The greatest number of deaths took place that summer; by the autumn the rates declined, and by the late winter and early spring of 1666, things had resumed a semblance of normalcy. A Harvard University article on the subject estimated the preplague population of London in 1665 at approximately four hundred and sixty thousand, and the Great Plague killed between seventy-five thousand and a hundred thousand of them. However, according to the contemporary Bills of Mortality, by the time the epidemic had run its course, the death toll of the Great Plague across the whole of England was 68,596, although Lord Clarendon, the chancellor, believed that figure should have been doubled at the very least. And the chaplain to the Duke of Albemarle, who had remained in the capital for the duration of the plague, estimated the total number of deaths nationwide from the epidemic at two hundred thousand. In any event, although there is little concurrence on the actual death toll, it represented a sizable percentage of England, and particularly London's populace. And the disasters kept coming.

While the court was still at Oxford, in January or February of 1666, Catherine suffered a miscarriage. By that time, Charles had returned to Whitehall in London and for some reason refused to believe it had occurred.

It would not be the only tragedy of 1666. Shortly after midnight on Sunday, September 2, a fire began in a bakery on Pudding Lane. London at the time was constructed primarily of wooden buildings densely packed together, often only a handspan apart. The blaze spread rapidly, driven across the city by a strong east wind, leaping the River Fleet and threatening Charles's court at Whitehall. By the next day, the conflagration covered a half mile. It was not brought under control until September 5, by which time thirteen thousand homes and eighty-seven churches, including St. Paul's Cathedral, had been destroyed. For days, King Charles and James, Duke of York, had pitched in, sleeves rolled up, joining bucket brigades until they were exhausted. Because the fire took place during the Second Dutch War, rumors spread that it had been started by French or Dutch immigrants; consequently, innocent residents of London were accosted and accused, beaten and lynched, while the firestorm raged around them.

The Great Fire of London forced the evacuation and resettlement of thousands, and crippled the tax yield at a time when the war was already sapping the lion's share of England's income. In 1667, the first year since her marriage that Catherine's royal allowance was finally paid in full, the Peace of Breda was signed with Holland, France, and Denmark. The Dutch got Surinam, Pulo Run in the Banda Islands of Indonesia, and parts of West Africa. England received New York, New Jersey, and New Delaware. By 1668, Charles was still on good terms with the Netherlands, signing a pact with Holland and Sweden—the Triple Alliance—intended to check French aggression.

In matters of international diplomacy, Charles realized that he had a secret weapon—his sister, Minette, who was married to the younger brother of Louis XIV. Minette was an obvious correspondent, as Charles had always written candidly to her about his marital situation. On May 7, 1668, the king confided to Minette that Catherine had miscarried that morning, writing, "And though I am troubled, yet I am glad that 'tis evident she was with child, which I will not deny to you till now I did fear she was not capable of." Samuel Pepys also wrote that day that the queen had miscarried "of a perfect child."

Unless Catherine was significantly further along in this pregnancy—sources say ten weeks—than she had been when she had miscarried previously, it's unclear why Charles would only now believe her capable of conceiving. One can only imagine that he must have assumed her prior spontaneous abortions were merely the "abundance of her menses" referred to earlier, or related to some other ailment.

For the past six years, Catherine's infertility had been a source of perpetual gossip and speculation. It was even more humiliating to her that she was the problem; Lady Castlemaine's increasing brood proved that it wasn't Charles who was deficient. After Catherine's May 1668 miscarriage, the rumors began anew that her husband might divorce her. Others suggested that he might legitimize his first bastard, the Duke of Monmouth, who was very popular in some court circles. A third rumor made the rounds that Charles and Lucy Walter had been legally wed, meaning that young Monmouth was legitimate after all. Lucy was dead by the time Charles was crowned, so his marriage to Catherine in 1662 would never have been considered bigamy. Yet the king adamantly denied any marriage to Lucy Walter. Nor, he assured Catherine, did he ever intend to divorce her, or send her back to Portugal for barrenness.

In May 1669, the queen believed herself with child again. Pepys wrote in his diary that she was pregnant, and his suspicions were confirmed when he spied her a week later dressed in a pinner and apron, Restoration-era maternity wear.

On May 24, 1669, Charles wrote to Minette, "She missed *those* [her periods] almost, if not altogether, twice, about this time she ought to have them, and she had a kind of colic the day before yesterday which pressed downwards and made her apprehend she would miscarry, but today she is so well she does not keep her bed. The midwives who have searched her say that her matrix is very close, though it be a little low; she has now and then some shows of *them*, but in so little quantity as it only confirms the most knowing women here that there is a fair conception."

Yet on June 7, the king sorrowfully told his sister that the thirty-year-old Catherine had miscarried, "after all our hopes" and "without any visible accident." Some sources believe that the miscarriage occurred late enough in the pregnancy to determine the sex of the fetus, but it has never been stated whether the queen was carrying a boy or girl.

Catherine of Braganza never conceived again. And after the tragedy of her 1669 miscarriage, Charles evidently did not expect her to do so.

Despite the king's misgivings, his courtiers continued to pressure him to divorce her. James was against it; as he was now the heir presumptive, a new, fertile queen would likely bear heirs that would knock him further down the line of succession—although he feared that his brother would keep Catherine, but declare the Duke of Monmouth his legitimate heir. The royal mistresses were also eager for the queen to stay put, as they were loath to entertain the possibility of their paramour falling in love with a beautiful and nubile replacement.

Divorcing a barren queen had royal precedent. In Catholicism, it was grounds enough for annulment. A number of suggestions were made: If Catherine volunteered to quietly retire to a convent, things could discreetly blow over. But if she insisted on remaining Charles's wife and refused to withdraw, the Duke of Buckingham had the gall to sketch out a scenario in which he would have her kidnapped and dispatched to some distant plantation after she left the palace to attend a fair. Charles was appalled. In 1670, Buckingham introduced a bill into Parliament that would grant the king the right to divorce Catherine and remarry. But Charles would not repudiate her. He halted the proceeding of the bill, declaring, "It was a wicked thing to make a poor lady miserable only because she was his wife and had no children by him, which was no fault of hers." Charles also refused to legitimize Monmouth. The status quo would remain.

The first decade of Charles II's reign was a period of freedom and hedonism, curiosity and inquiry. By the end of the 1660s, he had granted a charter to the British East India Company, and awarded a royal charter to the Hudson's Bay Company, which would control that vast swath of territory in North America.

But the next decade would be marred by religious tensions.

Charles was himself tolerant and had intended to make freedom of worship a cornerstone of his reign. However, England was not an autocracy. Among many of his subjects, including several members of Parliament, the mistrust of papists continued to run high, whether the Catholics were foreign (i.e., French, Spanish, or Portuguese) or domestic.

However, in 1670, under what would come to be known as the Secret Treaty of Dover, enabled by Minette on behalf of her brother and brother-in-law, Charles did get into bed with Catholic France, an alliance that Louis XIV had desired since Minette's marriage to his brother in 1661. After Minette's sudden illness and swift death just days after her return to the Continent, Charles also tried to get into bed with one of her maids of honor. On parting from her brother at Dover, Minette had refused to cede him one of her "jewels"—the virginal (or so she claimed) Louise de Kéroualle, a curvaceous Breton brunette with rosebud lips and a squint in one eye, having promised Louise's parents to keep the girl from the wolves. But later that year, Louise was bestowed upon Charles as a gift from Louis XIV, and made as much of a game of "keep-away" with her virtue as Frances Stuart had done. The French girl eventually succumbed after many make-out sessions with the king and another mock wedding staged by Barbara Castlemaine, as well as the promise of several gifts. Louise was as avaricious as Barbara; she was raking in cash and costly trinkets from Charles as her lover, and from her paymaster, Louis XIV, for whom she was said to be spying on the English king and court.

By 1671, Charles's affection for Barbara was on the wane. He had honored "la Belle Stuart," commanding that her profile personify the realm on his victory medals over the Dutch in 1664. This image of Frances Stuart would later become "Britannia," for three centuries on all British coinage. But Frances had not been as grateful for this distinction as Charles would have liked. To his fury, not only had she continued to refuse him, but she had gone and married *another* Charles Stuart, the 3rd Duke of Richmond and 6th Duke of Lennox. But the king now had Louise as his lover. And he still had the most adorable, and genuinely loving, of his mistresses, "pretty, witty Nell Gwyn," as Pepys dubbed her, a vivacious redhead with an irrepressible sense of humor whose father had fought for the royalist cause and died in debt. Nell, whose alcoholic mother ran a brothel, came from the underbelly of London. In her early adolescence, she became an orange seller at the newly reopened Drury Lane theater, and was soon discovered by the company manager, who offered her the opportunity to be an actress. The illiterate Nell learned her roles by rote, was a natural mimic, and became the toast of the London stage. Charles was also sleeping from time to time with another actress, Moll Davis. And of course there were numerous one-night stands, overseen by the king's Keeper of the Privy Closet, William Chiffinch. Over the course of just a few years, Chiffinch made more than ten thousand pounds, quietly funneled to him from Secret Service accounts, for discreetly escorting the king's nocturnal diversions up to his bedchamber and down again by means of a private staircase.

Charles was not promiscuous in the sense of being an indiscriminate sexaholic. He was a serial adulterer—although he did juggle multiple long-term mistresses simultaneously. He explained his temperament to Sir John Reresby with the disclaimer "because that his Complexion [meaning his personality, not his skin tone] was of an amorous sort," women often succumbed to his embraces.

But by 1671, Catherine of Braganza was sick of it. She moved out of her rooms at Whitehall and into Somerset House on the Strand overlooking the Thames, which had been Henrietta Maria's dower house; after the king's mother died in August 1669, he gave the property to Catherine. Continuing to fulfill her duties as queen consort, she accompanied her husband on his journeys outside London, where she was tremendously popular. But the stress created by the omnipresence of Charles's myriad mistresses, as well as the increasing anti-Catholic sentiments throughout the kingdom, began to have an effect on her emotional and physical health.

In February 1673, Catherine suffered a serious illness and believed she had been poisoned, sparking a fear of future attempts to poison her, which she thought were connected in some way with the Duke of York's conversion to Catholicism. Charles's brother had embraced popery, as the English called it, in 1672, although it did not become widely known until the following year, and James continued to attend Anglican services until 1676.

The whole issue of religion was heating up far more than the king had ever wanted. On March 29, 1673, Charles II reluctantly gave his assent to the Test Act. The act required all persons serving in civil or military office to swear an oath upholding the supremacy of the Anglican Church and denying the concept of transubstantiation (the conversion of the two elements of the Eucharist into the actual body and blood of Jesus Christ).

Catherine's Catholic servants were exempted from the Test Act, but James resigned his office as Lord High Admiral of the Royal Navy rather than take the oath. Charles evidently commented that he was willing to rid his own entourage of Catholics, with the exception of his barber, "whom he meant to keep in despite of all their [Parliament's] bills, for he was so well accustomed to his hand." It was the king's subtle way of conveying his trust of papists, no matter their proximity to the throne, as the hand that daily brought the razor to the royal throat practiced this now-proscribed religion.

During the Restoration, coffeehouses had replaced ale houses as loci for progressive, often dissenting political discourse. Coffee, drinking chocolate, even sherbet were considered signs of dissidence then. In December 1675, with religious tensions still running high, an order was issued to suppress the coffeehouses. That year, all English and Irish Catholic priests were commanded to leave the country. The queen was at least allowed to attend Mass conducted by her Portuguese clerics, and quietly opened her own chapel to English Catholics so that they could worship there.

By this time, the forty-five-year-old king had gone almost totally bald beneath his curly black periwig. His rakish air was tinged with a veneer of melancholy. He and Catherine were more or less separated. In 1674, the royal marriage had reached a nadir and she decided not to accompany her husband to the horse races at Newmarket as she had always done. Instead, she remained at Hampton Court "in retirement." The Venetian ambassador wrote, "Contrary to her usual custom, stifling the pangs of jealousy by which she is tormented, her Majesty made an effort to amuse herself during the whole of this last season with hunting and dancing," returning "unwillingly to London where the customary freedoms of the king and even more the flaunting of his mistresses dispirit her and render her incapable of disguising her sorrows."

Charles's conduct was demoralizing enough to Catherine; imagine how painful it must have been to know that all of the foreign ambassadors were sharing the details with their employers. She had never appreciated being waited on by one of her husband's lovers acting in her role as a lady of the bedchamber. In particular, the weepy Louise de Kéroualle, whom Charles had created Duchess of Portsmouth, and who had given him a bastard son, would stand behind Catherine's chair during dinner and mock her.

And yet as the years passed, the queen's tremendous character and fortitude had become much respected and admired by her subjects. These qualities were not lost on her husband, either.

In 1678, when Titus Oates, an anti-Catholic agitator, fomented the "Popish Plot," a trumped-up conspiracy to assassinate the king that falsely fingered the most highly placed papists in the realm, including Catherine and members of her household, it was feared that charges would be leveled against the queen herself. But Charles was entirely convinced that his wife had nothing to do with the plot, despite Oates's allegation that she both knew and approved of it as revenge for the king's infidelities. Not only was Catherine modest and discreet in her piety, and never urged her faith on anyone (especially Charles), she was hardly the sort of person to exact revenge, especially through her religion.

By this time, the royal couple had been married for sixteen years. Although the Popish Plot had engendered mass hysteria throughout the realm, Charles knew that Oates's allegations were bogus, particularly after he claimed that the plot was spearheaded by Catherine's physician, Sir George Wakeman, and had been hatched right in the queen's apartments. The king was so angry that he masterfully cross-examined Oates himself; the conspirator's description of Catherine's voice and her rooms clearly revealed that he had never seen or heard the queen, nor ever set foot inside her residence. He had invented everything.

Still, even as Oates's charges were being investigated, Charles remained uncertain that his wife's virtue and discretion would be enough to protect her. So he made a point of demonstrating that he supported and trusted Catherine entirely. Instead of dining with Louise de Kéroualle, the king took his meals with the queen, as well as enjoying his postprandial nap in her chamber. They appeared in public in coaches and on barges, presenting the picture of a loving, happy couple. Charles's message to his subjects was clear: Catherine was remaining by his side.

Of all the events that had transpired during their marriage, including Catherine's numerous miscarriages, the Popish Plot was the one that drew the royal couple most closely together.

The king's support for his wife continued throughout the anti-Catholic madness. In 1679, the Countess of Sutherland, a close friend of Louise, wrote snarkily to a relative of her husband's in Holland, "The King and Queen—who is now a mistress, the passion her spouse has for her is so great—go both to Newmarket, together with their whole court."

Catherine wrote to her brother, the king of Portugal, to tell him "how completely the King releases me from all trouble by the care which he takes to defend my innocence and truth. Every day he shows more clearly his good will towards me, and thus baffles the hate of my enemies. I cannot cease telling you, dear Pedro, what I owe to his benevolence, of which each day he gives better proofs, either from generosity, or from compassion for the little happiness in which he sees I live." That same year, the Earl of Shaftesbury had spearheaded the Exclusion Bill, intended to separate the royal spouses, thereby paving the way for Charles to marry a Protestant.

Charles had imprisoned Titus Oates, but after a brief period of incarceration, the House of Commons ordered his release under threat of a constitutional crisis. Oates, the ultimate con artist, went from being treated like a criminal to a hero, awarded a State apartment in Whitehall and a twelve-hundred-pound annuity.

As a result of the Popish Plot, fifteen innocent men, including some of Catherine's servants, were executed; the last of them died in 1681. It took three years from the launching of the plot before a backlash against Oates began. That year, he was ejected from his apartment, but continued to denounce the royal family, leading to a second period of imprisonment, this time on the charge of sedition.

The queen had incurred a reputation for goodness, and maintained a truly regal sense of serenity and poise, even during this frightening anti-Catholic period, and even as her husband continued to dangle his infidelities in her face. By now, he had added a former flame, the fabulously wealthy, and glamorously bisexual, Hortense Mancini, the niece of Cardinal Mazarin, to his stable of royal mistresses. Catherine's remarkable tolerance of Charles's affairs was the key to retaining his love, affection, and respect. He had more than political reasons for refusing to divorce the queen. Not only did Charles owe her a tremendous debt for suffering in silence while he committed countless infidelities, paraded his paramours around the court, and lavished more jewels and real estate upon them than he had ever given her, but he genuinely esteemed Catherine and enjoyed her company.

Unfortunately, the king would never feel the same kind of love for Catherine that she had for him. And by the spring of 1681, when the court was at Newmarket for Charles's beloved horse races, it was being reported that Catherine "entertaines better thoughts in her solitude, being retired most part of the day at her devotions and reading." The queen's tolerance for Louise de Kéroualle had reached its limit. In 1683, in the course of an argument with Charles, Catherine complained to him that "now the mistresses governe all."

In 1684, Charles fell ill. He and James kept the gravity of his ailment a secret so that neither their nephew, the statdholder William III of Orange, nor the Duke of Monmouth and his faction would get any ideas about instigating a rebellion. That year, James finally took his place in the Privy Council and was restored to his post as Lord High Admiral, a great boon for the navy. It was clear that with no child born to Catherine and Charles, the only legitimate successor was the Duke of York, despite his Catholic faith.

Following a night of cardplaying amid his mistresses, on the morning of February 2, 1685, after awakening feeling faint and nauseated, Charles had an apoplectic fit while his barber was shaving him. The sudden onset of his illness led to the suspicion of poisoning, although no plot was ever proven at the time. The results of Charles's autopsy were consistent with granular kidney disease, a form of Bright's disease, and modern medical theories have concluded that his symptoms were those of uremia, or kidney dysfunction. The king's initial fit, however, would seem like a ministroke or TIA (transient ischemic attack), which can leave the victim suffering from neurological symptoms that pass within a day.

For the next four days, while his doctors tortured him with frequent bloodletting, blistering, emetics, purgatives, and a broth laced with cream of tartar, Charles languished between lucidity and unconsciousness. On the fifth of February, with the Duke of York by his side, it is believed that Charles II received last rites, welcomed into the Roman Catholic Church by Father John Huddleston, the priest who had helped him escape after his defeat at the Battle of Worcester in September 1651. It has never been fully proven whether the king's deathbed conversion (if it indeed occurred) was his own idea, or if he had finally been persuaded by James, and/or Louise de Kéroualle (both of whom took credit for it). Louise, however, whose relationship to the king was considered no better than that of a prostitute, was not permitted anywhere near the dying monarch; nor were any other of Charles's mistresses. However, their ennobled sons, because they were now peers of the realm, might be allowed to see their father if they wished. Nell Gwyn's son, Charles, the little Earl of Burford (and later Duke of St. Albans), was the king's favorite child, and was by his side during his final days.

Aware that her husband never wished his private views on Catholicism to be made public, Catherine stayed out of any preparations or discussion surrounding his conversion. She came to say good-bye to Charles on February 5. Already tearful, she became convulsed with weeping when he greeted her tenderly. Prostrated with grief, she had to be carried back to her rooms. According to the poet-playwright John Dryden, "Which was nearest the Grave could scarce be seen / The dying Monarch, or the living Queen. . . ." She sent word to Charles, requesting his pardon if ever she had offended him. Nonplussed, the king exclaimed, "Alas, poor soul! She ask my pardon! I beg hers with all my heart."

After apologizing to his physicians and courtiers for being "such an unconscionable time dying," the fifty-five-year-old Charles II expired at noon on Friday, February 6. He was buried with no state funeral on February 14, St. Valentine's Day, in a vault beneath the Henry VII Chapel of Westminster Abbey. His body, which was encased in a lead coffin, did not even lie in state prior to his interment. Atop the coffin, a solid silver plate bore a lengthy Latin inscription that ended with the words, "in the thirty-seventh year of his reign," dating Charles II's accession from the year of his father's execution in 1649.

The late king's official mistresses were permitted to wear black, but were not allowed to put their households into mourning; that was specifically a royal prerogative. Upon the accession of James II, after first withdrawing to a convent she had founded in Hammersmith, Catherine retreated to Somerset House.

Diarist John Evelyn described Charles as "a Prince of many virtues, and many great imperfections" who instituted "a politer way of living—even if he turned later to luxury and expense." In his 1676 *Memoirs*, Sir John Reresby wrote that Charles was "not an active, busy or ambitious Prince . . . he seemed to be chiefly desirous of 'Peace and Quiet for his own Time.'"

Yes, he desired peace. But in the aftermath of the Great Fire of London, he was both busy and ambitious, tapping the great Sir Christopher Wren to help rebuild the capital. It was Wren whose design for a new St. Paul's Cathedral began construction in 1675. In addition to granting royal charters to the British East India and Hudson's Bay companies, in 1681 Charles also granted a vast tract in North America to William Penn, land that would eventually become Pennsylvania. Charles II also founded the Royal Naval Observatory and had plans to build a naval hospital for veterans modeled after Les Invalides in Paris; his dream was realized, but not during his lifetime.

At one point during Charles's reign, the Duke of Buckingham wryly observed that a king is supposed to be the father of his people, and His Majesty was certainly the father of a good many of them. Because Catherine was unable to carry a child to term, the king shared her anguish at not bearing him a legitimate heir. Had she given him a child, which the queen accepted would be raised as a Protestant, the religious tensions surrounding James's prospective ascension as a Catholic would have been mooted.

Instead, Charles fathered at least a dozen royal bastards with seven mothers, although there may have been more children as well. Barbara Castlemaine bore six children, but the king refused to admit paternity of her last child, a daughter. Nell Gwyn gave her royal lover two sons, one of whom died in France, where the little boy was sent for schooling. Louise de Kéroualle bore a son as well. Charles ennobled all of their children. Six of Charles's illegitimate sons received nine dukedoms: the present-day dukedoms of Buccleuch (still under attainder), Grafton, St. Albans, and Richmond and Lennox (joined together) all derive from those granted to the sons of the merry monarch's numerous mistresses. There were also children from his liaisons with Elizabeth Killigrew, Viscountess Shannon (a courtier and sister to the playwright and theater manager Thomas Killigrew), Catherine Pegge (who had two children by Charles while his court was in exile in Bruges), and the actress Moll Davis, who bore the king a daughter she named Lady Mary Tudor.

Things did not end well for Charles's first illegitimate son, Lucy Walter's boy, the Duke of Monmouth. After his uncle the Duke of York ascended the throne as James II, Monmouth staged a rebellion against the crown. Catherine, who had always nurtured a soft spot for her bastard stepson, unsuccessfully pleaded with the new king to spare his life.

During James's reign, Catherine had more freedom of religion, but she was an isolated figure with no purpose for remaining in England, now that "the Almighty hath seen fitt to set me free." Yet her brother, King Pedro II of Portugal, seemed reluctant to welcome her home, even though she offered to retire to a convent to avoid arousing the envy of his courtiers, who might fear her influence upon him.

So Catherine stayed at Somerset House. And she insisted that the treasury finally settle its financial obligations, paying her the allowance she had not received for so many years as queen consort. She had never complained of shortages and the necessity of economizing all those years, even when her husband continued to lavish untold wealth on his mistresses. Charles would have wanted her to receive her due. And so she fought for it.

In 1687, looking back on her royal marriage, Catherine ruefully wrote, "There were then Reasons for my coming to this Kingdom, solely for the advantage of Portugal, & for this cause & for the interests of our House I was Sacrific'd."

After thirty years in England, Catherine finally sailed back to Portugal in March 1692. In the words of the diarist John Evelyn, "She deported herself so decently upon all occasions . . . which made her universally beloved."

Catherine had no idea that in Portugal she was regarded as a living legend, the courageous infanta who married the king of a faraway land, a man whose navy had helped them defeat the invading Spanish several times. Stories of her patience, piety, and goodness over the decades had reached her homeland. Her countrymen did not revile her for never becoming a mother. And she would never again be made to feel unloved or unwanted.

Now over fifty, the former queen of England lived quietly and modestly with a small retinue at a series of Portuguese palaces. She emerged from her retirement in 1704, when she was appointed queen regent for the ailing Pedro. Like her mother, Luiza Maria, Catherine was an exceptionally capable regent. Although she had never taken an active role in the politics or administration of England, she had absorbed much by listening so attentively to Charles.

In fact, since her husband's death in 1685, Catherine governed her decisions by asking herself, "What would Charles do?" As one example, on his deathbed, he had implored James to look after the welfare of his mistresses, particularly Nell Gwyn, famously urging his brother to "not let poor Nelly starve." James did so, transferring the allowance to Nell's son, Charles, after she died in 1687. But after the Glorious Revolution made James an exile, William III saw no reason to continue to pay a pension out of the royal treasury to one of his uncle's bastards, even if the boy was Duke of St. Albans. So before Catherine left England, she made provisions for two thousand pounds a year to be disbursed out of the funds she brought back to Portugal, part of her own marriage settlement. Not only had Catherine been fond of the child, but Nell Gwyn had been the one royal mistress who was not avaricious and who truly loved Charles II as much as the queen did. Nell never wed and never cheated on him with another man, as the king's other significant paramours had done. With her inimitable wit, she always insisted that she would not "lay a dog where the deer had laid."

In 1704, during Catherine's regency, Portugal was forced to make war on Spain, which was then ruled by the French-born Philip of Anjou. Under Catherine's instructions, the Duke of Cadaval executed a brilliant strategic campaign and the Portuguese were triumphant. In the throne room at Lisbon, Catherine received the envoy from Madrid and signed the peace treaty on behalf of her native land.

She remained regent until her death on December 31, 1705, at the palace at Bemposta. The sixty-seven-year-old Catherine of Braganza was buried in the Jerónimos Monastery in Belém, near Lisbon. In the twentieth century, her remains were reinterred in the capital's Monastery of São Vicente de Fora, where the royal family of Bragança reposes.

The great Restoration-era playwright John Dryden praised the goodness and marital loyalty of Catherine of Braganza in an unrhymed couplet that wasn't, but might as well have been, her epitaph:

> *The best of Queens, the most obedient wife . . .*
> *His life the theme of her eternal prayer—*

How ironic that Catherine's own countrymen viewed her royal marriage as a glorious alliance for their kingdom, while her husband's subjects—poetic panegyrics aside—regarded the union as an inglorious one from the moment they'd discovered that her mother had played bait-and-switch with her dowry. From her mousy physical appearance to her Romish religion to her unfortunate inability to bear an heir, Catherine was considered an utter mismatch for their charismatic king, and their marriage a political misstep for England.

MARIA CAROLINA
OF AUSTRIA
AND
FERDINAND IV
OF NAPLES

....

MARRIED: 1768–1814

"*O*thers wage wars; you, happy Austria, marry," was the motto of the Hapsburg dynasty, the family into which Maria Carolina, archduchess of Austria, was born. Sadly, the motto would prove to be no more than wishful thinking: Maria Carolina's inglorious royal marriage to a philandering idiot was never a happy one.

Her mother was the formidable Maria Theresa, Empress of Austria and Queen of Hungary, Bohemia, and the Netherlands. Her father was French: the indulgent François of Lorraine, a grandson of Liselotte, the outspoken second wife of Philippe d'Orléans. In 1745, Francis, as he became known, was elected Holy Roman Emperor. However, it was Maria Theresa, whose father had held the title before him, who really wielded the scepter.

Maria Carolina was the third daughter born to the empress to be given that name, her first two namesakes having died in infancy. Our Maria Carolina was the thirteenth of Maria Theresa's surviving children, and would always be known within her large family as Charlotte. When she became queen of Naples, it was also the name she would sign beneath the letters written in French or German, although she called herself Maria Carolina in her Italian correspondence. Despite being a polyglot, she was never able to write in any language with academic perfection.

Maria Carolina was raised within a close-knit family at the Hapsburg palaces in and around Vienna. Although the empress's court etiquette was not rigid, she insisted on a high moral tone within and beyond the palace walls. Perhaps because Maria Theresa despaired over her husband's extramarital liaisons, she discouraged all flirtations and intrigues, imposing strict laws regarding the conduct of her subjects. She formed a commission to enforce purity, whose officers patrolled the Viennese streets twenty-four/seven, with the authority to arrest anyone behaving immorally.

Until it came time to "finish" Maria Carolina's education to prepare her for marriage, she was schooled primarily in the company of her youngest sister, the future queen of France, Marie Antoinette; as girls, they were inseparable and would always remain kindred spirits.

Yet Maria Carolina lacked her younger sister's porcelain prettiness. And while both girls were high-spirited, it was the headstrong and impetuous Maria Carolina who most reminded the empress of herself. The child always behaved as if she were born to rule.

It would happen far sooner than even Maria Theresa could have predicted. In October 1767, Maria Carolina's beautiful and dutiful sister Maria Josepha died of smallpox on the eve of her departure from Vienna to wed Ferdinand IV, the teenage monarch of the southern Italian kingdoms of Naples and Sicily. Consequently, Maria Theresa had a slot to fill. She had four remaining unwed daughters, but had already promised Maria Antonia, who was only twelve at the time, to the dauphin of France. Maria Elisabeth had survived the smallpox epidemic, but was too disfigured by the scars to make an attractive bride. Maria Amalia remained a possibility, but she was older than Ferdinand, who, it was alleged, was already immature for his years.

As the Neapolitan marriage was never intended to be a love match anyway, Maria Theresa left the choice to Ferdinand's father, King Carlos III of Spain, dispassionately writing to her fellow sovereign as though they were discussing chattel that had been destroyed due to some mishap. "I grant you with real pleasure one of my remaining daughters to make good the loss. . . . I do currently have two who could fit, one is the Archduchess Amalia . . . and the other is the Archduchess Charlotte who is also very healthy and a year and seven months younger than the King of Naples."

Carlos selected Maria Carolina. Rather than undertake the complicated process of renegotiating the marriage contract between his son and the Archduchess Josepha, the empress simply substituted Charlotte's name.

Although she wore the king of Naples's portrait affixed to her corsage as a symbol of their betrothal, the pinch-hitting bride-to-be fought her destiny with every ounce of strength. She'd heard enough about Ferdinand's unattractive appearance and crude manners from Josepha to dread marrying him. Worse still, he'd shown no respect for her sister's demise. Word had gotten back to Vienna that upon hearing of his fiancée's death, Ferdinand had staged a mock funeral, dressing one of his pages in a gown, stippling his face with melted chocolate to simulate smallpox, and solemnly parading him through the palace atop a bier. Hilarity ensued. But not in Austria.

Maria Carolina cried and screamed and pleaded with her mother to spare her the fate of such a husband. But the empress, who viewed her daughters as sacrifices to politics, had no intention of changing her mind.

So at the Church of the Augustinian Friars in Vienna, on April 7, 1768, wearing a cloth of gold gown, with a tissue overlay of white organza, her bodice studded with gemstones and her hair teased high off her forehead and dressed with seed pearls, Maria Carolina Louise Josepha Johanna Antonia, archduchess of Austria, was married by proxy to the seventeen-year-old Ferdinando Antonio Pasquale Giovanni Nepomuceno Serafino Genarro Benedetto. Her eldest brother, the Holy Roman Emperor Joseph II, gave her away to another of their brothers, also named Ferdinand, who represented the Neapolitan groom during the nuptials. Empress Maria Theresa, wearing the black widow's weeds that had become her habit since the death of her husband in 1765, witnessed the ceremony from her private pew.

The bride was so miserable that she might have considered wearing mourning herself. Incapable of concealing her dismay, she lamented that "they might as well have thrown her into the sea."

Afterward, the empress proudly and tenderly embraced Maria Carolina; in her view she wasn't losing a daughter: She was gaining a queen. Although Charlotte had yet to meet her husband, she was now queen of Naples and Sicily and, at the age of sixteen, the youngest reigning queen in Europe.

A wedding breakfast at Schönbrunn Palace on the outskirts of Vienna followed Maria Carolina's proxy nuptials. Immediately afterward, she embarked on her journey for Naples, aware that she would not be expected to return to her homeland. Maria Carolina was so unhappy at the prospect of heading off to a repulsive husband from whom there would be no escape that she was homesick before her carriage clattered out of the courtyard. She sprang from the coach and dashed across the cobbles in her gold-and-blue traveling ensemble to tearfully embrace Maria Antonia one last time.

The nearer she drew to Naples and Ferdinand, the more Maria Carolina's heart filled with dread. The Emperor Joseph despaired, too, fearing that his sister wasn't ready for her new role. He observed Maria Carolina during the early part of her journey to the south, and informed their mother that "she has a good heart, she willingly accepts advice, being anxious to do right, but she is impetuous . . . and has as yet too little experience of the world. . . . Of course, she is so young . . . she has never been trained to be Queen of Naples."

Joseph was right. In the months prior to her proxy wedding, Maria Carolina's education had been "finished" by her governess, the Countess von Lerchenfeld, but nothing had prepared the archduchess to rule over a boisterous, largely illiterate, and indolent populace whose behavior was vulgar in comparison with the Viennese, and a husband who had been deliberately brought up to lack all interest in the governance of his own kingdom.

Born in Naples, Ferdinand was the third son of King Carlos III of Spain and Maria Amalia of Saxony. At the time, Naples was governed as a satellite of the Spanish branch of the Bourbon dynasty, but a king of Spain was not permitted to rule both realms. Consequently, Ferdinand ascended the Neapolitan throne at the tender age of eight, after Carlos, who had been king of Naples, inherited the Spanish crown from *his* father. An excess of royal inbreeding had left its mark on Ferdinand's oldest brother, the epileptic Prince Royal. He was too mentally incapacitated to reign, characterized at the time as a congenital imbecile. Madness ran in the family; King Carlos's father was convinced that his mania for hunting every day would stave off the hereditary insanity, evincing, it seems, little awareness that the responsibility for it could be placed on his dynasty's numerous uncle-niece and first-cousin intermarriages.

With his parents in Spain, the boy-king Ferdinand was raised more or less by his prime minister, Bernardo Tanucci, who became regent in 1759 when Ferdinand ascended the Neapolitan throne. Tanucci wanted to rule Naples unimpeded, so he ensured that Ferdinand learned as little as possible about his own kingdom by instructing the monarch's tutor, the Prince of San Nicandro, to maintain Ferdinand's ignorance and encourage the boy to amuse himself. This seemed perfectly all right with King Carlos, as well as with his incurious son, who was raised without any responsibilities and little contact with his own regent. In consequence, Ferdinand grew up as an anti-intellectual. Unlike most royals of his day, he knew no foreign languages and could not even speak formal Italian, communicating only in the local Neapolitan dialect. At the age of fifteen, the king was still entertaining himself with his marionette theater.

Ferdinand's lifelong passions were those of his peasantry: He loved to spend his entire day hunting, or fishing at the edge of the bay alongside the *lazzarone*, Naples's half-clad, unshod underclass who were deeply loyal to him and considered him one of their own. He'd haul in a day's catch and hawk it on the pier, giving away his earnings. Some of his customers recognized their sovereign in the "tall and muscular" youth described by the Margravine of Anspach, due to the bulbous Bourbon proboscis that had earned him the affectionate nickname *il re nasone*—King Nose—from his subjects.

Ferdinand's loutish behavior and practical jokes had become the talk of other European courts and coffeehouses, including those in Vienna. To protect his dignity, Tanucci obtained an order forbidding all courtiers, except those on duty, from attending the young king's meals, because he was prone to rowdy behavior.

Ferdinand's minority had ended in 1767, the year before his marriage, but he evinced no interest in assuming any power or responsibility. Instead, he provided Tanucci with a stamp bearing his signature, content for the prime minister to govern in his name, although Bernardo was no longer Ferdinand's regent.

Naples was officially ruled by the Spanish Bourbons, and was therefore expected to parrot Spain's political ambitions. But there were vast cultural differences between them. The spontaneous, carefree, and superstitious Neapolitans could not have been less similar to the rigid, urbane, and learned Spaniards. When Maria Carolina arrived as their new queen, it was not her husband but Tanucci who was the de facto ruler of Naples, doing the bidding of his boss's father, Carlos of Spain, rather than the unsophisticated and barely literate King Ferdinand, whom the Neapolitans looked upon as one of their own. Consequently, the country she entered in May 1768 was still struggling to find its national identity.

After traveling for several days, Maria Carolina finally met her husband for the first time in the town of Portella, at an opulent pavilion that had been constructed for Ferdinand's parents thirty years earlier. Accompanied by her brother Leopold, the Duke of Tuscany, and his wife, Maria Luisa, the new bride was introduced to a scruffily attired teen who looked more like a peasant than a king. Later that day, the couple left Portella for Caserta, the location of Ferdinand's summer palace, to celebrate their Italian wedding ceremony.

Maria Carolina wrote to her former governess, the Countess von Lerchenfeld, about the lengthy carriage ride to Caserta, which afforded her the opportunity to become acquainted with her husband, admitting, "He is very ugly, but one gets used to that; and as to his character, it is all much better than I was told"; however, "I must tell you and confess that I don't love him except from duty, but I do all I can to make him think I have a passion for him. I conduct myself with great patience and gentleness. He says that he loves me very much, but he will not do anything I want."

The new queen's first glimpse of the twelve-hundred-room Palace of Caserta, where her nuptials were to be held, took place at night, when the vast baroque monstrosity looked its best, illuminated by the glow of countless candles and lanterns. On hand to greet Maria Carolina was a welcoming committee of ministers, courtiers, and the ambassadors from Spain, Austria, and France.

Shortly before midnight on May 13, the teenage royals were wed during a brief ceremony inside the palace chapel. According to Sir William Hamilton, Britain's ambassador to Naples since 1764, "Ferdinand manifested on his part, neither ardour nor indifference for the Queen." Given the groom's evident ambivalence, the wedding night was hardly romantic, although it appears the marriage was consummated. Up per usual at the crack of dawn to go hunting, Ferdinand had left his bride in bed the following morning. When asked by his courtiers how things had transpired between the sheets, he had ungallantly replied, *"Dorme come un' ammazzata, e suda come un porco"*—"She sleeps as if she had been killed and sweats like a pig."

The honeymoon was worse. "One suffers real martyrdom, which is all the greater because one must pretend outwardly to be happy," Maria Carolina wrote to her former governess. She was even more irritated that he considered himself extremely handsome and clever, and was utterly convinced that she had fallen in love with him. It was an effort to feign pleasure in his company, when she was disgusted, bored, and homesick. "I would rather die than endure again what I had to suffer. If religion had not said to me: 'Think about God,' I would have killed myself rather than live as I did for eight days. It was like hell and I often wished to die."

In addition to their language barrier, spending time with her spouse must have been a nightmare because part of this "hell" was a roundelay of celebrations—fetes and fireworks, operas and concerts, all in honor of the royal newlyweds. But the bride couldn't force herself to have fun.

On May 19, the teenage monarchs entered Naples "with royal pomp in the full light of a lovely day." Maria Carolina put on her game face and waved with poise and grace to the vast crowds eager to greet their new queen, but inwardly she was miserable. Her husband was more toad than prince. And despite the incomparable physical beauty of Naples, a gem overlooking the glistening blue confluence of the Mediterranean and Tyrrhenian seas, it was a far cry from the elegance and sophistication of Vienna. Moreover, the wealthy lived extravagantly, while the poor were desperately so. The kingdom's literacy rate was estimated at a mere ten percent. No wonder Naples was considered a backwater by the rest of Europe.

Maria Carolina's first few months of marriage were dreadfully unhappy. Friendless, in a strange country, she didn't understand her husband, literally or emotionally, nor could Ferdinand fathom her. Despite the enormity of her palaces and the beckoning Bay of Naples beyond her windows, the new queen felt stifled and suffocated. Ferdinand described a tantrum his wife pitched one day when "she became a fury . . . calling to all the servants who are maids, who could see nothing but that she was screeching like an eagle."

Maria Theresa's spies, including the Austrian ambassador, informed her about the queen of Naples's volatile temper, particularly when Maria Carolina unleashed it on her hapless attendants. This prompted a scolding from the empress, who told Maria Carolina to curb her rudeness, especially to her ladies. There was no excuse for such behavior in a queen. Maria Theresa also cautioned her daughter against falling prey to the Neapolitans' natural indolence and to find something with which to occupy her mind, as such a task would prevent her from acting rashly or immaturely.

A woman's reputation was everything. And a queen's character should always be above reproach, regardless of the king's behavior. Maria Theresa reminded Maria Carolina to [a]void coquetry," bearing in mind that "many things harmless in a girl are not so in a married woman, although contemptible in either. Love your husband," the empress advised her daughter, "and be firmly attached to him; that is the only true happiness on earth," conveniently forgetting that her own union had been that rare royal love match. Maria Theresa also urged Maria Carolina to endeavor to understand the "ill-educated but well meaning . . . King Ferdinand."

It is unclear whether Maria Carolina knew by this point that her husband commanded foreign ambassadors to attend him while he was sitting on the commode enjoying a postprandial poop. Or if she'd been acquainted with his habit of pouring steaming handfuls of macaroni upon the heads of the well-coiffed opera patrons beneath the royal box. Or that when he went hunting, he personally slaughtered beasts by the hundred, then insisted on field-dressing them himself, up to his elbows in gore. Ferdinand was exceptionally skilled at gutting his kill, a far better butcher than a king.

Maria Theresa also cautioned her daughter not to compare the customs and drawbacks of her new kingdom to the morals and merits of her homeland. The empress was quick to point out, "There is good and bad in every country." And then she dispensed the advice that would always confound her girls regarding the twin allegiances that she expected from them as royal wives. "In your heart and in the uprightness of your mind be a German," adding specifically for Charlotte's benefit, "in all that is unimportant, though in nothing that is wrong, you must appear to be Neapolitan."

In this, Maria Carolina would willingly obey her mother. "My first aim . . . is to render service to my adored brother the Emperor, for whom I would willingly shed my blood," the queen would declare even two decades later.

As a newlywed, Maria Carolina initially resented her mother's meddling. But the empress's letter ultimately sparked her ambition to steer herself out of the doldrums. From then on, she vowed to make the best of her destiny by taking control of it. Not only would she manage her husband, as her mother had instructed—she would become the real king of Naples.

In the words of historian Derek Beales, "Ferdinand was born to be ruled by others." Maria Carolina's sister-in-law, Grand Duchess Maria Luisa of Tuscany, coached her on how to be a caring, supportive wife to Ferdinand, while also gaining the upper hand with him. In his case, feminine wiles would go a long way. The queen cleverly gained ascension over Ferdinand by flattering his athletic prowess, feigning interest in his pursuits, and making him believe that her suggestions were his own ideas, then heartily congratulating him on executing them. In so doing, she also managed to convince the king that she was in love with him.

But the ultimate magic touch turned out to be the king's attraction, bordering on fetishism, to Maria Carolina's bare arms and opera-length gloves. The queen discovered that she could get just about anything she wanted, even politically, by tantalizingly removing her long kidskin gloves. Twentieth-century burlesque queens could have learned a trick or two from her technique.

As soon as Maria Carolina chose to take charge of her own happiness, even if she still didn't enjoy her husband, something positive occurred. "The affability and goodness of the Queen of Naples gives unusual satisfaction here," wrote the British ambassador Sir William Hamilton in June 1768. By the end of the summer, having decided to follow her mother's instructions to the letter, Maria Carolina had won the affection of her subjects and her spouse. Ferdinand was said to be "dazzled" by her self-possession. In turn, she considered him *"ein recht guter Narr,"* as she told her brother— a right good fool.

However, Maria Carolina required time to become acclimated to the sovereigns' primary residence, the Royal Palace, an architectural eyesore situated in the center of the city. The Palazzo Reale failed to impress her brother Joseph during his imperial visit to Naples in 1769, not so much because of its baroque decor, but because of the other residents. He was shocked to find the palace's "five or six frescoed and marbled rooms . . . filled with chickens, pigeons, ducks, geese, partridges, quails, birds of all sorts, canaries, dogs and even cages full of rats and mice, which the king occasionally sets free and enjoys the pleasure of chasing."

Joseph also minced no words in his description of his new brother-in-law, an inch taller than the emperor at five feet, seven inches, with a piercing falsetto voice that was painful to the ear. Maria Carolina's brother described Ferdinand as "very thin, gaunt and raw-boned . . . his knees always bent and his back very supple, since at every step he bends and sways his whole body. The part below his waist is so limp and feeble that it does not seem to belong to the upper part, which is much stronger. He has muscular arms and wrists, and his coarse brown hands are very dirty since he never wears gloves when he rides or hunts. His head is relatively small, surmounted by a forest of coffee-coloured hair, which he never powders, a nose which begins in his forehead and gradually swells in a straight line as far as his mouth, which is very large with a jutting lower lip, filled with fairly good but irregular teeth." Joseph also found Ferdinand's "low brow, pig's eyes, flat cheeks and long neck" unremarkable. "Although an ugly Prince, he is not absolutely repulsive: his skin is fairly smooth and firm, of a yellowish pallor: he is clean except for his hands; and at least he does not stink."

However, the emperor was troubled by the rumors he had heard about the king's violence toward Maria Carolina. Had he really punched and slapped her? The queen admitted that her husband had kicked her on occasion. Ferdinand had perhaps punched her more than a few times as well, half in anger and half in jest—sometimes when they were in bed, or when they were out riding in their carriage, but she felt that he had never been truly violent, even when she had been furious with him. Ferdinand evidently had a propensity for roughhousing. Finding his own antics wildly amusing, he caned and kicked his attendants, and spanked the ladies of the court during parlor games, and no one could gainsay his boorish behavior because he was their king.

After attempting to discern his brother-in-law's religious and moral temperament, Joseph ultimately concluded that Ferdinand hadn't any. Having ascertained that the king was afraid of the dark, believed in the supernatural, and thought that angels were white and the devil black, the emperor was also fairly convinced that Ferdinand was incapable of reciting the Ten Commandments, although he "explained that he only thought it wrong to sleep with another woman, to steal, murder and lie." This cherry-picked menu of morality did not prevent the king from frequently committing adultery. And yet Ferdinand assured the emperor "that he was satisfied with the Queen, but he could not conceal that he feared her, since she did not seem so infatuated with his merit or blind about his integrity as he would wish."

According to Joseph, Ferdinand's biggest complaint about his wife was that she was too fond of books. He personally detested reading and did not approve of others, especially women, doing so. As it was abundantly evident that Maria Carolina needed an outlet for her intellect, and her husband was not about to provide it, the emperor suggested that she form a salon. The queen eventually did so, cultivating the acquaintance of the Neapolitan elite, including the Freemasons, a society in which her late father, Joseph, and two of her sisters were members. Ferdinand's father had banned them in 1751, but under Maria Carolina's aegis, the Freemasons enjoyed a resurgence until the advent of the French Revolution, when she abolished everything that smacked of Enlightenment.

During his visit in 1769, Joseph did notice how much in love Ferdinand was with Maria Carolina. He reassured their mother that she had made a wise match, but when the time came for the Hapsburg siblings to say good-bye, the king mocked his wife for bursting into tears over her brother's departure. At this, Maria Carolina was on the verge of losing her temper when Joseph lectured her in German, after which she "mastered her feelings and said nothing." The imperial marriage counselor "preached to the King to leave her alone today and not torment her."

The Neapolitan royal couple's relationship would always be volatile. They endured numerous, and vociferous, squabbles. One subject of contention was that Ferdinand's eyes followed every woman in a skirt, regardless of her age, her looks, or her social stratum. He carried on torrid affairs with two opera dancers—signorinas Rossi and Bratella—both of whom were later married off to noblemen. The queen forced herself to tolerate these liaisons because her husband's lovers were from an inferior class. But when he became infatuated with the Duchessa di Lucciana, the daughter of the Neapolitan secretary of state, it was too much for Maria Carolina to bear. After catching the pair of them flirting during a ball, the queen called an abrupt halt to the entertainment and booted everyone out of the ballroom.

After this incident, Ferdinand learned to conduct his trysts with more discretion, and was better able to conceal his future infidelities, including his liaison with the Marchesa di San Marco—that is, until the queen discovered it and exiled the marchesa from Naples.

There was no question that the queen wore the metaphorical breeches in the marriage. By gaining the upper hand—or glove—in the kingdom's governance, as the months and years passed, she schooled herself to become "amused rather than depressed" by her husband's "eccentric habits," ultimately characterizing Ferdinand as "a really nice halfwit."

The queen tried to live with the bowls of hot macaroni coated in olive oil and melted cheese that her husband dumped onto the heads of opera patrons. It was his roving eyes and hands that most humiliated her. But Maria Carolina revised the court protocol so that during their all-too-frequent marital spats, Ferdinand had to request permission from the First Chamberlain to return to her bed after she had evicted him for an infidelity. The duration of his

banishment—which was judged by the queen—was usually propor-
tionate to the gravity of his offense. Nevertheless, the royal couple
was hardly lax in their marital duties.

The only thing they would always share was their unqualified
devotion to their progeny. Between the years of 1772 and 1793,
Maria Carolina gave birth to eighteen children, including a set of
twins; seven of their offspring lived to adulthood. During their first
several years of marriage, Ferdinand and Maria Carolina were
blessed with a peaceable kingdom. "Naples is a paradise, in it every
one lives in a sort of intoxicated self-forgetfulness," the visiting
writer Johann Wolfgang von Goethe famously observed. This las-
situde allowed the royal couple ample time to raise their growing
brood, and they were devoted parents. Superintending her children's education, especially that of her daughters, the queen was a
much more hands-on mother than Maria Theresa had ever been,
although, granted, the empress had a far greater realm to govern.

Yet Maria Carolina always insisted, "Nature made me a mother;
the queen is only a gala-dress, which I put off and on." However,
she was such an astute politician—even as a sixteen-year-old
bride—that a stipulation in their marriage contract guaranteed her
a seat on the powerful Council of State as a quid pro quo for bearing an heir. The queen's first son would be born in 1775, and she
wasted no time shaking things up and transforming Naples from a
chaotically governed satellite of Spain into an independent, and
unsurprisingly pro-Austrian, realm.

Yet even before then, Maria Carolina was gaining influence. By
the time she was twenty, while she still had a few detractors who
derided her for being "large, raw-boned and bulky . . . with a
pinched face and a severe expression," she was generally considered
to be very lovely, and capable of charming everyone around her.

Lady Anne Miller, an English noblewoman connected with the
British embassy in Naples, described the queen in 1771 as a "beautiful woman" with the "finest and most transparent complexion I
ever saw; her hair is of that glossy light chestnut . . . by no means
red; her eyes are large, brilliant, and of a dark blue, her eyebrows
exact and darker than her hair, her nose inclining to the aquiline,
her mouth small, her lips very red (not of the Austrian thickness),

her teeth beautifully white and even, and when she smiles she discovers two dimples, which give a finishing sweetness to her whole countenance; her shape is perfect: she is just plump enough not to appear lean; her neck is long, her deportment easy, her walk majestic, her attitudes and action graceful. . . ." Maria Carolina's political acumen garnered as much praise as her appearance. Elizabeth, the last Margravine of Anspach, praised Maria Carolina's innate ability to reign. The queen "appeared much better calculated to represent the majesty of a throne [than Ferdinand]. . . . It was natural to her."

Maria Carolina had even managed the near-impossible: winning the admiration of the Neapolitan ministers and generals. One of the latter observed that although the queen was "in the prime of youth, her mind was of the most powerful stamp, and her wit of the highest order. By nature she was both proud and haughty, and she nourished within her bosom the most inordinate love of power." In other words, she was a mini–Maria Theresa, viewing it as her destiny to follow in her mother's footsteps and to be a ruler in the same mold. As a Hapsburg, and queen of the largest dominions in Italy, Maria Carolina was certain that she was destined to play a role in history. She was—but not the one she foresaw. And the men who so lavishly complimented her acumen had as their basis for comparison her lumpish "halfwit" of a husband!

Soon it was an open secret that the queen, whom Ferdinand affectionately called *maestra mia*—my mistress (or boss!)—was the real king of Naples. Whoever had *her* ear made diplomatic headway, while Ferdinand attended council meetings only if he absolutely had to do so, but paid no attention, and spent the better part of his days hunting, fishing, and chasing other sorts of tail. He never developed a talent or taste for governing, so it was a good thing that his queen possessed those skills in spades. Whenever someone asked Ferdinand about a government-related topic, he would throw his hands in the air and reply, "Ask my wife, she knows everything!" The king was so uninterested in reigning that he had the inkstands removed from his council chambers, lest he be tempted to write something down.

As the years went by, while Ferdinand occupied himself with

hunting, flirting, pranks, and scatological jokes, Maria Carolina overhauled the court, removing the antiquated Spanish influence, much to the consternation of Ferdinand's father and the despotic Prime Minister Tanucci, whose ouster she engineered in 1777. The hapless king felt caught in the middle of a power struggle between his strong-willed, absent father and his equally formidable, and very present, wife. But Maria Carolina was skilled "in the art of man training" (in the words of her brother Joseph), and knew she had the upper hand. If Ferdinand failed to see things her way, she dramatically threatened to withhold sex. On one occasion, the queen was heard to exclaim, "for at least a year, whether you die or burst, I refuse to be pregnant." Whatever had set her off, Maria Carolina had not finished making her point. She punctuated her argument by biting her husband's hand.

When political appointments fell vacant, believing that the Neapolitans were too uneducated and unqualified to run their own country, the queen nominated Austrians and Germans, and still retained a retinue of forty-five German maids. An Anglophile, she cultivated a relationship with the British ambassador Sir William Hamilton, and later with his mistress-turned-wife, Emma, a stunning former courtesan. In the mid-to-late 1790s, Lady Hamilton became Her Majesty's closest confidante and eventual interpreter—England's minister without portfolio during Naples's efforts to enlist Lord Nelson's aid in keeping Napoleon at bay.

Infusing the court with a dash of Viennese glamour, in an effort to transform it from a Mediterranean backwater into an A-list European kingdom, the energetic, vivacious, and ambitious Maria Carolina developed ties with Naples's intellectual and cultural elite. Out of his element in the presence of the glitterati and literati, Ferdinand "never spoke, or at least very rarely," according to the writer Louis Dutens, who visited the court at Caserta. "[B]ut the Queen made ample amends for his silence by the affability and the engaging manners with which she received" her guests.

One of Maria Carolina's forward-thinking plans was to reorganize and strengthen the navy—vital, as Naples was a kingdom by the sea. To that end, her brother Leopold recommended Sir John Acton, a French-born English baronet who had made his mark with

Leopold's Tuscan navy. Variously described, depending on whether the source was a supporter or a detractor, as "a very pretty sensible young man" or "ambitious and covetous" and a "soldier of fortune," Acton became Naples's Secretary of State for the Marine. Within a few years of his 1778 arrival in Naples at the age of forty-two, he had worked his way through the governmental ranks, becoming commander in chief of the armed forces and the navy, so indispensable to Maria Carolina that he acted as her de facto prime minister.

But some, including Ferdinand and his father, were convinced that Acton was much more to the queen than her favorite minister, despite their fourteen-year age difference. In Naples, it was inconceivable that an attractive, charismatic woman should spend so much time in the company of an equally attractive and charismatic man and not be his lover. King Carlos of Spain used the rumors of an adulterous affair between Acton and Maria Carolina as a wedge to force his son to dismiss the powerful minister, insisting, "They have turned you into a pasteboard king, you must get rid of Acton at once, or send him out of your kingdom."

Despite his own frequent extramarital dalliances, the king needed little encouragement. Ferdinand's conviction that Acton was tupping his wife led, predictably, to another violent argument between the monarchs. For twenty-four hours, they shut themselves inside Maria Carolina's royal apartments, shouting at each other. "I am trying to surprise you together," Ferdinand warned the queen. "I will kill you both, and have your bodies thrown out of the windows of the palace!"

Naturally, Maria Carolina stood her ground and reminded Ferdinand about his own infidelities. After a full day of bickering, the queen emerged from her rooms triumphant. Acton remained; his influence even increased.

Never ask a boy to do a man's job, fumed Carlos of Spain. If Ferdinand couldn't get rid of Acton, he'd take care of it himself, dispatching a chargé d'affaires, one Señor Las Casas, "to persuade her to dismiss Mr. Acton from the business of the state, and from her intimacy." It didn't go over too well. Las Casas managed to offend both Maria Carolina *and* Ferdinand with his questions. Acton received her favor on *merit*, Her Majesty told the Spanish envoy, and when he had the temerity to openly accuse her of taking the minister as her lover, Maria Carolina, who at the time was in the first trimester of one of her numerous pregnancies, angrily retorted, "I will have his picture drawn by the best painter in Italy, and his bust made by the best sculptor, and both sent to the King of Spain, who may judge whether his is a figure for a woman to fall in love with."

Unfazed, Las Casas audaciously replied, "Oh, madam, my master has lived long enough to know there is no answering for the caprices of *des dames galantes*."

Maria Carolina attributed her subsequent miscarriage to her outrage over the envoy's arrogance and his unforgivable insult (essentially, he had called her a prostitute). When news of her miscarriage reached France, her brother-in-law Louis XVI intervened with Ferdinand on her behalf, and Acton remained as Naples's prime minister. But the damage to his credibility and reputation had been done, and Acton's detractors loathed him with renewed venom.

Even Ferdinand respected Acton's advice and was gaining the reputation, however fictional, as a ruler of his own dominions. As Maria Carolina wrote in the late 1790s, "Six years ago the name of the King of Naples was ignored or at most regarded as a viceroy sent from Spain to a subordinate province. Now he plays a fine role with glory and distinction."

Ferdinand's pet project was the silk factory at San Leucio near Caserta, where he made sure that the workers received a good wage, and that the employees and their families were provided with medical care and education. State-of-the-art machinery made their products competitive with those in other countries. But the king's critics accused him of founding the silk works for his own sexual gratification, because sturdy country girls were his favorite physical type, and Ferdinand's frequent visits to San Leucio afforded him an escape from his wife.

In general, however, Ferdinand received the glory whenever something was a success, even if the achievement was his wife's. Meanwhile Maria Carolina was blamed for every failure. She was given none of the credit for the myriad accomplishments of the couple's reign, even from those who knew perfectly well that the king was in no way personally responsible for them.

But history has frozen Ferdinand and Maria Carolina in amber, characterizing him as a popular hedonist and her as an ambitious harridan, conveniently forgetting her successful transformation of Naples during the first two decades of her reign.

In 1788, the same year that Ferdinand's father died, Maria Carolina began arranging marriages for her oldest offspring although she was still bearing children. Like her mother before her, the queen believed that one of her greatest duties was to negotiate brilliant matches for her brood. By placing them in every European court, she thereby extended Naples's influence. Many of the unions were with the offspring of the queen's numerous brothers and sisters. She had hoped to unite Ferdinand's heir, Francesco, to Marie Antoinette's seven-year-old daughter, Madame Royale, but the girl had already been promised to another first cousin, the oldest son of Louis XVI's youngest brother. Despite the horrors of the French Revolution, this marriage would eventually come to fruition.

Unfortunately, Maria Carolina and Ferdinand were not able to broker as many matches as they might have liked, because smallpox—the scourge of the eighteenth century—claimed the lives of so many of their children, despite the queen's progressive insistence on inoculation. Each death devastated her, yet she could scarcely spare the time to mourn. By 1789, pockets of rebellion were at the Neapolitan doorstep. Soon Naples would be flooded with royalist refugees.

While many of the issues of the French Revolution were indeed endemic to France, the events did not occur in a vacuum; nor was it solely a copycat uprising of the American Revolution fomented in the 1770s. The world was on fire in the months before the storming of the Bastille. By early 1789, the Hapsburg dominions were in revolt, because Emperor Joseph II's subjects were convinced that he had destroyed the economy of central Europe. Austria had already depleted its military resources in Eastern conflicts, and had been decimated by the Turks.

Then, as part of a westward-moving domino effect, the Austrian Netherlands exploded. Maria Carolina's sister Maria Christine and her husband, the Duke of Saxe-Teschen, watched in horror as Antwerp was flooded with revolutionaries venting their frustration on *all* Hapsburgs; the emperor was no longer the single target of their animosity. The insurgents in the Austrian Netherlands then encouraged their Dutch counterparts to rebel.

North of Italy, the Magyars were on the brink of revolt in Hungary, and peasants were leading uprisings in Bohemia (which comprised a portion of the present-day Czech Republic), as well as in other Eastern European regions. As Emperor Joseph lay dying, his own chancellor abandoned him. After issuing orders reversing all of his progressive reforms, Maria Carolina's brother died of tuberculosis on February 20, 1790. Joseph was succeeded by their brother Leopold, who was able to abate the crisis in Hungary later that year.

During the madness, a pregnant Maria Carolina was busy arranging marriages for three of her oldest children with a trio of Leopold's offspring. By this time, after fifteen births, the queen's health was understandably strained, and world events did nothing to soothe her frazzled nerves. She began to suffer bouts of dizziness. This had not deterred Ferdinand from his conjugal visits, so she was soon *enceinte* for a sixteenth time. Doctors did not want to treat her symptoms, for fear she would miscarry. Pregnant for half her life, Maria Carolina remarked, "I sincerely hope this will be my last child." She was wrong; there would be two more.

About to become a grandmother for the first time, the queen was more concerned about her first child Teresa's health than her own. Teresa, the wife of Leopold's widowed son Francis (who would eventually succeed him as emperor), bore a daughter, Marie Louise.

On December 17, 1792, a French squadron appeared in the Bay of Naples. The flagship dropped anchor within firing distance of the Neapolitan fortress of the Castel dell'Ovo. An immediate apology from Maria Carolina was demanded for her having insulted the ambassador from the fledgling French Republic—which had deposed her beloved sister and brother-in-law, imprisoning the royal family—or else the French navy would bombard the city. A craven Ferdinand hastily promised neutrality and the fleet weighed anchor.

The execution of Louis XVI in January 1793, followed that October by the judicial murder of Marie Antoinette, marked a sea change in Maria Carolina's personality, as well as in her governance of Naples. Determined to prevent the violence from spreading to her door, and aware that the progressive ideas that had fomented the Revolution in France had been spawned in the salons and coffeehouses frequented by the intelligentsia, the Neapolitan queen cracked down on the very groups she had once championed for their enlightened minds. She herself had been a member of the arcane Illuminati; the society was now banned.

Vengeance was Maria Carolina's byword; she became hell-bent on rooting out all revolutionary ideals within her realm, resorting to a network of spies and a secret police force comprised of informants from every stratum of society. Those in the highest echelon filed their reports via clandestine nocturnal visits to a chamber within the Palazzo Reale called the *sala oscura*—the dark room. Naples was in the grip of paranoia; her citizens were terrified of the twin threats of foreign invasion and the domestic secret police. Even siblings and cousins of members of the royal household were tried for treason.

"This infamous revolution has made me cruel," Maria Carolina wrote in 1795. She recounted an incident at one of the intellectual clubs "where many of the nobility spat upon, reviled and finally pierced my portrait with knives, inciting each other to repeat these gestures to the original." She defended her husband against their common enemy. "Personally I scorn the madness of these people, but when it rages against their King—and what a King!—an affectionate father, devoted to them, just and good, such as they do not deserve, I cannot forgive them for it."

Just as Marie Antoinette had become the locus of her subjects' hatred, Maria Carolina became the target of vicious innuendo and slander, the wildly mistrusted outsider who was the architect of all their misfortunes. This was the fate of many royal brides, who, in the opinion of their adopted countrymen, had overstepped their bounds and become more than the mother of an heir.

Rumors abounded that Maria Carolina had emptied the Neapolitan treasury for her own gains and self-indulgent political schemes. British ambassador William Hamilton observed that although Ferdinand remained as popular as ever, "the Queen of Naples is by no means popular, but as her power is evident, she is greatly feared."

In the space of a few years, Maria Carolina had gone from being an enlightened sovereign to a neurotic one, but not without reason. By the mid-1790s, French Republican troops had begun to press past France's borders, west into Hapsburg terrain, and south into Italy and Spain. Naples was within their sights, and despite the queen's efforts to quash them, many Jacobin sympathizers, home-grown Neapolitans as well as French expatriates, already dwelled within the realm. Maria Carolina had to continue to feign interest in her husband's amusements in order to maintain her influence over him. Even at this dire juncture, Ferdinand might have declared Naples a neutral territory, were it not for the queen's insistence on revenge for the murder of the French monarchs.

In 1796, Ferdinand finally decided to take control of his own kingdom, in the face of a Napoleonic invasion. That October, he signed the Treaty of Brescia, but the terms for Naples were so unfavorable, they placed his realm in an untenable position. To avoid being run over roughshod by the French army, he had agreed to "indemnify" Napoleon with the astronomical sum of eight million francs. Maria Carolina was outraged by her husband's capitulation to the treaty.

By 1797, Italy was embroiled in open warfare with the new French Republic. After Rome fell to their army, Ferdinand personally assumed command of the Neapolitan troops. It was his first taste of combat ever—and was an unmitigated disaster for his men and his monarchy, opening the door to the revolutionaries.

With the encouragement of Britain's preeminent naval strategist, Lord Nelson, who had been charged with protecting England's Neapolitan allies from Napoleon, Maria Carolina convinced her husband to launch a preemptive military strike. On November 29, 1798, Ferdinand led thirty thousand troops into Rome, with the aim of liberating the Eternal City from the French menace and forestalling Napoleon's troops from heading south into Naples.

Having lulled the inexperienced king into a false sense of security, Bonaparte's army quietly surrounded the equally amateurish Neapolitan soldiers on all sides. Within two days, they had retaken Rome. Ferdinand donned a disguise and fled home in disgrace. In retaliation for Ferdinand's violation of the Treaty of Brescia, Napoleon ordered an invasion of Naples.

The royal spouses disagreed on what course to take. Ferdinand insisted upon remaining on his Neapolitan throne. Backed by Lord Nelson and the Hamiltons, Maria Carolina endorsed a flight to safety in their sister kingdom of Sicily. With Emma Hamilton acting as a courier, in December 1798, plans were secretly hatched to spirit the royal family, their household effects, and approximately two thousand members of their retinue from the palace. The queen packed up, at one modern estimate, some £2.5 million worth of money, crown jewels, and treasure, and safely stowed it at the British embassy.

Other personal effects were being jettisoned, sold, or worse—as the royal family prepared for all eventualities. Maria Carolina wrote to her foreign minister, the Marchese Gallo, ". . . We have got rid of our silver . . . Not even coffee-pots, all is gone. The King has given up 392 horses and 300 dogs, and reduced his hunting grounds. . . . Yesterday he had the wild beasts of the menagerie killed. . . . From one minute to the next we expect the French squadron of fifty-four sails. . . . If the French exceed this number, we have informed them that the surplus will be regarded as hostile. . . ."

Despite Maria Carolina's despair over the fate of her nation and her family, Napoleon's undeniable genius would always impress her, regardless of their mutual enmity. "I wish this rare and extraordinary man to succeed . . . outside Italy," she wrote to Gallo, as the royal family prepared to flee Bonaparte's approaching troops. "I foresee that this world will resound with his name, and history will immortalize him. He will be great in all things, in war, diplomacy, conduct, resolution, talent, genius: he will be the greatest man of our century. . . . Cultivate in him friendly sentiments for Naples and the desire not to injure us."

Five days before Christmas, violence reached the gates of the Palazzo Reale, as loyalist mobs clashed with the Jacobin revolutionaries. The queen was convinced that their own subjects wished to take them hostage. Ultimately, she and Ferdinand were able to placate their supporters, but the mollification was short-lived, and Naples erupted into chaos.

Maria Carolina was not about to endure the fate of her sister and brother-in-law. When the going got tough, the Neapolitan monarchs fled. Unlike the French sovereigns, at least they were successful. But first they were compelled to hole themselves up in the palace for three days—essentially under house arrest—because their subjects, fearing they might escape, kept a vigilant eye on them. Under cloak of darkness, the royal family was finally able to sneak away during a masquerade ball, boarding Nelson's flagship, the H.M.S. *Vanguard*. Looking forward to his daily hunting in the sister kingdom he had ruled for four decades but had never before seen, Ferdinand had already sent the royal dogs ahead.

It should have been a short sea voyage across the Bay of Naples to Palermo, but the flotilla bearing the royal family, their personal property, and hundreds of retainers was caught in a horrific storm on December 23, 1798, causing tremendous damage to the *Vanguard*. The queen's favorite child, six-year-old Prince Alberto, became ill on the journey and died in Lady Hamilton's arms. By the time the ship limped into the snowy port on Christmas morning, the grief-stricken Maria Carolina no longer wished to live, let alone reign.

After the Neapolitans registered their shock and disbelief at the disappearance of their sovereigns, some judicious royal spin-doctoring recast their departure as an extended holiday: The king had never visited his other realm and had chosen to do so now. One purported reason for his Sicilian journey was to gather military reinforcements. Yet few believed the story. Although Palermo was the other capital of the Kingdom of the Two Sicilies, Ferdinand and Maria Carolina were perceived by royalist and revolutionary alike not as exchanging one capital city for the other, but as abandoning their Neapolitan thrones.

Following their cloak-and-dagger departure, the monarchs ordered the willful destruction of their naval fleet. All Neapolitan ships were to be torched, to prevent the French from capturing the vessels and enlarging their own navy, then turning the guns against the Neapolitan citizens. It was a maritime tragedy. Years of the queen's focus, money, and ambition went up in smoke in a matter of hours.

In Sicily, the royal family was in crisis; the monarchs' marriage was in a shambles; their children, as well as their offspring's spouses, were seriously ill. The king blamed his wife for encouraging him to attack Rome, thereby poking the Napoleonic hornet's nest—an action that he believed had led to their present situation in Palermo's damp and chilly Colli Palace, refugees from their own mainland home. Maria Carolina was exasperated by her husband's inaction and placidity. "Nothing is done," she lamented. "And soon, in spite of our privations, we shall be in financial straits, for we must create everything anew, marine, artillery, everything. . . . Alas, the thought of being dishonoured and disparaged throughout Europe kills me even more than my losses and misfortunes."

Their reign and their marriage were both failures. Deep in mourning for little Prince Alberto, Maria Carolina detested Sicily, whose "customs and ideas" she described as being "sixty years behind the times." She became permanently morose, although she should have had something to cheer. By the end of the eighteenth century, the queen had married off her oldest surviving children so astutely that she was being called the "mother-in-law of Europe." Members of Maria Carolina's immediate family sat on thrones reaching across one-third of the continent.

This might have brought a measure of solace, but not contentment. In the early weeks of 1799, the queen's winter cold and perpetual throat infections gave Ferdinand, fearing contagion, an additional excuse to avoid her company. Far less indisposed than she by their change in fortunes, he was glad to go out hunting "to spare himself the tedium of his wife's tears."

A simple man of simple tastes, after thirty-one years, he still couldn't handle being married to a drama queen, even when her losses—the deaths of their children and the downfall of Naples— were his as well. "Whether owing to religion, resignation, virtue or temperament, he is far more resigned to his fate than I," griped Maria Carolina. So fed up was Ferdinand with his wife's constant weeping and morbidity that he left the Colli Palace and took up residence in a coastal villa, cheerfully dividing his time between this sanctuary and the theater, and rarely visiting his wife or children. Maria Carolina lamented to Lady Hamilton, "I am neither consulted nor even listened to, and am excessively unhappy."

In the monarchs' absence, the French, abetted by the Neapolitan Jacobins, transformed Naples from a kingdom into the Parthenopean Republic, named for an ancient Greek colony that had existed in the same locale. Trees of liberty were planted, sympathizers wore the red Phrygian caps of the French Revolutionaries, and a new tricolor flag of red, blue, and yellow was raised. Any man unfortunate enough to be named Ferdinand hastened to be rechristened, or risked assault merely for sharing the king's name. The Neapolitan streets were renamed, too, in a similar vein to the Revolutionary-era Parisian *rues*, with absurd symbolic monikers such as Fortune, Triumph, Fecundity, Hilarity, Innocence, and Frugality.

From Sicily, Ferdinand and Maria Carolina supported a counterinsurgency, but things got horrifically out of hand. The former treasurer to Pope Pius VI and superintendent of Ferdinand's silk factory, Cardinal Fabrizio Ruffo, led a ragtag army known as the Sanfedisti (the Army of the Faith) against the French, but his rebels were just as bloodthirsty as Napoleon's troops or the Neapolitan Jacobins. Meanwhile, the *lazzarone*, the previously indolent underclass so devoted to Ferdinand, independently dispensed their own brand of justice to the political enemies of their beloved monarch, viciously slaughtering hundreds of innocent and defenseless men, women, and children. Cardinal Ruffo either encouraged or turned a blind eye to the carnage.

Finally, in an effort to halt the unremitting violence on both sides, Ruffo signed an unauthorized two-month armistice, infuriating the monarchs. Neither the king nor Maria Carolina could countenance the cardinal's capitulation of amnesty to those who had collaborated with the enemy—the occupying French Republican army. The queen wanted vengeance, not compromise. Yet Ruffo believed he had no alternative. Moreover, he *had* reconquered the monarchs' lost kingdom for them. Explaining his rationale for the truce to Acton, he wrote, ". . . Having to govern, or more precisely to curb, a vast population accustomed to the most resolute anarchy; having to control a score of uneducated and insubordinate leaders of light troops, all intent on pillage, slaughter and violence, is so terrible and complicated a business that it is utterly beyond my strength." Although he had nowhere to restrain them, "1,300 Jacobins" had nonetheless been handed over to him, men ". . . [who] must have massacred or shot at least fifty in my presence without my being able to prevent it, and wounded at least two hundred, whom they even dragged here naked." Accused of coddling the enemy, the cardinal came under suspicion of being a secret Jacobin.

Thanks in part to Ruffo's invasion with his Sanfedisti, in June of 1799 the Parthenopean Republic collapsed, within six months of its formation. But the real hero of the hour—at least to the Neapolitan monarchs—was Lord Nelson, acting beyond the scope of his commission by actively strategizing on behalf of a foreign government to keep them in power. Yet, with an inept and militarily inexperienced Neapolitan sovereign, and an unpopular queen who had lost all perspective and become a vengeful termagant bent on executing every revolutionary, Nelson's unthinkable alternative would have been to allow Naples to permanently fall to Napoleon.

The royalist crackdown was intense. While the queen stayed safely in Palermo, and Ferdinand remained aboard Nelson's flagship in the Bay of Naples, rough justice was dispensed in their names, as trials proceeded with the ruthlessness of a personal vendetta. Yet things were not quite as bad as Maria Carolina and Ferdinand's enemies have painted it. Out of eight thousand political prisoners, one thousand four were punished. Only a hundred and five of those were sentenced to death, although six of them were reprieved; two hundred twenty-two received life imprisonment; three hundred twenty-two were given shorter terms of incarceration; two hundred eighty-eight were deported; and sixty-seven were exiled.

The Neapolitan monarchy's previous constitutional freedoms were abolished in the zeal to cleanse the kingdom of revolutionaries. Yet even after order had been restored, Ferdinand was afraid to return to Naples, despite Maria Carolina's desire to do so immediately. The frustrated Lord Nelson wrote, "Plain common sense points out that the King should return to Naples, but nothing can move him." One reason for this was the disagreement between the royal spouses as to how the kingdom should be ruled, going forward. As Nelson put it, "[T]he King and Her Majesty do not, at this moment, draw exactly the same way."

After more than thirty years of marriage, Ferdinand had finally decided to put his foot down. From a man who had cared for nothing but the pursuit of his own personal pleasures, he became a martinet, parsimonious about household accounts, the one thing in his life over which he could assert full control. Maria Carolina groused, "We are all kept so sparingly as to lack everything."

The queen was disgusted with her husband, as well as with the prevailing political climate in Naples. She hated Sicily, which was more of a backwater than Naples had been before she'd given it a healthy dose of Viennese sophistication three decades earlier. Ever the mother hen, Maria Carolina gloomily declared, "Were it not for my daughters, I should wish to bid adieu to the world, and retire to a convent, there to terminate my days, a desire prompted by circumstances in which I am placed." Between her melodramatic lines could be read the balance of her message: There was no longer a place in her life for her husband.

Ferdinand felt the same way about her. After decades, he wanted to reign on his own, even if the results might be less successful. The Count de Damas had observed that Maria Carolina's power over her husband was entirely dependent on his taste for her, waning if his head had been turned by another woman. According to Damas, the reason the king returned to his wife in the wake of one of his frequent infidelities was not because he missed her, but because he'd tired of the tedium of governing. In the count's opinion, the queen championed so many ill-conceived plans because she advanced an agenda without taking the time to analyze the consequences of her actions, aware that she might forfeit her window of influence with her spouse if she didn't act quickly. Many of Maria Carolina's governmental errors were due to this perpetual race against time and her struggle with Ferdinand's caprices. Damas observed, "His brain becomes exalted when he sees a glove well stretched over a beautifully shaped arm. . . . The Queen has spent her life leading the King and Acton by seduction, holding out her glove before one, her arm before the other, and always ending in doing what she wanted, but without being able to modify the effervescence of her character by reasoning. . . . In one of her last letters she wrote to me: 'I have always foreseen that as I grew older my power would diminish. . . .'"

In the spring of 1800, Sir William Hamilton was relieved of his post as ambassador to the court of Naples after thirty-six years, in part because England had perceived that he (and the ambassadress) had actively meddled in Neapolitan foreign affairs and influenced governmental policy. Having made the decision to return with her children to Austria, Maria Carolina asked to tag along on their journey home, traveling with Lord Nelson and the Hamiltons as far as Vienna. Ferdinand remained in Sicily.

Maria Carolina stayed in Austria for two years, driving her son-in-law Emperor Francis II crazy with her political interference, which he blamed for another round of hostilities between Austria and France, known as the Second Coalition.

After the wife and child of Naples's Crown Prince Francesco died of consumption, the Neapolitan Bourbons chose to form a political alliance with the Spanish branch of the family, in order to shore themselves up against the French. But Spain had become a pariah throughout Europe after signing a treaty with the French Republic in 1795. Without Maria Carolina's consent, Ferdinand brokered a double union with the Spanish for two of their children—Francesco and "Toto," the Princess Maria Antoinetta, who at the time was still in Austria with her mother.

The queen was extremely upset about her husband's matchmaking behind her back. She had no love for his family and had wanted her children to marry "respectable Austrians" instead. She failed to recognize that their son and heir had fallen in love with his Spanish cousin, the infanta, and wanted to wed her. It upset her all the more that Francesco was willing to remarry "only ten days after the death of his virtuous wife. . . ."

Yet Ferdinand's unsanctioned interference in the nuptials of their children was still not enough to drag Maria Carolina back to Sicily. "I am waiting for the King to express in writing his desire to see me again, so as not to hear him tell me the next day: '*Chi ti ha chia-mato*' [who summoned you]—depressing to one who returns with intense repugnance," she insisted, even as her Austrian relatives couldn't wait for her to depart.

Ferdinand finally sailed back to Naples in June 1802, but Maria Carolina, who was recovering "stoically" from an "excruciating operation" for a hemorrhoid infection, did not join him there until August.

The amnesty guaranteed to the Neapolitan Jacobins after the revolution in 1799 encouraged many of them to remain in Naples, and attracted many more. The rebels had spent the intervening years regrouping and recommencing their antiroyalist activities.

Consequently, the queen dreaded the welcome she might receive in her adopted kingdom, averring, "I leave [Austria] as one con-demned to death and certainly to torment for the rest of my life. . . . I shall attend the Council [of State]; I shall deliver my opinion; but my door will be closed to every class and rank, as I do not wish to be accused of dealing with spies." Writing from Trieste, en route to Naples, she lamented, "[U]nless I had children to marry, no force human or divine would have brought me back." Clearly she antici-pated no romantic reconciliation with her husband. A friendship grounded on their mutual affection for their children was the most she could hope for. When their daughter Maria Luisa died in child-birth a few weeks after the queen's arrival, the couple bonded over their grief.

By 1803, Napoleon's complex system of pacts, cease-fires, and armistices had failed, and he began to gobble up European territo-ries like Pac-Man. That spring, with utter disregard for his treaty with Naples, he occupied two of their ports, Brindisi and Taranto. The rest of the continent seemed uninterested in helping to defend the kingdom from falling entirely and becoming a dependent of the French Republic. Ferdinand wanted to return to Sicily, but the queen was certain that if they were to quit Naples now, another revolution would erupt as soon as they left the shore.

Finally, swallowing every ounce of pride, Maria Carolina wrote to Bonaparte directly, asking him to relieve the Neapolitans of the burden of supporting his troops. Sources differ with regard to the emperor's reaction; Harold Acton writes that he assured the queen of his strict neutrality, while other historians claim that Bonaparte never deigned to reply. The queen complained to her eldest daughter, now Empress of Austria, "[I]t is as if we were assaulted on the public highway" by France.

Yet Maria Carolina seemed to be the only one fuming over the intolerable burdens imposed upon them. Her husband still had his own priorities in order. Baron Alquier, the French Republic's envoy to Naples, wrote, "Amid heavy taxation and financial distress, all is being prepared for the great hunts at Persano, which absorb from three to four hundred thousand francs."

On January 2, 1805, Napoleon finally responded to the queen's scathing assaults with a blistering scolding. Did she think he was unaware of her machinations to regain Naples? "I have in my possession several of Your Majesty's letters, which leave no doubt as to your real secret intentions. However great Your Majesty's hatred of France, how is it possible, after all your experiences, that the love of your husband, children, family and subjects does not counsel a little more prudence and a policy more compatible with your interests? Cannot Your Majesty, whose mind is so distinguished among women, cast off the prejudices of your sex? Must you treat affairs of state like affairs of the heart? You have already lost your kingdom once: twice you have caused a war which has nearly ruined your father's family. Do you wish to cause a third?"

In the wake of Bonaparte's triumph over the combined forces of two emperors—Czar Alexander and Francis II of Austria—on December 26, 1805, the Treaty of Pressburg dissolved the Holy Roman Empire founded by Charlemagne. The Hapsburg crown lands were united into a single empire. Maria Carolina and Ferdinand's son-in-law Francis, no longer the Holy Roman Emperor Francis II, was given a new title: His Imperial and Apostolic Majesty The Emperor of Austria Francis I. And he was also no longer the autocrat he had been. Although on paper Francis got to retain his lands, for all intents and purposes he was now a Napoleonic puppet, and the Hapsburg domains were really a part of Bonaparte's vast empire.

Having crushed Austria, Napoleon looked southward, vowing "to punish the Queen of Naples, and to cast from the throne that

guilty woman who has so often and with so much effrontery pro-
faned every law, human and divine."

On January 23, 1806, for the second time in a decade, Ferdinand fled to Palermo before the advancing French army could force
him to do so. The rest of the royal family, including Maria Carolina, remained in Naples. The queen channeled her mother's
indomitability as she prepared for the French onslaught. She organized the kingdom's resistance movement, an activity that finally
renewed her spirit even as she tamped down her terror and continued to pack up the royal treasures.

Maria Carolina bade farewell forever to the city of Naples on
February 11, addressing the court after Mass that day, her voice
choked with tears. Then she and her daughters, daughter-in-law,
and granddaughters, along with their entourages, boarded a frigate
for Sicily. But they suffered another disastrous shipwreck, in which
nearly all of their precious possessions were lost at sea. After that,
Maria Carolina was compelled to dismiss most of the family's attendants, lacking the funds to pay their wages.

Napoleon conquered Naples almost as soon as the queen de-
parted. Although the kingdom was known as the Two Sicilies, and
Palermo was the sister capital to Naples, the emperor declared that
Ferdinand and Maria Carolina had abandoned their thrones and
forfeited their crowns. Napoleon then appointed his brother Joseph
Bonaparte king of Naples "[b]y the legitimate right of conquest."

Times had changed since the rebellion and counterrevolution of
1799. The self-indulgent and lazy Neapolitans, not political by nature, were sick of bloodshed and revolt. According to Count Roger
de Damas, the general who had commanded the monarchs' vanquished troops, "The feeble, the discontented, the indifferent, and
the timid look upon Joseph Bonaparte as a king; and a people grows
more readily accustomed to a change of dynasty than to a republican constitution. . . . If habit is a second nature, that will be the only
thing that will make the people desire their former masters."

Ferdinand was still warming the Sicilian throne, but with a
catch. He remained king of Sicily at the sole discretion of his British
allies, who'd been keeping a weather eye on the Neapolitan royal
family for the past few years. In Whitehall's misogynistic view,

Maria Carolina had meddled once too often in political affairs for their amusement. Although they were content to permit the far less competent Ferdinand to keep his throne as their puppet king in the Mediterranean, the queen was warned to keep her nose out of politics.

The Neapolitan royal marriage now rebooted to endure Palermo 2.0. Maria Carolina shut herself in the Colli Palace and dosed herself with increasing amounts of opium to dull the pains of neuralgia. But the king—resigned to the loss of Naples, according to the new British ambassador to Sicily, Hugh Elliot—went hunting every day, delighted to enjoy the pleasures of the great outdoors without the burden of ruling.

The monarchs could run, but they couldn't seem to escape from tragedy. Illness was even crueler to Ferdinand and Maria Carolina than imperial France. In May of 1806, their daughter "Toto" succumbed to TB, although Maria Carolina was convinced that Toto's jealous mother-in-law, the queen of Spain, had poisoned her. The following April, the sovereigns' oldest girl, Teresa, empress of Austria, died of a chill ten days after bearing her fourteenth child, who also expired after three days. Teresa's death hit the queen particularly hard; she was Maria Carolina's first child, her closest tie to her homeland, and the one she had counted on to mother her younger siblings after the queen herself had passed on. When Emperor Francis remarried only ten months later, it broke Maria Carolina's heart that Francis and Teresa's dozen surviving children immediately fell in love with their stepmother.

Clearly, the queen was dismayed by the younger generation's short memories and lack of respect. The next suitor who came calling for a daughter's hand was the duc d'Orléans—son of the turncoat who had sided with the French Revolutionaries, changing his name to Philippe Égalité, and voting to execute Maria Carolina's brother-in-law, Louis XVI. Much as Her Majesty loved to see her daughters make good marriages, Louis Philippe was the last man on earth she would have wanted the Princess Maria Amalia to wed. But the young couple genuinely fell in love, and the queen took a liking to the duc, despite her intentions to despise him. Only on the condition that Louis Philippe tell her everything about her beloved sister's final years would she forgive him for *his* family's betrayal of *hers*.

Named for her paternal grandmother, the twenty-eight-year-old Maria Amalia was the last of Ferdinand and Maria Carolina's daughters to marry. Her 1809 wedding to Louis Philippe marked the final time her parents were together in an official, formal capacity. By now, Ferdinand blamed his wife for every ill that had befallen him. If there had ever been any love between the spouses, there was no longer a trace of it.

Whatever specific transgressions Napoleon referred to when he denigrated Maria Carolina, they could not have been worse than his own. Adulterer and arch-hypocrite, he toppled monarchs while besmirching their reputations. Yet when he wished to shore up his self-actuated imperial status, he sought a bride from the same royal house he had impugned, ingratiating himself with the relatives and descendants of the very people he had made his career by destroying.

In 1810, another embarrassing marriage took place when Emperor Francis of Austria sacrificed his daughter Marie Louise, Ferdinand and Maria Carolina's first grandchild, on the altar of peace. He yoked her to Napoleon Bonaparte, thereby making Marie Louise empress of France. Maria Carolina would never accept this spawn of the French Revolution as one of the family, and it was a further affront to both the Hapsburgs and the Bourbons that Napoleon attempted to legitimize his claim to France's imperial throne by wedding the daughter of a genuine emperor. Ironically, Joachim Murat, Napoleon's brother-in-law, and by then the king of Naples, was against the imperial remarriage as well. Now that Maria Carolina and Ferdinand were Napoleon's grandparents-in-law, Murat feared it would hinder his own plans to conquer Sicily.

But Marie Louise quickly enchanted her husband and implored him to leave Sicily alone and not add it to his conquests. And so, to impress his new bride, Boney obliged her, on behalf of his "grandmother, the Queen of Sicily."

Some people, however, don't appreciate favors. Maria Carolina viewed her Sicilian subjects as country bumpkins, second-class compared to the Neapolitans, who were already inferior to the Austrians. She was clearly biding her time until she and her husband could reclaim the throne of Naples. Yet Ferdinand had become cozy with his English puppet-masters. By 1812, they were so tired of the queen's meddling in governmental affairs that William Bentinck, Britain's minister on the island, gave Ferdinand an ultimatum: If you want to retain our aid, abdicate in favor of your son Francesco and banish your wife from the kingdom.

On January 16, 1812, Ferdinand signed the deed of appointment, naming Francesco his vicar-general in Sicily with the words ". . . I yield and transfer to you with the ample title of 'Alter Ego' the exercise of all the rights, prerogatives, pre-eminences, and powers which could be exercised by myself. . . ." It had been agreed between Ferdinand and Bentinck that Francesco had the keys to the kingdom as long as he remained free of his mother's influence.

Having quit the palace, the royal spouses dwelled apart. Maria Carolina relocated to Santa Croce, a mile or so from Palermo. Ferdinand retired to Ficuzza, twenty-four miles from the capital, where he lived in sin with his mistress, the Princess of Partanna, a former lady-in-waiting to the queen.

By agreeing to cede his power to his son, Ferdinand was ultimately able to squeeze himself out from under the pressure of Bentinck's British thumb. The queen was not so fortunate. Maria Carolina reacted as one might expect to Bentinck's demand for her banishment, confronting him when he delivered the news. "Was it for this that I helped Nelson to win the Battle of the Nile? For this, that I brought your army to Sicily? General, is this your English honor?" she railed. Her reputation had been undeserved. She had "been poisoned" with a "burning, incessant, persistent calumny. . . . They have represented me as cruel—after I had saved hundreds of ungrateful people! They have portrayed me as ambitious. Yes, so I am, if it is ambitious to defend the crown received from God."

Her bitterness was boundless. "I have been deprived of the government of my own country, of the dignity of my character, of the affection of my husband and children!" the queen told Bentinck. "But *he* has never been a father—*he* has never been a sovereign, and cannot therefore have the feelings of insulted majesty. And then I am accused of treason because I wish to recover my just rights as a sovereign, a wife, and a mother."

Everything dear having been ripped from her, Maria Carolina, frail and ailing, was heard to remark in her waning months, "For a long time I have believed that I knew how to govern, and I have only found out my mistake when it was too late. In order to rule men wisely one should study and understand them; this I did not do. If ever God should restore me to the throne, I will begin a new life." But can one blame her for not knowing how to rule when the power and authority were first thrust upon her at the age of *sixteen*, as a stranger in a strange land with a husband who had abrogated all responsibilities to govern?

The queen filed a formal protest against her banishment with England, claiming they had no right to separate her from her family, effectively deposing her as queen. But for their sakes, she ultimately acquiesced to Britain's request and her husband's demands.

However, even Ferdinand believed that exile was too harsh a punishment, and regretted the necessity of this enforced estrangement after forty-four years of marriage. It was one thing to separate from his wife of his own volition, but quite another to have it mandated by a foreign entity and their tone-deaf viceregal minister.

In Maria Carolina's parting letter to her husband, she expressed her pity for him and told Ferdinand that she forgave him, but added that she would never forgive the "wretches" that surrounded him, and warned the king that the fate of his reign rested on a knife's edge. She closed the note by offering Ferdinand her prayers for himself and for Sicily.

The sixty-year-old queen was most grief-stricken at the prospect of being parted from her children. Her only consolation was that Prince Leopoldo, who refused to be separated from his mama, accompanied her into exile.

Emperor Francis had approved of his former mother-in-law's ouster from the Sicilian throne, but was too embarrassed by her request for refuge in Vienna not to grant it. Maria Carolina had become an international outcast; her children had to beg Francis to extend her a cordial welcome.

Even Ferdinand wrote to the Austrian emperor urging him to receive Maria Carolina and Leopoldo, because "for reasons very displeasing [to me], my dear wife [was] being obliged to leave this kingdom . . . to avoid greater misfortunes to us both."

Traveling as always with her precious family portraits, including those of the murdered French monarchs, Maria Carolina took the scenic route, finally arriving in Vienna on February 2, 1814, eight months after her departure from Sicily. This last living daughter of Empress Maria Theresa was granted the courtesy title of Queen of Sicily, and took up residence at the pastoral Hetzendorf Castle on the outskirts of Vienna.

How ironic that she would spend her final months dispensing advice to her favorite grandchild, Marie Louise, the wife of her greatest nemesis. As much as Maria Carolina had despised Napoleon, by now her enmity was a decade in the past and she was able to view him with respect, admiration, and even sympathy. She scolded the young French empress for refusing to follow her husband into exile after his downfall. Upon hearing that Marie Louise's father had forbidden her to do so, the queen declared that *she* would have tied her bed curtains together and escaped out the window to join her vanquished spouse. "At least, that is what I should have done in her place, for when one is married it is for life." Appalled that Marie Louise did not even have her husband's picture on display, Maria Carolina impressed upon her granddaughter the honor a wife owes to her husband, despite absence and adversity. She convinced her to retrieve the portrait, which Marie Louise placed atop her writing desk.

On September 7, the sixty-two-year-old Maria Carolina spent an exhausting day greeting visitors and courtiers at the glittering Congress of Vienna, the first major display of movers and shakers of Europe's new world order following the fall of Napoleon. She retired to bed at ten o'clock that evening, so tired that her son Leopoldo asked that she not be disturbed before seven the next morning.

But shortly after midnight, Maria Carolina's maid thought she had been summoned. She entered the queen's bedchamber to find her mistress dead on the floor, a number of letters scattered about her, her hand reaching for the bellpull. She had died of a stroke, or as it was termed then, a fit of apoplexy.

Laid out across a mantle of silver tissue, Maria Carolina's corpse was dressed in silver-colored slippers and a black taffeta gown, with a matching veil worn over a white lace cap. According to custom, a fan and a pair of gloves were placed at her feet, as well as a casket containing her entrails and a cushion that displayed the Order of the Starry Cross, an honor bestowed on noblewomen of uncommon virtues. She was buried in the Kaisergruft, the Hapsburgs' imperial crypt, where her parents are also interred.

The kingdoms of Naples and Sicily were directed to observe strict mourning for six months. Ferdinand ordered his secretary to read the following statement: "The dreadful blow struck at my soul by the fatal news which came as a thunder-bolt on the morning of the 22nd left me so dispirited that I could do nothing but retire to the country plunged in the most extreme affliction."

It was too little, and far too late, but in her death, Maria Carolina finally earned the praise of her nemesis, Napoleon, who eulogized his "grandmother" from exile on Elba. "That woman knew how to think and act like a queen, while preserving her rights and her dignity."

Violating his own mandated half-year period of mourning, on November 27, 1814, less than three months after Maria Carolina's death, Ferdinand wed his forty-four-year-old, raven-haired mistress Lucia Migliaccio, the widowed Princess of Partanna. Upon her royal nuptials, she was made Duchess di Floridia. It was a morganatic marriage, meaning that she could never formally or legally bear the title of queen. The placid-natured duchess, who knew nothing about politics and could not have been less interested in governance, was the temperamental opposite of Maria Carolina. "How happy I am! with a wife who lets me do what I will, and a minister who leaves me nothing to do," declared the delighted Ferdinand.

After Ferdinand's brother, King Carlos IV of Spain, had abdicated in 1808, Napoleon replaced him with his brother Joseph Bonaparte. The emperor then filled the vacancy on the Neapolitan throne with his own brother-in-law Joachim Murat. Seven years later, during the Neapolitan War against Austria in 1815, which coincided with Napoleon's Hundred Days return from exile, Murat was dethroned. Ferdinand returned to Naples, and in 1816, he reunited his sister realms into the Kingdom of the Two Sicilies, ruling both of them until his death.

Although he had been viewed as a fairly benign, if not kindly ruler in the prerevolutionary days, and had always been the king of the *lazzarone* (the darling of Naples's lowest classes), his postrevolutionary cruelty was well-known. After the demise of Maria Carolina, Ferdinand became a repressive autocrat, reigning as an absolute monarch and granting no constitutional reforms within his domains. This triggered a revolt in Sicily, but it was quickly quashed by Neapolitan troops. In 1820, Ferdinand was compelled to sign a constitution, which he repeatedly violated. The following year, Prince Metternich, chancellor of the Austrian Empire, authorized the Austrian army to enter Naples for the purpose of restoring order.

On January 2, 1825, Ferdinand went hunting for the last time. The following day, he suffered the symptoms of a cold, and by that evening he struggled to remain alert during his nightly card game with his wife, Lucia. His speech became slurred. He refused a bloodletting by the royal physicians, preferring to retire for the night with the request that he not be roused at his usual time of six a.m. After that hour had come and gone, at eight o'clock, Ferdinand's valet entered the king's room and asked whether His Majesty wanted the windows open. When he received no reply, he parted the bed hangings to discover the seventy-four-year-old monarch lying dead, his mouth slack, one arm hanging limply off the bed. Like Maria Carolina, Ferdinand had died of a stroke.

He lay in state for three days, during which time the theaters of Naples were closed in his honor. Mourning Ferdinand's demise, Lady Blessington, an English expatriate who had lived in Italy for years, wrote, "He is much regretted, for if not a sovereign of superior mental requirements, he was assuredly a good-natured man."

None of the Neapolitan royal family regretted the passing of the Duchess di Floridia the following year. Maria Carolina's children had never approved of their father's remarriage, a royal mismatch of social unequals.

Ferdinand was succeeded by Francesco, who had temporarily ruled Sicily in his stead during the period of British babysitting earlier in the century. Prince Leopoldo, who had accompanied his mother into exile, had remained in Vienna, marrying a daughter of Emperor Francis in 1816.

Each of Ferdinand and Maria Carolina's surviving daughters became a queen consort. After all the tragedies of the French Revolution, their daughter Maria Amalia, duchesse d'Orléans, became queen of France when her husband was chosen to reign after the abdication of Charles X (Louis XVI's youngest brother, the former comte d'Artois). Louis Philippe I, King of the French, and the Neapolitan-born Maria Amalia, a niece of Marie Antoinette, reigned from 1830 until 1848, when another French revolution overthrew them.

Empress Maria Theresa had, in her own words, sacrificed her daughter Maria Carolina to politics because the necessity of forging a strategic alliance between Austria and Spain in order to gain a measure of control in southern Italy trumped her child's marital happiness. And like it or not, the Austrian archduchesses were aware of the roles they were destined to play, not only within the Hapsburg dynasty, but on the international stage. Yet Maria Carolina's royal marriage to Ferdinand of Naples is an inglorious one, not only because it was so unhappy. When it came to the actual governance of the kingdom, in the misogynistic culture of eighteenth-century Naples, the traditional gender roles were reversed. This led to widespread dislike and distrust of Maria Carolina, despite the many progressive reforms she accomplished toward the beginning of her reign. By the time revolution had reached their borders, she was perceived as a harridan whom her husband could not control.

But Ferdinand and Maria Carolina had never been given the choice of a different partner. Nor would the concept that teenage royals had the right to marry for love have been an acceptable one. These two were forced to play the hand their parents dealt them till death (or in their case, the British government) parted them, making babies and making the best of it, regardless of whether their temperaments were compatible.

Most of the time, young royal spouses never met before their wedding day, and had learned nothing about each other, so they never knew whether their personalities and affinities would mesh. But Maria Carolina and Ferdinand are a rare exception to this rubric: Their parents, especially the Austrian empress, who was fully aware of the character and habits of both children, pushed her daughter into an inglorious mismatch with a boy she already knew to be a coarse and illiterate lout. Nevertheless, the security of her empire came first.

The fact that Maria Carolina and Ferdinand didn't kill each other over the course of four decades of matrimony, despite all their rows, is a testament to something we rarely see today: a deep religious faith (at least on the queen's part), and an unswerving devotion to their children, combined with a sense of duty and obligation to something larger than themselves. Not only did the hopes of their respective families rest on the success of their marriage, but the fate of their subjects and—during the era of Napoleon's campaigns—a significant portion of the world was in their hands. As Maria Carolina herself understood, despite the pitfalls of an inglorious union, "[W]hen one is married, it is for life."

PRINCESS MARIE
OF EDINBURGH
AND
FERDINAND I
OF ROUMANIA

MARRIED: 1893–1927

"*And* Love is a thing that can never go wrong; / And I am Marie of Roumania," the acerbic Dorothy Parker sardonically versified in her four-line "Comment" on life and love in the mid-1920s. Parker's poetic witticism illustrates the glamorous Balkan sovereign's popularity during the first quarter of the twentieth century, employing Marie's then–immediately recognizable identity as a personage of wealth and exoticism in the same way some people still sarcastically say, "Yeah, and I'm the queen of Sheba."

Typical of Parker's razor wit, her couplet was double-edged. At the time the poem was published, the whole world would have known that Marie's royal marriage, never a love match to begin with, had gone terribly wrong.

Marie Alexandra Victoria was born three years before the country she was destined to rule came into existence. A granddaughter of Queen Victoria, Missy, as she would always be known within the family, was the second of five children born to Victoria's second son Alfred ("Affie"), the Duke of Edinburgh, and his duchess, Marie Alexandrovna, a daughter of Czar Alexander II.

A devotee of fashion and beauty from the age of five (according to her own recollection), Missy spent her earliest years at the family estate of Eastwell in Kent. Blond and blue eyed, she was close to her siblings, especially her sister Victoria Melita ("Ducky"), who was taller and darker, and only thirteen months her junior. The Edinburghs were a more peripatetic family than many royals of the day because their father actually had a job. In 1886, when Missy was going on twelve, Affie was named commander of the Mediterranean fleet. He moved the family to his posting in Malta, where they remained for three years.

During their sojourn at Malta, the adolescent Missy experienced first love with her short, bearded, first cousin George, a naval lieutenant already in his early twenties. They flirted and kissed and exchanged affectionate correspondence when he was away at sea.

Even after the family moved again in 1889, this time to Coburg, Germany, in preparation for the day when Affie would inherit his uncle Ernest's duchies of Saxe-Coburg and Gotha, the general expectation, or at least the great hope, was that Missy—who was only fifteen at the time—would marry George. At this point, George was merely the Prince of Wales's "spare"; his older brother Prince Albert Victor ("Eddy") was second in line to the throne after their father. Even though he was a second son, George would nonetheless have been a prestigious catch, and Protestant princes were at a premium. Marriage to an English prince would have been considered a major alliance for Missy. Unfortunately, her Anglophobic mother was adamantly against it.

Another match that might have been was with the snub-nosed, "red-haired, freckled and impudent" Winston Churchill, who happened to pay a visit to Osborne, Queen Victoria's retreat on the Isle of Wight, while Missy and her family were also vacationing with her grandmama. "He and I had a sneaking liking for each other. At first we did not dare to show it openly, but by degrees our redhaired guest threw away all pretence and brazenly admitted his preference for me, declaring before witnesses that when he was grown up he would marry me!"

But marriage to a commoner would have been out of the question, regardless of his pedigree. A passionate Germanophile, the duchess, who abhorred London's society, food, weather, and most of all its dissipation, was determined to wed her eldest daughter to the kaiser's cousin Ferdinand, Crown Prince of Roumania, in a bid to pave the way for her own family, the Romanovs, to extend Russia's influence into the Balkans. Her own Anglophobic prejudices (as well as her Russian Orthodox beliefs against the intermarriage of first cousins—a credo that would nevertheless be violated with the marriage of Nicholas and Alexandra)—prevented her from acknowledging that the prospective match with Missy's cousin George would by far have been the more glorious union. And there would have been an unforeseen bonus to it as well. George's older brother died young, moving the prince up a notch in the line of succession. Missy would eventually have become queen of England, instead of queen of Roumania.

Ferdinand wasn't even Roumanian; nor was the country's king, Carol I. In 1861, the Roumanian Parliament voted to invite a foreign royal to accept their throne as a deterrent to the rampant squabbling among the nobility. Fighting on behalf of the Roumanians, Carol (formerly Karl), from the Sigmaringen branch of Germany's Hohenzollern dynasty, had defeated the Turks in 1877, completely freeing the Roumanians from Ottoman tyranny. But by decree, the king of Roumania could not wed a native, for fear that such a union would lead to a return of the former corruption. So Carol married a German princess, Elisabeth of Wied, who in due time became a free-spirited patron of the arts, and a mediocre dilettante in her own right, assuming the pseudonym Carmen Sylva. Their only child, a daughter, had died at the age of four, and Carol adopted his nephew, Ferdinand, as his heir.

Ferdinand Viktor Albert Meinrad was the second son and favorite child of Carol's older brother, Prince Leopold, and his wife, Princess Antonia of Hohenzollern-Sigmaringen, a Portuguese infanta. Unfortunately, he was shy to the point of being inarticulate. Although Ferdinand possessed an encyclopedic knowledge of botany and a corresponding passion for flora—one of the only interests Missy would share—biology had betrayed him. His legs were too short for his long torso, and when he was a child, his parents had instructed his nurse to bandage his head in an (unsuccessful) effort to pin back his protruding ears. When Ferdinand became an adult, his head would indeed resemble a two-handled pitcher.

Carol had first offered to make Ferdinand's older brother, Wilhelm, his heir, but after a year in the Balkans, Wilhelm found the lifestyle there unrewarding and was ready to come home. Ferdinand lacked the guts to take a stand regarding his own destiny. He was the perfect good soldier, diligent and obedient, and too weak-willed to question authority. Off he went to Roumania to become schooled in their history and politics. A rigid autocrat, Carol drilled Ferdinand night and day, refusing to let him socialize with anyone beyond the immediate family.

Consequently, the crown prince spent a considerable amount of time in the company of the queen, which left him ample opportunity to fall in love with Hélène Vacaresco, her favorite lady-in-waiting. Hélène was clever and witty, a talented writer, but plump and homely, a commoner, and moreover Roumanian, which made her absolutely off-limits. The kingdom's constitution contained an ironclad clause compelling its kings to marry foreign-born princesses of equal rank.

After Ferdinand was given an ultimatum—Hélène or the throne—much as he believed he loved the girl, he gave her up, with abject apologies to his parents and his uncle for causing them so much angst. To cure his broken heart, he was sent on a Grand Tour of Western Europe to meet *eligible* young princesses, bearing in his pocket a handwritten list of candidates that King Carol had compiled for him.

Missy was the first name on Carol's list, so Ferdinand requested her photograph before their first meeting. A decade older than the fifteen-year-old princess, Ferdinand had already become enchanted by her photo by the time they saw each other in Cassel; it was the occasion of Missy's first adult appearance in society. She thought the family was merely visiting her cousin Kaiser Wilhelm. Little did she know, after her mother bought her a new mauve gown (her favorite color), and slyly schemed to have her seated next to Ferdinand at dinner, that she was being scouted.

But nothing came of it, at least not immediately. Berlin was filled with worldly belles, and although she was slender and fair, the sheltered Missy, a mere *Backfisch*, or teenager, failed to make an impression with any of the sophisticated grown men she met during her visit. After one week, she was whisked back to the less cosmopolitan confines of Coburg.

Meanwhile, over in England, the Waleses wondered why their

boy George hadn't heard from Missy in two years. Owing to the death of his older brother in January 1892, he was now second in line to Victoria's throne. What was not to like? George wrote to Missy to reopen the lines of communication. Unbeknownst to him, her mother had intercepted his correspondence and responded on Missy's behalf. The duchess ghostwrote a Dear John letter to George, informing him that he should not have taken their Malta flirtation seriously.

George would go on to wed his late brother's fiancée Princess Mary of Teck, while the duchess brought Missy to Munich and spent the spring of 1892 finding ways to throw her daughter and Ferdinand together: at dinner parties, outdoor excursions, visits to galleries, theater parties, and shopping ventures. The elder Marie never passed up a chance to enumerate the merits of Eastern Europe. Being Russian herself made her feel infinitely superior to other mortals, but Roumania was the next-best thing, being at the time the easternmost country in Western Europe.

The duchess—who firmly believed that princesses should marry when they were young, before they began "to think too much and to have too many ideas of their own which complicate matters"— was relentless in her intent to demonstrate the merits of wedding a cultivated German prince. All her daughter needed to do was say yes to the match. Ultimately, Missy's maternal instincts, untested as they were, were aroused by Ferdinand's overwhelming shyness. Even though he was a decade older than she was, it gave her "a longing to put him at ease . . . in fact you wanted to help him." Missy was also charmed by the prince's unpretentious and amiable character.

Despite their ten-year age gap and the fact that Ferdinand spoke no English, he had been given no more preparation for marriage, or evidently for anything else, than Missy had. As she would later write in her memoirs, "We were brought up in a Fool's Paradise. . . . We had been kept in glorious, but I cannot help considering dangerous and almost cruel, ignorance of all realities . . . it was . . . a deliberate blinding against life as it truly is, so that with shut eyes and perfect confidence we would have advanced towards any fate."

The couple became engaged at the Neue Palais in Potsdam.

Missy wrote, "How he ever had the courage to propose is . . . a mystery to me; but he *did* and I accepted—I just said 'Yes,' as though it had been quite a natural and simple word to say . . . and with that 'Yes' I sealed my fate." The duchess was "radiant" that her plan had come to fruition.

The match had been an inside job, instigated and prodded by the Duchess of Edinburgh. Missy's father had not been present at the announcement of her engagement and had yet to meet her fiancé. The princess's conscience was troubled that the English side of her family was not on board with her prospective marriage. Queen Victoria would ultimately realize what a dismal, inglorious union it was, her clever, vivacious granddaughter sacrificed to be a breeding cow in Europe's hinterlands. She would privately speak of Missy as "a great victim . . . to be enormously pitied."

More troubling to the "victim" herself was the ever-present shadow of King Carol, *der Onkel*, as Ferdinand referred to him, inserting his autocratic uncle's name into every conversation. The crown prince couldn't even visit the privy (or so it appeared) without *der Onkel*'s permission. According to Missy, "When he spoke of him something very like anxiety and not far removed from dread came into his eyes; one felt that a shiver ran down his spine."

At least, according to Missy, the fiancés got along like gangbusters during the period of their engagement. "Nando and I were two loving companions advancing towards perfect bliss, towards plenitude and fulfillment, beneath the kindly, indulgent smiles of those who were going to make our road easy for us and our life all joy. . . ."

Having secured the marriage she desired for her daughter, the Duchess of Edinburgh then began to wrangle over Missy's wedding plans. The Sigmaringen branch of the Hohenzollerns were Catholics and the British royal family were Protestants; by wedding Ferdinand, Missy would have to renounce all claims to the English throne, even though she was miles down the line of succession. Additionally, the official religion of their mutual adopted country was neither of their own; they would be expected to raise their future offspring in the Roumanian Orthodox Church. Queen Victoria, who wanted her grandchild wed at Windsor, was none too pleased that Missy could not have the ceremony there, because she was not marrying another Anglican. The pope was miffed, because the Hohenzollerns were blowing off their Catholicism for the sake of the Roumanian throne. Then there was a bit of a hiccup when Victoria asked King Carol whether it was true that his nephew had previously been engaged to another girl. Embarrassed that HRM had somehow gotten wind of the Hélène Vacaresco episode, the king lied through his teeth and blamed it on his wife's fanciful imagination. As the flighty Carmen Sylva was legendary for her whimsy, Queen Victoria swallowed Carol's fib. Missy, too, had no idea that there had indeed been a prior love and that Ferdinand "was supposed to be travelling about with a broken heart."

Ultimately, the main reason the wedding ceremony was postponed until January 1893 was to wait for Missy to grow up a bit. As it was, she would wed at the ripe old age of seventeen. Meanwhile, 1892 was spent paying visits to various branches of both sides of everyone's family. Although she was thrilled with all her new clothes, Missy felt "excruciatingly shy and ridiculously self-conscious" during all the requisite changes of wardrobe throughout each day, as if she were just a girl playing dress-up. "Occasionally I felt nothing but a negligible accessory to my voluminous sleeves, in which I almost entirely disappeared. I may have been smart but I was certainly not *chic*. I do not think Mamma considered it quite proper or *bon ton* for a princess to be *chic*."

"Nando," as everyone called Missy's dark-haired, mustachioed fiancé, doted on her with puppyish ardor, but the more she grew acquainted with him, the more she realized how ill-suited they were. As Marie of Roumania recollected in her memoirs, ". . . on my side all my feelings, ideas and visions were based upon an entirely erroneous conception of life. I was happy in a slightly troubled way. I was strangely incurious. I did not fear the future, I was too much a born optimist and idealist to fear anything. . . ." Not only that, "I was to be led utterly innocent up to the altar. . . . But there were occasional moments when it suddenly came to me that Nando and I had not perhaps exactly the same tastes about everything. . . ." Marie was an outdoorsy, sporty girl who adored horses; Nando preferred the cultured refinement of indoor pursuits.

Nonetheless, the pair mutually enjoyed a significant amount of premarital kissing when they were together; when they were apart, they exchanged numerous billets-doux. Lonely without her, Ferdinand wrote daily to his fiancée, assuring Missy that there never before had been a duo that "loved each other more and were more happy than we two." He insisted that they demonstrate to their respective sets of parents how grateful they were for arranging their marriage, adding that he had already promised his own father and mother that he and Missy would be "good and obedient children"—this from a man nearly twenty-seven years old.

A few days before the royal wedding, the Duke of Edinburgh spoke privately with his daughter to inform her of two things: that he was giving Missy a dowry of a million French francs, and that he'd always harbored different plans for her future (perhaps an unspoken allusion to the much-desired match with her cousin George).

On the wintry morning of January 10, 1893, Missy and Ferdinand suffered through a trio of wedding ceremonies: civil, Catholic, and Protestant. Missy discovered that the Latin chants during the Catholic ritual had a hypnotically relaxing effect on her. This ceremony was much grander than the subsequent one. A British naval chaplain conducted the Anglican rite in a small anteroom of Sigmaringen Castle's Ancestors' Hall.

Missy's still-flat teenaged bosom was tightly laced into her wedding gown with its bell-shaped skirt and stylish leg-of-mutton sleeves. The dress and train were constructed of corded white silk embellished with crystals, pearls, and silver sequins. She disliked lace veils, and therefore had received a special dispensation to wear one made of tulle. It was secured to her fashionably frizzled hair with a diamond tiara wreathed in the orange blossoms her grandmother had henceforth made a tradition for English brides. Throughout the long day, dressed according to her mother's taste and not her own, Missy felt as though she were in a dreamworld, playing a role and lacking the dignity to live up to the weightiness of her "overpowering finery" and the gravity of the occasion.

Ferdinand's father gave the newlyweds the nearby hunting *Schloss* of Krauchenwies for their honeymoon. The castle was picturesque and romantic in a German fairy tale sort of way, but Missy, more properly Marie of Roumania now, was terribly home-sick for her family and was immediately overwhelmed with the burdens of being a wife. It was winter, with nothing to do. Both spouses were just getting to know each other and too shy to ex-periment. "Nando was not a man of high spirits, nor was he imag-inative, so he was quite at a loss how to entertain so childishly young a wife."

Evidently, their maiden efforts at marital sex were a disaster. Ferdinand was in love with Marie, but clearly more exuberant than sensitive to her needs in bed. She described him as "terribly, almost cruelly in love. In my immature way I tried to respond to his pas-sion, but I hungered and thirsted for something more. . . . There was an empty feeling about it all; I still seemed to be waiting for something that did not come."

Marie was waiting for the magic and fireworks. The tingling of arousal that she had naively dreamed might happen. The tender-ness of marital lovemaking. She had hoped for a fairy tale. She got it, but the story was closer to *Beauty and the Beast*. Embarrassed at the way his clumsy attempts at passion were received, Ferdinand felt rejected by his child bride. Marriage was, as Marie would later describe, "a bad shock," and it took her a long time to "adjust my . . . mind . . . to accept it."

As Marie would soon discover, real life had hard edges. The palace in Bucharest that was to be her new home was surrounded by iron railings. The dimly illuminated "*Altdeutsch* and bad ro-coco" rooms, which Marie pronounced a "disaster" of bad taste, were hung with depressing religious paintings, although several of the canvases were El Grecos. The autocracy and austerity of King Carol's persona permeated every aspect of life in the royal precincts of Roumania. No one was permitted to enjoy themselves. In fact, Carol had suggested that his nephew take only a *Honigtag*—a honey *day*, rather than a honeymoon, or month, to celebrate his nuptials.

According to *der Onkel*, the purpose of life was work and devo-tion to the governance of the realm. Ferdinand and Carol spent all day, every day, in governing; every night was spent *discussing* governing over "such huge cigars, you never could hope that they would come to an end," while Marie grew sick from inhaling their fumes. Her only purpose was to make babies. At the formal balls and receptions, the king forbade her from dancing with any of the young men. Compelled to accept invitations only from the old geezers, the tall, blond, athletic, and free-spirited princess soon lost her desire to dance as well.

Neither Ferdinand nor Marie could choose their own servants; nor were they allowed the society of friends or acquaintances, because everyone in Roumania, except for the annoying bohemian queen, was a social inferior. Friends were dangerous, argued Carol. He decreed that his heirs should form no attachments outside the immediate family, as it might lead to their becoming allied with one or another of Roumania's political parties. The crown prince and princess were not even permitted to visit anyone's private residence or to set foot inside a foreign embassy. As a consequence of *der Onkel*'s rigidity and Ferdinand's early disappointment over the Hélène Vacaresco incident, Marie wrote that "Nando . . . had lost his faith in people: he had become painfully suspicious and was on the defensive even against those who were attached to us. This attitude on the part of my young husband did much to make our early years difficult and painful; he trusted no one and felt that isolation was my only safety."

While Ferdinand meekly acquiesced to his uncle at every turn, Marie chafed against it. "Cast out from Paradise," and wallowing in self-pity, she "felt like a prisoner behind iron bars peeping out upon" the "impossibly happy world" she'd left behind. Her lazy husband was tiresome. Her daily routine, taking nearly every meal with King Carol, relieved by only a few breaks for kissing and fondling with Nando, was tiresome. Eager as the Duchess of Edinburgh had been to marry her off to Ferdinand, she had neglected to educate her daughter about the birds and the bees. After only two weeks of marriage, the crown princess complained to her lady-in-waiting that she felt sick and miserable. The older woman immediately diagnosed her condition, and Marie was shocked to discover that she'd already become pregnant. Royal mothers are supposed to be delighted at the prospect of bearing an heir; it's the raison d'être for their marriages. Not so Marie of Roumania. She took the news "tragically," feeling as though she "had been trapped."

During Marie's first pregnancy, a tremendous family contretemps took place behind the scenes regarding her delivery. The Roumanian clergy wanted to control the birth of the potential heir to their throne and insisted that the crown princess endure a natural childbirth, suffering in agony for the sins of Eve. Queen Victoria and Marie's mother wouldn't hear of it. They secured the services of one of England's royal physicians, Dr. Playfair, who had been successfully tranquilizing his patients with the innovative painkiller chloroform.

Thanks to chloroform, Marie had "a very easy time," in Playfair's words, giving birth to a son on October 15, 1893. The doctor, however, wasn't the one enduring her labor pains; Marie herself reported that the chloroform availed little. Missy "felt like turning my face to the wall, unwilling to take up a life again in which such pain could exist." She didn't share her adopted subjects' enthusiasm for the new heir, and was annoyed by the thunderous cannon fire that announced Prince Carol's safe arrival into the world. She felt no sense of elation or accomplishment, but rather that she was the victim of a grand conspiracy—the collaborators being her biology, her family, and her destiny. It was the same fate as every female royal—to be a well-dressed, bejeweled broodmare. Perhaps Marie also believed she had been led to the sacrifice too young. Prince Carol's christening day on October 29, 1893, was also her eighteenth birthday.

Despite Marie's determination at the time to never become pregnant again, within three months of giving birth to the prince, she was once more *enceinte*. "One feels so humiliated at being so ugly. I don't know if all women suffer so much under it as I do! Perhaps it is not right but I cannot help it," she lamented in a letter to her mother. On October 12, 1894, Marie bore a daughter—this time without anesthesia, at the insistence of the Roumanians, including their queen Elisabeth, for whom the baby, Elisabetha, was named.

But even after two children with Ferdinand, Marie had yet to find her moorings in Roumania. At the time, she felt she had "no real identity; people seemed to dispose of me according to their will. . . ." She was ". . . in harness . . . merely a little wheel in a watch which was keeping Uncle's [King Carol's] time but a little wheel which had to do its part, relentlessly, and no one tried to surround that part with any glamour or make it seem worth while; it was all work and no play, I was with a vengeance the stranger in a stranger land. Everything I did seemed always to be wrong and no one understood that when you were young and life runs like fire through your veins, you wanted . . . to laugh, to be foolish with companions of your own age, to use your own faculties, to be a separate entity, someone with a mind of her own, with her own thoughts, her own habits, tastes, ideals, desires." This is the lament of every princess in Marie's shoes, before and since.

Marie was finally able to take a break from her restrictive social life in the summer of 1896, during a trip to Russia with her husband for the imperial coronation of her cousins Nicholas and Alexandra. Romanovs made Nando nervous, but Marie, dressed in gold lamé to witness the solemn ritual, was enthralled. This vacation was a revelation. By day, she dazzled everyone with her equestrienne daring. During the evenings, she was the belle of every ball, and it was then and there that she discovered her power to attract and enchant men. Modesty did not come easily. "I rejoice in my beauty. Men have taught me to," she boldly told one of her many admirers.

Later that year, Marie and Ferdinand received a visit from her brother, Alfred, who had brought along their cousin, Russian Grand Duke Boris, two years Marie's junior. The duo stayed long enough for Marie and Boris to commence a flirtation that did not pass unnoticed. The news of a possible royal affair even reached Coburg. Marie was smitten by her Russian cousin's carefree personality and sentimental nature, his tremendous charm, enchanting smile, and his husky voice with its slight lisp that she loved to mimic. They would remain friends for many years, and, according to Marie's memoirs, Boris would "occasionally declare with a deep sigh that I had been the first love of his life."

Defending her conduct to her mother, Marie explained how different her temperament was from her husband's. "Perhaps," she wrote, "I have not been as nice to Nando as I ought to have been, and am too easily irritated. . . . What is so difficult is that he always first says no to everything." Marie assured the duchess that she still loved Ferdinand—she just wasn't *in* love with him anymore. At the same time, she conceded that there was no other man she'd prefer to be married to, and admitted that "the pleasant thing . . . with other men is just that they have no right over you . . . . I am born with a desperate desire of my own physical bodily liberty," she would later insist. "My husband sees me cry, he is awfully sorry, he wants to console me, he has every intention to do so, his heart is full of love, he begins to kiss me then he forgets that, and tries to console me by giving way to just that, that I dread most on earth."

Was Marie admitting to her mother that she abhorred having sex with her own husband? How un-Victorian to speak of such matters! How un*royal* to admit her unhappiness!

Of course, Marie was married to a very Victorian and very royally entitled man, and therein lay the crux of their connubial problems: "What does one find, a man intensely in love with you, & who has the right to ask everything of you, when you ask him to read to you in the evening he hurries over it only to get to bed for other amusements which he does not perhaps think is a one-sided amusement, when one wants to talk with him, he is reading the newspapers, when one says one is lonely, he says you have the children, he is perfectly devoted to you, and yet he will not give up even a cigar to sit a moment with you!"

The devoted, yet clueless Ferdinand came down with typhoid fever in May of 1897, and the family prepared for his imminent demise. He had the strength to pull through, although the disease, and his lengthy convalescence, left him much altered in appearance. Nando's physique was gaunt, his face pale and haggard, and he had lost almost all of his hair. Only thirty-two, he appeared significantly older.

Ferdinand was an invalid for so long that King Carol had assigned an aide-de-camp to attend to Marie's needs as crown princess. It was a pure case of sending the fox to guard the henhouse. The dashing Lieutenant Zizi Cantacuzène was already an officer in Marie's regiment of Hussars. He was short, dark, and a flamboyant dresser, and his sense of mischief at a time when Marie sorely needed her own spirits lifted made for a combustible combination. Soon the pair were spending a good deal of time together, a fact duly noted by a governess to the royal children, who reported to the king the crown princess's untoward behavior with her aide-de-camp.

In Roumania, extramarital affairs, even royal ones, didn't raise more than an eyebrow and a shrug. It was a lusty society and such things were de rigueur. However, Marie's German and English relations found it utterly unacceptable (despite the fact that nearly all of her male relatives had mistresses). Women were expected to behave with complete propriety. And Marie's antics with her aide-de-camp engendered gossip across Europe. As Marie's aunt Vicky (the German empress, and Kaiser Wilhelm's mother) wrote to her daughter, who was then crown princess of Greece, "I think Missy of Roumania is more to be pitied than you. . . . The King is a great tyrant in his family, & has crushed the independence in Ferdinand so that no one cares about him, & his beautiful & gifted little wife, I fear, gets into scrapes, & like a butterfly, instead of hovering over the flowers, burns her pretty wings by going rather near the fire!"

The king had granted the crown princess permission to chaperone Zizi's thirteen-year-old orphaned cousin about Bucharest, which permitted Marie to spend even more time with her aide-de-camp. But after she was criticized for using the child as a screen to shield her adulterous affair, and she had lost the letter proving that the visit had been vetted, Marie's romance with Zizi Cantacuzène became a cause célèbre. Queen Victoria scolded King Carol for letting the gossip spread across the globe. His Majesty warned Marie, "We of course all know that Nando may not be so very entertaining. But that does not mean that you may find your entertainment elsewhere." Zizi was transferred to a different regiment that was posted out of the country.

The king sent Marie and Ferdinand off to Coburg for an enforced vacation and commanded them to reconcile. The crown prince returned to Roumania first. Soon after his arrival, he sent urgent word to Marie that their oldest child, Prince Carol, had been stricken with typhoid. She rushed back to Bucharest, only to have her way barred by the same governess who had ratted out her liaison with Zizi.

But Nando defended his wayward wife. For perhaps the first time ever, he stood up for *something*, ordering the governess to "Stand aside. The Crown Princess is the child's mother."

If only this remark had been the beginning of a true understanding between the spouses. Each owned a share of the responsibility for the failure of their marriage. Marie did not keep her passions in check. But she was yoked to someone it was so difficult to admire. As her mother wrote to King Carol, Ferdinand's "laziness, his . . . antipathy for all work, for any serious endeavor and . . . worst of all, his sensual passion for Missy [which] finished by . . . repulsing her," were hardly a recipe for success. "Nando will himself avow that he treated his wife like a mistress, caring little for her emotional well-being in order to constantly assuage his physical passions." Lest Carol should imagine that Marie's adultery with Zizi, if indeed their flirtation had gone that far, condemned her more than Ferdinand, the duchess reminded the king that "as a positive fact," she knew Nando had enjoyed his own extramarital liaisons.

When Marie became pregnant for the third time in 1899, she personally begged King Carol's permission to bear the child in Coburg, surrounded by her family. When he predictably refused, she made the stunning declaration that it was her cousin Boris's baby she was carrying. At this, the king relented, and at Gotha on January 9, 1900, Missy gave birth to her third child, Marie, who would always be nicknamed "Mignon" in honor of the opera the crown princess had attended that evening.

Although Marie of Roumania had never felt much love for her first two children, with Mignon, there was a rush of maternal instinct. Because Mignon was born during a time when she had been deeply unhappy, Marie always referred to this daughter as "the child of my flesh." Whether Mignon was really his child or Boris's, Nando never disavowed her paternity, and she would become his favorite child—but he reproached his wife for the girl's birth in more subtle, passive-aggressive ways than openly accusing her of infidelity.

For years after her return to Roumania with the newborn Mignon, Marie was treated like a prisoner. "Nando shuts me up completely," she wrote to her mother in 1902. "[P]erhaps I am paying for former mistakes, but it is almost unbearable . . . it really is an exile down here. . . . And there is not only one jailor, they are all jailors."

Marie's social life could not have been quite as dire as she made it out to be, because during this period, she became great friends with the American-born British expat, future politician, and business tycoon Waldorf Astor and his younger sister, Pauline. The Astors were devoted Roumaniaphiles. And Marie found Waldorf, then in his early twenties and younger than she, uncommonly handsome, and his manners impeccable. She clearly fell in love with him, and her affection and admiration were in some measure reciprocated. However, no substantive proof has yet been discovered that would confirm the torrid affair alluded to in the gossip of the day. Their relationship more than likely remained platonic, replete as it may have been with overt flirtation and naughty verbal innuendo. Yet even a whiff of sexual scandal was enough to mar Marie's character; a very married European crown princess had to watch every step, regardless of her husband's conduct.

During his bachelor days, Waldorf Astor, along with Pauline, schooled Marie by example in how to practice economy. So it was the crown princess, and not the fearful Nando, who in the winter of 1903, having discovered the atrocious state of their finances, demanded explanations and accountability for their debt. Marie, in particular, was a fashionista, comprehending the importance of style, especially as an element of diplomacy, and accepting as gospel her mother's maxim that "Clothes play a great part all over the world . . . so never forget to dress carefully for festive occasions, it belongs to a princess's duties." Marie had always asked for whatever she wanted and been given it; but then the bills came, and she was shocked to be informed that there was no money to pay them. Why hadn't she been told ahead of time that they lacked the funds to afford all the luxuries she requested? Had she known this, she never would have asked for them! Their creditors must be paid on time, arrears erased, and a lifestyle of perpetual debt must cease. For the first time, Carol was impressed with something Marie did, least of all to summon the courage to approach his forbidding mien.

Nando was little help. Self-effacing to a fault, he had adopted the tactic of concealing his impressive intellectual gifts in the areas of botany and languages, both modern and ancient. Maddeningly, he was playing the fool so as not to appear superior to anyone. Nando had been so browbeaten by his uncle that he hid his light under a bushel in every aspect of his life. Someone had to step up and take the reins in the marriage, or the royal household would fall to pieces and be governed by the staff. Pauline Astor noted that it was Marie who ran Bucharest's Cotroceni Palace, because Ferdinand was unable to give orders or make decisions.

Neither spouse was perfect, but the Roumanians seemed far more willing to give Marie a pass. During a military parade, when Ferdinand clumsily fell off his horse right in front of the reviewing stand, the public stared, *der Onkel* glared, and Nando received a round of derisive applause the way a pimply adolescent would if he dropped his tray in the middle of a crowded cafeteria. The police had to help the hapless prince to his feet. The king had Ferdinand so cowed that he would stammer when he greeted people, his hand trembling with unregal trepidation.

In contrast, Anne-Marie Vavaresco, Princess Callimachi, who knew Marie her entire life, had the highest praise for her, and reflected the Roumanians' general attitude toward adultery. "I believe she was the most beautiful woman I ever saw, held her in total admiration, and . . . [e]ven her faults, moral or physical, turned out to her advantage. . . . Her love affairs and caprices were never considered a grievance by the people. On the contrary . . . the Roumanians, with their natural lack of morality, felt relieved at not having a saint for their Queen."

Even Marie's cousin, England's Edward VII, who enjoyed his own share of infidelities, shrugged at the rumors of her extramarital dalliances. Lecturing his nephew, Kaiser Wilhelm (whom no one in the family liked), Bertie, as the king was known, said jocularly, "A little coquetry and a flirtation every now and then were surely permissible in a young and pretty woman. Moreover rumours were always exaggerated." Ferdinand was getting what he deserved for behaving like a pedant, particularly with a wife like Marie. "It is not wise to play the schoolmaster everywhere," Bertie added.

Bertie was right, especially about the exaggeration. The Roumanians, for whom infidelity was commonplace, ascribed many more romances to their crown princess than she actually enjoyed. This presented a problem in the summer of 1903, when she was pregnant with her fourth child and expecting the annual visit of Waldorf and Pauline Astor. Would people assume that Waldorf was the baby's father?

Marie gave birth on August 7 to her second son, whom she and Nando named Nicholas, after her cousin, the Russian czar. Of all their children, with his light blue eyes and hawk-shaped nose, Nicky most resembled Ferdinand's Hohenzollern side of the family.

After four children and nearly eleven years of marriage, Marie had ceased writing to her mother that she didn't love her husband. By now she was informing the duchess that they were "very good friends," and hoped they could "work together in spite of what is missing." Yet Nando, now Roumania's Inspector of the Cavalry, remained a social stuffed shirt, a stickler for court etiquette, in awe of King Carol, and scolded his wife for every imagined breach. She, meanwhile, remained exasperated and infuriated by his indecisiveness. Unable to control Marie's headstrong impulses, Ferdinand vented his own frustration on her, which only made Marie react all the more, perpetuating the vicious cycle.

But in 1907, the royal couple was compelled to think of something other than themselves. The peasants revolted, and that spring Marie's eyes were finally opened to the world outside the high walls of their palaces and the gilded railings of their opera boxes. She met the man who would awaken her slumbering innocence, or ignorance, of the plight of her subjects, and instill in her not only an understanding of Roumanian politics, but of patriotism. His name was Prince Barbo Stirbey—and finally Marie had something to be passionate about. In more ways than one.

Tall and slender, Stirbey hailed from one of the oldest aristocratic families in Roumania; his ancestors had ruled the region of Wallachia long before Carol and Ferdinand's Hohenzollern dynasty warmed the Roumanian throne. Two years Marie's senior, with a dark mustache and a mysterious air, he was handsome and cultured, educated at the Sorbonne, where he had studied law. In a country of glib self-aggrandizers, he was celebrated for his modesty. Although Stirbey was married to a stunning cousin, he was a renowned lady-killer; the women of Bucharest rhapsodized about the "strange hypnotic quality" of his bedroom brown eyes. A former parliamentarian, he had turned his attention to cultivating his estate into a financial empire, investing the profits from his land into banking and venture capital.

Marie of Roumania became the great love of Stirbey's life, although it took some time for her to be conquered. She visited him often at his estate, and when they were apart he sent her numerous letters praising her beauty. She eventually immortalized him in the guise of a fictional character in *Crowned Queens*, one of her many literary works. In public, they had to silently communicate their attraction through layers of royal protocol.

Meanwhile, Marie was having trouble with her children. She had never been an effective disciplinarian, and in any event, her two eldest had been whisked away to be raised under *der Onkel*'s aegis, denying both parents any input in how, or by whom, their own offspring were to be educated. This was having a highly detrimental effect on both children, but particularly on Prince Carol, who had been brought up from the cradle to believe that he was the most entitled creature on the planet. Marie did not mince words about her progeny; in fact, she described their deficiencies graphically. By the age of sixteen, Carol had developed his grandfather's mania for order and rules, evinced a fascination for military uniforms and protocol, and demonstrated a marked cruel streak. Elisabetha was already monstrously overweight, and cared for nothing but jewelry and no one but herself. Haughty and unloving, she was such an unpleasant piece of work that Marie despaired of finding her a suitable husband. And Mignon, the third child, was also growing fat, and alarmingly indolent, lacking attention to her personal appearance, and so passive that Marie feared the girl needed protection from the malice of her older siblings.

Nicky, child number four, was not only hyperactive and sickly, he was ugly, with a pinched face that reminded his mother of the visage of a wild beast. Nevertheless, when he was a little boy Marie found him "quite the most amusing creature alive," impossible as he was to control or reprimand.

In 1909, at the age of thirty-three, Marie bore her fifth child, Ileana; the crown princess had hopes that with her dark blue eyes, snub nose, and rosebud mouth, the girl would develop into a beauty. Perhaps because Marie referred to Ileana as "the child of my soul," it was rumored that Prince Stirbey was her father; he and Marie had become close two years earlier. But there is nothing in the prince's correspondence to Marie that would prove his paternity. This is not the case with her final child, Mircea. Named for a fourteenth-century Wallachian hero, he was born in January 1913, after a difficult pregnancy, and is generally believed to be Stirbey's son.

Because Ferdinand and King Carol treated Marie as though she were nothing but a womb that changed clothes several times a day, as the occasion permitted, she was under the impression that she was "not intelligent" enough to understand politics and government or to do anything about them. Prince Stirbey and his sister, who was married to Roumania's prime minister, set out to change Marie's mind, convincing her that she'd merely been too indolent to apply herself. Now, instead of resenting all the evenings of postprandial cigars, she remained in Carol and Ferdinand's presence to hear them discourse on Roumania's vital interests, both foreign and domestic, receiving a crash course in governance, policy, and economics.

In 1913, Carol appointed Prince Stirbey Superintendent of the Crown Estates, a position that brought him into almost daily, and wholly sanctioned, contact with the crown princess. The king intended for Stirbey to educate and guide Marie, so that she and Ferdinand, with Stirbey's sagacious and pragmatic counsel, would govern Roumania prudently after his demise. It was the smartest thing Carol could have done for his country, if not for his nephew's marriage.

In the years just prior to the First World War, Roumania endured a series of conflicts known as the Balkan Wars. Bloodshed and disease were brought to the royal family's doorstep. Marie stepped out of her comfort zone to help. Finally, she found a purpose. Desperate to be of use to her subjects, and unafraid of contracting the cholera raging about them, she tended to the sick, wounded, and dying, in muddy, makeshift hospital wards amid appallingly primitive and unhygienic medical conditions. The crown princess would also devote herself to nursing when the Great War upended their world not too many months later.

Central Europe reacted like a row of dominoes to the assassination of Archduke Franz Ferdinand in Sarajevo on June 28, 1914. On the twenty-eighth of July, Austria formally declared war on Serbia, and Germany declared war on Russia four days later. The following day, Kaiser Wilhelm invaded Luxembourg and demanded that Ferdinand of Roumania's first cousin, the king of Belgium, permit the German army to march straight through on its way to invade France. King Albert of the Belgians refused. On August 2, 1914, the Kaiser asked King Carol to support the German offensive against Russia.

Ailing and weak, Carol was torn. He was all for supporting Germany, as was his queen, Carmen Sylva, who had also been born a German. Marie recognized that England would not remain on the sidelines for long, and would eventually fight against Germany. Her heart sympathized with Britain, which she was convinced would prevail. Irresolute as ever, even as he faced his uncle's imminent demise and his own ascent to the throne, Ferdinand was in favor of Roumania remaining neutral for as long as possible, a position the kingdom would indeed retain through the first two years of the Great War.

It was Prince Stirbey who brought Marie the news of King Carol's death on the morning of October 10, 1914, making Ferdinand the new king (Carol's artsy wife, now the dowager, would die on March 2, 1916). "I was Queen. I felt wholly capable of being a Queen," Marie declared after Carol's death. Her husband, however, was not so ready for prime time. Marie confided in a letter to one of her sisters, "Poor Nando, it is hard for a character like his to take up such heavy responsibilities, and having been so long the humble follower it's difficult for him to realize that he is master." Ferdinand himself had no illusions about the crown, referring to it as a "legacy which I would not wish on my arch enemy."

During the first two years of World War I, Roumania was being pressured from all sides to enter the conflict. Marie's favorite sister, Victoria Melita, supported the Germans, and passionately urged her to do the same. Marie was equally related to the Russian czar, the German kaiser, and King George V of England. Being everyone's cousin gave her a different sort of entrée as a diplomat and, when necessary, allowed Marie to use her considerable powers of persuasion, where a minister or mere civil servant would never have made any headway.

Remarkably, Ferdinand didn't realize how much of an influence his wife had on Roumania's foreign policy at the time, and how cleverly she was steering him toward manifesting the pro-English results she desired. Only seven months before the kingdom entered the war, Nando had naively declared, "Missy is not one bit interested in politics." Meanwhile she had averred that his "habit of counting upon me for his material comforts had been unconsciously extended also to brainwork. I grasped things easily, even those not really within my province, and my old attitude of not taking myself overseriously allowed him to ignore how great a help I really was. . . ."

Confident that "England always wins the last battle," Marie won over her husband, his government, and their subjects to her point of view. The queen recognized that an Allied victory could guarantee them more than they would get by casting their lot with the Germans. On August 17, 1916, Roumania entered the war on the Allied side—with conditions. In exchange for her support, assuming an Allied victory, at the war's end Roumania would receive the following territories (which historically had once been hers, but had in the past been gobbled up by other eastern bloc nations): all of Transylvania, the Banat, Bukovina as far as the River Prut, Bessarabia, and Dobruja.

Three-year-old Prince Mircea, Marie's youngest child and probably the only one fathered by Prince Stirbey, died at the beginning of November 1916, after suffering from typhoid fever for an agonizing four days. As an example of chivalry lasting even into the twentieth century, during the boy's funeral at Cotroceni Palace in Bucharest, the kaiser had the opportunity to massacre the entire Roumanian nobility and their government, but out of respect for his cousin in her time of loss, he ordered a cease-fire and sent his condolences instead.

Geographically surrounded on all sides by the enemy, Marie fled the capital for Jassy in Moldavia. Ferdinand soon followed. Roumania subsequently spent the next two years under occupation. Heat and food became luxuries. Denying culpability, the Germans, Austrians, and Bulgarians blamed one another for the rapes and robberies of the Roumanian citizens. The winter of 1916–17 was the coldest in half a century. The people of Jassy dropped like flies from hypothermia, starvation, typhus, smallpox, and other epidemics. Even the royal family subsisted on a diet of beans. Roumania's army ate horse meat. Their "coffee" was composed of dried acorns. Meanwhile, Marie's Russian-born, Germanophile mother, the Duchess of Edinburgh and Coburg, illogically and hysterically accused her of starting the First World War and bringing all this misery to their people with her English sensibilities.

Crown Prince Carol was giving Marie grief as well, emigrating to Jassy with his tootsie, Zizi Lambrino. Zizi came from an aristocratic Roumanian family, but the prince knew perfectly well about the constitutional prohibitions against marrying a Roumanian. A few years earlier, at the start of 1914, Marie had endeavored to arrange a marriage for him with the Romanov Grand Duchess Olga, the daughter of her cousins Nicholas and Alexandra, but there had been no spark between them. Neither mother was keen on forcing a loveless match, but had Olga wed Carol, she would have been spared her family's bloody fate in 1918.

While the crown prince was inclined to shirk his royal responsibilities, and her husband was a lackluster sovereign, the new queen was intent on becoming the inspirational leader of her people during their darkest hours. The Jassy railway station had been transformed into a triage unit. It was dark and lice-ridden and stank of filth and disease; yet Marie was the angel of mercy, visiting the wounded and doling out religious icons, medals, and crosses, feeding the starving patients herself with hard brown bread she had personally hacked off the loaves and spread with jam. Unafraid of illness or gore, she bathed the eyelids of one soldier whose face had been "shot to pieces," and routinely offered her bare hand to enamored typhoid patients. "I really cannot ask them to kiss India rubber!" she insisted, after the doctors pressured her to protect herself. Every night, the queen of Roumania returned to her lodgings, and, clad only in rubber boots, she stood in a bucket of boiling water and shed her clothes to rid them of the lice she had attracted that day.

When she wasn't comforting wounded soldiers, the not-quite-so-glamorous queen of Roumania was penning propaganda in the form of sentimental magazine articles and travelogues about her adopted kingdom. She had already turned her hand to poetry and fiction, writing fairy tales inspired by those of Hans Christian Andersen. During the war years, sales of her book *My Country* raised funds for the Red Cross, for which the queen herself volunteered as a nurse. Marie was also instrumental in securing an American loan for Roumania, employing her friend the dancer Loie Fuller as a go-between. The young woman from the U.S. Embassy who couriered Marie's request to Fuller happened to be the former ward of America's secretary of war, and steered the queen's request for funds through the proper diplomatic channels.

By mid-September of 1917, Roumania's active role in the war had come to an end. A few weeks later, the Germans and Russians were talking of an alliance. But Roumania lay dangerously sandwiched between these two superpowers. George V offered Marie's family sanctuary, but there was no guarantee they could make it to England alive. On the same day the queen received her cousin's offer, they heard a rumor that the Russian soldiers intended to murder Roumania's royal family and disrupt the country's government and the infrastructure of railways, and telephone and telegraph lines. Much had been devastated already. Even the Allied Powers took part in the destruction; they had bombed Roumania's oil fields to prevent these precious resources from falling into enemy hands.

In January of 1918, during the same week that Marie and Ferdinand were celebrating their twenty-fifth wedding anniversary, England's prime minister, David Lloyd George, moved the football, compromising Roumania's 1916 treaty with them. Great Britain was no longer prepared to honor the territorial gains originally pledged. On the last day of the month, the Russians declared war on Roumania and claimed possession of the crown jewels. Roumania was in an untenable position, the country ravaged by years of war, and more or less abandoned by her greatest ally. The options, neither of them pleasant, were to surrender to the Germans, or face further destruction. Kaiser Wilhelm demanded that Ferdinand begin negotiating a peace with Germany and the other middle European countries (plus the Ottoman Empire) that formed the enemy bloc known as the Central Powers. Marie refused to concede to her hateful cousin, and the women of Roumania, as well as the crown prince, supported her. The royal spouses had a horrific argument in which Marie publicly accused her husband of "selling his soul, his honour and with it the honour of his family and country . . . not because he was a fool but because a man with his character is always the instrument and the dupe of those stronger than he."

Ferdinand became so enraged "he would have certainly beaten me," Marie later admitted. Nevertheless, she continued to berate him, insisting that by placing his signature on the proposed Treaty of Bucharest, a peace treaty with the Central Powers, he would be signing all of their death warrants. Prince Stirbey tried to restrain the queen and explain that Ferdinand couldn't function in a vacuum; his position had to be "upheld by . . . responsible men"— which only further infuriated Marie. There were "no men in this country," she fumed, adding that she was "ashamed of being the Queen of nothing but cowards!" Even the French minister to Roumania, the comte de Saint-Aulaire, commented, "There is only one man in Roumania and that is the Queen."

Still infuriated with her husband, "no one rallies for resistance," she lamented. And their opposite views on how to handle the wartime situation were tearing the couple further apart. "Nando and I could hardly face each other, he was a completely broken man." She finally stopped trying to argue with him, recognizing that she had been "defeated"—let down not only by her ally, England, but by her own husband and his craven government. The Allies couldn't even guarantee Marie that Ferdinand would retain his Roumanian sovereignty, should he be deposed or compelled to abdicate—a request that the king's dignity could scarcely permit him to make on his own. A new government of pro-German ministers was formed, and Marie announced that far from considering herself a "beaten Queen," she was "the leader of a glorious army which has *not* been vanquished, but had to submit to a fearful and preposterous peace because it was betrayed by its Ally, Russia." Russia was in the throes of its own internal conflict, and had withdrawn from the war at the end of 1917 as a result of the October Revolution that had overthrown the Provisional Government. After Russia's defection from the Great War, Roumania was left geographically isolated, surrounded by enemies affiliated with the Central Powers.

By spinning the tragedy this way, Marie became an international heroine, and the world sympathetically rallied around Roumania—if they could find it on a map. Thanks to the queen's ability both to captivate an audience and to capitalize on her assets, those far beyond Roumania's borders began to see Ferdinand's kingdom as a David in a battle among Goliaths. But the royal spouses' divergent views on how to handle the war were tearing them even further apart. Marie wrote in her diary, "I am . . . much too violent and then he gets angry. He is also angry because people come to me. I try to explain to him *why* they all come to me even the generals." Yet her husband didn't want to hear that his temper, or worse, his indecision, was off-putting. In the meantime, the queen had charmed Colonel Joe Boyle, a rugged, Canadian-born, aging Renaissance man and former Klondike prospector, who, among other things, used his numerous talents to secure a peace treaty between Roumania and Russia's new Bolshevik government. Marie came to depend upon Boyle to help save her kingdom. In 1918, the married, fifty-one-year-old Boyle, recuperating from a stroke, confided to the queen that she was the love of his life.

On September 15, 1918, as Ferdinand and Marie were figuring out how to handle the shifting balance of power—with the occupying Germans growing more demanding and increasingly crueler to the Roumanians even as the Allies gained ground—the sovereigns were dealt a stunning personal blow: The twenty-four-year-old crown prince had eloped with a commoner, having secretly wed his lover the previous night. Carol was prepared to renounce his claim to the throne for his new bride, the petite and graceful brunette Jeanne Marie Valentine ("Zizi") Lambrino. Although he'd been romancing Zizi for several months, the prince had clearly not been thinking with his head. Such a marriage played right into the Germans' hands. Not only did Carol flee Jassy for the border with his bride; in doing so he had deserted his military regiment, which was a treasonable offense.

In his own youth, Ferdinand had been talked out of marrying a commoner; yet now he had no time for empathy, and no choice but to punish his son. Although the king was no longer the commander in chief of Roumania's army, he sentenced Carol to two and a half months' imprisonment for deserting his post and for crossing the frontier without permission. A defiant Carol insisted that the punishment would ruin his reputation. But Marie told her son that she had survived worse damage to her own name; he'd bounce back soon enough.

On September 22, 1918, Crown Prince Carol was packed off to a remote mountain monastery. Zizi refused to sign the divorce papers, but the royal marriage was annulled without her cooperation. Carol was liberated after Armistice Day, November 11, 1918, so he could lead his regiment triumphantly into Jassy on the same day Marie was greeted by her subjects with a surprise reception at the rail station.

The royal family's return to Bucharest was delayed until December 1, because the Germans had blown up every bridge leading into Roumania's capital. Ferdinand asked his wife whether she would do him the honor of riding at his side as he led the Roumanian and Allied troops into the city. "If ever a queen was one with her army, I was that queen! This I say without any modesty!" Marie exclaimed, costumed for the occasion in a military tunic, fur-collared cape, and gray curly astrakhan hat strapped under her chin like a helmet. Marie of Roumania always knew what to wear to a coming-out party. This was, after all, the person of whom it was written, "Marie of Roumania—one of the most wonderful women in the world. A woman like that is born once in a century." She had penned the lines herself.

But behind the glamour lay a woman trapped in an unhappy marriage, whose grown children were turning out to be a dreadful disappointment, and whose adopted kingdom had for the past two years been raped and ravaged by the occupying Germans.

During the postwar peace talks at Versailles, Roumania's prime minister ruffled too many feathers. It was the brainchild of the kingdom's French minister to let the queen represent the kingdom instead. After all, she was related to half the participants. Who

better to charm the superpowers into granting her country the reparations it deserved? Marie was thrilled. "Roumania needs a face
and I will be that face," she declared. This statement, possibly the
most famous remark Marie ever uttered, made her even more of a
heroine in the eyes of her subjects.

Prince Stirbey coached her thoroughly for her new diplomatic
role. Yet in March 1919, when Marie arrived in France, because she
was merely a consort and not a reigning sovereign, nor was she a
member of Roumania's government, there was no seat for her in
Versailles' Hall of Mirrors. Undaunted, Marie negotiated from her
flower-filled, twenty-room Paris hotel suite. She practiced couture
diplomacy, putting her mother's sartorial wisdom to use at this
critical moment for her kingdom by matching the perfect ensemble
to each meeting with a foreign dignitary. The queen had traveled to
Paris with sixty gowns, thirty-one coats, twenty-two fur wraps,
twenty-nine hats, and eighty-three pairs of shoes. "I feel that this
is no time to economize," she averred. "Roumania . . . has to have
Transylvania . . . Bessarabia too. And what if for the lack of a gown,
a concession should be lost?"

If Marie met with obstructions or condescension, she opened her
handbag and whipped out the secret treaty of 1916—proof that the
Allies had promised specific, and massive, territorial gains if Roumania entered the war on their side. When Lloyd George balked,
the queen found herself educating the English on the geography of
the Balkans. During her youth, Marie had come to realize that she
had a powerful effect on men; back then, she used her charisma to
conquer the men themselves. Now, at forty-three, although she
hadn't lost a bit of her charm, she parlayed it differently, convincing
men to yield *territory* to her instead. In essence, Marie was now
flirting for Ferdinand's sake—but mostly for that of Roumania,
which was in desperate straits. Russia had fallen to the Communists and was an imminent threat to her kingdom. Roumania
needed those lands Marie had been promised in order to expand
and safeguard her borders.

Flooded with invitations, the self-proclaimed "most beautiful
queen in Europe" became the toast of Paris. Marie then took the
show on the road, to London. There she became frustrated with the

self-effacing politeness of her English cousins and their hidebound traditions, telling George V, "Try not to be shocked at me. . . . Forgive me if I am different from what you think a queen ought to be." But she pressed on. "[W]e want action, not just fine words," Marie insisted, and the satirical magazine *Punch* got her point, publishing a cartoon of a rag-clad old woman labeled Roumania, begging by the railroad track as an Allied food transport passes. It is laden with reparations that are tagged for the Central Powers, the enemy that had left Roumania so bereft in the first place.

While Marie was playing the diplomat in Western Europe, a Russian military buildup was amassing on Roumania's eastern borders. Ferdinand was relying on his wife's ability to secure foreign aid. Their kingdom was beset with problems from within and from without. If she could not guarantee the return of Transylvania, their subjects would revolt. If Crown Prince Carol abdicated the succession for love of Zizi Lambrino, it would weaken their dynasty's claims to the throne.

On December 19, 1919, Marie got her treaty, enabling her to return to Roumania with everything she asked for and more: all of Transylvania, almost all of the Bukovina, Bessarabia, two-thirds of the Banat, and the southern part of Dobruja. Roumania's square mileage went from fifty-three thousand to a hundred and fourteen thousand, more than doubling her population as well. The treaty made Roumania, at that time, the fifth-largest nation in mainland Europe after France, Spain, Germany, and Poland.

On January 20, 1920, Zizi Lambrino bore the crown prince a son. Carol had formally renounced the throne the previous August while his parents were touring Roumania's front lines. Relations between the sovereigns and their heir had sunk to a level of outright hostility. Because Zizi could never have a proper marriage with a member of the ruling house, Marie deemed her an interloper intent on destroying the dynasty. Ruthless as it was, for the sake of Roumania the only way to salvage the situation was to enforce a separation between Zizi and Carol. Although the prince had once again changed his mind about the succession and returned to the familial fold, his parents sent him on an eight-month world cruise.

At least Marie and Ferdinand's oldest daughter was making a

good match. In the autumn of 1920, at the age of twenty-five, the fat, selfish, and indolent Elisabetha became engaged to Crown Prince George of Greece. Marie invited George to bring his siblings to Roumania with him for the announcement of his marriage. By that time, the tall, blond, mustachioed Carol, twenty-seven, had returned from his cruise. He promptly fell in love with George's twenty-four-year-old sister, Princess Helen, a willowy brunette known within the family as "Sitta."

Predictably, things didn't sit too well with Zizi when Carol told her about Sitta. Zizi demanded a massive settlement and a title for their son, whom Carol had never even bothered to visit. She did not receive the latter request.

Elisabetha wed Prince George on February 27, 1921. On March 10, in Athens, Carol was united with Sitta. She was the first princess of Greece to be married in her own country. After a tremendously difficult birth, on October 25 she produced a son, Prince Michael, named for Mihai, the hero who had united Moldavia, Wallachia, and Transylvania in the sixteenth century. Recuperating from the ordeal of childbirth, and with their marital home not yet fully renovated, Helen remained in Greece with the new baby for several months. By the time she returned to Bucharest, Carol had already been unfaithful.

Meanwhile, on June 8, 1922, Marie and Ferdinand married off their modest and unfashionable daughter Mignon to Alexander, the king of Yugoslavia. That September, following the overthrow of Greece's King Constantine, Crown Prince George became the new monarch, making Ferdinand and Marie's oldest daughter the queen of Greece. With Marie on the Roumanian throne and two of her daughters now occupying the thrones of Yugoslavia and Greece, even though it was the twentieth century, she was making advantageous geopolitical matches as if the world had never changed for the royal houses of Europe, proud of her nickname, "Mother-in-Law of the Balkans."

Ironically, Marie and Ferdinand had not yet been formally crowned. King Carol had died in October 1916, during the Great War, and Roumania's dire circumstances during the conflict had not permitted any sort of coronation festivities.

The event finally took place in 1922, but not without some religious wrangling. The Catholic Church (Ferdinand's Hohenzollern dynasty were Catholics) would not permit the king to be crowned in a Roumanian Orthodox Church by a Roumanian Orthodox priest, but it was the *kingdom*'s official religion. Marie solved the problem by staging their coronation outdoors, in the shadow of the church, cleverly spinning their public relations so the monarchs could claim that they wanted as many of their subjects as possible to be able to witness the spectacle.

The queen now became a producer; glamour was her specialty, and the coronation, already without precedent (for taking place outside of a church, and six years after the monarchs' ascension), was going to be one for the history books. "I want nothing modern that another Queen might have. Let mine be all medieval," she declared. All of the royal women in the procession were asked to wear gold. The other women were directed to wear silver and mauve, Marie's favorite color. The coronation assumed a Byzantine flavor when the other European princesses invited to participate in the ceremonies wore mantles of royal blue, crimson, or brilliant orange over their golden gowns. Over Marie's reddish-gold sheath, she wore a heavy mantle embroidered with metaphorical emblems—local crests and sheaves of wheat that represented "the chief richness of our land."

No look would be complete without the jewelry. The queen accessorized with her coronation present from Ferdinand: a lengthy diamond chain from Cartier, with an enormous sapphire dangling at the center. Placed over a veil of delicate gold mesh, also in the Byzantine fashion, Marie's four-pound crown was a copy of one worn by Princess Despina, the wife of a sixteenth-century Wallachian prince. Heavily embellished with emeralds, rubies, moonstones, and turquoises, it featured huge gem-studded golden pendants that hung down over each of Marie's ears. In her own words, she carried off her weighty ensemble "splendidly."

In the center of the public square in Bucharest, a colorfully carpeted platform had been erected below a dramatically swagged and tassled canopy decorated with the royal coat of arms. There, in the presence of three hundred thousand of their subjects, Ferdinand, wearing a purple velvet mantle over his ensemble of red velvet and ermine, and Marie in her glittering wardrobe, were crowned. Although the queen described the festivities as modest compared to some she had experienced (and they probably paled in comparison to the one she had attended in 1896 for Russia's Nicholas and Alexandra), Ferdinand and Marie's coronation cost Roumania roughly the equivalent of a million dollars.

Officially king and queen nearly thirty years after their marriage, and now grandparents, Marie and Ferdinand were no more compatible than they had been back in 1893. But at least they had settled into a routine. Marie deferred to her husband in public so that he no longer felt inferior, not only in her eyes, but in everyone else's opinion. Privately, he had come to acknowledge that her extroverted nature made her better equipped than he to cope with the world. Marie had even come to terms with Ferdinand's long-standing, yet purely physical liaison with Mrs. Martineau, their stout landscape gardener, assuring the horticulturist that she was the only woman Marie could trust with the king. Perhaps Her Majesty was forgetting another one of her husband's paramours, Aristitza Dissescu, the elegant wife of a university professor who, according to Marie, had declared Ferdinand to be the "love of her life."

The Roumanians couldn't conceive of their boring, asexual king being interested in anyone, or vice versa. Ironically, because everyone loves a love affair, it was Marie and not Ferdinand who became internationally renowned for rampant infidelity. Owing to the queen's beauty and vivacity, stories of her adultery made sense to people, so they refused to believe they hadn't read or heard the whole truth. As Marie would tell a friend in 1929, "It is only through books and certain things that have been said of me that I realized that such immense importance was given to that one thing which has played little part in my life, that chase after 'sexual excitement,' if that is the right technical expression?"

The genuine sexual predator was Crown Prince Carol, whose own royal marriage was now on the rocks, thanks to his new mistress, a half-Jewish, blowsy redheaded commoner named Elena Lupescu, who had deserted her own husband for another man before she'd met Carol.

It was the last thing Ferdinand and Marie needed, as the king's health began to decline in 1925. That January he had a hernia operation, and two months later he was diagnosed with a pulmonary embolism. Marie sent for his favorite child, Mignon, to cheer him up. Aware of Mme. Dissescu's devotion to Ferdinand, Marie even permitted her husband's sometime-mistress to visit his bedside.

Four days before Christmas, Carol deserted his family and ran off with Elena Lupescu. Just as he had done when he eloped with Zizi, he cast himself in the role of the persecuted victim. But by now, his parents were fed up with him. On December 31, Ferdinand convened a special meeting of the Crown Council and made plans in the event of his imminent demise for a regency council to rule on behalf of Helen and Carol's then-four-year-old son, Prince Michael.

But what should have been an internal transition became a national crisis. Carol's forfeiture of his succession brought every Ferdinand-and-Marie hater out of the woodwork, criticizing them politically and personally, and threatening to permanently topple their dynasty. No one had confidence in an ailing man and a toddler. In the wake of the backlash, Ferdinand was obliged to form a new government. The troublesome prime minister was swept out of office and his replacement was compelled to form a new cabinet.

The crisis didn't prevent Marie from touring America in 1926, the same year Dorothy Parker published her four-line poem "Comment," with its tart allusion to the glamorous queen. But Marie's U.S. appearance received mixed reviews. Some people wondered why she didn't seem to be rushing home after getting word that her husband was ill. By the time she returned to Roumania at the end of the year, the doctors confirmed the worst: Ferdinand was suffering from terminal cancer of the lower intestine. His condition was inoperable, although silver tubes were inserted into the small intestine to draw out the poison. Marie informed their children that he had only a few months to live, but they decided not to tell the king, who handled his painful illness with grace and dignity.

In January 1927, realizing that she and Ferdinand were about to celebrate their thirty-fifth wedding anniversary, Marie wrote in her diary, "May God allow that it not be our last . . . we have lived to become firm and faithful friends, two wildly different characters that have managed to produce harmony out of what might have been something quite else . . . we have lived for the country & for our children and always knew how to keep passion sufficiently under so as never to harm these two loves of our lives."

Perhaps she was drawing the distinction between her own marriage and their son's. While Ferdinand slowly deteriorated, receiving radiation treatments at the end of January, Elena Lupescu issued the monarchs an ultimatum: She would renounce Carol if he were reinstated in the succession. Marie wanted to love and indulge the prince, but the government had no desire for him to return, because they thought he would make a dangerous king.

By this time, Marie had Ferdinand moved to the Pelişor Castle at Sinaia, where she believed the mountain air would be beneficial. She had become accustomed to sleeping outside his sickroom so that she could rise and go to him the moment she heard a sound. Around midnight on July 19, 1927, Ferdinand tried to get out of bed. "I am so tired," he lamented to his wife. She took him in her arms and he died a few minutes later with his head resting against her shoulder.

The following morning, Prince Michael, not yet six years old, was taken to Bucharest to be proclaimed king of Roumania in front of the country's Parliament.

Ferdinand's body lay in state for four days. Marie decreed that no black should be used, so his coffin reposed on a red velvet pall. How different he looked to her in death. "Such a beautiful face with his noble features frozen into a stillness which gave him a grandeur which was not his in life," Marie noted. "In life he was too modest, too timid, he always seemed to be excusing himself for everything he did. Now, without any more gestures he was calmly . . . accepting all the honours paid, all the flowers, prayers, tears." Sentiment had cast a rosy glow over a rocky marriage of thirty-four years.

The king was buried at the monastery of Curtea de Argeş, a ninety-five-mile rail journey across the mountains. Carrying candles, a thousand peasants in colorful native costume participated in the funeral procession that escorted Ferdinand's body to the church. His coffin was as modest as he had been. Laid across it was a single bouquet of faded pink roses with a card inscribed simply, *Marie*.

After a brief outdoor service, Ferdinand's coffin was interred in the vault. "One volume shut forever," Marie wrote in her diary after she returned to Sinaia, "and now forward with courage, and with what remains to me of health and strength. . . ."

The years immediately following Ferdinand's death were unhappy ones for Marie. Sitta became determined to estrange her from little King Michael. Ferdinand and Marie's second son, Prince Nicholas, who was one of Michael's regents, had become a bad egg, resorting to street violence. And then, in June 1930, Prince Carol returned from his self-imposed exile—and successfully staged a coup, proclaiming himself King Carol II of Roumania.

For the next several years, Marie's relationship with her first-born son grew tense, and her other children presented problems of their own. Carol greatly reduced his mother's income, although he was aware that she had inherited no funds from his father. Then he delayed the payments, collecting the interest himself. He reduced her staff and tightened the security around her as if she were a spy, ordering her movements and conversations reported to him. A repressive autocrat, he refused to accept Marie's advice, despite her decades of experience.

His queen, Sitta, left Roumania forever on July 17, 1931. Ten days later, Marie attended the wedding of her favorite child, Ileana, to Archduke Anton of Austria. Carol had introduced the couple, and orchestrated their lavish nuptials.

That October 28, Prince Nicholas illegally eloped with Jeanne Doletti, a Roumanian divorcée. When he returned to Bucharest a married man, King Carol II declared that Nicholas could no longer be a member of the royal family or a Roumanian citizen. Marie was disgusted by Carol's hypocrisy. Nicholas left the country, but when he returned in 1932, Carol had him arrested and sentenced to one year's exile. Carol also refused to allow his sister Ileana to give birth in Roumania, because her husband was a Hapsburg, and the Austrians had been Roumania's enemy during the First World War.

In the early 1930s, as Carol grew more unpopular with his people, Communism threatened from the east; to the west Hitler was on the rise; and in the south, the dictator Benito Mussolini's Fascisti were changing the face of Italy. Marie, who had been born a Victorian and had seen so many shifts in Europe's political landscape over the course of her life, began to pen her memoirs, and spent her time traveling. Failing to see the perils of Nazism, Marie insisted on withholding judgment of the party until she saw how things transpired, although two of her younger sisters had already become pro-Hitler. There had even been rumors that Victoria Melita had attended Nazi rallies with her husband, Kirill, and had sold "some of her remaining valuables [after the war] . . . to raise funds" for the party.

Marie was in London attending a flower show on October 9, 1934, when she received the news that her son-in-law, Mignon's husband, King Alexander of Yugoslavia, had been assassinated in Marseille by a Macedonian terrorist. He was succeeded by his eleven-year-old son, Peter, then just a schoolboy at Sandroyd in Wiltshire. Peter II would be Yugoslavia's last king.

As the years between the two World Wars progressed, Marie continued to be disappointed in her children and their spouses. Prince Nicholas, whom she described as "entirely & sinfully indifferent to his duties," had returned to Roumania with his acquisitive wife, Jeanne, who "can only sit upon historical chairs or eat off tables that ought to be in a museum and drink out of historical glass & eat off historical china."

Queen Elisabetha of Greece was creating a scandal by divorcing her husband, George, to wed a Greek businessman. Ileana, and the freshly widowed Mignon, dwelled elsewhere. Had Marie and Ferdinand failed as parents, or were the lives of royal children, or the pitfalls of royal marriages, just as fraught as those of commoners?

In the spring of 1935, the second volume of Marie's autobiography *The Story of My Life* was published to mixed reviews. The following winter, it was translated into Roumanian. Requests followed for foreign-language editions in Polish, Czech, German, French, Hungarian, Swedish, Italian, and Japanese. "I feel rather like a hen who has hatched ducklings!" Marie exclaimed proudly.

During the winter of 1936–37, King Carol II perpetrated such a humiliating restriction on his mother—barring her from all communication with the Roumanian government—that she felt compelled to send him a lengthy letter spelling out every abuse she had suffered at his hands since he took the throne. He had kept the income Ferdinand wished her to have after his death. Carol had, without her knowledge or consent, deprived her of the title of queen, demoting her to Queen Mother. The infuriated Marie, who once had world leaders eating out of the palm of her hand, was abasing herself before her firstborn son and heir. "I was Queen of this country and have my definite position recognised by parliament, it is my right also to the title of Regina Marie which Papa wished me to have." After enumerating everything she had withstood, Marie held out the olive branch, hoping for a reconciliation; Carol never seems to have replied to her letter.

At the age of sixty-one, Marie collapsed with internal bleeding in March of 1937. Unable to locate the source of the hemorrhaging, her doctors hypothesized that she might be suffering from cirrhosis of the liver, although she rarely drank alcohol. While Marie was bedridden, Carol exiled his brother Nicholas again for the sin of contracting a morganatic marriage with a commoner, the same transgression he had himself committed with Zizi Lambrino—not to mention his elopement with Elena Lupescu while he was still married to Princess Helen of Greece! The king's hypocrisy was staggering. Rumors flew that Marie's condition was caused from a stomach wound she received when she tried to break up a gunfight between her two sparring sons. The incident never happened.

On December 29, 1937, Marie suffered a relapse; for six days the doctors were unable to stanch her internal hemorrhaging. Eventually she recovered enough to travel to a sanatorium in Italy, where a specialist from the Weisser Hirsch Clinic in Dresden was asked to look in on her. Dr. Stoermer was horrified. Declaring that Marie had been misdiagnosed from the start, he insisted that she be moved to his clinic ASAP for the treatment that could prolong, but unfortunately not save, her life.

Marie did indeed have cirrhosis of the liver (a rare type not caused by alcohol abuse). But according to the German physicians, her primary ailment was a condition that had resulted from it— esophageal varices, dilated blood vessels that encroached on her esophagus. Dr. Stoermer's colleague, Dr. Warnerkrose, was convinced that Marie had "been given the wrong treatment from the beginning. I can only say that the doctor who did that had to have done it purposely. He can't have been that stupid."

And then, with his mother's life in the balance, Carol sent word that he could not permit her to journey to Dresden for treatment unless it was sanctioned by Roumanian doctors. Marie vehemently protested this decision, but Carol nonetheless delayed her departure until she was examined by her adopted countrymen, who eventually approved her admission to the clinic in Dresden. From this facility, just prior to her July 15, 1938, return to Roumania, Marie wrote a farewell letter to Barbo Stirbey, her mentor, and perhaps former longtime lover. When she'd first told him of her incurable illness the previous July, he wrote from Switzerland to say how sorry he was not to be able to be there for her. ". . . [N]ever doubt the boundlessness of my devotion," he assured Marie, adding the acronym "Ilymmily"—for, *I love you, my Marie, I love you.*

The return from Dresden to Sinaia, Roumania, by rickety train caused Marie to bleed again almost immediately. Always knowing how to dress for every occasion, she cleverly disguised her body, wasted away with illness, beneath a filmy pearl gray gown. Too weak to walk, but too proud to be carried on a stretcher, she was borne out of the rail station in a chair.

She lingered for a day at Pelişor Castle in Sinaia, watching the door of the former nursery and waiting for her favorite children to arrive. But Carol had deliberately not notified them of the gravity of her condition in time for final farewells. Instead, only her two oldest children were present at the end, those whom she loved least and who had been the most self-absorbed.

On July 18, 1938, at 5:38 p.m., eight minutes after requesting the Lord's Prayer to be recited in English and whispering to Carol to be "a just and strong monarch," Marie of Roumania peacefully died. Within the hour, the news was broadcast to her former subjects, at which, according to a contemporary reporter, "[a] moving silence reigned in the streets."

Now that she was gone, Carol decided to honor his mother. Marie had requested that her mourners wear mauve, her favorite color, and that all flowers placed on her coffin be red. Carol complied with her wishes.

Her body was taken to Bucharest on July 20, where it lay in state in the white drawing room at the Cotroceni Palace, guarded by a quartet of officers from Marie's regiment, the Fourth Hussars. Over the next three days, thousands of people filed past her bier to pay their final respects. The third day was reserved solely for factory workers.

But the pomp-filled funeral was delayed for three days to allow foreign royals and dignitaries time to travel to Roumania. To the sound of low-flying aircraft, trumpets, and church bells, a grand cortege comprised of Orthodox clergy, crippled veterans, sisters of the Red Cross, and Knights of the Order of Michael the Brave accompanied the gun carriage bearing Marie's catafalque to the rail station for her final journey to Curtea de Argeş. Six black horses pulled the carriage. One of Marie's own favorite horses, its saddle empty, pranced behind it.

The train's five-mile route was lined with peasants holding lit candles to pay their respects. They tossed so many flowers onto Marie's coffin that the soldiers guarding it were nearly smothered with blossoms.

Marie's bier, covered by a plain slab of white marble engraved with the sign of the cross, was interred in the vault beside Ferdinand's at the monastery of Curtea de Argeş. But according to her wishes, her heart was placed in a golden casket embellished with the emblems of the provinces of Greater Roumania, and taken to the Orthodox chapel in the gardens of the home she had built in Balcic overlooking the sea. The box was transferred to a wooden church at Marie's beloved Castle Bran in Transylvania after the Bulgarians took over the Dobruja region in 1940. Communist sympathizers defiled the marble sarcophagus and the coffer containing Marie's heart in 1968. After that, the jeweled casket containing her heart was brought to Bucharest and eventually placed in the custody of the National Museum of Roumanian History, although it is not on public display.

Not too many months after Marie died, Roumania fell to the Fascists. After the end of the Second World War, the country became a victim of Communist expansion. Two years after Marie's death, on September 6, 1940, the same year Roumania lost several of the gains Marie had scored after World War I—including Bessarabia, the northern part of Transylvania, and Southern Dobruja—Carol was forced to abdicate his throne. Without a country to rule, he fled Roumania and sought refuge from Hitler. Der Führer denied him, because Carol's mistress, Elena Lupescu, was half-Jewish. Carol and Elena went on the run through Europe, then traveled to Mexico, and ultimately ended up in Brazil, where Carol finally made an honest woman of Elena.

The day after Carol's abdication, his son by his second wife, Princess Helen of Greece, technically became King Michael I of Roumania for the second time, although the country was then governed by the pro-Nazi dictator Ion Antonescu, who had allied Roumania with the Axis Powers. In August 1944, Michael staged a coup, ousting Antonescu and claiming his family's throne. On August 23, now under King Michael's sovereignty, Roumania declared war on Germany and joined the Allies. Michael did not attend his father's funeral when Carol died in 1953.

Once upon a time, in some circles the mere words "Marie of Roumania" conjured a certain magic. As the late English writer and historian Lesley Blanch put it, ". . . she formed a whole generation—every man was in love with her, every artist inspired by her, every woman wished to look like her."

While juggling the responsibilities of sovereignty, motherhood, and marriage, as well as steering her country through a world war, Marie published numerous magazine articles and more than fifteen books—allegorical romances, attempts at more literary novels, fairy tales, short stories, poetry, and finally her own memoirs in various iterations. Some of Marie's short stories were adapted for other media, including ballet, theater, and film. In the sixteen syndicated articles she wrote in 1925, all under the title "A Queen Looks at Life," Marie dished just enough royal gossip to keep readers interested, and dispensed advice that nowadays would be viewed as feminist, championing equality of the sexes in everything from marriage to infidelity. "I am not a conventional Queen, I admit, I must often make your dear old royal blood curdle, but my heart is in the right place, Georgie, dear," she told her cousin and former adolescent flame George V of England in 1926.

Marie had come to Roumania for her royal marriage as "a foolish, pliable, clinging, credulous innocent." And it took her years to fall in love, if not with her husband, then with her adopted kingdom instead. In time, as she ripened and matured, Marie came to realize that she had made another marriage as well: to her subjects. Their health and welfare were as important to her as those of her own husband and family. Rarely has a royal woman who was intended to be a mere consort made such a journey. She became queen "at a moment when the whole of Europe was on fire and flames were licking our every frontier." And until she drew her final breath, she was Roumania's wife and mother as well, "with every drop of [her] blood!"

The marriage of Ferdinand and Marie, like that of an earlier Ferdinand—the king of Naples—and his wife, Maria Carolina of Austria, as well as the mismatched union of Henry VI of England and Margaret of Anjou, have earned their inglorious stripes primarily because the spouses' traditional gender roles were reversed for most of their lengthy marriages. The queens were the warriors and the decision makers.

When the going got tough, it was the formidable and charismatic Marie and not her diffident husband who stepped up to the plate and went to bat for the adopted homeland she had grown to love. And she did so in spite of the facts that her marriage was personally unrewarding and her husband and in-laws did not treat her kindly. Given her astounding success in Roumania, one can only imagine what Marie might have done had she been permitted to wed her childhood crush instead—the future George V of England! Would her other youthful swain, Winston Churchill, have been able to control himself?

PRINCESS VICTORIA MELITA
OF SAXE-COBURG AND GOTHA

AND

ERNEST LOUIS,
GRAND DUKE OF HESSE

....

MARRIED: 1894–1901

AND

KIRILL VLADIMIROVICH,
GRAND DUKE OF RUSSIA

....

MARRIED: 1905–1936

*M*arie of Roumania would forever recall a remark her favorite sister once made about the institution of holy matrimony. Victoria Melita had declared, "To be entirely happy in marriage, the same things must be important to both." Unfortunately, it mattered little to royal parents whether their children and their prospective spouses possessed common interests, which is one reason so many of these marriages were doomed to failure and nearly perpetual unhappiness. At least Victoria Melita got a second chance at a happy ending, but the heavy cost may not have been worth the price of her connubial bliss.

Victoria Melita was named after her paternal grandmother and for the island on which she was born—Malta (formerly Melita, the ancient Greek word for honey). Sadly, her journey through life was far from sweet. This princess, always called "Ducky" within the royal family, was the second of four daughters born to Queen Victoria's second son, Alfred ("Affie"), the seafaring Duke of Edinburgh, and his wife, Marie, a daughter of Czar Alexander II. Ducky was a year younger than her blond, glamorous, and highly romantic sister Missy, who became the queen of Roumania. She was also the taller of the two, with chestnut hair, and large blue eyes set into an olive complexion. Her sober disposition, even from girlhood, gave the impression that she was the older one of the pair. Unlike many royal sisters who rarely, if ever, saw each other after their marriages, Ducky and Missy remained best friends, traveling across Europe to reunite during times of need, when illness or the calamities of war did not prevent their journeys.

Ducky's parents did not have a happy marriage. The Russian-born Marie, Duchess of Edinburgh, later Duchess of Saxe-Coburg and Gotha, was a squat, homely, no-nonsense woman, certain of her supremacy over anything English or German, especially her husband's family, even though the Romanovs had married German women for the past two centuries. (By Victoria Melita's generation, only one percent Russian blood coursed through their veins.) The duchess was quite a character: She smoked in public and was the only member of the Royal Mob, as Queen Victoria referred to her vast brood, their spouses and offspring, who was not cowed by Her Majesty. Ducky's father, who spent most of her childhood at sea, was a foul-tempered hedonist, a raging alcoholic, and a philanderer. Affie's personality, described as "[r]ude, touchy, willful, unscrupulous, improvident and unfaithful," was so objectionable that his own mother found it difficult to like him. The Duchess of Edinburgh would admit that she never felt like anything more than Alfred's "legitimate mistress," a degrading position for the daughter of a Russian czar.

Although Ducky was her mother's favorite child, sharing her passion for all things Russian, and eventually converting from the Anglican faith in which she was raised to the duchess's Orthodox religion, she physically resembled her father, inheriting Affie's slender figure and chiseled features. Ducky also inherited—from somewhere—a strong sense of justice. Austere and unbending, even as a girl, she would always be a defender of the weak and an espouser of lost causes.

Victoria Melita and her siblings were brought up in Malta as well as in England, at their father's Kentish estate, Eastwell Park, and their London residence, Clarence House. Yet after Alfred prepared to inherit his uncle's duchy and the family moved to Coburg, the duchess embarked on a crusade to Germanize her children. This met with considerable criticism from her husband's English relatives—even though Queen Victoria herself had wed a German first cousin. Moreover, Her Majesty had married for love. Despite her own Russian ancestry, Ducky's mother planned to unite her offspring to Germans. Because Marie's religion did not permit the intermarriage of first cousins, none of her children would be wedding any Romanovs.

However, in the early autumn of 1891, when Missy and Ducky accompanied their mother to St. Petersburg for a family funeral, Ducky, then nearly fifteen, fell in love. It was not only Russia that infatuated her, but a Romanov first cousin—Kirill, a son of her mother's brother, the Grand Duke Vladimir. The feeling was mutual. But the duchess was a strict mother hen. She cautioned her girls against damaging their reputations by succumbing to the dark charms of their persuasive Russian relations, who were undoubtedly also "kissing the maid behind the parlor door."

At the time, Ducky could never have known that she'd be meeting both of her husbands that fall! Shortly after the funeral, the family traveled to Balmoral to visit Queen Victoria. There, Ducky was introduced to another first cousin, Ernest Louis of Hesse, the son of the queen's late daughter, Alice. Ernie, who shared the same birthday with Ducky (though he was eight years her senior), was lively and spirited and, well, gay, but at the time everyone just assumed he was lively and spirited. Quick-witted, intelligent, and the life of every party, Ernie also shared Ducky's passion for art and interior design. The cousins got along like gangbusters, giving Victoria the impression that her two favorite grandchildren would make a perfect couple.

The Duchess of Coburg was eager to marry her daughters off when they were as young as possible—before they began to think too much for themselves. But Queen Victoria thought it was best to wait another year and a half before she began pressuring her "dear Ernie" to propose. By then, Ducky would be almost seventeen.

The duchess had been against the match until the spring of 1892, when, upon his father's death, Ernie ascended his throne, becoming Grand Duke of Hesse and by Rhine. Now Ducky would be a sovereign, a role the duchess had always envisioned for her daughters. Marie snobbishly agreed to overlook the fact that Ernie was a grandson of Queen Victoria, meaning that he had English blood in him. But Ducky's mother was a mass of self-contradictions where royal marriages were concerned. Just about *everyone* eligible to wed Ducky was related either to Queen Victoria or to the Romanovs. And Marie clung tightly to her religious beliefs when it came to nixing first-cousin weddings where one party was a Romanov, although she expressed no qualms about uniting her children with another first cousin from a different royal house! From the duchess's perspective, holy water was more viscous than blood.

And yet in 1884, Ernie's sister Elisabeth (known as Ella) had wed a Romanov grand duke. A decade later, his sister Alexandra of Hesse would marry their first cousin, Nicholas Romanov. So the Russian Orthodoxy's religious strictures about first-cousin intermarriages, which were ostensibly for the same modern reasons we cite, went up in holy smoke on the occasion of *their* royal nuptials. It's best not to try to make sense of the religious rigidity on this issue, because there were historical exceptions to every rule.

Ernie had been a sensitive child with a poet's temperament, and had endured a considerable amount of trauma during his early years. The superstitious citizens of Darmstadt believed in the Curse of Hesse that was purportedly leveled upon the royal house centuries earlier by a mad monk. Angry that the dynasty placed ambition over faith, the monk condemned them to perpetual misery. Like Ducky, Ernie's parents' marriage had also been soured by infidelity. But adultery was the least of his family's problems. Ernie's younger brother suffered from hemophilia, the dreaded disease of the blood that Queen Victoria had passed down to her youngest son, Leopold, and to two of her daughters. One afternoon, the four-year-old Ernie had been playing a game with his brother Frittie, a year younger, when the toddler hid behind the drapes in their mother's bedroom. Moments later, Frittie fell through the open window. A healthy child might have recovered from his injuries, but a hemo-

philiac can easily bleed to death. Frittie was hemorrhaging inter-
nally, and within a few hours the child was gone. Frittie's death
would forever haunt Ernie; he would always blame himself for his
brother's fatal accident.

Tragedy struck again in 1878, when his mother died of a diph-
theria epidemic that swept through their family. Only ten years old,
Ernie was shattered. Queen Victoria took it upon herself to raise
Alice's half-orphaned children long-distance, and they became particular favorites of Her Majesty. But as she was unable to bring
herself to discipline her "dear Ernie," he grew up childlike and
feckless, an indifferent student who coasted on his considerable
charm and exceptional good looks. By the time Ernie reached maturity, he was tall and well-proportioned, with high cheekbones
and a square jaw, deep blue eyes, and an abundant head of auburn
hair.

If Ernie had been allowed to make his own path in life, he might
have been an artist. At the universities of Leipzig and Giessen he'd
been tremendously influenced by the Arts and Crafts movement
championed by the Englishmen John Ruskin and William Morris,
and he was an exceptionally accomplished painter and a talented
poet. But duty and the military called, and Ernie was obligated to
follow in his father's footsteps. In 1884, he was made a second
lieutenant in the Hessian Life Guards; two years later he joined the
Prussian Foot Guards. Barely passing his military exams in 1888,
he gave up the soldier's life in 1892, when his father, Louis IV,
Grand Duke of Hesse and by Rhine, died of a stroke. Ernie acceded
to the throne at the age of twenty-three.

As grand duke, Ernie pursued a lifestyle of constant amusements. He designed the scenery for the Court Theater, which he
personally funded. There was no end to his parties and practical
jokes. Life at his court was a perpetual whirlwind, as if he were
breathlessly running from something, in the frantic hope that the
nonstop diversions would chase away the demons that haunted
him. Ernie was indeed hiding something, but his secret was even
deeper than his unfathomable grief for his late mother and baby
brother.

Queen Victoria couldn't understand why Ernie remained a bachelor. Several young maidens of Hesse had lost their hearts to the handsome grand duke. Why had there been no movement with Ducky? The queen's only concern about their prospective match was the specter of hemophilia that hovered over the family tree, so she consulted her personal physician, Dr. William Jenner. According to the queen, ". . . I spoke to him about the possibility of Ernie's marrying one of the Edinburgh Cousins, and he said there was no danger and no objection as they are so strong and healthy. . . . He said if the relations were strong intermarriage with them only led to greater strength and health. . . ." The queen was under the wildly misguided notion that, as she insisted to Ernie, "the same blood only adds to the strength and if you try to avoid it you will marry some unhealthy little Princess who would just cause what you wish to avoid."

After these words of encouragement from her trusted medical expert, it was full speed ahead on the Ducky-Ernie marriage. The queen urged Ernie's oldest sister, also named Victoria, to "hint" to her brother "to be very kind and posé [sedate] and not tease Ducky or make silly jokes, which might destroy our hopes and wishes."

But Ducky spiraled into a depression after her older sister's January 1893 marriage to Ferdinand of Roumania. The girls were accustomed to being inseparable, and Ducky had a naturally jealous nature and envied anyone else claiming Missy's attention. To ease her mind over the parting, the Duchess of Coburg brought Ducky to St. Petersburg for a holiday. The excursion worked wonders. Snapping out of her melancholia, Ducky became newly enraptured with her handsome and soulful sixteen-year-old cousin, Kirill. During long walks, the pair held hands and poured out their hearts. By the end of Ducky's vacation, they were deeply in love. Her mother was none too thrilled; aware of the free-spirited, lusty nature of all the Russian grand dukes, the duchess was convinced they made unfaithful husbands.

But back in Hesse, Ernie was getting cold feet about proposing to Ducky. His sister, Alicky, the future Empress Alexandra of Russia, threatened to leave court if he wed Ducky. Alicky hated the idea that Ernie's wife would take social precedence over her. Nor did she welcome the prospect of Ducky's pushy mother "playing the dictator around Darmstadt." Being doubly related to Ducky, Ernie privately feared that the family trait of hemophilia might be passed to their children. But the grand duke had an even greater secret: He was finally beginning to acknowledge that he "preferred male company." For all his cousin's loveliness in others' eyes, he was not sexually attracted to her.

As for Ducky, her feelings for Ernie were fraternal. They were nothing compared to the passion she felt for Kirill. The latter, whose smoldering looks and temperament made her nervous, was the dangerous choice. Ernie was safe. Ernie didn't make her uncomfortable by generating physical sensations that were too scary to confront.

But Queen Victoria kept up the pressure, insisting that Ernie show cousin Ducky some interest. And finally, in early December 1893, a few days after Victoria Melita's seventeenth birthday, Ernie paid a surprise visit to Coburg to discuss his intentions.

It must have been a difficult decision. But royals were raised to accept and fulfill their dynastic duties, regardless of the promptings of their hearts or their sexual proclivities. "After the gravest heartsearchings," Ernie returned to Coburg to celebrate the New Year. And on January 9, 1894, Affie sent his mother a telegram announcing, "Your and my great wish has been fulfilled this evening. Ducky has accepted Ernie of Hesse's proposal. . . ."

The match was universally praised in the print media as brilliant, and from a dynastic standpoint, Ducky's parents would view it as the most illustrious of their daughters' unions.

Ordinarily sleepy Coburg bustled with activity as it prepared to welcome the great crowned heads of Europe and their extended families for Ernie and Ducky's wedding. Their nuptials were considered the social event of the year. Even the septuagenarian Queen Victoria, who rarely ventured beyond Buckingham Palace (unless it was to escape to her beloved Balmoral or Osborne) never would have missed it! And the bride's sister Marie, Crown Princess of Roumania, ever the fashionista despite being four months pregnant, was resplendent in a white satin gown embroidered in gold, even though she was "looking pale and thin," according to their aunt Vicky, the kaiser's mother.

The morning of Thursday, April 19, 1894, was golden and blue. At eleven a.m., Ernie and Ducky were wed in a brief civil ceremony in Queen Victoria's apartments at Alfred's Edinburgh Palace. Then the family and their guests packed into the small chapel within the Schloss Ehrenburg, which had been festively decorated with flowers and fir garlands.

Dressed identically to their mutual cousin, the uniform-obsessed Kaiser Wilhelm (who many believe was also a repressed homosexual), Ernie wore the full regalia of a Hessian general and a gleaming helmet with red and white plumes. In a simple white gown with a judicious absence of Victorian embellishments, and her late mother-in-law's wedding veil secured with an emerald diadem and a sprig of orange blossoms, "Ducky looked very charming and 'distinguée,'" Vicky wrote to her daughter Sophie, the Crown Princess of the Hellenes. Aunt Vicky became teary-eyed during the ceremony, as did the bride's father, and their mother, Queen Victoria. Ducky's mother remained unsentimentally dry-eyed.

Only when the Duchess of Coburg kissed her daughter good-bye after the wedding breakfast did the bride notice the first tears she had ever seen in her mother's eyes. The newlyweds climbed into their carriage bedecked with flowers and drove off in a hailstorm of rice. Still a teenager, Ducky was now Grand Duchess of Hesse.

And now what? Queen Victoria had pushed her into Ernie's arms. Neither of them knew what love was; neither had any experience of a sexual relationship. On their first night of marriage, Ernie admitted to his cousin-wife that he "was not attracted to her." What was she to think after that? Ducky had to bear an heir for a husband who had trouble with the process because he found her physically repellent, and their first experiences between the sheets were so disastrous that she felt "completely shattered and disillusioned." With no basis for comparison, all Ducky could do was doubt herself.

So the grand duke and duchess opted to pretend that nothing was amiss. Instead they lived and laughed and partied and played as hard and fast as they could, behaving flamboyantly and spending money as if it were water. Queen Victoria despaired of her namesake's rudeness in neglecting to respond to her letters and telegrams. Ducky had not even demonstrated the good grace to thank her wedding guests for their gifts.

Still a few years shy of her twentieth birthday, Ducky was in rebellion. In her mind, the only way to assert her independence was through overindulgence. To the outside observer, the grand duchess's life in her new home at Darmstadt was glamorous and colorful, a nonstop merry-go-round of amusements with a husband who shared every interest. But in the privacy of their marital bed, their proclivities could not have been more different. Nevertheless, within three months of their wedding vows, Ducky was pregnant.

Ernie was delighted at the prospect of an heir. So were their subjects. The only one who couldn't summon a smile was Ernie's diffident sister, Alicky, who disliked her confident cousin, and resented losing her status as the first lady in Hesse and playing second fiddle to Ducky. Eager to wed Grand Duke Nicholas Romanov in a genuine love match, she couldn't leave Hesse fast enough. But Alexandra would never lose her antipathy for her sister-in-law, and one day would actively strive to destroy her happiness.

In the throes of a difficult pregnancy, Ducky remained in Darmstadt while Ernie journeyed to Russia for Alicky's November 26, 1894, wedding to the newly created Czar Nicholas II, which came on the heels of the funeral for Nicky's father. The old czar, Alexander III, had died of nephritis on November 1.

On March 11, 1895, Ducky bore a daughter, the first royal birth in Hesse in nearly two decades. Everyone was delighted, from their subjects to Queen Victoria, who believed the successful birth had vindicated her pairing of these two cousins. But no one was more exhilarated or relieved than Ernie. The birth of baby Elizabeth, controversially named after his Hessian grandmother, rather than for his wife or maternal grandmama, proved what the grand duke feared he'd been unable to accomplish. Ernie had become a father. And he transferred every shred of his attention to his tiny daughter, denying Ducky the warmth and—dared she hope—love she expected as his wife. At first she tried to compete with her own infant for her husband's affection, but soon realized it was fruitless. Ernie and Elizabeth formed a special bond from the day she was born. Elizabeth was all of six months old when her father began redecorating the nursery. Ernie held up various wallpaper samples in front of her like flash cards, choosing the mauve-colored swatch after Elizabeth's eyes lit up when she saw it.

In 1895, Ducky decided to take her daughter for a holiday in England—without Ernie. But when he bade them farewell in the palace courtyard, smothering Elizabeth with tearful, tender kisses, and giving Ducky only a perfunctory peck on the cheek, it was a crushing heartbreak from which she never recovered. During her sojourn, despite the gaiety of Ascot and a joyful reunion with her sister, Missy, she had plenty of time to reflect upon her marriage, concluding that it had been a horrible mistake.

She realized that Ernie had been interested in her for only two purposes: as a breeder, and to fill the vacancy in Hesse made by his mother's death in 1878—that of *Landesmutter*, or Mother of the Land. But the former rulers of the duchy had been unwilling to embrace progress, and Ducky, more cultured and sophisticated than her subjects, resented the fact that she was now expected to please them. Bored with the Hessians' rigid social constraints, she pleased *herself* instead, by deliberately neglecting the duties expected of her as first lady of the realm. She "forgot to answer letters; she postponed paying visits to boring old relations; at official receptions she often caused great offense by talking to someone who amused her, and ignoring people whose high standing gave them importance." Ducky also decreed that her court was a place for young people only; anyone over thirty was "old and out." This behavior is straight out of the playbook Marie Antoinette employed as soon as she became queen of France, conduct unbecoming that began her tragic journey from heedless to headless. But with the lessons of history and the upbringing of an eagle-eyed mother, Ducky should have been mature enough to know better.

Her dereliction of duty had the desired effect. She got her husband's attention, and Ernie was outraged that she should insult their subjects. Ducky's subsequent bursts of "ungovernable temper" led to numerous rows, replete with flying Pfaltzgraff, as she aimed for Ernie's head with pieces of china, silver tea trays, and "any handy object." Her cousin Kaiser Wilhelm nicknamed her the Little Spitfire. Others at his court in Berlin called her the Fighting

Grand Duchess. These nicknames weren't intended to be compliments.

Parenthood had fulfilled neither Ducky nor Ernie. Darmstadt earned the reputation for being the most hedonistic court in Europe, as the Hessian spouses tried to drown their unhappiness in the pursuit of pleasure. Adultery was still frowned upon between aristocratic social equals, but the nobility freely went slumming with lovers from the lower orders. Nevertheless, there were exceptions to every rule. Most royal husbands had mistresses, who were occasionally from their own class, and some of their wives took lovers, as well. But the ruling classes endeavored to be discreet about their adulterous liaisons.

According to Missy, Ducky would not have strayed from her marriage bed, no matter how unhappy she became, because she always "hated frauds and insincerity more than anything else." Fidelity was important to her.

Not so to Ernie, however. There had been whispers that he was satisfying his passions elsewhere—with a young woman from Darmstadt—and rumors circulated about his unconventional friendships with men from Hesse's flourishing artistic community, of which he was a major patron.

In May of 1896, Ducky and Ernie traveled to Moscow for the coronation of Nicholas and Alexandra. Ducky and her older sister, the two glamour girls of European royalty—Missy fair and blithe, and Ducky dark and melancholy—were the life of every event, to the dismay of their dowdy mother. As the czar's aunt, she had fully expected to be the center of attention. More important, Ducky fell in love all over again with Russia's golden and bejeweled Orientalism—and with her nineteen-year-old cousin, Kirill.

For three weeks of banquets, balls, and parades, while the married Missy enjoyed a torrid flirtation with Kirill's brother, Boris, Ducky and Kirill acknowledged that their own mutual passion was undeniable. And highly problematic. Although royals had always done so, Ducky was not the type to have an extramarital affair. In any case, what was winked at for men made women social pariahs. Divorce was unthinkable. And even if Ducky *were* to divorce Ernie, how would she and Kirill legitimize their relationship, when imperial Russian law *and* their Orthodox Church (which officially sanctioned three marriages for every person, no matter how many exes still survived) had nonetheless placed an interdiction on the union of first cousins?

Ducky left Moscow convinced of the futility of her illicit love. Having witnessed the happiness of Nicholas and Alexandra's marriage, she and Ernie promised each other to try harder. He vowed to be more considerate of her feelings, and they both endeavored to analyze what had gone wrong. Hindsight reveals what was abundantly clear even then: Ernie had always loved men, and Ducky had always loved Kirill.

A month and a half Ducky's senior, Kirill was the oldest of four children born to the gruff and outspoken Grand Duke Vladimir, the most erudite of her mother's brothers. Kirill's mother, Ducky's stylish and witty aunt Miechen, was the daughter of the Grand Duke of Mecklenburg-Schwerin, a duchy in northern Germany that bordered the Baltic coast. Thanks to a British nurse, Kirill had learned Ducky's native language from the cradle. A boyhood English teacher instilled a lifelong passion for the works of Shakespeare and Sir Walter Scott. Kirill was also an accomplished athlete and a talented pianist whose passion for music would never wane. In the autumn of 1891, he'd applied the same devotion to the study of math, science, mechanics, and navigation, in preparation for enrollment in the naval college and a career at sea. His maiden voyage a year later as a midshipman shaped his career. After finding conditions Spartan and the discipline brutal, Kirill was nonetheless determined to make friends; the experience provided him with the empathy necessary to be a commander.

By 1897, while Ducky fretted over her miserable marriage to Ernie, Kirill's charm, generosity, and grace on the dance floor became legendary from St. Petersburg to Paris. Described by his cousin the Grand Duke Alexander Mikhailovich as "kind-hearted" and "built like an Apollo," Kirill was the most envied member of Russia's imperial family, "the idol of all women and the friend of most of the men."

Ducky was, of course, one of those women. But her sister, Marie of Roumania most decidedly was not. Already predisposed to be hostile to men who were "too handsome," Missy jealously referred to Kirill as the Marble Man: majestic, yes, but cold. She was also worried that Ducky's love affair would not survive the long haul, because Kirill might someday regret his decision to defy the czar and blame Ducky for the personal sacrifices he had made for their relationship.

In 1897, Ernie and Ducky enjoyed a holiday in Roumania with Missy and her husband, Crown Prince Ferdinand. Ducky extended her visit; when she returned to Hesse, she was startled by the change in Ernie's demeanor. He seemed remote. Ducky suddenly felt like an unwelcome guest at their home, the Wolfsgarten Palace. Several servants now refused to meet her gaze; they whispered and laughed among themselves when she passed.

Ducky was completely confounded by the shift, until one day she caught Ernie in bed with a boy from the palace kitchen. The shock left her physically ill for days. She refused to see anyone, especially Ernie. Ducky had no idea such behavior existed, and it disgusted her. She had no way of knowing that their cousin the kaiser may also have been secretly homosexual and that his Second Reich was rife with gay relationships, even though the punishment for such "criminal" behavior was several years' hard labor in prison.

In her own private hell, Ducky could not discuss "the love that dare not speak its name" with anyone, because the revelation would bring down the dynasty. She unhappily acknowledged the importance of being discreet; five years after her discovery of Ernie's predilections, another German noblewoman would be thrown into a madhouse and locked inside a padded cell for outing her husband. His life ruined as well, he committed suicide.

Ducky finally unburdened her soul about Ernie three decades later, after Missy's daughter Ileana learned that her fiancé was gay. As she would then tell her niece Ileana, Ernie's indiscretion was far from a solitary fling. "No boy was safe, from the stable hands to the kitchen help. He slept quite openly with them all." People had suspected the truth for years.

After the royal families returned to their respective courts following the 1897 celebrations of Queen Victoria's Diamond Jubilee, there were also rumblings about the undeniable attraction they'd witnessed between Ducky and Kirill, now fueled by the rumors of Ernie's homosexuality and his penchant for stable boys and kitchen hands. Hesse itself was small enough for word to spread quickly from the center of the court into the echelons of the military and out among the citizenry.

Queen Victoria, who had expressed the desire that Ducky might "become of more and more use to Ernie" and might eventually bear him a son, finally saw the light after receiving an uncomfortably detailed description of the reasons for their connubial tension. With a heavy heart, Her Majesty remarked, "I arranged that marriage. I will never try and marry anyone again." And she never did.

But when Ducky and Ernie approached her for permission to divorce, Victoria strenuously objected. Marriage was a sacred and permanent bond that only death could sever. Moreover, the couple had the well-being of a child to consider. After Ernie contracted smallpox and hovered for a time between life and death, grateful to have survived, he enjoyed a temporary reconciliation with Ducky. But it didn't take long for him to revert to his hole-in-the-corner affairs with the handsome young men at the palace, although he became more discreet about them, now that his wife—and so many others—knew his secret.

Aware that divorce was no option, Ducky tried to remove thoughts of Kirill from her mind, and chose to rededicate herself to her marriage. Ernie was doing his best as well. They began to sleep together again—on occasion—and for some reason Ducky found the experience a bit more pleasant than she had when they'd been newlyweds. But there was now another reason she couldn't consider jettisoning her marriage. The revelation of Missy's sensational affair with a dashing Roumanian military officer, Zizi Cantacuzène, had sent shock waves through the family, as well as half the courts of Europe, before the damage control began. Never mind that their husbands had both been unfaithful: *Two* sisters could not be embroiled in marital scandals, or it might herald the collapse of the respective monarchies. So Ducky had to take one for the team.

The results of her renewed relations with Ernie were unfortunate. She had a miscarriage in 1900, and later that year, she prematurely gave birth to a stillborn son. It was the final blow to the

Hesse marriage. Ernie would never change. And Ducky had not overcome her revulsion to his homosexuality.

In the autumn of 1900, Kirill, who had been serving with the Russian fleet in the Black Sea, visited Ducky at Wolfsgarten for three weeks. He would later describe the time in his memoirs as "decisive for the whole of my life." The couple planned for the future, even if marriage seemed a pipe dream. From then on, their intention was "to meet as often as possible." At the end of Kirill's visit to Hesse, he and Ducky went off to Paris. Although they were accompanied by his sister, Helen (the future queen of Greece), their rendezvous created a scandal among polite society.

The death of Queen Victoria in January 1901 eliminated the major obstacle to Ducky's divorce. The clandestine planning began. Kirill visited her that summer at Wolfsgarten before embarking on a yearlong voyage. One morning in October, Ducky packed most of her clothes, telling Ernie she was going to Coburg to visit her parents; the servants wondered why she so tightly, and tearfully, hugged her daughter when she left the palace.

Ducky informed her mother that she'd left Ernie and had no intentions of returning. After the duchess protested, and Ducky finally explained everything she'd endured for the past eight years, Marie promised her support. It was Ernie who resisted at first. He preferred to remain married, accepting Ducky and Kirill as discreet lovers while he continued to pursue his secret lifestyle. Divorce would air the filthiest linen and ruin the family's respectability. Royal sovereigns did not divorce.

Ducky acknowledged the gravity of their situation and the massive scandal a divorce would create in their social sphere. It was far worse than being secretly gay or clandestinely adulterous. But even though Ernie was capable of living a lie, she was not.

Finally, he relented, admitting in a letter to his oldest sister that the past few years had been "a living hell. . . . Now that I am calmer I see the absolute impossibility of going on leading a life which was killing her and driving me nearly mad." Ernie did not divulge the true reason for the split. Unbeknownst to him, his sister had already divined it.

The extended royal family weighed in as soon as they received the dreadful news. The Czarina Alexandra, who knew nothing of her brother's lifestyle, saw him as the victimized saint and her sister-in-law as the villainess who had irrevocably disgraced the family. Her husband was infuriated, writing, "In a case like this even the loss of a dear person is better than the general disgrace of a divorce. How sad to think of the future of them both, their poor little daughter—and all his countrymen."

Princess Elizabeth of Hesse and by Rhine may have been the first royal child to become the subject of a joint custody agreement: six consecutive months a year with each parent, and the proviso that she permanently return to Darmstadt on her eighteenth birthday. Unfortunately, the child wouldn't live that long; she would die of typhoid in 1903 at the age of eight, when the alleged Curse of Hesse struck again. Her daughter's death heralded Ducky's final, and permanent, break with the grand duchy.

A divorcée in 1901 at the age of twenty-four, Ducky had prepared for the inevitable backlash. But she had not expected to become an outcast within the royal family, and the cold shoulder she received shocked and angered her. With Ernie's homosexuality unknown to most of the family, it was Ducky who was blamed for the failure of their marriage.

While Ernie was busily erasing all traces of Ducky's presence from the grand ducal archives of Hesse, the condemned grand duchess fled into exile with her mother and youngest sister, briefly reuniting on the French Riviera with Kirill, who had obtained shore leave. Yet behind the scenes, prompted by Alexandra's thirst for revenge, the imperial family closed ranks, determined to thwart their love affair and, in Kirill's words, to "ruin any chance" of their meeting in the future.

The cousins had one ally: Kirill's father. Grand Duke Vladimir, who loved his son unconditionally, finally came around when he realized that Kirill was never going to abandon Ducky. But Vladimir's support availed little when the czar was hell-bent on upholding the laws that had knit their society together. Kirill would never be permitted to wed his divorced cousin whose husband was still alive—particularly when that husband was the czarina's beloved brother.

In February 1904, after the Japanese attacked the Russian fleet at Port Arthur, Kirill reported for active service as a naval officer to do his part in the Russo-Japanese War. On the night of April 13, during a violent blizzard, an explosion from a Japanese mine destroyed Kirill's ship, killing 631 of the *Petropavlosk*'s 711 men. Badly burned and bruised, Kirill jumped from the wreckage into the sea; caught in a maelstrom, he injured his back as well. Kirill managed to cling to a piece of flotsam from the burning ship until he was rescued. His wounds would heal, but he would never recover from shell shock, or his newly developed fear of the water—a devastating blow for a naval officer.

As lovers, Ducky and Kirill had weathered ostracism and war, scandal and repudiation. The acknowledgment of the fragility of life in the wake of Kirill's accident reinforced their decision to wed, despite the insuperable obstacles. And in August 1904, after Empress Alexandra finally bore a son and heir, which removed Kirill from the direct line of imperial succession, he grew less afraid of agitating his cousin Nicholas.

The lovers waited as patiently as they could for the Russo-Japanese War to end. Finally, in the autumn of 1905, the Treaty of Portsmouth put a cessation to all hostilities. Japan had come out on top in the first of a series of severe blows to the Russian Empire that would lead to the revolution, the rise of Bolshevism, and the overthrow of the monarchy in 1917. The Romanovs' tragedies would culminate in 1918, with the violent deaths of the immediate imperial family and many of their relatives.

On the afternoon of October 8, 1905, in the midst of a blizzard, Victoria Melita of Saxe-Coburg-Gotha and Grand Duke Kirill Vladimirovich decided to present the emperor with a fait accompli. The trembling Father Smirov, fearing both "the wrath of the Holy Synod and the Emperor," conducted their wedding ceremony in the private chapel at the home of one of Ducky's personal friends, at Tegernsee, outside Munich. None of the witnesses had been told why they'd been invited until the ceremony began. Ducky's mother and youngest sister, Beatrice, were in attendance, as well as their host, his housekeeper, and three other servants. Caught in the blizzard, Kirill's uncle, Grand Duke Alexis, arrived late.

Kirill never regretted nor looked back on his risky decision to wed Ducky without the czar's permission. Toward the end of his life, after much had passed between them, he would write, "There are few who in one person combine all that is best in soul, mind, and body. She had it all, and more. Few there are who are fortunate in having such a woman as the partner of their lives—I was one of these privileged."

Ducky was just as confident in their decision to wed, but not in the outcome. Soon after her wedding to Kirill, she confided to a friend, "I hardly know to what sort of happiness it will lead."

While the newlyweds enjoyed an Alpine honeymoon, the entire Russian Empire was paralyzed by a general strike. Cossacks had rioted. The cousins could not have chosen a less auspicious time to announce their nuptials to the Imperial Majesties, let alone expect their heartfelt felicitations. Kirill traveled to the Vladimir Palace to share the news with his parents, expecting to do the same with Czar Nicholas the following day. Instead, that night the minister of the court, Count Frederiks, delivered an ominous message: Leave Russia within the next forty-eight hours. Not only was Kirill to be outlawed—banished from the entire Russian Empire—but he was to be stripped of his honors and decorations, as well as his titles and privileges, including his commission in the navy. His imperial allowance was to be discontinued, effective immediately.

Kirill and his parents had not anticipated such a drastic reaction. The czar at least owed a debt of gratitude to his uncle Vladimir, Kirill's father, who had been the head of the imperial army for the past twenty-five years. Having never liked the imperial couple, Vladimir and Marie blamed the czar's decision primarily on Alexandra's vindictiveness, believing that she had pressured her weak husband into meting out a punishment that far exceeded the crime, particularly given Kirill's own service to the empire.

But to Nicholas, it was precisely the fabric of the empire that was being ripped apart by Kirill's marriage. The czar was morally and legally bound by his empire's laws. Some of his relatives, including his younger brother Michael, had already transgressed them and disgraced the family with their scandalous liaisons. Faithful and honorable in his own marriage, Nicholas II was not about to grant special concessions to his cousin. Had Russia not lost the recent war to Japan, and were she not threatened by strikes, uprisings, and pogroms, beset from all sides by unhappy and disenfranchised students, workers, and peasants, Nicholas *might* have had a more open mind. Instead, he treated Kirill's disobedience as a crime against the state.

Kirill's parents were livid: In their opinion, he deserved a slap on the wrist at the most. Instead, the czar was making an example of him. Grand Duke Vladimir marched into a meeting with Nicholas, and in a characteristic display of his legendary temper, he ripped the medals and decorations from his uniform and renounced them before the ungrateful emperor. On Vladimir's departure, he slammed the gold-studded door so hard that he demolished it. A few days later, Nicholas conceded that he had been too hasty. He agreed to reinstate Kirill's titles, but refused to rescind the rest of the punishment, including the grand duke's exile.

Two weeks after Kirill's banishment, on October 30, 1905, Nicholas was compelled to sign an Imperial Manifesto that effectively transformed Russia from an autocracy into a semiconstitutional monarchy, establishing a parliament, the Duma. From now on, the czar would be unable to pass any laws without their consent. His thirteen-year march to a firing squad in Ekaterinburg had begun.

Perhaps it was better that Kirill and Ducky were personae non grata in a disintegrating empire. Raised on French culture, the grand duke decided that they might be happy in Paris. Having been impoverished by his cousin, Kirill and Ducky were financially supported in the City of Lights by his parents and her mother. By the summer of 1906, when they emerged from obscurity to visit Missy in Bucharest, Ducky was two months pregnant. She gave birth to a girl on January 20, 1907, at the Edinburgh Palace in Coburg, naming the baby Marie, after her mother. Just a few weeks earlier, Ducky had been received into the Russian Orthodox Church.

After his only son was diagnosed as a hemophiliac, Czar Nicholas began to have second thoughts about his mistreatment of cousin Kirill. The czarevich's precarious health meant that Nicholas would have to seriously consider the probability of relatives further down the line of succession inheriting his throne. Next in line after his son, Alexei, was Grand Duke Michael, who had all but eliminated himself by living in sin with his mistress. After Michael came Kirill, a promising candidate but for his marriage to Ducky. However, at least theirs had been a union of royal equals. And, having become a victim of circumstance, Nicholas reversed his opinion on Kirill's marriage, viewing it now as a mere breach of imperial etiquette, rather than high treason. When Kirill's father became gravely ill in January 1909, Nicholas felt ashamed that Vladimir might die while his oldest son remained dispossessed. And so, over the objections of the czarina, during the first week in February 1909, Nicholas conveyed the information to Kirill, through the grand duke's mother, that he and Ducky were welcome within the imperial family, with the brief message: *"Ta femme est grande duchesse"*—"Your wife is a grand duchess." Grand Duke Vladimir died a few days later.

Ducky was now formally the imperial Grand Duchess Viktoria Feordorovna. Because of Nicholas's tremendous respect for their grandmother, Ducky's namesake, Queen Victoria, she was granted the rare honor of retaining her own name, rather than adopting a Russian one, according to their custom and tradition. Yet Ducky was still not permitted to set foot in Russia. She remained in exile for another year while Kirill resumed his naval duties, and she was still in Paris in April 1909, when she bore him a second daughter, Kira.

Finally, in the spring of 1910, the family was allowed to move to Russia. Ducky enthusiastically reembraced the land she had adored as a girl. For the pampered and privileged royals, the next few years leading up to the start of the Great War were a glittering whirligig of balls, concerts, and dances. Women in furs shopped for Fabergé and thrilled to the high-flying Nijinsky at the Imperial Ballet. Ducky's taste in fashion and interior design was admired and copied, and everyone clamored for an invitation to her always lively entertainments.

But behind the abundant vodka, sturgeon, and caviar, Grigori Rasputin, a scruffy peasant and self-proclaimed starets (or faith-healing holy man), had insinuated himself into the royal family's inner sanctum by convincing the czarina that he had the power to heal her son. Through Alexandra, Rasputin's influence eventually permeated the corridors of government.

The assassination in Sarajevo on June 28, 1914, of Archduke Franz Ferdinand, the heir presumptive to the Austro-Hungarian Empire, precipitated a domino effect of war declarations that quickly escalated into the First World War. Yet, owing in part to Queen Victoria's global matchmaking, the crowned heads—whether they were hostile or allies—were interrelated. Nearly a demimillennial leap in time from the Cousins' War that pitted Lancaster against York, international geography suddenly made foes out of formerly amicable family members in what was initially called "the War of Cousins," because the king of England, German kaiser, and Russian czar were all first cousins.

Overlapping relationships from intermarriages over the years also tested the bonds of familial loyalty over allegiance to one's sovereign. Ducky was first cousin to each of the leading players. She was now married to a Russian whose position was obvious. But her mother was the daughter of a czar, had married an Englishman, yet had lived in Germany for most of her life, and was staunchly on the other side, supporting the kaiser.

Ducky made herself useful during the Great War. The imperial family financed and supported the Red Cross, and she was one of the first to mobilize an auxiliary ambulance corps, personally visiting the front lines near Warsaw with supplies from the Red Cross, while Kirill worked with the naval department in Poland braving crude wartime conditions.

Nineteen seventeen was a difficult year for Ducky and Kirill. They were in St. Petersburg when the city capitulated to the revolutionaries; mob violence increased by the day. Now forty-one, with a history of miscarriages and difficult pregnancies, Ducky was carrying Kirill's third child, hoping this time for a son. Her husband was still in command of his naval guards; their unswerving loyalty kept him alive through a number of terrifying touch-and-go ordeals. From Kirill's perspective, the mob was not particularly antagonistic or disloyal toward the czar, but they were hungry, and they did want an end to the war and a fair distribution of land and wealth. He believed that they didn't even understand the revolutionary rhetoric they were parroting; it had been fed to them by the demagogues who were the agents of the Revolution.

Three hundred years of Romanov rule came to an end on March 15. Czar Nicholas was forced to abdicate his throne, relinquishing the rights of the young czarevich as well. By the order of succession, the imperial crown then passed to Nicholas's ne'er-do-well younger brother Michael, who, terrified of assassination, abdicated the same day. Kirill considered March 15, 1917, "the saddest moment" of his life, although the triple renunciation had made him the heir to the Russian throne.

Except there was no more throne. Kirill and Ducky had been stripped of their titles and lived in increased deprivation. As the Revolution had continued to close in around the imperial family and their Romanov relatives, Kirill chose to declare his allegiance to the Provisional Government. This decision spared his own nuclear family, but also made them objects of contempt to other Romanovs. They considered Kirill a traitor who had sold out to the Revolution. Kirill also used his connections to spirit Ducky and their children out of the hotbed of rebellion. Forbidden to take "anything of value" (although Ducky cleverly sewed her most precious jewelry into the family's garments), and permitted to bring only "such clothes as they could carry," at the end of May, they quietly departed for Finland, an autonomous grand duchy of the Russian Empire since 1809. On August 30, 1917, Ducky gave birth to a boy they named for Kirill's father. Their son, Vladimir, was the last Romanov to be born within the borders of the old empire.

Meanwhile, to the east, the Revolution became a clash of ideologies, as the Communist Bolsheviks (the "Reds") clashed with the moderate and conservative opponents of the royalist regime (the "Whites"). How ironic that concurrent to the War of Cousins, a civil conflict raged in Russia between two opposing philosophies of government that was named for the same two colors delineating the combatants in the Wars of the Roses—that other Cousins' War.

A full-scale civil war erupted in Finland at the end of 1917. Kirill and Ducky endured frightening raids on their home and property, saved only by the former grand duke's reputation as a beloved military commander, and the knowledge that Kirill had pledged his allegiance to the Provisional Government.

In March 1918, the Bolsheviks signed a peace treaty with Germany, bringing those hostilities to an end, but the Russian civil war continued. In late July, Ducky and Kirill collapsed at the news that Nicholas and Alexandra, their children, their few devoted household attendants, and even the family dog had been summarily executed. That month, as part of the Bolsheviks' agenda to rid Russia of its imperial past, several of Kirill's relatives as well as Ducky's cousin Ella (sister to Alexandra and Ernie, and the widow of a previously assassinated Romanov grand duke) were murdered.

Ducky pleaded with her cousin, England's George V, for aid in destroying the monster of Bolshevism, writing,

> *Is it possible that great political men such as England has at the head of her government fail to realize that the Bolsheviks do not represent the democracy of Russia and that they are not socialist, even in the remotest sense of the word; that they are nothing but the scum of the earth profiting of a momentary madness to maintain their power by a reign of terror against which all humanity and civilization cry aloud. . . . Petersburg at the present moment has reached the limit of human endurance, the population reduced to some seven hundred thousand souls who are dying of starvation and want. The remaining supplies of food are entirely in the hands of the Bolsheviks and not allowed to reach any of the population not belonging to Bolshevik organizations—all the bourgeoisie and higher classes and a great part of the working classes, not employed by the Bolsheviks are literally dying daily by thousands for want of food, clothing and warmth. Their lodgings are taken from them—all former officers and officials are thrown into prison and forced into Bolshevik service by drastic measures such as*

the shooting of their entire families, wives and children.

Replying to Ducky's impassioned plea, George V denied that England was refusing to become involved, but explained that Russia's chaotic military morass made British interference nearly impossible.

By 1919, the First World War was over, and three massive royal empires had collapsed, relegated to the history books. The Austro-Hungarian Empire, once the Holy Roman Empire founded by Charlemagne, was gone forever. The Romanovs and their imperial splendor had been replaced by the triumphant Communists, who began to push westward into Central Europe. And the Kaiser's Prussian hegemony had been broken, replaced by the socialist Weimar Republic; the petty potentates of all those German duchies with hyphenated names still had fancy titles, but had nothing left to rule.

Ducky and Kirill joined the ranks of postwar peripatetic royalty. They moved from Switzerland to France and back to Coburg, where Ducky had spent so much of her youth. The couple kept homes in more than one country, all the while maintaining the hope that the Russian throne would be restored to the Romanovs.

It was difficult for Kirill and Ducky to adjust to the new world order. As her onetime friend Meriel Buchanan explained, "After years of unhappiness she had married the man she loved, and, having at last got all she wanted, saw it destroyed, and herself faced a future of despair and bitterness, an exile in poverty and humiliation." Approaching the age of forty-three, she had even lost her beauty. Deprivation and fear had taken it from her.

Kirill, however, had retained his looks and was as handsome as ever. Rumors circulated around Coburg that unbeknownst to Ducky he was indulging "his passion for . . . beautiful women."

Kirill—and Ducky—were searching for an identity after the war. Everything they were raised with had been demolished. They were unwelcome in many parts of the world. Cousin George, who still presided over the familiar comforts of a monarchy, feared the Bolsheviks would come scratching at the White Cliffs of Dover if he extended asylum to a Romanov. They certainly couldn't return to Russia; the Soviet government had no intention of admitting them; nor were there to be any postwar reparations, or recognition of their personal rights. And yet, Ducky fed Kirill's dream of ascending the throne. He was the last of the Romanovs—if you didn't count his older and authoritative cousin Grand Duke Nicholas, the former commander in chief of the Russian army, who contested Kirill's rights of succession, absurd as both claims were after the triumph of communism. Yet in 1922, the same year Kirill claimed the artistically inventive title of "Curator of the Imperial Russian Throne," a royalist faction choosing a new czar proclaimed the childless Nicholas "Emperor of All the Russias."

In 1923, Kirill suffered a nervous breakdown that left him so shattered he was unable to cross streets without Ducky's assistance. She devoted herself to rehabilitating him, body and spirit, chiefly by encouraging his fight to restore the Romanov monarchy and, in her husband's words, "save his country from suffering and misfortune." Her sister, Marie of Roumania, thought it was a fool's errand and a lost cause, but Kirill was completely committed to it. On August 8, 1924, from his rented house in Saint-Briac-sur-Mer on the coast of Brittany, he issued his first "Manifesto," declaring himself "Guardian of the Throne." The following month, a lengthier manifesto urged the Russian people to "rise together with the army and recall . . . [the] lawful Tsar." That would be him—as he made plain in the manifesto, setting forth his claim as "the senior member of the Czarist House and sole legal Heir of the Russian Imperial Throne, [taking] the title of Emperor of all the Russians which without possible doubt is mine." He went on to "proclaim My Son, Prince Vladimir Kirillovich, as Heir to the Throne with the title of Grand Duke Heir and Czarevich."

Kirill faced a surprising stumbling block: his aunt Minnie—the mother of the murdered czar, who adamantly refused to believe that Nicholas II and his family had been killed. If her son was still alive, then Kirill had no claim!

Other detractors raised their objections to Kirill's assertion of his imperial rights; most other surviving members of the family felt that his declaration of loyalty to the Provisional Government during the war had been tantamount to treason. A Soviet newspaper tarred him with the nickname "Cyril Égalité," an allusion to Louis XVI's cousin, the duc d'Orléans, who became a friend of the French Revolutionaries.

Then another, stranger voice piped up. An impostor claiming to be Grand Duchess Anastasia had the audacity to declare Kirill and Ducky traitorous "pretenders" to the throne!

Kirill paid none of them any heed. He brought his family back to Coburg at the close of 1924, from then on behaving in thought and action as an emperor. His two teenage daughters, zaftig Marie (known as Masha) and slender Kira, became grand duchesses. Ducky had reached the apotheosis of her mother's ambitions: By virtue of being Kirill's consort, she became Empress Viktoria Feodorovna of Russia.

But her own ambition had yet to be entirely fulfilled. While Ducky seemed born for her new regal role, Kirill remained a czar without a throne, and she would not be fully content until it was restored, maintaining her conviction that her husband's ascension was inevitable; it was all a matter of time. To that end, she vigilantly monitored his conduct. When he laughed too uproariously at a joke one evening, she reprimanded, "Remember, Kirill, you will be Emperor one day!"

On November 29, 1924, Ducky left Le Havre for the U.S., sailing off to promote Kirill's monarchist agenda, despite her repeated denials to the American press and her insistence that it was purely a social visit. It was also a speculative fund-raising mission. On her husband's behalf, Ducky had hoped to dip into the country's deep pockets, but she had miscalculated the rigidity of America's dedication to isolationism in the wake of the First World War. Ducky enjoyed herself in New York City, but when she arrived in Washington, D.C., the Coolidge administration—aware of the awkwardness inherent in honoring the consort of the self-proclaimed Russian emperor, when they had officially recognized the Soviet government—diplomatically avoided her. The first lady managed to be out of town for the duration of Ducky's visit. The Washington press was downright derisive of both Ducky and Kirill. Although she had written to her husband daily from America,

Ducky tried to conceal her disappointment when she returned to Coburg. The trip had not been a success.

On November 25, 1925, the same day Ducky turned forty-nine, her oldest daughter, the eighteen-year-old Grand Duchess Marie, married Friedrich Karl, hereditary prince of Leiningen, a tiny principality near Hesse-Darmstadt that had managed to remain in existence after the Great War. As far as Ducky and Kirill were concerned, Masha had married beneath her, but at least her husband was a genuine prince and their union was a love match.

After the Bavarian government established cordial relations with Moscow during the mid-1920s, Germany's homegrown Communists demanded that Kirill remove his imperial court, unformed as it was, "to some place where monarchies are more popular." So Ducky and Kirill quit Coburg and returned to Saint-Briac-sur-Mer, resuming their residence at Ker Argonid, which translates to Villa Victoria in English. There, Ducky gardened and Kirill golfed, while they continued to plan for the future. Ironically, their imperial prospects suddenly seemed brighter after the death of the dowager empress in October 1928. With his aunt Minnie gone, Kirill was now the most prominent surviving member of the Romanov dynasty. And after his cousin, the Grand Duke Nicholas, died on January 5, 1929, Kirill's claim to Russia's throne was uncontested.

A groundswell of support for Kirill was now bolstered by legions of Russian émigrés, underscoring the validity of his rights of succession. He and Ducky organized a "general secretariat" in Paris to keep track of monarchist sympathizers and timely developments.

The secretariat was transferred to Ker Argonid in 1929. While Ducky painted and pottered about the garden, Kirill diligently worked from nine to six on imperial business, but as his cousin Alexander observed, he was a "highly overrated" Shadow Emperor. His subjects, former royalists, had been dispersed in the vast diaspora of Russian émigrés, ". . . driving taxis in Paris, serving as waiters in Berlin, dancing in the picture houses on Broadway, providing atmosphere in Hollywood, unloading coal in Montevideo or dying for Good Old China in the shattered suburbs of Shanghai." Former judges were employed as factory workers; military officers were working as dishwashers. Yet all of them optimistically considered Kirill the czar and wrote him passionate pleas for his aid and guidance.

Ducky and Kirill marked their silver wedding anniversary on October 3, 1930, with a celebration attended by most of their extended family. Looking back on this quarter century of marital happiness, their son Vladimir later wrote, "It was a marriage which was based entirely on the mutual love of my parents, and which took place in spite of the circumstances in which they found themselves. For twenty-five years they lived together with one heart and mind, and our family could well be an example to all. . . ."

The early 1930s united Ducky and Missy in sisterly solidarity after Marie of Roumania's son Carol began to treat her abominably. Then it was Ducky's turn to require Missy's solace after a horrific revelation during the early months of 1933 sent her to bed with a raging fever. At first the empress dared not confide, even to her sister and best friend, what had devastated her; nor would Missy ever divulge the reason for her "errand of mercy." It clearly concerned Kirill, because for the rest of her life Ducky refused to sleep with him or even to permit him to touch her. However, for the sake of everyone's reputation and dignity, they decided to preserve the appearance of the happy couple they had previously been. Even their children never suspected that a dark secret had come between them. Marie of Roumania did confide to a friend that her younger sister "had an overwhelming soulgrief which has shattered her conception of life and humanity," but never specified what it was.

Ducky may have already known that Kirill had an eye for the ladies. She had caught her first husband in the arms of a stable groom, which at the time, had stunned her to the core, and later in their marriage, she was humiliated by Ernie's numerous homosexual liaisons. But her reaction to Kirill's betrayal was exponentially stronger. What sin was so great that it destroyed Ducky's "conception of humanity"?

Whatever it was, it began to destroy her as well. Missy reported that from the time Ducky discovered her husband's betrayal, she began to die "by inches," spiraling into a depression from which she could not, and stubbornly would not, be rescued. She had devoted three decades of her life to Kirill; he had been everything to her. Now the Shadow Emperor and empress had a shadow marriage. Missy wrote to her friend Lord Astor, ". . . Through the horror of what happened to her in her married life, she has learnt to doubt . . . all men. . . ."

Shortly after Ducky's fifty-ninth birthday, she traveled to Germany, where her oldest daughter, Marie, was about to give birth to her fifth child. On January 2, 1936, she bore a daughter. Ducky, who had not been well, insisted on tending to the new mother and child, and caught a chill that worsened as the month progressed. Her spirits sank further at the news of the passing of her first cousin, King George V, on the night of January 20. "You know, we have rights on the Russian throne and some on the English; how splendid it would be if our two Empires could be joined, we would dominate the world," she told a friend sadly, still dwelling, if only in her mind, in the bygone era of imperial splendor.

The day after her infant granddaughter Matilda's christening, Ducky suffered a stroke, paralyzing one side of her body and destroying most of her powers of speech. Her immediate family arrived to share her final days. Fortunately, Marie of Roumania had been granted permission to leave the country from the sovereign, her abusive oldest son, Carol. When Ducky was asked whether she was pleased that Missy had come, although it was an incredible effort to reply, she managed to form the words, "It makes all the difference."

Missy held her younger sister's hand through the end, softly reminiscing about their golden days. Finally, at twelve fifteen a.m. on March 2, 1936, Ducky took her last breath.

Writing to Nancy Astor (her friend Waldorf's wife) after Ducky's death, Marie referred to her sister as "our Conscience." Yet she added that when Kirill had "betrayed her, she did not know how to forgive, so she allowed him to murder her soul. From then onwards, her strength became her weakness, her undoing—she was too absolute, she could not overcome herself. And now she had to die, unforgiving! Her lips were sealed because of the stroke which had felled her to the ground—but although she knew we were there and the first day she found a murmur of recognition for each of us in turn, she shuddered away from his touch— Whilst we sat, in turns holding her hand, he stood like an outcast on the threshold of her door not daring to enter her room—"

Ducky's corpse was wrapped in a white silk robe. Marie laid some white lilies about her head and shoulders, and their sister Sandra placed a few stems of white freesia in her hands.

According to Ducky's wishes, the burial was a simple family affair. Her body was brought to Coburg on March 5. The following day, while a winter storm raged outside, a modest funeral was conducted, after which Ducky's coffin was interred alongside the remains of her parents and her brother Alfred in the family vault of the dukes of Saxe-Coburg-Gotha.

Kirill and their children returned to Saint-Briac after Ducky's funeral, but her spirit so pervaded Ker Argonid that it was difficult for him to go on without her. Kirill never recovered from the shock of his wife's death; after Ducky was gone, he began to prematurely age, spending the rest of his days poring over her letters and photographs and speaking of her frequently and glowingly.

In 1938, though ailing, he insisted on traveling to Potsdam to attend their daughter Kira's wedding ceremony to Prince Louis Ferdinand of Prussia. His health deteriorated through the summer, and by September he was too physically weak for surgery to remove the extensive gangrene consuming his body. After another month of suffering, surrounded by his family, Kirill died on October 12, 1938, at the age of sixty-two.

His death was viewed as a "national sorrow" by the diaspora of Russian exiles across the globe. Requiems were held around the world, but he, too, had a quiet funeral in Coburg, where he was laid to rest alongside Ducky.

Ducky's first husband, Ernie, remarried in 1905, wedding a social inferior, the frumpy Princess Eleonore of Solms-Hohensolms-Lich. She knew nothing about Ernie's homosexuality going into her marriage, but evidently made her peace with it, and bore him two sons, in 1906 and 1908. Ernie and Eleonore considered themselves happily married until his death in October 1937. Ernie was buried alongside Elizabeth, his daughter by Ducky. One month later, his widow, Eleonore, died in a plane crash.

As for Ducky and Kirill's children, Masha's husband became the

6th prince of Leiningen in 1939. They had seven children, one of whom died in infancy, before the prince was forced to join the German army during the Second World War. Taken prisoner by the Russians at the end of the war, he died of starvation in 1946 in a Soviet labor camp at Saransk. Masha died of a heart attack in 1951. Their third child, also named Marie, would eventually wed her first cousin, Prince Andrei of Yugoslavia, Marie of Roumania's grandson.

The beautiful raven-haired Kira and her husband, Louis Ferdinand of Prussia, also had seven children. During World War II, the prince collaborated with the underground, working against the Nazis, but he and Kira were both arrested and sent to the concentration camp at Dachau. They were finally liberated by U.S. troops in 1945. In 1951, upon the death of his father, Louis Ferdinand became the titular emperor of Germany. A woman with an essentially cheerful nature and a zest for life, Kira unfortunately died too young. She suffered a heart attack in 1967 at the age of fifty-eight, while she was visiting her brother.

During the Second World War, the anti-Nazi Vladimir remained under their watchful eye. He was essentially under house arrest at Ker Argonid until 1944, when the Nazis feared he might fall into the hands of the Allies, and compelled him to move to Germany. Vladimir had inherited his father's throne, nebulous as it was, but, unlike Kirill, he never referred to himself as emperor or czar, instead retaining his title of grand duke. When the war ended, he returned to Saint-Briac, marrying Princess Leonida of Bagration-Moukhransky, the widow of a Jewish American killed by the Nazis. After the collapse of the USSR in December 1991, monarchists believed he might still have a voice in Russian politics. Unfortunately, Vladimir died of a heart attack during a news conference in Miami on April 21, 1992.

His parents' marriage had been that rare royal love match. But Ducky and Kirill's illicit passion and eventual nuptials had broken rules of God and law, the sacred beliefs of their families, and the tenets of polite society, and for one reason or another, it remained a scandal throughout its thirty-one-year duration, casting it in a decidedly inglorious light. Moreover, whatever sin Kirill had committed against Ducky toward the end of their marriage was so shameful that she literally could not reveal or discuss it.

Another of Queen Victoria's granddaughters, Ducky's former sister-in-law Princess Victoria of Hesse and by Rhine, de-Germanized her name in the wake of the First World War to become Victoria Mountbatten, the widowed Marchioness of Milford Haven. She eloquently explained such long-held objections to this particular unholy marriage of first cousins, even after the world had changed so much. "I dare say Royalty is nonsense and it may be better if it is swept away. But as long as it exists, we must have certain rules to guide us."

Acknowledgments

Thanks as always to my brilliant agent, Irene Goodman: This makes twenty books together—and counting! A huge thank-you to my terrific editor, Claire Zion, and the fabulous team at NAL for the wonderful work they've done, and always do, for all the books in my nonfiction *Royal* series. Thank you to my own prince—my remarkably patient husband, Scott, who heard the phrase, "I'm on deadline, honey!" more than anyone has a right to within the space of a year. And most of all, to my readers, without whom there would be no books, and to royals, past and present—without whom there would be no stories.

Selected Bibliography

Acton, Harold. *The Bourbons of Naples.* London: Prion Books, Ltd., 1998.

Archer, Rowena, ed. *Crown, Government and People in the Fifteenth Century.* New York: St. Martin's Press, 1995.

Barker, Nancy Nichols. *Brother to the Sun King: Philippe, Duke of Orléans.* Baltimore: The Johns Hopkins University Press, 1989.

Barnes, Ishbel C. M. *Janet Kennedy, Royal Mistress: Marriage and Divorce at the Courts of James IV and V.* Edinburgh: Birlinn Ltd., 2007.

Bearne, Catherine Mary. *A Sister of Marie Antoinette; the Life-story of Maria Carolina, Queen of Naples.* London: T. Fisher Unwin, 1907 (BiblioLife, LLC reprint).

Bernier, Olivier. *Louis XIV: A Royal Life.* New York: Doubleday, 1987.

Brand, Emily. *Royal Weddings.* Oxford: Shire Publications, Ltd., 2011.

Buckley, Veronica. *The Secret Wife of Louis XIV: Françoise d'Aubigné, Madame de Maintenon.* New York: Picador, 2008.

Cartwright, Julia. *Madame: A Life of Henrietta, Daughter of Charles I and Duchess of Orleans.* London: Seeley and Co. Limited, 1900.

Cawthorne, Nigel. *Sex Lives of the Kings and Queens of England.* London: Prion, 1994.

Constantine, David. *Fields of Fire: A Life of Sir William Hamilton.* London: Weidenfeld & Nicolson, 2001.

Daggett, Mabel Potter. *Marie of Roumania: The Intimate Story of the Radiant Queen.* New York: George H. Doran Company, 1926.

De Lisle, Leanda. *The Sisters Who Would Be Queen: Mary, Katherine, and Lady Jane Grey. A Tudor Tragedy.* New York: Ballantine Books, 2008.

Elsna, Hebe. *Catherine of Braganza: Charles II's Queen*. London: Robert Hale Limited, 1967.

Fraser, Antonia. *Love and Louis XIV: The Women in the Life of the Sun King*. New York: Nan A. Talese/Doubleday, 2006.

———, ed. *The Lives of the Kings & Queens of England*. Berkeley, Los Angeles, London: University of California Press, 1999.

———. *Royal Charles: Charles II and the Restoration*. New York: Alfred A. Knopf, 1979.

———. *The Stuarts*. Berkeley, Los Angeles: University of California Press, 2000.

———. *The Tudors*. Berkeley, Los Angeles: University of California Press, 2000.

Freer, Martha Walker. *The Married Life of Anne of Austria, Queen of France, Mother of Louis XIV*. New York: Brentano's, 1913 (BiblioLife, LLC reprint).

Griffiths, R. A. *The Reign of King Henry VI*. Phoenix Mill, Thrupp, Stroud, Gloucestershire: Sutton Publishing, Limited, 1998.

Herman, Eleanor. *Sex with Kings*. New York: William Morrow, 2004.

Ives, Eric. *Lady Jane Grey. A Tudor Mystery*. West Sussex: Wiley-Blackwell, 2009.

Kleinman, Ruth. *Anne of Austria: Queen of France*. Columbus: Ohio State University Press, 1985.

Langdon, Gabrielle. *Medici Women: Portraits of Power, Love, and Betrayal*. Toronto: University of Toronto Press, Incorporated, 2006.

Lee, Sidney. *Dictionary of National Biography, volume 36*. New York: Macmillan and Co., 1893.

Mandache, Diana. *Later Chapters of My Life: The Lost Memoir of Queen Marie of Roumania*. Phoenix Mill, Thrupp, Stroud, Gloucestershire: Sutton Publishing, Limited, 2004.

Marie, Queen of Roumania. *Ordeal: The Story of My Life*. New York: Charles Scribner's Sons, 1935.

———. *The Story of My Life*. New York: Charles Scribner's Sons, 1934.

Marvick, Elizabeth Wirth. *Louis XIII: The Making of a King*. New Haven and London: Yale University Press. 1986.

Maurer, Helen E. *Margaret of Anjou: Queenship and Power in Late Medieval England*. Woodbridge, Suffolk: The Boydell Press, 2003.

Meyer, G. J. *The Tudors: The Complete Story of England's Most Notorious Dynasty*. New York: Delacorte Press, 2010.

Mitford, Nancy. *The Sun King*. London: Penguin Books, 1994.

Moote, A. Lloyd. *Louis XIII: The Just*. Berkeley and Los Angeles: University of California Press, Ltd., 1989.

Murphy, Caroline P. *Murder of a Medici Princess*. New York: Oxford University Press, Inc., 2008.

Packard, Jerrold M. *Victoria's Daughters*. New York: St. Martin's Press, 1998.

Pakula, Hannah. *The Last Romantic: The Life of the Legendary Marie of Roumania, the Most Famous Beauty, Heroine, and Royal Celebrity of Her Time*. New York: Touchstone, 1986.

Perry, Maria. *The Sisters of Henry VIII: The Tumultuous Lives of Margaret of Scotland and Mary of France*. New York: St. Martin's Press, 1998.

Plowden, Alison. *Lady Jane Grey and the House of Suffolk*. New York: Franklin Watts, 1986.

Porter, Linda. *The First Queen of England: The Myth of "Bloody Mary."* New York: St. Martin's Press, 2007.

Prescott, H. F. M. *Mary Tudor: The Spanish Tudor*. London; Phoenix Books, 2003 (originally published in 1940 as *The Spanish Tudor*).

Rowse, A. L. *Homosexuals in History*. New York: Carroll & Graf Publishers, Inc., 1977.

Strickland, Agnes. *The Queens of England: A Series of Portraits of Distinguished Female Sovereigns. Drawn and Engraved by Eminent Artists, with Biographical and Historical Sketches*. New York: D. Appleton & Company, 1854.

Symons, John Addington. *Renaissance in Italy: The Catholic Reaction*. New York: Charles Scribner's Sons, 1900.

Thompson, Oliver. *The Impossible Bourbons; Europe's Most Ambitious Dynasty*. Stroud, Gloucestershire: Amberly Publishing, 2009.

Van der Cruysse, Dirk. *Madame Palatine, princesse européene*. Paris: Fayard, 1988.

Van der Kiste, John. *Princess Victoria Melita: Grand Duchess Cyril of Russia 1876–1936*. Phoenix Mill, Thrupp, Stroud, Gloucestershire: Sutton Publishing, Limited, 2003.

Vovk, Justin C. *In Destiny's Hands: Five Tragic Rulers, Children of Maria Theresa*. Bloomington: iUniverse, Inc., 2010.

Weir, Alison. *The Wars of the Roses*. New York: Ballantine Books, 1995.

Whitelock, Anna. *Mary Tudor: Princess, Bastard, Queen*. New York: Random House, 2009.

ARTICLES

Chalmers, T. G. "James IV (1473–1513)." T. G. Chalmers In *Oxford Dictionary of National Biography*, edited by H. C. G. Matthew and Brian Harrison. Oxford: OUP, 2004. Online ed., edited by Lawrence Goldman, October 2007. http://www.oxforddnb.com/view/article/14590

Dunn, Diana E. S. "Margaret (1430–1482)." Diana E. S. Dunn In *Oxford Dictionary of National Biography*, online ed., edited by Lawrence Goldman. Oxford: OUP, . http://www.oxforddnb.com/view/article/18049

Eaves, Richard Glen. "Margaret (1489–1541)." Richard Glen Eaves In *Oxford Dictionary of National Biography*, online ed., edited by Lawrence Goldman. Oxford: OUP, http://www.oxforddnb.com/view/article/18052

Griffiths, R. A. "Henry VI (1421–1471)." R. A. Griffiths In *Oxford Dictionary of National Biography*, edited by H. C. G. Matthew and Brian Harrison. Oxford: OUP, 2004. Online ed., edited by Lawrence Goldman, September 2010. http://www.oxforddnb.com/view/article/12953

Hoak, Dale. "Edward VI (1537–1553)." Dale Hoak In *Oxford Dictionary of National Biography*, edited by H. C. G. Matthew and Brian Harrison. Oxford: OUP, 2004. Online ed., edited by Lawrence Goldman, January 2008. http://www.oxforddnb.com/view/article/8522

Loades, David. "Dudley, John, duke of Northumberland (1504–1553)." David Loades In *Oxford Dictionary of National Biography*, edited by H. C. G. Matthew and Brian Harrison. Oxford: OUP, 2004. Online ed., edited by Lawrence Goldman, October 2008. http://www.oxforddnb.com/view/article/8156

Merriman, Marcus. "Douglas, Archibald, sixth earl of Angus (*c*.1489–1557)." Marcus Merriman In *Oxford Dictionary of National Biography*, edited by H. C. G. Matthew and Brian Harrison. Oxford: OUP, 2004. Online ed., edited by Lawrence Goldman, January 2006. http://www.oxforddnb.com/view/article/7866

Miller, John. "Henriette Anne, Princess, duchess of Orléans (1644–1670)." John Miller In *Oxford Dictionary of National Biography*, edited by H. C. G. Matthew and Brian Harrison. Oxford: OUP, 2004. Online ed., edited by Lawrence Goldman, January 2008. http://www.oxforddnb.com/view/article/12946

Pakula, Hannah. "Marie, Princess (1875–1938)." Hannah Pakula In *Oxford Dictionary of National Biography*, online ed., edited by Lawrence Goldman. Oxford: OUP. http://www.oxforddnb.com/view/article/64674

Plowden, Alison. "Grey, Lady Jane (1537–1554)." Alison Plowden In *Oxford Dictionary of National Biography*, edited by H. C. G. Matthew and Brian Harrison. Oxford: OUP, 2004. Online ed., edited by Lawrence Goldman, October 2008. http://www.oxforddnb.com/view/article/8154

Redworth, Glyn. "Philip (1527–1598)." Glyn Redworth In *Oxford Dictionary of National Biography*, edited by H. C. G. Matthew and Brian Harrison. Oxford: OUP, 2004. Online ed., edited by Lawrence Goldman, May 2011. http://www.oxforddnb.com/view/article/22097

Reid, Stuart. "Acton, Sir John Francis Edward, sixth baronet (1736–1811)." Stuart Reid In *Oxford Dictionary of National Biography*, edited by H. C. G. Matthew and Brian Harrison. Oxford: OUP, 2004.

Online ed., edited by Lawrence Goldman, January 2008. http://www
.oxforddnb.com/view/article/76

Richardson, G. J. "Dudley, Lord Guildford (c.1535–1554)." G. J. Richardson In *Oxford Dictionary of National Biography*, edited by H. C. G. Matthew and Brian Harrison. Oxford: OUP, 2004. Online ed., edited by Lawrence Goldman, October 2008. http://www.oxforddnb.com/view/article/8149

Seaward, Paul. "Charles II (1630–1685)." Paul Seaward In *Oxford Dictionary of National Biography*, edited by H. C. G. Matthew and Brian Harrison. Oxford: OUP, 2004. Online ed., edited by Lawrence Goldman, May 2011. http://www.oxforddnb.com/view/article/5144

Thomas, Andrea. "Stewart, Henry, first Lord Methven (c.1495–1553/4)." Andrea Thomas In *Oxford Dictionary of National Biography*, online ed., edited by Lawrence Goldman. Oxford: OUP, http://www
.oxforddnb.com/view/article/26472

Weikel, Ann. "Mary I (1516–1558)." Ann Weikel In *Oxford Dictionary of National Biography*, edited by H. C. G. Matthew and Brian Harrison. Oxford: OUP, 2004. Online ed., edited by Lawrence Goldman, January 2008. http://www.oxforddnb.com/view/article/18245

Wynne, S. M. "Catherine (1638–1705)." S. M. Wynne In *Oxford Dictionary of National Biography*, edited by H. C. G. Matthew and Brian Harrison. Oxford: OUP, 2004. Online ed., edited by Lawrence Goldman, January 2008. http://www.oxforddnb.com/view/article/4894

Web Sites

http://www.inveraray-castle.com/home.html
http://www.lib.rochester.edu/camelot/teams/duntxt2.htm#P30
http://www.undiscoveredscotland.co.uk/usbiography
http://englishhistory.net
http://www.englishmonarchs.co.uk/stuart_23.html

Leslie Carroll is the author of several works of historical nonfiction, women's fiction, and, under the pen names Juliet Grey and Amanda Elyot, is a multipublished author of historical fiction. Her nonfiction titles include *Royal Romances*, *Royal Pains*, *Royal Affairs*, and *Notorious Royal Marriages* as well as *The Royals*, a brief overview of English royal history containing removable reproductions of famous documents, commissioned by Sterling, the publishing arm of Barnes & Noble. Leslie is also a classically trained professional actress with numerous portrayals of virgins, vixens, and villainesses to her credit, and is an award-winning audio book narrator.

A frequent commentator on royal romances and relationships, Leslie has been interviewed by numerous broadcast, online, and print media, including MSNBC.com, USAToday, the Australian Broadcasting Company, NPR, Hearst Television, Inc., and she was a featured royalty historian on the *CBS Evening News* in London during the royal wedding coverage of Prince William and Catherine Middleton. She also appears as an expert on the love lives of Queen Victoria, Marie Antoinette, Catherine the Great, and Napoleon on the Proper Television series *The Secret Life of . . .* [fill in the name of famous figure] for Canada's History Channel, and as an expert on the French royal family's ill-fated flight to Varennes for the Travel Channel's "Greatest Mysteries" series. Leslie and her husband, Scott, divide their time between New York City and Washington, D.C.

CONNECT ONLINE

lesliecarroll.com